# Memoir of the
# Rev. Edward Bickersteth

## Volume 2

# Memoir of the
# Rev. Edward Bickersteth

### By the Rev. T.R. Birks, M.A.

### Volume 2

REGENT COLLEGE PUBLISHING
VANCOUVER

Memoir of the Rev. Edward Bickersteth, Volume 2

Photo-reproduced from second edition published by Seeleys, 54 Fleet Street, London, 1852. First edition published June 1851.

This edition published 2001 by Regent College Publishing
5800 University Boulevard, Vancouver, B.C. Canada V6T 2E4

The paper used in this publication meets the minimum requirements of the American National Standard for Information Sciences—Permanence of Paper for Printed Library Materials, ANSI Z39.48-1984.

Printed on demand in the United States and the United Kingdom

ISBN 1-57383-204-9 (Vol. 2)

# CONTENTS OF VOL. II.

# CHAPTER XIX.

A. D. 1836, 1837.

PUBLIC ENGAGEMENTS, 78—120.

# CHAPTER XX.

A. D. 1837—1839.

MISCELLANEOUS LABOURS, 121—152.

# CHAPTER XXIV.

## A. D. 1844.

### JOURNEY TO SCOTLAND, 255—288.

# CHAPTER XXV.

## A. D. 1845.

### MAYNOOTH, AND CHRISTIAN UNION, 289—321.

# CHAPTER XXVI.

## A. D. 1846.

### DANGEROUS ILLNESS, AND EVANGELICAL ALLIANCE, 322—362.

# CHAPTER XXVII.

## A. D. 1847, 1848.

### SPECIAL APPEAL, AND MISSIONARY JUBILEE, 363--404.

# CHAPTER XXVIII.

## A. D. 1849.

# CHAPTER XXIX.

## A. D. 1850.

# MEMOIR

## REV. EDWARD BICKERSTETH.

# MEMOIR OF EDWARD BICKERSTETH.

## CHAPTER XVII.

### REMOVAL TO WATTON.

#### A. D. 1830—1832.

THE presentation of Mr. Bickersteth to the living of
Watton opened a new period in his personal history.
Concurring with that great and sudden revolution, which
convulsed the whole of Europe, and seemed even in
England to threaten the dissolution of the social fabric,
it was more than simply a relief from conscientious perplexity, and the opening of a new sphere of pastoral
labour. It withdrew him from the stir of London, and
the heavy pressure of many official engagements; and
placed him on a quiet watch-tower, where his practical
zeal and energy might be combined with a wider view of
the prospects, duties, and dangers of the Church of Christ.
He availed himself of the privilege thus afforded him. He
felt the importance of his new charge, and his interest
in that beloved Society, which had employed so many
years of his life, was undiminished; but he was now led
to observe more diligently the signs of the times, and to

lend an impartial and active support to every work of Christian benevolence. Using the talents entrusted to him with quiet and steady diligence, he gradually became a watchman to the whole Church, and an honoured coun- sellor of his fellow-ministers. Every year brought with it more various claims of public duty, and a silent acces- sion of moral influence.

His first entrance, however, on this new sphere, was attended with many anxieties. The patron of the living, with a simple desire to secure at once the fittest pastor for the flock, had offered it to him, as soon as Dr. Dealtry had announced his purpose of resigning it in June. When, after some delay, a strong wish was expressed to retain it, and resign another living instead ; or, if this were impossible, to defer parting with it until the close of the year, an unforeseen difficulty arose. Mr. Bickersteth had already tendered his own resignation, both to the Trus- tees of the Chapel, and to the Society ; while domestic circumstances rendered a removal late in the autumn very undesirable. His journal shows the burden he felt, and how earnestly he sought to cast all his care upon his heavenly Father.

" *April* 9, 1830. *Good Friday.* There are at present difficulties in the way, as to my speedy and secure settle- ment at Watton. Lord Jesus, I commit them all to Thee. Roll away every impediment, that Thy name may be glorified."

" *April* 11, *Easter.* How many are the unmerited mer- cies that surround me ! not, O my God, for my righteous- ness, but for Thy name's sake. All glory be to Thee.

" And there is that mixture of darkness and light over the future, which is best adapted to the exercise of all Christian graces, as a stranger and a pilgrim." . . .

" *April* 18. My mind has been much exercised by the way I have been led, in the last few weeks, and more especially by the uncertainties of the future ; but it is all very sinful, because it all arises from want of faith in God.

" These uncertainties seem to be meant to prepare my heart for my new scenes of duty, and for my new labours.

" I was too much elevated, too buoyant. I must walk humbly. I was looking too much at the temporal good. I must regard only the spiritual charge. I was too secure. I must learn the frailty and uncertainty of this world's good. I was looking rather at man than God. I must wait *only* on the Lord. O thou gracious Father, to Thee I commit my way."

Before these uncertainties had arisen, he wrote to his much-esteemed patron. " The more I look back on the whole way by which our gracious God has led me, the more I see of His loving-kindness, and do unfeignedly desire that I and mine should be entirely devoted to Him. I hope that His grace will teach me to give all my time and strength to the immediate duties to which He calls me. I can truly say that my whole heart is in the pastoral work of the ministry, and the enlargement of the Redeemer's kingdom. . . . . I shall deeply feel giving up a Society that will ever be dear to me ; and a most affectionate congregation, on which, one of my communicants the other day observed, that he thought there had latterly been a remarkable effusion of the Divine Spirit. But circumstances have been preparing the way for my leaving the Society ; and in my chapel I hope to obtain a successor, who will follow up all my plans. I shall enter on my labours at Watton with the joyful conviction, that with our God is the fulness of the Spirit, and He can there also abundantly bless."

" *April* 23. The motto I desire in my future course is, ' Holiness to the Lord,'—devotedness to God my Saviour.

" It has been a comfort to me to think, that what is uncertain to me is all certain to Him who has loved me, and given Himself for me, and that it is ordered by Him.

" *April* 29. It pleases the Lord still to exercise my mind, by the continued uncertainty of my future plans. O the extent of corruption within! Its out-breaking is, I think, by far the most depressing part of the present dispensation. I want to see in it, not man, but God ; and then all is wisdom, and truth, and love, and kindness, and everything that is delightful. ' My soul, wait thou only on God, for my expectation is from Him.'

" In the meantime, how absurd to be anxious about future settlements, when weighty present duties are before me ! O Lord, enable me to roll my burdens on Thee! Let Thy name be magnified, in using a poor feeble worm like myself, for good to Thy cause, both in my ministry, and in the Society."

" *May* 30. *Whitsunday.* Dr. Dealtry has fixed October 8th, for giving up Watton. May I then go there in the fulness of the blessing of the gospel of Christ ! To God be glory in all these changes."

During the interval of delay, thus occasioned, Mr. Bickersteth took his last journey in his official character, as Secretary of the Society, and laboured in its cause with his usual diligence, though his thoughts were now often turning to his new charge.

*Newcastle, June* 12.

My BELOVED WIFE,

I arrived here about an hour ago, and take the first opportunity of writing to one with whom I have left so much of my heart.

. . . . We arrived at Aylesbury a few minutes before three, and I preached for the Society for propagating the Gospel. We had afterwards a meeting of the Collectors of the Church Missionary Society. We reached Claydon Hall about eight. Yesterday, I addressed, first, the schools; secondly, a meeting; thirdly, a congregation at Claydon; and, fourthly, another at Gawcott; and then went to Stoney Stratford, slept for three hours, and then got into the mail for Newcastle. Thus you have my journey.

*June* 15.

. . . I am anxious that our own minds should be quickened now to prayer for a special blessing on our going to Watton. A fervent spirit of prayer will be a gracious token that God means to use us there for much good. . . . And let us not be too anxious about having things complete at first. This world is too full of uncertainties, for us to be careful about any thing but the one great concern of life.

I shall be anxious for your next letter, to hear about my Wheler Chapel flock. May the God of all grace provide a faithful pastor for that people; it will wonderfully relieve my mind.

I preached three times on Sunday. The evening congregation was such as I expect at Watton, in a country village;—farmers, labourers, and a few of the higher classes. I quite enjoyed laying aside my sermons, and talking simply and affectionately with them. . . .

O beloved wife, how mercifully and lovingly has the Lord hitherto dealt with us as a family! May we walk gratefully and humbly, never once repine or complain in our little sorrows, but abound in thanksgiving for our many and great blessings.

*Preston, June* 26.

. . . I am really anxious about my dearest J.'s health. He told me, he thought he should soon be gone, and the care of all his family would devolve on me; but how little do we know who will go first, or who shall care for those we leave behind! And why? that we may place all our confidence, not in the creature, but wholly and only in our heavenly Father, who loves all, cares for all, and will never fail them that trust in Him.

The meetings and collections at Liverpool were good, and a fine spirit of piety and love seems to be given to the people—though on these occasions we see things in their holiday suit. It is a mercy, however, to witness and quicken the zeal of the churches; and if God uses me for this, to Him be all praise. . . .

May I return to you with a blessing, and may the intervening time be profitably employed, with reference to all we leave, and all to which we have to go. I hope that we shall settle principles and plans, that may guide us now, and be looked back to with comfort on a dying pillow. All should be with reference to eternity.

We shall have an opportunity of talking together about our dear children's education. It is the one thing that terrifies me, when I look at the trials of A——, and other good men. O may our God make our children His children! All other things are not, comparatively, worth a thought.

I heard Dr. Chalmers preach a very able and profitable sermon from Isaiah xxx. 10, at the Scotch Church in Liverpool; and bless God for raising up men, with his talents, to plead his own cause. But I must close. The Lord give you a happy Sabbath to-morrow, and ever bless you, prays

Your affectionate husband,

E. BICKERSTETH.

The separation from the Wheler chapel flock was a very great trial. He wished once more to set before them fully and plainly, the great truths of the gospel, and with this view preached a series of parting sermons, which

were soon after published, with the title, " The Chief
Concerns of Man." His last sermon before leaving them
was on the words ;—" Finally, brethren, farewell. Be
perfect, be of good comfort, be of one mind, live in peace ;
and the God of love and peace shall be with you."
" I would apply to you Jacob's consolation to Joseph. ' I
die, but God shall be with you.' Though I remove, God
does not. It pleased God to bless among you a sermon
on the words—' Cease ye from man, whose breath is in
his nostrils.' We are now called to practise the duty
there presented to us. Oh ! it is good to look wholly away
from the poor creature, and to glory only in the Creator.
And what grounds of comfort there are for you ! True,
you are needy, the very fulness and extent of God's promises may shew this, for there are no useless promises ;
but you cannot have a want for which there is not a supply in the promise ; nor a fear, but there is a suitable
encouragement. . . . . . . O my brethren, well may you
spare the feeble light of a taper, if you have the bright
shining of the full Sun of glory ; well may you part with
a messenger, if you have his Master himself as your guest
and friend. All human aid is but as that derived from
a cistern ; you have a fuller, an inexhaustible source, for
' my God shall supply all your need according to his
riches in glory by Christ Jesus.' I commend you all to
the God of love and peace."

These Discourses were greatly blessed at the time of
their delivery, and still more widely in their publication.
Mr. Bickersteth could thus look back on the trials of the
summer, and the unexpected delay of his removal, with
deep gratitude and joy. The following were his reflections when the time drew near.

" *September* 4. . . . . Looking forward to the brief span

of life before me, I know not whether it shall be a day, or many days,—a year or many years. O Lord God my Saviour, I entreat thee to give me sufficient grace, that I may serve Thee, and glorify Thy name !

" The snares around my future path appear to be these. Sinking into a worldly, self-indulgent, pleasure-seeking life. Sinking into a mere literary, reading, and studious habit. Overwhelming myself with too many employ- ments, none of which would be well done. Entering into much religious visiting, and dissipation of mind. Enter- ing into the secular concerns of a parish.

" O Lord my God, preserve me from these snares, and from every spiritual danger, whether now foreseen, or not at all thought of, or known by me ! Now, O my God, the grace I ask of Thee is—

" 1. To devote myself ardently and fully to the work of the ministry. In preaching the glorious Gospel diligently and laboriously. In visiting unweariedly every part of my parish, from house to house, with many tears, with much prayer.

" 2. To foster the spirit of religion in the county. By clerical meetings and intercourse. By religious associa- tions, and meetings in different places. By opening my house to every plan for doing good.

" 3. To pursue religious publications, as God shall ena- ble me, first trying to improve my present works. To write an Address upon Missions. To write a Treatise on Baptism, and on visiting the poor.

" 4. To attend specially to the religion of my own household. My wife, children, and servants, must have more of my thoughts, prayer, and time, as it regards their spiritual welfare.

" 5. To give that time to the Church Missionary Society

which does not interfere with other duties. The most important aid will be in journeys and committees. And in all, and above all,

" 6. To walk closely with God, content with nothing, but as I have communion with God in the duty, and seek not my own glory, but His, whose I am and whom I serve. And here of special importance—prayerful reading of the Scriptures, close self-examination, and much fervent prayer.

" *September* 26. I feel this to be a crisis in my life. The time for going to Watton rapidly approaches, and with it the giving up of my present scenes of usefulness, my chapel, the Society, my London residence, my two nieces. O how dependent I am on the Lord, and how soon, without Him, will all be blighted that seems fairest ! Lord, it is my joy to leave all with Thee.

" *October* 3. Again I go with my dear people to the Lord's table, probably the most unworthy and sinful of all. There are many, who are now first, that shall be last. Lord, only let me enter to dwell in Thy light for ever, though it be among the last and least."

Three days after this entry in his journal, Mr. Bickersteth went down to Watton, to take the first steps for his removal ; and the same day, during his absence, his youngest child was born. On the 17th he preached his first sermon in Watton church, was instituted on the 19th, and inducted on the 23rd, and the following day read himself in, when he thus records his gratitude to his heavenly Father.

" *October* 24. To my gracious God be all praise. The more I trace of His loving-kindness in this matter, the more I am amazed at His condescension and grace to one so unworthy.

" O Lord, now it is that I need Thy grace ! Here are
800 precious souls committed to me, to watch over, to
feed, to nourish. What a responsible trust ! Let me
never be weary of entreating them to come to Christ ;
let me pray over them and for them ; let me set them a
blessed example, and walk among them in Thy fear, and
in constant love to their souls.

" Many collateral mercies have accompanied this. The
free, disinterested kindness of the Christian friend, who,
with a single eye to his Master's glory, presented the
living to me, can never be forgotten. May the Lord
richly return into his own soul multiplied mercies and
blessings ; and to his whole family, especially his aged
parents and children.

" The kindness with which I have been received in
the parish, and the hopeful prospect of doing good here,
from the large preparation made through faithful curates,
and Mr. Smith's bounty in the establishment of schools,
call again for warm thanksgivings.

" Yet let me rejoice with trembling. I know what I
merit in myself ;—only wrath. I know where I am,—in
a world of tribulation. I know who hates me and my
Master—the devil ; and how malignant and powerful
and active he is. But though I merit only wrath, Jesus
merits for me great and weighty blessings ; though we
enter heaven through tribulations, we may be joyful, as
well as patient in them ; and though Satan is mighty,
Jesus is mightier, and will for ever bruise him under our
feet."

On November 7, Mr. Bickersteth preached his farewell
sermons at Wheler Chapel, and at the close of the same
week his family removed to their new home.

The village of Watton is five miles from Hertford, and

twenty-six miles from London, on one of the main north
roads, through Stevenage, Biggleswade, and Huntingdon.
It lies in a valley, pleasantly wooded, and watered by a
small stream which joins the river Lea ; but the church
and rectory are on a rising ground, at a small distance
on the western side.　At the foot of the hill, and at the
southern end of the village, the roads from Ware and
Hertford meet each other.　Between them, to the south-
east, is Woodhall, the seat of the patron, Abel Smith,
Esq., surrounded by a park several miles in circuit ; and a
private walk of half a mile leads to it from the village,
through a small copse by the side of the stream.　This
walk, through Mr. Smith's kindness, was always open to
Mr. Bickersteth and his family.　It was one of his favourite
resorts, when wearied with his incessant labours.　He
used often, at mid-day or in the summer evening, to enjoy
this quiet retreat, and took sweet counsel there with many
a dear friend who came to see him, and to be refreshed
by the communion of Christian love.

In a letter to his mother, soon after his removal, he
describes to her his new residence.

I wish you could now be with me in my capacious study.　Out
of one window I see the church-tower, through the trees of the
shrubbery ; and out of the other we see, at a short distance, my
village, with the sun shining upon it, and the hill rising on the
other side above it.　Only may the Sun of Righteousness beam His
life-giving rays on us, and we shall be a happy people.　I never expected such an issue of this year, which has been full of mercies,
trials being turned to blessings.

I have good reason to hope also, that my sphere of usefulness will
not be diminished, if I have but grace to be diligent and prayerful,
but rather increased.　At present I have a superabundance of work,
and much is left undone.

Mr. Bickersteth entered at once on new plans of usefulness. On Sunday, November 14, after the two usual services, he began a catechetical lecture to the boys in the evening ; and a week-day lecture on the following Wednesday, both of which were continued through his whole ministry. In the course of the month he also began a prayer-meeting at the Rectory on Saturday evening, like the one which he had set on foot at the Mission-House, and which had been found so profitable. This was often a season of refreshment to his family, his friends, and pious parishioners, and gave a deeper tone to the services of the following day. Other duties, however, continued still to rest upon him. In the middle of December he wrote to his brother at Liverpool, "I begin to be interested in my precious charge, and am getting to work among them. There is a vast deal to be done, and nothing but the energy of the Divine arm can prosper my work. There are a few devoted Christians, but very few,—the Lord increase them a hundred-fold ! I have still a great deal to do for the Society, as I wish to write a farewell letter to each of the missionaries, and am Secretary till Christmas.

"What times are these ! Let us watch and live near to God. His people alone are safe and happy."

The close of 1830 was a time of trouble throughout Europe, and the uneasy spirit in our own country, with the unusual number of incendiary fires in the autumn, caused many gloomy forebodings. These national dangers gave Mr. Bickersteth a deeper sense of his own mercies. "Our country," he wrote, "is full of sin, and in the midst of plenty abounds in wretchedness. The Lord spare us in His great mercy. My own sins have added to the load of national transgressions. God has bestowed

on me great mercies, but I have not rendered to Him
accordingly." He seems, indeed, to have experienced, in
some measure, the truth of his own frequent remark, with
reference to the histories of Noah, David, and other
servants of God, that a time of great temporal blessing is
generally one of spiritual temptation, if not of actual decline. His journal bears witness of the danger, to which
he felt himself thus exposed.

" *December* 24. . . . I greatly need reviving grace, none
more. There is great danger of sinking into an indolent,
negligent, literary course, full of self-indulgence. O Lord,
give me large portions of Thy Spirit. Teach me to do
thy will. . . .

" Never had any one more temporal mercies than I
have recently had showered upon me. . . . My cup runneth over. O may abounding gratitude and devotedness
to the Lord be given to me. Give me grace in Thine
own ordinance."

" *December* 31. . . . The good hand of God has led me,
and I have occasion for much thankfulness to my heavenly Father, though great room for deep humiliation
before Him. . . . My soul is by no means prospering, and
chiefly from want of diligence in the use of means. I
enter not into heaven in prayer : how then can my mind
be heavenly ? I am living on past experience, rather than
on present communion. O my God, revive Thy work !"

With the new year he issued a Pastoral Address to his
parishioners, and repeated it in the three following years.
He there set the Gospel plainly and simply before them,
exhorted them to a diligent use of the means of grace,
warned them of the besetting sins of the parish, and invited them to come to him, in private, with all freedom,
as their sincere friend, whose greatest joy would be to

promote their spiritual welfare. The whole of the services for the first year rested entirely on himself; and he entered on them in the spirit of the counsel given him at the time by his venerated friend, Mr. Pratt, who was then suffering from disease. " Give your spirits,, and health, and ease, and strength to God, my dear friend, while God continues them to you ; not lavishly, but vigorously ; and then be sure that He will supply, and more than supply, the want of any or all of these, should He see fit to suspend or withdraw them."

The labours of Mr. Bickersteth, in his own parish, did not differ, by any striking feature, from those of any other faithful clergyman. He was constant and affectionate, though, from the pressure of public duties, less abundant than some others, in his private visits ; but his chief strength lay in the ministry of the word. His sermons were less adapted to arouse the careless by the terrors of the law, or to probe deeply the consciences of men, than to attract them by an earnest exhibition of the love of God in Christ, and to establish believers by a glowing description of their privileges and their hopes, and of the peace and joy to be found in the Gospel. His expositions in the school-room or in the family were peculiarly striking and impressive, from their simplicity of style, heartiness of tone, and rich fulness of Divine truth. The general character of his teaching may be described in his own words, in a Visitation Sermon, which he preached in June this year, before the Bishop and clergy, and which continues to this day a most seasonable lesson of ministerial duty. The text was 2 Tim. iv. 1, 2.

" A bold, prominent, decisive line is marked for us— ' Preach the word.'

" THE WORD. Not a mere code of morals, not the

doctrines of men, not a mere remedial law, nor heathen philosophy, nor the infidelity of rationalism, nor the blandishments of antinomianism, nor the novelties of those who are tossed to and fro, and carried about with every wind of doctrine, nor the decrees of human councils, nor the superstitions of Popery. None of these will ever effectually reach and subdue the proud and prejudiced heart of fallen man. Preach the Word. . . .

" That word is full of momentous truth; but its chief glory is, that it reveals a Saviour suited to all our wants. Jesus Christ is the sum and substance of the whole. . . The epistles of Paul are full of Christ. This blessed name shines through every address, and in every chapter; nay, you can hardly find two periods together, in which it does not appear. It is used for every ministerial object; to teach truth, to refute error, to animate to duty, to console in distress, to pacify the conscience, to rejoice the heart, to enliven our hopes, to confirm our faith, to inflame our love, and to raise our affections to heaven. He sets forth as the scope of the ministry, to ' preach Christ.' Jesus Christ is all his logic, and all his rhetoric, and the soul of all his discourses."

The standard, which he set before him in his ministry, though he often mourned in secret his defects in seeking to attain it, and the motives which he kept in view, appear at the close of the same sermon, by which he desired, at his first entrance on his work, to quicken his own heart, as well as to exhort and stimulate his brethren.

" The day of judgment is one of joy and triumph to all God's children. How blessed and glorious will the reception of the faithful minister be! What tongue can utter, and what heart imagine, his joy in meeting his Saviour! When the chief Shepherd shall appear, ye shall

receive a crown of glory, that fadeth not away. What
will it be to hear from His lips the joyful welcome, ' Well
done, good and faithful servant, enter thou into the joy
of thy Lord.' Methinks as he enters his Saviour's joy,
leading those to whom his labours have been blessed, he
says, ' Behold I, and the children whom God hath given
me.' And each of those converts will testify, ' Lord Jesus,
he was a faithful minister of Christ to me. He toiled,
and laboured, and persevered, day after day, in seeking
my salvation. Long I refused to obey Thy word, though
often touched by his earnest addresses, and fervent
prayers, and repeated conversation ; the world had too
much hold on me, and year after year I neglected and
trifled, or ridiculed and opposed. But he was not weary.
He knew that the redemption of the soul is precious, and
ceaseth for ever, and he tried again and again ; he was
full of plans and expedients for doing me good, till at
length Thy omnipotent grace, O Jesus, sent the truth to
my heart, turned me from sin, and I was everlastingly
saved.' O my brethren, may each of us have many such
to be our joy and crown of rejoicing, in the presence of
our Lord Jesus Christ at His coming ! O glorious recompence ! O surpassing bliss and glory."

The influence acquired by fifteen years' labour in the
cause of missions, was too precious a talent, however, to
be thrown away. Mr. Bickersteth took two journeys this
year, one in March, and another in May, for the Church
Missionary Society. His zeal soon involved him in the
difficulty, from which he thought that he had just escaped,
but which always attends that Christian grace as its
shadow. the conflict of rival duties. He had not as yet
the help of a curate, and notices, on his first return, how
serious a thing it was to leave the parish, and that it

must not be done without manifest and urgent cause. But the urgency of the call rather increased than diminished in succeeding years. The harvest-field was large, and labourers, qualified like himself to awaken and sustain missionary zeal, were but few ; and hence, although these journeys involved a real self-denial, and a sacrifice of present comfort, he dared not shrink from the work to which he believed that the providence of God was still calling him. He returned from his long journey in May, feverish and overwrought ; and the frequent recurrence of these labours, in later years, gradually exhausted his strength, and wore out his vigorous constitution.

His diary of this year contains many complaints of spiritual coldness and barrenness. A comparative drought seems to have rested on him, in his inward and sensible experience of the Divine love.

" *October* 9, 1831. My mind is in a very cold, distracted state, and my ways are far too self-indulgent. My privileges, and blessings, and comforts, have led me, not to more devotedness to God, but to more negligence in His service. Oh, I infinitely need the quickening Spirit of God to rouse me, as well as the atoning blood of Immanuel to cleanse me !

" I preached last Sunday an Introductory Lecture on the Ten Commandments. The Lord, in tender mercy, grant a full blessing."

" *November* 5. I feel in a very cold, dead, dull state, and make no adequate efforts to recover myself from it : and yet every thing speaks loudly now to ministers, and all others, to be watchful and prayerful.

" There have been in the last week great riots at Bristol, and immense loss of property. The Lord is shaking these kingdoms, and leading all to see how uncertain

every thing here below is ; but my heart is most unim-
pressible.   I feel the truth of that hymn—

> " O for a glance of heavenly day,
> To take this stubborn stone away ;
> And thaw, with beams of love divine
> This heart, this frozen heart of mine.
>
> " The rocks can rend, the earth can quake,
> The seas can roar, the mountains shake,
> Of feeling all things show some sign,
> But this unfeeling heart of mine."

" The sins that chiefly burden me are—cold, negligent,
and formal private prayer ; not giving due attention to
visiting my people ; indolence and self-indulgence.   O
Lord, bless Thine own ordinances to my soul's good.

" *December* 24. . . The cholera morbus has entered the
country, and at Sunderland, Newcastle, and other places,
above two hundred have died.   It will probably spread,
and bring multitudes to their great account.   O my soul,
art thou prepared ?

" O my God, I have to lie low, very low before Thee !
Fair to the eye of man, but, O how vile in my own eyes,
and in Thine !  God is forgotten, even in doing the things
of God, and having the help of God.   While carried on in
my duties by His aid, the eye to His glory is wanting. . .
Hence I am justly kept at a distance from my Father,
and have seldom communion with Him.   Even in retired
devotion, I can kneel and pray, and yet not have fellowship with the Father of my spirit.

" *December* 31, 1831. . . .When shall I begin to breathe
freely in the Divine life !   When shall I rise to full communion with God ?   O Lord, teach me Thy way, and lead
me in a right path !

" It is my anxious desire—the Lord strengthen that

desire which He has given, and bring it into life and
action, to begin a new course with a new year.   I am but
half a Christian, but half a minister, but half a Christian
husband, or a Christian father.   I redeem not time, I
live not in the presence of God.   I study not, I pray not,
I visit not my poor, as I should, or, as I desire, or as
living on the borders of eternity, I ought.

" O Lord, help me to plan, help me to execute more for
Thee, than I have yet done, or thought of doing.   Open
doors of usefulness for me."

On Christmas-day, which was the last Sunday in the
year, his voice failed from the exhausting nature of the
public services, and he was led to see the necessity of procuring a helper in the work of the parish.   He alludes to
this in a letter, a few days after, to Mr. and Mrs. Smith,
from whom he had received much kind help in promoting
the temporal and spiritual welfare of the people.

*December* 29, 1831.

MY DEAR FRIENDS,

I cannot see you going to town at the close of another year,
without endeavouring a little to pour out the fulness of my heart,
for all the kind assistances you have rendered to me, and to my
ministerial work. . . . . . How much I owe you for upholding me in
every effort for the religious welfare of the parish, so that I seem to
have room for nothing but thanksgiving to the Fountain of all
good.

Need I be surprised, in the midst of so many blessings, at the
memento, last Sunday, of the poor earthen vessel?   I have no
doubt that it was in every way sent in love ; to me, to keep me in
my proper place, of entire dependence on the Lord ; and to you,
my dear friends, in every way to cease from man.

I judge it right, however, to guard as much as I can against the
recurrence of such a weakness, which I mainly attribute to lengthened
services, and am therefore turning my attention seriously to finding

a curate. I fear losing anything of that little ministerial zeal and interest I may now have, by devolving duties on another; but there are so many desirable things, such as cottage lectures, a weekly meeting with the young men on Sunday morning, and a Sunday evening meeting at Wempstead, which can only be accomplished by another labourer, that I have nearly determined to lose no time in seeking for an assistant. . . . . .

We are fast entering on another year—but who, knowing the Lord, and knowing His word, and knowing the world, can look forward to it without mingled feelings? Increasingly do I feel— all that is in the world is a vanity; and except to do good, and thereby glorify God, and help to save immortal beings, there is nothing worth an anxious thought. May your varied talents be all employed, just as our God would have them to be, and as we shall wish they had been employed in the last day.

For yourselves I shall not cease to pray, that you may be abundantly filled with the Divine Spirit, that you may ever have the utmost singleness of eye in the service of God, and the most entire devotedness to Him, that you may enjoy most intimate communion with the Father, the Son, and the Holy Spirit, and have constant grace to confess your Saviour before men. My hearty prayers shall also continue to be offered for your three sweet children, that from their childhood they may be under the influence of that grace which God gives to His children.

Ever most affectionately yours,

E. BICKERSTETH.

With the new year the progress of the cholera became more alarming. The novelty of the disease, its frightful rapidity, and its mysterious nature, which seemed wholly to baffle the skill of physicians, conspired to produce a deep, and almost panic terror. Minds which before had remained utterly careless, were now awakened to the fear of death, and the sense of a Divine judgment. These feelings were so powerful, that the Government of the

day, even amidst the excitement of the Reform agitation,
was compelled to yield to them ; and though some voices
were found in Parliament, which dared to speak of any
acknowledgment of God's hand as cant and hypocrisy, a
Fast was appointed on March 21st, to deprecate the anger
of the Almighty, and entreat him to remove the pestilence from our shores.

Mr. Bickersteth was deeply thankful for this seasonable call to humiliation and prayer.  He was reflecting
how to use it for good, when he received a note in February, from his friend, the Rev. R. G. Baker, telling
him that he had looked in vain for such a tract as he
wished to give his parishioners ; and ending with the
appeal—" While the unbelieving and irreligious press is
busily at work with its scoffs and sneers at the appointment, ought such a pen as yours to remain idle ? "  Mr.
Bickersteth responded to this call with his usual promptness in seizing special opportunities.  Just a fortnight
from the day when he received the note, we read in his
Journal :—" I have written a Tract on the Fast-day,
which has already had a circulation of several thousands.
May it please the Lord to own it for extensive good !  It
was very hastily written, but He delights to use weak
means, that all the glory may be His."

These desires and hopes were not disappointed.  By the
close of March, a hundred thousand copies were in circulation ; and probably half a million of readers had listened to his simple and earnest appeal, at a moment
when they would be more than usually open to serious
impressions.  His tract was one main help and guide to
the due observance of the day, in hundreds, probably in
thousands, of parishes ; and swelled largely those accents
of united confession and prayer, which obtained a gra-

cious answer, and procured a lengthening of our national
tranquillity for so many years.

During the same month he engaged the services of
Mr. Garwood as his Curate, now the Secretary of that
invaluable Society, the London City Mission. Their con
nexion was one of mutual comfort and blessing. A kindness, on the one side, almost parental, was repaid, on the
other, by an almost filial honour and esteem. Though
Mr. Bickersteth sometimes recoiled, with great sensitive-
ness from rude and unbecoming familiarity—the only
case in which his natural reserve re-appeared, no one
was more free from the assumption of superiority, or delighted more to unbend freely in his intercourse with his
younger brethren. This feature is seen in the following
letter to Mr. Garwood, a few weeks before he entered on
the curacy.

*February* 13, 1831.

My dear Friend,

Your letter gave me sincere pleasure, and the best hopes that
your coming to us will be a mutual comfort and benefit. You will
have a cordial welcome from all here, and I shall rejoice to labour
with you as a true yoke-fellow, in the work which our one Master
gives us to do. . . .

It will be a great joy to me to help you forward, as God shall
enable me, in the ministry. I am not sorry to see you jealous of
any thing interfering with that work. We have here eight hundred
and thirty immortal souls to watch over, most of them, I fear,
walking in the broad road; and we have enough to employ our
constant prayers and labours for them, with the more special duty
of bringing up my children for the service of the Lord Christ. It
is for this united work, which I find far too much for my single
efforts, that I rejoice to have the help of a Christian brother, like
yourself; and my hope is, that while with me, you may not only
be helping on this great work, but maturing and ripening for such

further scenes of usefulness, as it may please our Lord hereafter to open before you. Just in a similar way, I found my own labours, under Mr. Pratt, help me in those scenes to which I have since been called. . . .

My strength is not what it was—this leads us often to say, "We wish that Mr. Garwood was come." May our Lord bring you to us in the fulness of the blessing of the gospel of Christ.

Affectionately yours,<br>E. Bickersteth.

The connexion, thus formed, lasted until September, 1833, when Mr. Garwood was appointed to Wheler Chapel, and thus succeeded Mr. Bickersteth in the earliest scene of his pastoral labours. Its name, a few years later, was changed to St. Mary's Church, Spitalfields, where he has exercised his ministry to the present day, besides taking an important part in the London City Mission.

In November, 1831, Mr. Bickersteth was invited by the Church Missionary Society to preach their Annual Sermon. He accepted the task, and prepared for it with his usual diligence, by collecting information from various sources, to illustrate and enforce the duty of British Christians. His sense of the great importance of the occasion led him to bestow much pains on the sermon, and his elder children can recollect his reading it aloud to them in private, more than once, to discover any defects, and be more familiar with it in the public delivery. His text was Psalm lxvii. 1, 2 ; which he applied to the British nation, to the Church of England, and to the Church Missionary Society. He enlarged on the high privileges of our country, its providential opportunities, and grievous sins ; the past revival of the Church, and its remaining weakness and corruption ; the growth of missionary zeal, and its scanty means, compared with

the immense expenditure on mere luxuries and sinful
pleasures ; the fearful wants and darkness of the heathen
world, and the blessings that would flow to it from an
extensive revival of true religion in our church and nation ; with the means by which these blessings might be
secured—prayer, personal devotedness, and their combined influence on the hearts and minds of others.   His
remarks on this last head received a striking illustration
in his own history.

  " You may do something by your own devotedness, but
you will do inexpressibly more by the Christian influence
of that devotedness.   Devotedness is but the first seed ;
influence is the whole future produce.   Look at St. Paul.
Thousands may have been the converts of his personal
ministry, but his influence has extended to millions after
millions ; it has reached every Christian in each successive age, and is boundless and lasting as eternity.
. . . . We inquire not, have you much or little property, much rank, or none.   There is something higher,
that alone gives an eternally-beneficial influence, even
the constant daily working out of devotedness to the
Lord, in the self-denying exercise of every Christian
grace."

  The entries in his journal, in the early part of this
year, show the secret consciousness of temptation, and a
constant struggle against it.

  " *January* 15, 1832.   My mind has been much exercised latterly by some of the novelties of Mr. Irving entering into my parish, and possessing two or three of
whom I hoped the best.   The Lord, in tender mercy, preserve me and mine from all error, and guide us into all
truth, whatever be the cost.   I see no scriptural warrant
for these novelties, and many things that seem directly
against them ; therefore I feel it my duty to oppose them,

with all the wisdom, and firmness, and love, that God may bestow.

" I have very important duties before me : the Church Missionary Sermon, the commencement of the " Christian's Family Library," the Confirmation in June, the engagement with a curate, and a fresh governess for my children."

" *February* 24. The times are very stirring and awakening. The cholera spreads : above a thousand have already been carried off by it. But the ungodliness of the nation, the divisions of the Church, the heresies afloat, the worldliness of professors, the state of my own heart, make me tremble. . . .

" Blessings that ought to be more fully realized : Communion with God in public and private prayer ; realizing more His presence ; directly aiming to please Him in all things, a more grateful heart, looking for the coming of the Lord Jesus."

" *March* 10. I have to bless God for the circulation of the Tract. May the Lord, by this weak instrument, teach many precious souls. As for myself, nothing can be more weak and worthless than I am. I can only cast myself on the merit of the Lord Jesus. I have no other plea than His blood, no other covering than His righteousness. . . ."

" *March* 19. Through mercy I am brought to the close of my 46th year. O that sovereign grace might reign, in turning me from my sins, negligences, and infirmities, and leading me to a new course of devotedness to the Lord !

" I find alterations and improvements a great snare. They take up much precious time in looking after them, and shut out self-denying and important duties. Yet

they furnish employment to the poor, and they are a relaxation to my own mind. Lord, guard me from the
snares of them.

"Two things I find most difficult—to keep up real
communion with God in worship, and to visit patiently
and fully the poor in my parish. . . . What an unprofitable servant I am! Why am I not cast off? Only from
infinite mercy. O renew a right spirit in these things!

"I expect a curate to join me in my labours here, to-
morrow. O Lord, let it please Thee to bring him here
for good to me, to himself, to the parish, and to my dear
boy, whom he is to educate. Give me wisdom, and love,
and fairness, and kindness, and equity, in all my dealings
with him. Bless him, and make him a blessing in this
place.

"I ought, on a birth-day, and when the pestilence is
abroad, to look well into my own heart, and place myself
in the situation of one on the verge of eternity. O my
soul, suppose thou wert this night to enter the unseen
world of spirits, and to appear naked and alone before
thy God! what is thy readiness for thy Lord? I can
only say, 'Enter not into judgment with thy servant, O
Lord!' I can only say, 'In the Lord is my righteousness
and strength.'

"Blessed Jesus, my only hope is in Thee; and I do
now again, for time and for eternity, cast my immortal
spirit on thy grace and salvation, as my only refuge.

"But O my heavenly Master, is it not thy blessed office
to purify the sons of Levi, that they may offer to Thee
an offering in righteousness? Graciously fulfil that office
in me. Thou knowest how poor and needy I am. O
blessed Jesus, purify me unto Thyself, as one of Thy
peculiar people, zealous of good works!

" *April* 1.  I went to London last week, partly about the Bible Society.  I feel the way of truth and peace there to be difficult to find.  The Lord keep me from error.

" I went one morning to Mr. Irving's church, and heard the speakers with tongues.  It did not appear to me a real work of the Spirit.  I was depressed by it, as a delusion on the minds of eminent Christians.  The Lord preserve me and His Church from every thing contrary to His mind.

" What I feel I mainly want is, communion with my God.  Lord, above all givings give me this—never may I rest, but in Thee !  Thy favour is better than life.  Surrounded with every earthly blessing, I want one thing above every thing else, even the Giver of all these gifts, the light of His countenance, and the joy of His presence.  But O how cold and dry and barren are my prayers and service !  Surely if I may hope, none need despair ! "

" *April* 29.  On the morrow, if God will, I preach the Anniversary Sermon.  A most fearful and responsible duty, considering all its varied connections.  O Lord, I am oppressed, undertake for me !  If Thou usest Thy feeble creature, let it be to thy glory, and not for mine.

" My old friend, Daniel Wilson, is this day to be consecrated Bishop of Calcutta.  The Lord himself anoint and consecrate him as a chosen vessel, to bear His name before the Gentiles."

" *May* 20.  My beloved mother died at Burslem in Staffordshire on the 4th of this month, aged seventy-nine. I attended her funeral at Liverpool on the 10th.  So one generation passes away. She died in the Lord—the latter years of life, though weakened by disease, being tranquil

and peaceful, spiritual, devout and heavenly—her mind
always alive to Christ and the things of Christ.

" God carried me through my duties in town with
much mercy.   I preached an hour and three quarters—
the longest sermon I ever preached in my life—but the
interest seemed to be kept up in the crowded congregation to the end.

" O revive my soul, heavenly Father, with Thy grace,
for thy Church's sake, for my people's sake, for Thy
Name's sake.   Nothing do I need so much as quickening
grace, to walk more closely with God."

This year Mr. Bickersteth undertook a work of much
practical utility, as Editor of the CHRISTIAN'S FAMILY
LIBRARY.   The object he proposed, in concert with his
publishers, was, to diffuse sound religion among the
middle classes.   Old and valuable works of Divinity
were to be republished, and new treatises written, with
a large proportion of religious biography, and the whole
to be presented in a cheap and popular form.   Among
the works first proposed were the lives of Luther, Brain-
erd, and Payson, Flavel's " Saint Indeed," Serle's " Christian Remembrancer," and an abridged Martyrology.   The
series extended to rather more than fifty volumes, and
has conveyed to its many readers a large amount of solid,
scriptural truth, mingled with some choice examples of
religious experience.   In this work he felt deeply the
importance of a wise selection, and earnestly sought the
counsel of Christian friends.   In a letter to Mr. Budd, his
former pastor, he thus expressed his feelings.

I venture to claim your aid in this matter, because, if the Lord
spare me to carry it on, it may materially affect the tone of Divinity
in an extensive circle.   I am truly anxious, as the Lord gives me
wisdom, that any influence I may have should be wholly used to

advance His truth in the present work. . . . Now, just tell me
what you would tell your children—what books I should exclude—
what books, in forming the mind of those committed to you, you
would give them to read.  I intreat you, my dear friend, to help
me with your judgment, that our common Lord and Master may
not have hurt, but help, by any thing which I do in this matter.
You cannot be too free with me, because I know the love you have
to Him who is dearest of all to us, and your love to me in Him.

The correspondence of Mr. Bickersteth, at this time,
was much occupied with another subject, of great importance, and equal difficulty, which occasioned a painful
division of judgment among pious and thoughtful men.
This was the Bible Society controversy.  That noble
Institution might be said to have been cradled in storms.
The simplicity of its object, and the grandeur of its results, had now secured it, for many years, the general
and warm concurrence of Protestant Christians.  Yet
the width, or as others would call it, the laxity of its
constitution, exposed it from the first to serious dangers,
as soon as any question of practical delicacy arose.  About
the year 1825, the Apocryphal controversy awakened very
bitter and angry feelings, and led to the secession of most
of the Scotch auxiliaries.  The wise decision, however, to
abstain in future from circulating, directly, or indirectly,
any copies which contained the Apocrypha, restored peace
to the Society, and regained the confidence of the great
body of its supporters.  Like an oak which has lost some
of its leaves and branches in a storm, it rooted itself more
deeply than ever in general esteem, and enlarged yearly
the range of its operations.

But the shock which was now convulsing the political
world, was also felt deeply by the religious institutions
of our land.  A mere appeal to precedents and results

would no longer suffice, to secure the full sympathy of
Christian men.  There was a craving for spiritual reform, a renewed appeal to the first principles of Christian
duty, a resolution to sift every human institution to its
very foundations.  The Bible Society again became a
theatre of conflict.  The recognition, as fellow-Christians,
and Christian ministers, of those who held and taught
fundamental heresy, and the want of any united prayer
for the Divine blessing, were felt by many excellent men
to be serious blots in its constitution, and difficulties in
the way of their conscientious adherence.  A motion
was made at the Annual Meeting of 1831, to exclude
Socinians from the management, and to open all public
meetings by prayer, and reading the word of God.  This
alteration was rejected by a great majority, and a formid-
able controversy at once arose.  The extremes of opinion
were wide asunder.  Some denounced the proposed change
as a piece of factious bigotry, and a breach of contract,
which would be fatal to the honour and existence of the
Society.  Others, again, viewed it as a plain and absolute
law of Christian duty, which no fancied expediency could
set aside, so that its rejection would brand the Society
with the guilt of bearing false witness against Christ, and
render secession and active opposition inevitable.  One
class seemed ready to maintain that the excellence of the
object rendered all inquiry into the lawfulness of the
means superfluous ; while others in their zeal for a hardly
attainable perfection in the means employed, were in
danger of sacrificing the great object itself; or at least of
breaking in pieces the most powerful and effectual instrument, which the world had ever witnessed, for the diffusion of those Holy Scriptures, which are the chief light
and blessing of our fallen world.

There were many, however, on both sides of this painful
controversy, who took a middle and more temperate
course. Some of them thought any change unnecessary,
and in itself inexpedient, but desired under the altered
circumstances, a partial concession to be made to the sen-
sitive conscience of many of their brethren. Others,
again, while they held strongly that the actual constitution was in principle defective, believed that the defect
was rather in theory than in practice ; and while they
sought to reduce the suggested changes within the nar-
rowest limits, did not feel that the continued rejection of
them would justify their creating a schism in so noble a
work, or demand more than a temperate and friendly
protest. To this last class Mr. Bickersteth himself belonged, and though at the time he found himself in a
small minority, he lived to see his convictions, on one
point at least, spread widely among the friends of the Society, until they were echoed by a large majority, at the
last Annual Meeting he attended, the year before his
death.

The controversy at the time was well adapted to sift
the spirits of men, and to call into exercise the graces of
Christian wisdom and forbearance. Intimate friends
were found, perhaps for the first time, opposed to each
other. The correspondence of Mr. Bickersteth contains
letters of encouragement from one friend, of rebuke or
deprecation from another ; complaints, on one side, that
he had gone too far, and on the other, that he was not
decided enough in his protest against the actual constitution. The difference reached to his nearest and
choicest friends. Thus, whilst Mr. Bridges wrote to him
in December, 1831,—" How remarkable is the continued identity of our sentiments on the Bible question,

without mutual communication : it is literally seeing eye to eye,"—his aged friend and predecessor, Mr. Pratt, wrote a few months later ; " Consider, my dear friend, that your paper will be seized upon by the weak and wicked, to run down the noblest institution which the world ever saw. You do indeed incur a fearful responsibility. I am truly anxious that you should not, in your advancing years, be betrayed, under what appears to me an utterly erroneous view, to thwart, retard, and hinder that cause, which your earlier years were spent in promoting. I grieve at the whole procedure, but am ever affectionately yours, J. Pratt."

Again, while his fellow-labourer and successor in the Secretaryship of the Church Missionary Society, Mr. Woodrooffe, concurred fully in his views, the lay Secretary, Mr. Coates, wrote to complain of an intended protest, as a wrong done to himself, in his character as a member of the Bible Society. The lines of defence, as well as the grounds of objection, were various. Some, like Mr. Bickersteth's former pastor, Mr. Budd, justified the actual constitution, on the plea that the circulation of the Bible was a moral, and not a religious work ; while others maintained that Socinianism was virtually excluded, by the law which prescribed the exclusive adoption of the authorized version. When, at the close of 1831, a new Society was formed, called the " Trinitarian Bible Society," fresh complications of opinion and practice arose, and it became hard for the wisest Christian to see his way clearly amidst the excitement of thought and feeling which prevailed. A letter of Mr. Bickersteth to his valued friend the Rev. E. B. Elliott, now so widely known as the author of the " Horæ Apocalypticæ," in reply to a pamphlet which he had forwarded, will explain his views on this difficult controversy.

*March* 16, 1832.

MY DEAR FRIEND,

I thank you, both for your pamphlet and your letter. The sweet spirit of both is just what I expected from you. The Bible Society controversy is to me a most painful subject, and to open my mouth upon it is a thing I shrink from; because I differ from brethren whom I love most heartily in our common Lord.

There are many things in your speech which I fully concur in, and I am aware of the difficulties of the position in which I and a few friends stand, who differ both from the old and the new Society.

I conceive the doctrine of the Trinity to stand by itself, as the great fundamental article of the Christian religion, running through the Bible, but specially stamped upon every Christian. (Matt. xxviii. 19.)

I conceive the Socinians to be distinguished from all others, by professedly denying this doctrine, and being therefore professed unbelievers.

I consider that the work of the Bible Society, in the translation of the Scriptures, is one which has to do with the principles of religion.

I consider, therefore, a passage which you have not quoted, but which has always been one of my principal difficulties—"Be not unequally yoked with unbelievers,"—to be my Master's direction to avoid being yoked together with them, in drawing the same religious institution, having to do with the principles of religion.

I feel the difficulty the greater, as every Socinian minister is entitled to be on the Committee, with every Socinian subscriber of five guineas a-year.

The very principle of the Bible Society is a giving up of the main principle of Popery, and a protest against open transgressors of the laws of the Bible. But the Socinians avow the most fundamental of all errors; are professed unbelievers; and yet are, in principle, yoked with us in a common work, in which the principles of the Gospel have in translations to be determined upon.

Yet, feeling the conscientious difficulties of many as to a test and

C 5

prayer, and turning much in my mind how the breach might be
healed, and the purity of Christian principle be maintained, it has
occurred to me and other friends, that an explanatory confession of
Christ might be so worded as to meet the views of all good men,
and be appended to the laws of the Parent Society, in words
similar to these—" That the Society feels itself called upon to
acknowledge the Father, the Son, and the Holy Ghost, to be the
one living and true God, and declares and avows this great principle
of the Christian faith to be the basis of its union and labours."

With regard to prayer, the devout reading of a suitable portion
of Scripture, containing a prayer, would satisfy me, and those who
think with me.

You will easily see that there is a broad line of distinction between a voluntary union, like that of the Bible Society, and a providential one, formed before men had heard the Gospel. This
meets some of your suppositions. I cannot get over 2 John 10, so
easily as you seem to do. The doctrine of Christ, when we recollect how much St. John dwells on His Godhead, must emphatically
include that which is its peculiarity and its glory.

It appears to me that the British and Foreign Bible Society has
now a noble opportunity, in the midst of an ungodly world, of
bearing testimony to this fundamental truth of the Gospel, and
true centre of union of real Christians. God would be honoured by
it, and the conscientious scruples of very many be removed, and a
higher point of union and blessedness be reached, than has ever
yet been attained.

These are my deliberate sentiments. But I shrink from controversy as a fearful danger, and have therefore kept as much as possible in the back-ground. Yet I cannot deny what, in the best
exercise of my judgment, appears to me the scriptural path ; and to
afford a basis, as broad, I think, as any Christian can desire, for
union in this long-cherished Society.

With these views, I was sorry, my dear friend, to see your
pamphlet, which justly exposes many mistakes, but is calculated, I
fear, to put off, rather than to accelerate, the much-to-be-desired
re-union of the servants of Christ in this great and blessed work.

I have not left the old Society. Though I think it wrong in
principle, I think it has in the main, in practice, not been unequally yoked with unbelievers; but if the practice is correct, surely
the principle may be avowed.

I have thus, with all frankness, confessed my principles to you.
We love and serve the same Saviour, and heartily love each other
in Him, our one Head.

Ever affectionately yours,

E. BICKERSTETH.

I must add a few words, with reference to those from whom I
have differed. I have the sincerest love and esteem for them. I
believe them to be wholly upright in this matter before God. I
conceive it to be very possible that I may be in error, in mistaking
the sense of God's word; and nothing grieves me more than that
my poor name should be in any way implicated in the matter, to
strengthen any thing like divisions among brethren. I grieve that
the new Society was formed so precipitately.

To the views of this letter Mr. Bickersteth always adhered. He never ceased to regret the seeming recognition
of Socinians as Christian ministers, by a law of the Society, and the absence of united prayer in its meetings, as
serious defects in its practice and constitution. But he
thought them far outweighed by its real merits, by the
Christian tone which prevailed in its Reports and general
management, the vast importance of the object, and the
clear tokens of the abundant blessing of God, which rested
on its labours. He continued, therefore, to give it a
zealous, practical support, as the Secretary of its local
Auxiliary. He also subscribed, however, to the Trinitarian Society, that he might show his desire for a plainer
confession of that holy name, into which all Christians
are baptized, and his deep sense of the duty, in such a
work, of united and open prayer for the blessing of God.

When his view on this point had gained a partial acceptance, the year before his death, his love for the Society
received a fresh impulse, and some of his last days were
employed in a hearty and zealous advocacy of its claims.
We return to his journal :—

"*July* 15.   To-morrow I take my young people to the
confirmation.   I have endeavoured diligently to instruct
them ; but some of them seem to have got little good.

" The Cholera has spread very widely in this country,
and has been in the neighbouring towns of Ware and Hertford.  O that these things may bring us nearer to God !

" *August* 21.   I go to-morrow, the Lord willing, on a
long journey for the Church Missionary Society, to Lan-
cashire, Westmoreland, Cumberland and Norfolk.   I
doubt not it is the Lord's work, and therefore desire
to go willingly ; but I have a sick child seriously ill at
home, and my mind shrinks now from the fatigue and
anxieties of travelling ; but O my Father, let Thy will
be mine !   Seeing Thou hast redeemed me in Jesus, I desire to be wholly Thine.

" *September* 30.   By God's great mercy I have been
carried through my long journey, and have returned in
peace to my dwelling : my dear child is restored to health.
O how good the Lord is !   O that His Spirit may work in
me, to render grateful returns to Him !   To-morrow, the
Lord willing, I go to Cambridge, to attend Mr. Simeon's
jubilee of his ministry.   Lord ! bless my going out and
coming in, to Thy glory and the good of many !

" We had fourteen to our clerical meeting on the 25th
—the largest number that have met.   The Lord increase
them more and more.

" *October* 13.   The privilege of attending Mr. Simeon's
jubilee was very great.   He preached on Monday, Octo-

ber 1st, from 1 Peter i. 12—15. On Tuesday there met
in his rooms Mr. J. and Mr. F. Cunningham, Mr. C.
Bridges, Mr. Nottidge, Mr. Carr, Mr. Close, Mr. Tacy,
Mr. Edwards, Mr. Hankinson, Mr. Carus, Mr. Sargent,
Archdeacon Hodson, Professors Scholefield and Farish,
Mr. Clarkson, Mr. Marsh, S. Wilberforce, W. Jowett, &c.
Mr. Sargent brought forward humiliation, Mr. Edwards,
Isa. vi., Mr. Hankinson, thanksgiving, and I, the spread
of the Gospel. On Wednesday we discussed subjects, the
coming of Christ's kingdom, the prayer of faith, and
reform in the Church, in which we generally agreed we
could not intermeddle. It was a season much to be
remembered.

" My own soul does specially need reviving grace, and
quickening in prayer. Many things call me to this ;—
changes in my family, changes in the parish, and the long-
continued lukewarmness of my soul in spiritual things.

" I have lately been enlarging my tract ' On Prophecy,'
with a special reference to the coming of Christ's kingdom. I have also been preparing a new hymn-book for
my people."

The work, thus alluded to in his journal, occupied much
of his time and thoughts, and has borne very abundant
fruit to the Church of Christ. On his first removal to
Watton, his attention was soon drawn to the defective
state of the church-psalmody. Of the various hymn-
books in use, there was none which met his own ideas of
what was desirable for all the wants of the Christian
family and congregation. He now set about supplying,
if possible, this want, which was felt also by many others.
He procured copies of a very large number of previous
collections, and compared them together, consulted vari-

ous friends, digested a full system of arrangement, applied in several quarters for new hymns, where particular
subjects were unoccupied, and submitted the whole to a
careful revision, that no statement, objectionable in
point of doctrine, or otherwise offensive, might appear.
With his strong practical sense, he saw clearly that a
hymn-book, drawn up for general use, stands on a footing
entirely distinct from a literary edition of an author's
work, where the first excellence is historical fidelity ; and
that there was no good reason why a beautiful hymn
should be sacrificed, because of some doctrinal or critical
flaw in a single verse ; or why real faults should be per-
petuated and imposed on thousands of congregations, in
order to secure the integrity of a brief, and perhaps hasty
composition, as it first came from the author's pen.    Perhaps the principle, sound in itself, was at first carried
rather to excess in its application, and in later editions his
riper judgment dispensed with some of the alterations
which had originally been made in hymns, already well
known.    Perhaps, also, the comparative absence, in his
mind, of the poetical element, with his deep sense of the
preciousness of gospel truth, obtained admission for a small
number of hymns, not quite worthy of a place in such a
collection.    But, with these slight drawbacks, his spiritual
feeling, practical judgment, and zealous diligence, produced their natural fruit.    The " Christian Psalmody "
has since undergone two successive enlargements, and a
sale, up to the present time, of nearly 160,000 copies, is
a sufficient proof of the high estimation it has deservedly
gained.    The index was drawn up by his esteemed and
honoured brother-in-law, the late Rev. R. Mayor, formerly
a missionary in Ceylon, whose ardent mind saw from the
first the importance of the work, and the certain prospect

of a wide circulation. His letter, in transmitting it, shows
the warmth of his heart, and the result has proved the
correctness of his judgment.

MY DEAREST BROTHER,

Does your patience still hold out, or have you sent your index
to press, without waiting for a tardy brother ?   I have found it no
such easy matter to complete it, as I anticipated, and completed it
is not, even after so long a delay.   The truth is, the treasures of the
Watton Hymn Book are inexhaustible.   The more I explore their
contents, the more I am astonished and delighted ; but as it will
not soon pass under the public eye, as it has been day after day
revolving before mine, you should have a full index, to tell way-
faring men where some of its riches are concealed.   I fully calculate
on the Hymn Book's becoming, in a short time, quite a standard
work.   But at present, when good people hear of " Bickersteth's
Hymn Book," they have hitherto loved you so much in prose, that
they cannot give you credit for pleasing them with poetry, and they
enquire with some degree of scepticism—Is Edward Bickersteth
also among the poets ?   But when they have searched for themselves, they will find that the making of a good selection depends
on something more intrinsically valuable than an ear for soft flowing language—that a spiritual taste and discernment, a mind to
catch what is grand in thought, are qualifications more needed than
a musical ear, or poetic genius.   In time, therefore, your Hymn
Book must circulate, wherever truth is loved. . . . . . . I have been
feeding in green pastures, while making the index.   I would rather
be the author of the Watton Hymn Book, than all your other publications, valuable as they are ; for I trust that many thousands,
rich and poor, will be nourished, elevated, comforted, and edified by
them. . . . I would disregard the clamour of those who are waiting
for the next edition, and would take time to make it perfect.   With
regard to the index, I would add to the price, rather than have a
meagre one.   All who care for souls will not be prevented from
giving the best book, because some other may be had 3d. cheaper.

There is such a power of moving in the book itself, that nothing can prevent its insinuating itself everywhere. This is not the solitary opinion of a sanguine brother, who forms hasty judgments, but many wiser heads and warmer hearts will confirm it.

Yours ever,

R. Mayor.

That Mr. Mayor was not mistaken in his estimate of the work, and its prospect of wide acceptance, was proved, not only by its growing circulation, but by many private testimonies. One of the most striking and gratifying of these occurs in the following letter from his old and valued friend, the Bishop of Calcutta.

The Palace, Oct. 16, 1833.

My dearest Brother,

At the very time your kind present of your new Psalm Book arrived, Mr. Dealtry * was engaged in reprinting the Psalm Book of the Old Church. I looked over yours with sincere approbation. I think it decidedly the most copious, practical, devout, and well-arranged, with which I am acquainted. The order of the subjects, embracing a body of divinity, particularly pleases me, and I cannot but hope, will help much the infant cause of Christianity among our native converts. I sent down your volume to Mr. Dealtry and Mr. Boys. They highly approved also; their book, half prepared, is laid aside, and they beg you to send 500 copies as soon as you can. Five hundred I also beg for myself. . . . What a pleasure it will be to me to see my dear brother Bickersteth's Psalm-Book the current work for celebrating the praises of God in this new scene. . . . . . . We entreat your prayers, and remain

Your most affectionate

Daniel Calcutta.

It is needless to add that the desire so lovingly expressed, has been very extensively fulfilled, by the use of the Hymn Book in most of the Indian churches.

* Now the Bishop of Madras.

The journal of the year closes with these entries :—

" *December* 24.  I have been preaching a course of sermons on the advent of Christ, and have been led to see the importance of the subject, and how needful it is to be ready.  The Lord give me grace to have oil in my vessel with my lamp, as well as to all committed to my charge.

" I trust that I have found preparing the Hymn-Book profitable to my soul.  It is now going through the press.  O Lord, prosper this effort for the good of thy Church !  O manifest thyself as a Purifier and Reviver of my soul !  O for communion with Thee, and holy thirstings after Thee.

" *December* 31.  . . . In looking back, how very many have been God's mercies in the past year !  It began in darkness and sorrow, and it ends in peace.  The help afforded in the Missionary Sermon was very gracious ; and I have been carried in health and strength through my varied duties.  To God be all praise and glory !

" As to my soul, some things are more bright ; but others are still dark.  O for more real communion with God in private, in family prayer, and in public worship !  I think that I enjoy it most at our social meetings ; but is it from excitement, or the work of the Spirit ?  Jesus is all my confidence and all my boast.  I cannot for a moment rest anywhere but in Him.

" What I want most is for my soul to be growing in grace, and preparing for the coming of the Lord.  Without this, what good will anything else do me ?"

# CHAPTER XVIII.

At the close of January, 1833, Mr. Bickersteth wrote in his Journal: " My mind has latterly been much directed to the coming of Christ. The signs of the times are such as may well lead Christians to a more serious and thoughtful consideration of that glorious event. O may I be found ready, when He comes, to give up my account with joy; and may I go to dwell with Him for ever! O Jesus, help me to walk with Thee, every day, and every hour, and then Thy coming will indeed be unmingled joy and blessedness to me."

These words are one of the earliest signs of that change in his judgment, on the doctrine of the Second Advent, which gave a deeper tone, through all his later years, to his writings and ministry. When he was first brought, in his youth, to the knowledge of the gospel, he adopted the view which was then popular among serious Christians; and looked forward to the gradual conversion of the world, by the spread of missions, and a larger blessing on the ordinary means of grace. His occupation, and the peculiar character of his mind, which was practical and earnest, but not imaginative, seemed likely to confirm him in the view he had so early embraced. His whole strength, for many years, had been given to the work of missions; and perhaps no single person had done more to awaken an interest in labour for the heathen through the length and breadth of the land. On the other hand, the excitement of the unknown tongues, and the dogmatism and extravagance often connected with the study of unfulfilled prophecy, would naturally repel a mind like his from all such inquiries. In a letter a few years earlier, he had mentioned his fears for the missionary cause, from the eager attention given to prophetic discussion. Again, in May, 1831, he wrote to Mrs. Bickersteth from one of the midland counties: "Things are in a most dead and cold state here : may the Lord revive his work! Dr. F——— keeps aloof from religious societies ; the good men are all afloat on prophesying, and the immediate work of the Lord is disregarded for the uncertain future. These things ought not so to be. But I think any one who has known this place for the last seven or eight years might have foreboded all we now see." Indeed his " Remarks on the Prophecies," in their original form, were chiefly designed to quiet the minds of those Christians, who were in danger, as he thought, of forsaking plain and immediate duties for the path of thorny and doubtful speculation.

The feeling, however, always predominant in his mind, was a deep reverence for the supreme authority of the word of God. The public events which followed his removal to Watton, were of an awakening and unusual kind. He was naturally led to make the inquiry, Does the word of God enjoin attention to all prophecy, whether fulfilled or unfulfilled ? and, if so, what, according to the Scriptures, are the real prospects of the church of Christ ?

The result of this inquiry, carried on for several years, was a decided change in the outline of his expectations.

He became what is popularly, but rather vaguely called, a Millennarian. To speak more precisely, he was led to believe that the second coming of Christ will precede the Millennium ; that the first resurrection is literal, and that Christ will establish a glorious kingdom of righteousness on earth at His return, before the resurrection of the wicked, and their final judgment. He believed that the whole tenor of Scripture was opposed to the idea, which had latterly prevailed in the Church, of a fixed interval of a thousand years, before the promised return of Christ. But while he thus renounced the opinion, that missionary agencies would secure the gradual conversion of the world, he continued to believe that they were the plain duty, and one of the highest privileges, of the Christian ; and he found new motives for diligence in the shortness of the time, and the prospect of a speedy recompence from the Lord in the day of His appearing.

He preached four sermons on the subject, in August 1832, and published them early in the next year, with the title " Preparedness for the day of Christ." Their practical, earnest tone, and the confidence widely felt in his sound judgment, procured them an attentive perusal, even from many who had regarded the whole subject with fear and jealousy. His correspondence, from this time, shews the attention which was drawn to the hope of Christ's coming, by these sermons, and by his later publications. There was no one whose character and example had so wide an influence in rescuing the study of prophecy, alike from the censure of its opponents, and the perversions of mistaken friends, as a nursery for censoriousness and dogmatism, and of crude, unprofitable speculation. The tone of all his writings on the subject was practical, loving, and holy. Without hiding his own views on secondary questions, he always kept before his readers the great things of the gospel, and the simplicity of those Divine warnings, which were the text of these first discourses. " Behold ! I come as a thief—Blessed is he that watcheth, and keepeth his garments ! The night is far spent, the day is at hand."

One effect of this change was to bring Mr. Bickersteth into correspondence and personal intercourse with Mr. Cuninghame of Lainshaw, whose labours as an expositor are well known. Mr. C. had forwarded a copy of his work on the Apocalypse, with a friendly note, and received an invitation to Watton, where he spent a few days in June 1833. The visit was repeated for several years, and was made the occasion for a gathering of clergymen and other friends, to confer on the word of prophecy, and to listen to the statements which so zealous and able a writer might lay before them. The mutual affection and regard thus awakened, continued to the last ; though Mr. Bickersteth's high esteem for his aged friend, and sense of obligation to his writings, were mingled with some regret for the asperity of tone by which they were occasionally disfigured, and which tended seriously to lessen their practical influence. In the preface to a later edition of his sermons, he stated clearly and modestly his own views, with his unchanged attachment to the great truths of the gospel, which he so long proclaimed.

" Prophetic truth, deeply but humbly studied, does not weaken our hold of any saving doctrine of Revelation, but rather enlarges the mind to fuller views of Divine righteousness and goodness.

" The author trusts that he holds, with greater simplicity and firmness than ever, those holy truths, which it has been his endeavour to embody in his past writings

for twenty years,—of our fallen nature in Adam, our total
ruin in ourselves, and the infinite love of God, in the gift
of His Son, and the promise of His Spirit. He desires to
maintain, with increasing stedfastness, the recovery of
God's people in and by Christ ; their election in him
before the foundation of the world ; their regeneration by
His Spirit, through His word ; their free justification by
faith alone ; their sanctification in the use of the means
of grace, such as hearing the word, prayer, and the sacraments ; and the life of faith, hope, and love, nourished
and maintained by the application of Divine truth in
God's ordinances to the heart, through the Spirit. He
rejoices in the thought, that they who are thus given to
Christ, are upheld by Divine power to the end, shall have
victory over Satan, death, hell, and the grave ; a glorious
resurrection, acceptance in the judgment to come, and
final and everlasting felicity, at the coming, and in the
kingdom, of their Lord and Saviour. With these views
are ever to be connected, the unspeakable danger of neglecting the truth, and the certain and everlasting destruction of those who " know not God, and obey not the
gospel of the Lord Jesus Christ."

" Respecting the period of the coming of our Lord, he
has been led latterly to the conclusion, that it does not
follow, but precede the Millennium. But after the mistakes of so many in ages past, the differences of the most
diligent modern students, and the positive declaration of
our Lord, Matt. xxiv. 36—44, he dreads attempting to fix
the exact time. Heartily does he love the many dear
brethren who hold the view with which he himself was
so long satisfied : nothing but his deliberate conviction
of the truth of the sentiment here avowed, and of its
vast importance at the present æra of the Church, would

lead him to make it known, and to urge his fellow-Christians to a diligent study of the sacred records on this subject."

Under the influence of these truths, the new year opened with the following reflections and resolutions.

" *January* 6, 1833. . . . . O that all my talents this year may be laid out for God. I desire to have this as my motto for the year,—OCCUPY TILL I COME.—Let me look backwards and forwards, then, for help to do this. My talents are money, time, influence, ability, the ministry.

" MONEY. In what is past, I have not laid it out wisely. Too much has been spent on self, in literary gratification, and pleasing my family.

" In what is to come, I desire to think more of the poor, to be more ready for cases of necessity, to count it more a privilege to give, and not to procrastinate, when there is opportunity.

" TIME. I have been very guilty here, in not giving my time, as I ought, to my people. It has been too much spent in desultory study, and too little in active duties.

" In what is to come, O Lord, help me to redeem time, giving to each hour its appointed work, as I believe that Thou wouldest have it occupied ; and to adhere as much as may be to a fixed plan. O preserve me from waste of time !

" INFLUENCE. I have but little thought how I might, by this, benefit others—my servants,—my children,—my friends. It has been a talent little improved for God.

" In what is to come, O Lord, help me to be more circumspect and diligent, seeking to lay out all my influence to benefit the souls and bodies of my fellow-creatures.

" ABILITY.   O for more fidelity to all the powers
entrusted to me! Let nothing be neglected that can
glorify my God, and benefit His church.   O may I be
faithful over what I have!

" THE MINISTRY.   Here I am most guilty.   When I
look at my parish, and see how many I have never personally warned and instructed—how many are living in
drunkenness and ignorance, I may well mourn over
them, and over my own unfaithfulness.   May this year
be distinguished by a new course of labours for the good
of the people.   O that my own Visitation Sermon were
my animating spring and my daily practice!   Lord,
make me a faithful minister of Thy word!"

His monthly journal gives a brief outline of the chief
employments of the year; though his correspondence
occupied also much of his time, and embraced a large
variety of subjects, connected with the progress of the
gospel.

" *February* 23.  . . . My family plans are now on a
much more comfortable and profitable footing.   I believe
we have secured a truly valuable governess for our children, and they are becoming much attached to her.   I
have much more constant daily prayer with my dear
wife.   But I cannot say that I have similar comfort in my
fulfilment of duties in the parish.   O Lord! revive Thy
work in my soul, and quicken me to holy diligence among
my people."

" *March* 19.  . . . . I am preparing for the press the
Sermons on ' Preparedness for the Day of Christ.'

" On Monday next I go to town and to Bristol, to
attend the Church Missionary Anniversary there.   The
Lord make it a blessing to me, and to many others.   It
is always a cross to me to leave home.

" My health has been more affected than in previous
winters, and requires constant attention. What mercies I
have had in forty-seven years of almost unbroken health !
Well may I be content now with some sicknesses, sent in
love."

" *April* 6.   I have been carried through my journey
in comfort, but am not so strong as I was in bodily health,
and must expect more infirmities, as I advance in years.
My dear wife also suffers from deafness.   May all our
troubles be sanctified !   They are infinitely outweighed
by countless blessings.

" My Hymn-book is now published—the blessing of
the Lord go with it."

" *May* 5.  . . . . I have just been spending the Anniversary week in London—Missionary, Bible, Tract, and
Jews—and have spoken at several of the meetings.   The
Lord pardon what has been amiss, and accept all in the
mediation of Jesus.   I hope the tone of the meetings is
improved.

" *May* 12.   I have had a gracious experience of God's
goodness in the past week.   I set off for Cambridge with
my two eldest children, their governess, and my servant.
We had not gone three miles, when the horse set off at
full gallop down a hill, and, at a sharp turn at the bot-
tom, the carriage was overturned, and we were all thrown
out ; but though the carriage was broken to pieces, we
were all preserved, and received no serious injury.   God
grant that it may be to serve and praise our merciful
Deliverer !

" I have since pleaded the cause of the Church Missionary Society at various meetings in Cambridge, Stapleford,
Bedford, and Kettering, and been brought in peace to my
home again.   To God be all the praise."

"*July* 7.   I have had several journeys for the Church
Missionary Society ; a fortnight into Lincolnshire, and to
Chenies, &c.   The Lord pardon and accept.

". . . . I have much reason to bless my heavenly Father for the acceptance of my Hymn-book, which has
already been introduced into many churches, and is likely
to be into many more.   If I can help my Saviour's disciples even with a cup of cold water, I have reason to be
thankful."

A letter to his eldest daughter from Lincoln, on this
journey, throws light on the character of his private intercourse with his children.

*Lincoln, May* 28, 1833.

MY DEAREST CHILD,

I think that Mamma will excuse me writing to our dear child
instead of herself, as I wrote to her yesterday.   It is only by little
bits of time that I can write at all on these journeys, and I trust
that my dear girl has learnt the importance of the direction, to redeem the time, that all may be employed for good.

I have had an interesting and, I hope, useful journey, and am
thankful that I was made willing to leave my dear, happy home,
for the sake of Christ. . . .   There is a beautiful cathedral in this
city, and a little company that love our Saviour, far more beautiful
in Papa's eyes than all the beautiful cathedrals and churches in the
world, and living stones of a temple far more glorious and lasting.
That is true taste, which leads us to love what God loves, prize
what He prizes, and follow that which He approves.

I hope, my dear child, that God is giving you this spirit, to set
your affection on things above.   To be spiritually-minded is life
and peace ; and in order to this, we must be in Christ Jesus, and
abide in Him.   He is the only source of spiritual and holy affection ; just as the branch gets all its sap and juice, its verdure and
blossom and fruit, by its union with the tree,—we also get all our
fruitfulness by abiding in Christ.   He is beyond compare more

important to you than your parents, though He teaches and helps you by them. But He will remain when they are gone; He will be our joy and portion for ever. Your father would now with all affection commend you to Him, and entreat you ever to live very near to Him.

Your father every where meets with the greatest kindness and hospitality, because he goes among those who love our Redeemer, and therefore love those who seek to promote His cause. Make the ground of your attachment to others, my dear child, the love they bear to the Saviour; and never be anxious after the friendship of those who do not care for His glory and His kingdom. The friends of Christ are the best, the truest, and the most beneficial friends to us.

I suppose that Lincoln Cathedral would cost £500,000 to build. Well, the Religious Societies of England are doing far better than if they built such a cathedral every year, in raising that sum to scatter in every direction the light of Divine truth. This will do far more for the honour of God our Saviour, and the salvation of our fellow-creatures.

Your ever affectionate father,<br>E. BICKERSTETH.

"*August* 4. I have again been journeying, partly for the Church Missionary Society, and partly for other objects, to London, Cheshunt, White Roothing, and Acton, &c. Blessed be Thy name, O my Father, for the many mercies of these journeys! O that my heart were duly alive to God, and His kingdom, and glory!"

"*September* 1. I have been to the Isle of Wight, and have enjoyed many mercies with my beloved brethren Sibthorpe and Woodrooffe, and I hope have gained some help in the Christian life.

"I wrote three letters to my dearest wife on practical points in which we failed, as concerned our souls, our children, our household, our parish, the Church of Christ,

D 2

our trials, our temptations, our mercies.   O that the Lord may give us grace to act on the principles there laid down,—the principles of his blessed gospel ! ''

One or two extracts from these letters will show the principles which Mr. Bickersteth sought to apply constantly in all the various details of domestic life.

*Isle of Wight, August* 14—17.

Every thing good must begin with our own souls, in an entire surrender of our hearts to the Lord ; to His will, His word, and His glory, as our highest interest and clearest duty, our richest privilege, our only happiness, and by free grace the path in which we may walk, as well as ought to walk.

Now, though fellow-heirs together of the grace of life, we have not been adequately fellow-helpers on the way to Zion ; by neglect of conversing on spiritual subjects, of reading the word and praying together.   May we have grace hereafter to walk more closely with God in these respects.   We can only be happy in each other, as both our souls are wholly surrendered to the will of Christ.

Our children call for much thought and prayer, not mainly as regards their education for this world, but their education for eternity ; ever remembering that to teach them self-denial is to lay the right foundation for their future happiness, and to indulge them now in self-gratifying things, is the way to make them miserable in all their after-life.   To be the disciple of Christ is to be truly happy for time and for eternity ; and in aiming at this, we are the wisest and kindest parents to our children ; and all that seems kind and considerate, when not according to this, is really in the end unkindness and cruelty.   Now to be disciples of Christ, we and they must deny ourselves, take up our cross and follow Him.   O may we ever have grace to bring up our dear children on these principles with united heart, that they may be a comfort to us, a blessing to the church and to their country, and to families that may spring from them ; so that our joy through eternity may be greatly enlarged by their Christian education. . . .   May we lead them early to Christ, lead them to cry earnestly to Him for His Spirit, and show them that there is now, in this day of grace, free, full, and complete deliverance, salvation, life, and glory for them. O may our God fulfil His promise : " I will pour my Spirit upon thy seed, and my blessing upon thine offspring," &c. May you and I, my love, plead those precious promises in prayer for our dear children. They are our jewels, if they be Christ's jewels. They will be our thorns, if it be not our constant aim to bring them up in the nurture and admonition of the Lord. I know you agree with me in this, but we need to have our minds stirred up by way of remembrance. . .

In our household, may God ever give us Joshua's determination, —" As for me and my house, we will serve the Lord." I believe that this has been our aim, but it has been feebly executed. It includes *our property*, to be all laid out, as we shall wish it had been in the day of Christ. Here I have been guilty of vain expence about books. . . . It includes the religion of *our servants ;* and here I think I have not duly attended to the males, nor you to the females, so as to be often speaking for their spiritual good. There has not been a neglect in the family religious duties, except as to their full improvement ; but there has not been that private and personal application, which is the most efficient mode of making the public means really profitable.

Our parish, however, is the point in which we have, I think, most failed, and where the failure is more especially to be regretted, as it is our primary duty. The want has been, of a more steady personal inspection of the poor. Breaking through obstacles and difficulties in the way of this is a material part of that self-denial to which our Saviour Christ calls his people. The root of it is a want of lively zeal for the salvation of the souls around us. When we become cool about our own souls, we cease to be anxious about the souls of others. I fear there has been something of this creeping over us. Our chief care, next to our own souls and our families, should be our parish, where Christ has placed us specially to labour for Him, and to glorify His name. I am persuaded, much might be done to enlarge the attendance on the means of grace, and to bring home the Gospel personally to the people, by far more extensive intercourse with them, such as marks the parishes of Hayne and Bridges.  I think that our two eldest children should now begin to think of the poor, and see them with their governess or parents.  It is an habit which they should acquire early.  As to the temporal relief of our poor, I believe that as much is done for them as is in general desirable, though perhaps we have not so fully looked after them as to be competent to form a judgment ; and much might perhaps be done by putting them on better plans in their domestic economy. . . . My leaving home for the Church Missionary Society is, I fear, a serious impediment to the due care of the parish ; and I must aim rather at curtailing all absences from home,  Yet this leads to another material point—

The CHURCH OF CHRIST at large claims a most important share of attention.  God has, in different ways, placed me in a leading and influential position ; and the talent of influence must be used for Him, and the good of His Church.  I desire grace that I may have wisdom, disposition, and ability to glorify His name, by devotedness to Him in this respect.  Money, time, writings, preaching, speeches, visits, all bear on this point.  It is the highest use of money to lay it up in Christ's treasury, for the spiritual good of our fellow-creatures.  God has so accepted my writings that I think it still a duty to give attention to them, if I may in any way hereby benefit His Church.  As to preaching, speaking, and visiting out of the parish, it requires, I am persuaded, a clear and manifest call from our heavenly Father, before I let them interfere with home.

Now in all these things, my dearest wife, I wish to act simply on the principles of the Gospel of Christ, and to give to each duty its due share of attention.  You must help me in this, by sacrificing lesser desires and pleasures, that might interfere with primary duties, and by praying that I may have grace and strength, amidst all corruptions within, and all seductions from without, steadily to walk, by the strength of Christ, in that path which will bring peace at the last, and most promote our Father's glory, and the good of all around us.  Depend upon it, the more I am devoted to Christ, and the more you help me in this, the more I shall be a blessing to you and to our family ; and all that troubles us at any time may be traced originally to a neglected Christ, and a disobeyed Gospel.

. . . . The Lord bless you, my love, and enable us to walk more closely with him.  Love to all my dear tribe at home.

Ever affectionately yours,

E. BICKERSTETH.

The confession made in these letters, of a comparative failure in parish duties, is one which often recurs in Mr. Bickersteth's private journal ; and since it might occasion, with prejudiced minds, a false impression of the real facts, it seems to require a few words of explanation.  His pastoral intercourse with his people fell short, it is true, of the standard of his own desires, and perhaps also of that which is sometimes attained in a few eminently favoured parishes, where a zealous and earnest minister of Christ devotes his whole time and thoughts to this one work alone.  But when tried by the ordinary measure of pastoral diligence, even among good and pious men, he may truly be said "to have purchased for himself a good degree," as a faithful shepherd of the flock immediately committed to his charge.  The quiet and regular course of his home duties, compared with the frequency of his journeys, and the variety of public work in which he was engaged, is very likely to mislead those, who judge of their amount by the confessions of his journal, or their relative prominence in his biography.  The time occupied in his journeys was usually not more than two months in the year, and he scarcely ever allowed himself any other holiday.  He was therefore hardly absent from his parish so long as many devoted clergymen, from a regard to their health alone, after ten months' active labour, find to be desirable and almost necessary.  During his absence, there was very rarely any interruption, either in

the public services of the Lord's Day, or in the week-day
lectures. Two full services and an evening lecture on
the Sabbath, and from two to five lectures in the course
of the week, were the usual average of these means of
grace. When he was at home, a part of the day was
almost always spent in his schools, or among the poor.
His pastoral visits to the sick were constant and assidu-
ous. A system of district visiting was constantly maintained, which made him at once acquainted with any
cases requiring special attention ; and he was always
prompt to visit, even where there was no actual sickness,
when there seemed reason to hope for special benefit from
a word spoken in season. This constancy of his interest
in their welfare, with the kindness of his manner, and
the clear marks, in his whole conduct, of real love to the
souls of his people, endeared him even to those who had
not learned fully to appreciate that gospel of grace, which
he delighted to set before them. However frequent and
sincere his confessions of guilt as a pastor, accustomed
as he was to try himself by a perfect standard, and the
pattern of his Divine Lord and Master, yet the fourfold
increase in the number of the communicants during his
ministry, the tears of the poor abundantly shed over his
grave, and the deep love and reverence for his memory
which are still cherished among them, are proofs that he
attained a high degree of ministerial faithfulness, and
that, even where he felt himself most tempted to neglect,
and liable to comparative failure, his labours were not
in vain in the Lord. This explanation seems due to his
memory, and to the friendly remonstrances of his own
parishioners, since the Memoir was first published, some
of whom have expressed regret that fuller justice was not
done to this aspect of their beloved pastor's zeal and

fidelity. But the constant and gentle love of such a ministry is like the dew of heaven, which falls in silence, and may readily escape the eye of an observer, in the pages of a biography, though rich fruits in the garden of the Lord bear witness to its reality and power.

Besides the journeys of Mr. Bickersteth, a variety of public duties occupied him at this time, and appear in his correspondence. Arrangements were made with a friend for re-publishing select works of Charnock and Goodwin. A letter was written to the Secretaries of the Bible Society, with minute suggestions for relieving the scruples of many Christians, by placing its constitution, more explicitly, on a basis of religious faith. Several relate to Wheler Chapel, where he took much pains to secure a faithful ministry in the scene of his former labours. A Sermon, afterwards published, was preached for the District Visiting Society. His monthly journal, to the close of the year, relates chiefly to his private and personal experience.

" *October* 6. The Lord has graciously strengthened me hitherto for my public work. Mr. Garwood left me September 2, and I have since taken all the duty myself, in a good deal of weakness, having been on a system of diet for the recovery of health. The Lord bless the means !

" My mind has been much, and I trust profitably, directed to the subject of prophecy ; and I gather increasing convictions of the importance of being prepared for His coming, who is my only hope, Lord, and Saviour.

" I want minute conscientiousness in thoughts, words, and actions.

" I want parental wisdom, watchfulness, patience, and labour for my children.

" I want a realizing recollectedness of Christ's presence, with hearty dependence on him.

" O how quickly is all here fading ! May my part, my home, my hope, my joy, be in the heavenly Jerusalem ; and may I never be ashamed of confessing my blessed Master now before all men, as the only King, Lord, and Head of heaven and earth, whose favour is better than life itself."

" *November* 3. . . . My conviction increases that Christ's coming is at hand, and I pray that I may confess His truth, and myself be ready for His return. Sure I am, that I can only stand in Him. His righteousness is my only plea, His owning me as a believer my only hope. But may I be, by His grace, a wise and faithful servant, giving His household their portion of meat in due season. O Lord, I cast myself on thee, to be moulded and fashioned, as a vessel meet for the Master's use. Oh ! out of this lump of clay, by Thine almighty power and all-sufficient grace, form a vessel of mercy to Thy praise ! "

" *December* 1. I have again been thrown out of my gig, and made lame by the blow my foot received, and so kept at home; but through mercy no other material evil has happened to me, nor to those with me. O how great is the goodness of God, in sparing, preserving, and every way using so sinful a creature as I am !

" I have begun a course of sermons on the coming of Christ. The Lord bless it to much good to my dear parish !

" *December* 24. My wound still disables me. Last Sunday I got the duty fulfilled for me, but to-morrow I hope to preach. The will of the Lord be done !

" *December* 29. I am still kept a prisoner in my house,

though, the Church being at hand, I hope, the Lord
strengthening me, to do my public duty. . . . O Lord,
surely my soul is more diseased than my body ! There
indeed my wounds are corrupt—my unbelief, my formality, my worldly mind, my distance from God."

" *January* 25, 1834.   My lameness still continues,
though, through mercy, there is now greater hope of my
recovery.

" On the morrow I hope to administer the Lord's
Supper, and myself to partake of it.   In what spirit ?
Alas ! on the very same day I appear to be in the most
opposite spirits ; sometimes almost raised to the very
height of my desires, in thirsting after God, and at other
times wholly dead and dull.   I can rest nowhere but in
the righteousness of Immanuel, and in His rich and great
and free promises to the unworthy. . . .

" This day my new assistant, Mr. Greig, is to be ordained to the ministry.   May he be filled with the Spirit,
and come here to be a blessing to me and to many ! "

*March* 19.   God, in His loving-kindness, has now carried me through forty-eight years of my life ; in all of
which I have been a rich partaker of daily mercies. . .

" This has been, in many respects, a year of affliction.
Three overturns, my E——'s arm broken, my own knee
disabling me for eleven weeks, my two eldest children's
prolonged illness, my wife's many bodily infirmities.   O
may they be sanctified !   I need all, I deserve far more.
To the Lord be praise !

" But it has been a year of great loving-kindness.   The
success of my Hymn-book, and of " Preparedness for the
day of Christ," call for warm gratitude ; and some of my
people have glorified God by holy and happy deaths.

" As to what is before me, though I calculate on labours

and trials, yet if the Lord only give me His soul-quickening Spirit and nearness to Himself, I may gladly welcome
every cross."

"*March* 30. *Easter Sunday.* My blessed Saviour's day
of resurrection. O raise my soul from the death of sin,
from a cold, lukewarm, careless profession, to a life of holiness, self-denial, devotedness, and heavenly love. When
shall it indeed be ! When shall my private devotions be
full of earnest, fervent, heart-going-forth prayer and
praise ? When shall my soul study more prayerfully and
feelingly the word of my God ! When shall my public
worship be something more than outside decency—even
heart-communion with my God ! When shall all my
walks and my rides, all my works, and all my ways, be
a walking before God, and living constantly with Him !
Lord, here is my desire. O bring it to a good issue !

" I have every earthly comfort and blessing, and only
trials to remind me of their transitory nature. O that
these earthly comforts may be sanctified, and draw my
heart to God ! Thou art able to do this, O my God,
and to give me a large heart, like David's, for Thee
and Thine. I want a large, liberal heart for God, who
gives me all things. Let me be continually laying out
for Thee."

" *March* 27, 1834. . . . . . . I have found the doctrine of
the personal coming of Christ before the millennium
quickening and profitable to my soul ; and, believing it
to be Divine truth, I pray that I may see it with greater
clearness and power, hold it more firmly, confess it more
boldly, and live in its joyful hope, as well as in its awakening and stirring influence.

· " O for grace to fulfil self-denying duties ! Here no
expression suits me better than that,—' O wretched man

that I am, who shall deliver me from the body of this
death ? '

" O Lord, direct me in the disposal of time, talents,
influence, property, and every thing I am and have, that
all may be used for Thy glory, and so as may give me joy
and not sorrow in the day of Thine appearing."

Early in 1834 Mr. Bickersteth was requested by the
London Jews' Society to preach their Anniversary Sermon. He gladly undertook a task, which was so thoroughly in harmony with his newly-acquired convictions
respecting the hopes of Israel ; and alluded to the change
of his feelings in the opening of the discourse. " Engaged for many years," he said, " in the work of promoting missions to the Gentiles, my mind was but little
directed towards the Jews ; but having since been enabled to give more consideration to the Divine testimony
concerning them, I have increasingly seen how plainly,
in these momentous times, our God requires His people
to care for Israel, and how great is the blessedness of
helping forward their salvation."

Some years before, he had been on the same platform
with Mr. Simeon at a meeting of the Jews' Society, when
that venerable servant of Christ spoke of the object for
which they were met, as the most blessed among the
various works of Christian benevolence. Jealous for his
own Society, Mr. Bickersteth wrote on a slip of paper,
which he handed to him—" Six millions of Jews, and six
hundred millions of Gentiles—which is the most important ? " Mr. Simeon promptly rejoined in the same way
—" But if the conversion of the six, is to be life from the
dead to the six hundred millions—what then ? " Mr.
Bickersteth had now learned to appreciate the force of
this pithy reasoning of his venerable friend, and to esti-

mate the importance of the Jewish cause, not by a mere comparison of numbers, but by its prominence in the word of God. Without the least abatement in his zeal for missions to the heathen, he now rivalled Mr. Simeon himself in the special and deep interest he felt for the conversion of Israel ; and his missionary journeys, from this time, were shared very much between the two Societies. His text, on this occasion, was Isa. lxii. 10—12, and was made the basis of a powerful appeal on behalf of Israel, which will be found in his volume on the Restoration of the Jews.

Soon after the Jewish sermon, Mr. Bickersteth took two journeys, into Yorkshire and Buckinghamshire, for the Church Missionary Society. On his return he was called to preach a funeral sermon for his beloved sister-in-law, Mrs. Thomas Bignold, who, after a lingering illness, slept peacefully in Jesus. The text was 1 Thess. iv. 13, 14, and the title which he gave it, " Comfort in Sorrow." It is eminently marked by that glowing, earnest tone, which made his sermons, without any special graces of delivery, or ornaments of style, so refreshing to every pious hearer, and so widely useful in their published form. He thus alludes to her death in his own Journal.

" *July* 23, 1834. I this morning committed to the silent tomb in Watton church, the remains of my beloved sister-in-law, Priscilla Bignold. I have for thirteen months attended her as her pastor, and seen the fruits of the Spirit beautifully growing and ripening, till quite matured for her Master. The last time I visited her, she said to me, ' Now that we are quite alone, I wish to have your sincere opinion of my state, whether you think me right before God.' I told her, I did believe from my heart,

her works of faith remarkably proved that hers was a
living faith, leading her to renounce all hope but in
Christ, and filling her with love to Him and His. She
replied, 'I know it is so, not only because you say it, but
because I feel the same things in my heart.' "

In August the health of his family rendered a visit to
the sea-side desirable, and he removed with them for a
month to Broadstairs. These times of seeming relaxation were not seldom among those of his busiest activity.
His general purpose in leaving home, to recruit his
strength by a season of quiet, could seldom hold out
against the importunity of friends who sought and prized
his ministrations, and his own zeal to be employed in his
Master's service. " It is better to wear out than to rust
out," was his frequent reply to the affectionate cautions
of his family. On his return he was journeying again,
first to Bristol and then to Cambridge, for the Jews'
Society. A year later, the Secretary wrote to him that
the impression of the latter visit was still bearing fruit,
in the deepened interest awakened in the university for
the cause of Israel.

He had indeed many proofs that the blessing of God
continued to rest both on these journeys and on his publications. In November he received an anonymous letter
from a lady, who ascribed her conversion to God to his
work on the Lord's Supper, which she had read seven
years before. Another, in August, from Lady Lucy Whitmore, is an example of the blessing which rested on his
ministry, in eight or nine hundred churches where he
pleaded the cause of missions.

*August* 4, 1834.

MY DEAR MR. BICKERSTETH,

It is so long since I heard anything of you, and your dear family,

that I must write, and beg a few lines in return. The valued tie
you so kindly proffered me, as godmother to your dear boy, gives
me courage to plead a kind of privilege, to intrude occasionally on
your precious time.

Last November I seemed just on the borders of the eternal
world. I hoped that I was just about to depart, and to be with
Christ. But it was not so, and here I am still, a weak and fainting
pilgrim, and perhaps may be for long. God knoweth, and may His
will more and more be mine.

I returned the week before last from spending a few weeks at
Cheltenham, and purposed to write immediately, but was taken ill.
I cannot say Cheltenham benefited my body, but my soul was
sweetly refreshed, by being permitted again to join the congregation
of God's people, and listen to the words of life. . . . . . . . Since I
heard you at Worcester, I think in the year 1820, I have never
seemed so strengthened by the preaching of any of God's ministers.
You were the instrument from whom (I speak not of the Bible
itself) I first received deep and lasting comfort. I can never forget
it, and daily my poor petition rises, for the Lord's blessing to descend
on you and yours. . . . The Lord be with you, now and ever, prays,

Your ever-faithful, and affectionate friend,

LUCY E. G. WHITMORE.

A clergyman, soon after, thus acknowledged a gift of
books. "We could not have received a more delightful
present. We love them, first, because of the truth of
which they are full ; and next, because we feel so strongly
and tenderly knit in Christian love to him who penned
them. I have also long felt greatly interested in your
publications ; remembering, that in my youth, when the
first glimmerings of spiritual light were arising in my
mind, when I had no friend to counsel me in divine
things, and no worthy supply of religious books, I was
led, I know not how, to purchase your ' Treatise on
Prayer.' It was the first work that received my serious

attention, and so deep was the attention I paid it, that
the whole book has been indelibly fixed on my mind;
and on looking into it, almost every page recurs fresh to
my memory, even at this time. I remember presenting
the prayers at the end, again, and again, and again, in
secret at the throne of grace, and have no doubt that this
exercise received the divine blessing."

At the same time, another thus alluded to his Sermons on the Advent. " I have often wished I could·
tell you, that your Sermons on ' the day of Christ,' were
received with uncommon pleasure in this neighbourhood.
I think forty-seven copies passed through my own hands;
and a neighbouring clergyman read the whole in succession from his pulpit. Pity it is that anything should offend
men's minds, and induce a disregard of this glorious and
soul-animating subject. But the prejudices of many are
subsiding, and on every side the announcement of the
Bridegroom's approach is spreading. What is the hope
set before us, if it be not the final triumph of the Lord
and His people? I have been deeply interested in all that
concerns you, since I heard and saw you in the parish
Church of my native place, many years ago."

A letter from his old and honoured friend, the Bishop
of Calcutta, in the following spring, shews the influence
his works were exercising in that distant part of the
world.

*May* 8, 1835.

MY DEAREST BROTHER BICKERSTETH,
    Though time, duty, and health forbid, I must and will write a
line. I cannot expect the comfort of letters from you, if I do not
at least acknowledge, though I cannot answer in detail, the sweet
endearing communications I receive. Your case of Psalm-Books
arrived when I was on my Visitation in the South. They are already

in full use in two of our Calcutta churches, and I have not more than a couple of hundred left. They are generally approved. I have received also the present of your publications, which are always acceptable to me, not only for my own edification, but for the purpose of recommending them to others. Books of practical devotion are rare among us. Every help that can be obtained we need in this country, where the climate unnerves body and soul, where the impossibility of intercourse, from a burning sun, for eight months in the year, cuts one off from the communion of the faithful, and where the exceedingly low tone of morals, in almost all quarters, is of the most insinuating and pernicious character. It may be truly said of us; " They were mingled among the heathen, and learned their works." Warnings, therefore, from dear friends in Europe, —admonitions, comforts, counsels, are of immense importance.

Things are, we hope, going on for good. The religious hold of Hinduism is loosened. . . . Then the Bible is marching through the land, and the patches of Missionary stations are leavening, here and there, considerable numbers. The divisions of Christians and Christian Societies sadly weaken the general impulse of divine truth, just as they do at home. . . . But enough, God's will be done! Pray for your affectionate

DANIEL CALCUTTA.

Amidst the tokens of the extensive acceptance of his publications, Mr. Bickersteth's journal, towards the close of 1834, seems to betoken growing earnestness, humility, and peace.

" *September* 29, 1834. One great use of the Lord's Supper is in the free and ingenuous confession of all our sins, and a holy determination, formed in dependence on the Lord, to go afresh to the blood of sprinkling, receive afresh the atonement, and, all jarring feelings between the soul and God dispelled, to return to duty, refreshed and strengthened, with spiritual joy.

" Just as I am, then, most sinful and most ungodly, I

come to Thee, O Father of mercies, and God of all comfort, thirsting after that fountain of living waters which Thou hast opened in Jesus ; free pardon for the most guilty, the righteousness of God accounted theirs—the Spirit of God imparted to them, the grace of adoption bestowed upon them, and the gift of eternal life freely given.   O wonderful loving-kindness, provided in a way still more revealing its wonders, the sufferings unto death of Thine own Son !

" And, O my Lord and my God, strengthen me now to break through all evil of every kind.   O that my personal conduct may be sober, my relative conduct righteous, my soul godly in all my doings, words, and thoughts, under the conviction that I am bought with a price, and belong wholly to Thee !

" The guilt which has most struck my mind lately is that of neglecting the body of Christ, His church, those for whom He died.   He would easily forgive personal sins ; but neglect of His people, unfaithfulness to the trust committed to me, not to seek out and feed those whom He loves so greatly, is not so easily pardoned. A mother can bear a personal slight, but cannot bear that a servant or teacher should neglect her children. O blessed Jesus, who hast appointed me as a monitor over Thy household, help me to give them meat in due season."

" *November* 29.  . . . I have been preparing enlargements of my ' Scripture Help,' especially the chapter on ' Prophecy,' and the first number of a set of Tracts for my parishioners, on ' Christian Truth.'   The Lord own it for good.

" My mind has been led very much to a contemplation of the coming of the Lord, with hearty desires that I may

have the oil in my vessel, and be ready for His coming.
The Lord quicken these desires in my soul, and bring
them to a good issue, both for myself and my poor dead
parish."

"*December* 25. I have been preaching a course of
Sermons on the Advent, on which I beg the Lord's blessing for the good of my poor people.

"O how painful appears the actual state of the world
at large, of the professing Church, of the spiritual Church,
and above all, of my own heart! When shall that brighter
day of glory dawn, in which we shall be relieved from
the body of sin and death !

"I look on the most devoted servants of Christ whom
I know. I admire the grace of the Saviour in them. I
would sit at their feet with joy, to learn their graces.
And yet I see verified in them, ' Every man living at his
best estate is altogether vanity,' to a degree, that I never
at one time could have anticipated.

"I look at my own heart—it is all full of evil. I look
at my profession—it is all formality and hypocrisy—at
least to such an extent, that I am shut up in utter despair
of life by works. O Lord, deliver me from this body of
sin and death ! Lead me in Thy way and Thy truth, for
Thy name's sake. Give me the liberty of Thy children,
and help me to rise, through the outward form, into the
life and power of godliness."

The public employments of Mr. B., in 1835, differed
from those of previous years, chiefly by their greater
abundance. Early in the year he was occupied in enlarging his " Remarks on Prophecy," so as to embody his
later and more deliberate convictions. It was published
about May, with the new title, " A Practical Guide to
the Prophecies," and obtained a large and rapid sale, be-

sides involving him in a great variety of interesting private correspondence.  Four public journeys were undertaken ; in March, May, and August, for the Church Missionary Society, and for the Jews in October.  A Herts Auxiliary for the Jews had been set on foot by him in the previous Autumn, and was succeeded this year by a similar effort for the Religious Tract Society.  Before the close of the year, five numbers of the " Cottager's Guide" had also been published, in which the great truths of the gospel were unfolded in a very simple form, for the sake of his own parishioners, and of the poor in general.  His correspondence at the same time was of a most varied and extensive character.  Among those who thus conferred with him, are many well known to the Christian public—Power Trench, the Archbishop of Tuam, the Bishops of Lincoln, Winchester, Calcutta, Illinois, and Ohio, Mr. Simeon, Mr. Bridges, Mr. Carus, Professor Scholefield, Mr. Biddulph, Dr. McCaul, Dr. McNeile, Archdeacon R. Wilberforce, Mr. Brooks, Mr. Faber, Mr. Cuninghame, Dr. Marsh, Dr. Pye Smith, Dr. Wolff, Mr. Grimshawe, Mr. Habershon, Sir G. H. Rose, Mr. A. Gordon, Lord Ashley, Lord Wriothesley Russell, Lady Powerscourt, Mrs. Sherwood, Charlotte Elizabeth, and other names connected with the public events, and religious literature of the day.

These multiplying public duties did not interfere with the quiet and ceaseless influence of parental love in the bosom of his own family.  Towards the close of 1834, his eldest child left home for Clifton, and the following summer her two sisters joined her at the same school.  Some extracts from the letters written to them, during their absence, will show the consistency with which his principles were carried into private life, while they illustrate the constant pressure of his more public engagements.

December 11, 1834.

MY DEARDET B    ,

As Mamma tells you all the news on the earth, I must dwell on those good tidings of the heavenly kingdom, which God reveals in His word. . . . The Lord keep your mind fixed on that kingdom. Remember, " the violent take it *by force*," every one that gains it *presses* into it. You are to seek it *first;* and do not, sweetest love, let the enemy gain the advantage, which he will gain, if you are unwatchful and slothful in spiritual duties, to make you loiter in the heavenly race. Press forward to the mark, in the Divine strength. Christ is near to you in spirit, and nearer to us, I believe, in His personal coming, than many of his people think. Be ready, love, for Him, as your richest joy and only full happiness.

I am glad your companions are interested in such questions as the glory to be revealed, Rev. xx. 6, which I believe to be a literal description, in the main, of what is yet to take place, and a blessing of which, I pray, you and your dear teachers, and all your school-fellows may richly partake. But we must make great allowance for the holy and devoted men who think otherwise, and at whose feet I should rejoice to sit, to listen to other parts of divine truth, which God, by His Spirit, has revealed to them, as I believe he has, by the same Spirit, revealed this to me. So you see we are all to be subject, one to another, in the fear of the Lord. Always your own Papa.

E. BICKERSTETH.

May, 1835.

MY DEAREST C——,

And so it pleases God still to keep my dear child a weak, sickly, feeble creature! And why? because he loves you not? So the world would think. But those who know the word of God, and have seen the ways of God, as your parents and friends do, say the very reverse—because He does love you, and desires to make you

His own dear child, and to call you to His heavenly kingdom. Say then to Him: "O my loving Father, I leave myself entirely in Thy hands, to be ill, or to be well, as Thou, who art all wisdom, and all love, seest best. Only do Thou, who gavest me Thy only Son, to be my precious and complete Saviour, give me now Thy blessed Spirit, to be my Guide, Sanctifier, and Comforter, and waken me to be, and to do, all that Thou wouldest have me to be, and to do, for Jesus' sake."

Here is a little prayer for you, my child, which perhaps you can soon get off, and repeat by heart, and from the heart, till your will, and God's will, are wholly one, and then your will must be done, and you must be happy, for all our misery flows from having a different will to God's will. . . .

From your most affectionate father,

E. BICKERSTETH.

"*February* 22, 1835. Every thing in Providence and Prophecy calls me to watchfulness, and prepared-ness for the day of Christ. The return of Sir R. Peel to power, and his inability to stand, seen by the first division in the house, and then, if he fails, the appa-rent inlets of the overthrowers of our national institu-tions, may well fill the Christian patriot with fears for his country, and these must be greatly increased by the predictions of God's word.

"Lord, where shall we look for refuge, for ourselves, our families, and the Church, but unto Thee?

"My mind is much exercised in preparing a work on 'Prophecy,' respecting the state of the times. I fear lest it should hinder more immediate duties. O give me the unction of the Holy One! nearness to Thyself, deadness to the world, delighting in Thee, my portion and joy! And as my way is very humbling through my sinfulness, so let grace reign in triumphing over it.

"*April* 18. *Easter.* I have been on a journey to Bristol and Bath, and was mercifully carried through varied duties. But my heart is dead, my prayers cold and formal. I have been struck with that passage, Jer. xiii. 23. What is impossible with man, however, is possible with God. I feel that nothing but Divine power can renew and revive me. Lord, work in me to will and to do !

"I am most grievously deficient in intercessory prayer. Lord, deliver me from my hateful selfishness !

"*May* 17. . . . . . I perceive, that the whole life of God in my soul would be speedily choked, and I should be drowned in cares, and lusts, and outward things, if my Lord Jesus, whom I so little know and love, were to leave me to myself for a little time. Much reading may be a great hindrance to a godly life. O my Saviour, impart Thy grace to my soul. O my Father, draw me to Thy Son Jesus. O blessed Spirit, come and sanctify my heart.

"*July* 25. Since May, I have published the 'Practical Guide,' and No. 2 of the 'Cottager's Guide.' and taken thirty-three young persons to Confirmation. . . . . . I must mention, to the praise of the Lord's goodness, that a Herts Tract Society has been formed, (June 8,) which I hope may do much good.

"I have again been lamed, and am hindered from walking. In all these things the Lord speaks. May I hear his voice and obey it.

"*August* 30. I have been safely carried through journeys to Liverpool, Manchester, Wigan, &c., in which many hundreds have been collected. To the Lord be all praise.

"I have come home with a wearied body, and some-what dissipated in mind. Lord, thou knowest all my

poverty, blindness, and vanity.  O supply all my wants
out of that fulness which is in Christ Jesus.

"*September* 26.   Since my return I have been attacked
with serious illness, but through mercy am restored.

" I determined, early this month, in faith and prayer,
to send my three eldest girls to Miss Finch at Clifton.  It
has been a great sacrifice of feeling, but the advantage
was too great to be slighted, and I trust the Lord will
overrule all for good.

" As to my own soul, I trust that there are symptoms
of beginning to seek the Lord more earnestly.  The Lord
himself carry it forward.   O that I may walk more closely
with Him from this time. . . . O for that character,—
' Walk in the Spirit, and ye shall not fulfil the lusts of
the flesh.'   O for that privilege—' If ye through the
Spirit do mortify the deeds of the body, ye shall live.' "

*Liverpool, August* 24.

MY BELOVED B.

A father's love must express itself in a few more lines to his dear
child, at a distance.

I am rather weary of travelling ; but it is well to be weary in
our good Master's work, and not in our own.   Everywhere His
dear servants, for His sake, welcome me ; and this is a great joy,
in the midst of much speaking, preaching, and travelling.

On Sunday the 16th, I got £50. for the Society, in three ser--
mons.   Last Sunday only £12 ; and yet the latter might be as
liberal and acceptable to God as the former ; for if there be first a
willing mind, that is what He regards !   How full of love is Jesus !
Honour Him by placing your full confidence in His wisdom and
love.

The Lord bless you, and make your return to school eminently
useful to yourself and to others.   Only think of present duties, the
*moment's* work.   Our life is given in *moments,* and you shall have
joys for each.

*September* 28.

MY DEAREST B.

. . . . . . And so it has pleased our Heavenly Father at length to remove our blessed Thirza, and take her to His holy and happy presence.   How thankful we ought to be that this dear child, the companion of your infancy, is taken from this evil world, and admitted to the glorious company above. . . . So another tie to earth is broken, and another call to seek the things above is given.

How precious, then, is the Saviour, our sole ground of hope, our own righteousness, our complete Deliverer.   Christ the end of the law for righteousness to every one, not that worketh, but that *believeth*.   O how I feel this, after all my attempts to serve God. They are, even to my eyes, such *sins*, instead of *services*—what must they be to Him?   I tell you this to comfort you, and show you that God's children must place all their trust in the death, righteousness, and intercession of the Lord Jesus.   Stand on this rock ; the Lord himself fix you firmly upon it. . . . . .

May our God order all our outgoings and incomings to His glory.   We daily pray for you.

Your ever affectionate father,

E. BICKERSTETH.

*November* 13.

MY BELOVED B.

. . . . . You have, we conclude, left your "Triumph," and returned, not to the valley of humiliation, but to the school of instruction, up the hill Difficulty.   Well, it is worth-while suffering a little now for a future benefit.   That is the great lesson of the gospel of Christ, to suffer now, in and for well-doing, and then to reap hereafter.   The Lord himself put this into all our hearts. " Walk in the Spirit, and ye shall not fulfil the lusts of the flesh ; " this is the great secret of the Christian life.

When we become cold, how can we get warm?   when we lose our former love, how can we recover it ?   We must go to the great fire of Divine love, which burns so brightly in the gospel of the grace of God.   See how God our Father loved us before time began, loved us when enemies, reconciled us to Himself, gave his Son, his only Son to die for us, while we were sinful and without strength ; much more, now being reconciled, we shall be saved by His life.   See how He intercedes for transgressors.   Mark every thing that shews His love in all His dealings with His people—what wonderful forbearance and long-suffering He has with them.   Think of His more abounding grace, even where sin exceedingly abounds, and how He puts it twice within a few verses, as His very title—' God is love.' Think, then, how in the constellation of His glories, Ex. xxxiv. 6, 7, forgiving love is again and again most prominent, and His justice all satisfied in atoning blood ; His judgments to the third and fourth, but His mercy kept for thousands of generations.   Think how He delights in pardoning mercy, Micah vii. 18, 19, and then pray that the Holy Ghost may shed abroad all this love of God in your heart ; shew you all its height, and depth, and length, and effectually root you and ground you in this amazing love.   O my child, see this love, feel this love, let it warm every corner of your heart.   He gave you all else that you value—father, mother, brother, sisters, teachers, friends, knowledge, means of grace, sabbaths, temporal, spiritual, eternal blessings.   All flow from His boundless, never-ceasing, never-changing love.   Enter into this, my dearest child, and then the heart is touched, and the tongue speaks—"I will go unto God, unto God my exceeding joy."   " I will delight myself in God my Saviour."   His loving-kindness is better than life itself.   O that I could more fully commend His goodness to you, and tell you better, not only of the love He has already shewn, but of the glories which that love is preparing for His people, and the return of our Divine Saviour.   Then, and not till then, shall we fully see Him as He is.

But how is the sense of love to be maintained in the midst of fagging lessons and mental exertions ?   This is the way in which He calls now for proofs of your love, and these must be rendered as tributes of love to the Lord.   I do this lesson, and go through this labour, because I would thus shew love to Jesus.   Love delights in sacrifices and labours, and grows strong in them.   Only get the

Divine gift of love, by them, from them, and in them, and all shall help you to serve Christ.

The Lord bless you all three, and your dear friends, and all your companions, prays          Your own papa,

E. BICKERSTETH.

*December* 28.

MY DEAREST CHILDREN,

. . . . . It will soon be the close of the year. I will give you all a few hints.

Let the past year shew you—1. What evil and sinful hearts you have, in departing from the Lord. 2. How perfectly unable you are of yourselves, to help yourselves. 3. What a long-süffering, forbearing, most tender, and compassionate Father you have. 4. How true His word is, and how infinitely needful for you His glorious gospel.

Let the next year see you—1. Going to God, with entire confidence, through Jesus, in His infinite love. Remember, He so loved the world ; that is, you should say, *Me*, a most vile sinner. 2. Praying that all unbelief may be taken out of your heart. It is a hateful sin, it wrongs the God of love, and ruins our souls. 3. Thirsting to be filled with the Holy Spirit, and earnestly pleading the promises of this gift. 4. Rejoicing in the Lord always— all He is, all He has, yours, received by faith.

May these little hints be helpful to you. O how my heart thirsts for your spiritual happiness ! I brought you much this morning before the throne of grace, in earnest prayer that our heavenly Father would have mercy on you, and greatly bless you all. You too, must pray for me, for I am like the Israelites fighting on the plain, and ready to fail when prayer ceases. But our High Priest is always on the mount, and never ceases praying for us.

Your affectionate papa,

E. BICKERSTETH.

" *December* 24. I have been writing Nos. 3, 4. and 5 of the ' Cottager's Guide,' for my poor. The Lord bless these means to their good, for Jesus' sake. Amen."

This notice closes the private journal for 1835. In a note, a few days before, to his children, he had told them, " As for Papa, he is busy as a bee; the winter is his summer for making honey, that is, books, and he is getting through as many as he can. The ' Cottager's Guide,' No. 3, on Creation, and No. 4 on Providence, are printing, and No. 5, on Redemption, is being written. I am also preparing a selection from the English Reformers for a new volume of the Christian's Family Library. My subjects for Advent have been 2 Peter i. 16 ; ii. 9, 10 ; iii. 3—7."

The character of the little work here mentioned is well described in a note from his friend, Dr. Pye Smith ; with whom, amidst a decided difference of judgment on many social and ecclesiastical questions, he maintained for years a friendly and very affectionate intercourse.

" Having returned home last Friday, it was not till this morning that I got to the lowest tier of my letters, and there I found a No. II. of the ' Cottager's Guide,' sent by your kind hand. I have read perhaps the largest part of it. With No. I. it will be one of my aids in retirement. Blessed be the Spirit of God, that He has directed you and enabled you to labour in the best and richest part of the field ! How do such stars shine above the smoke of our wearisome controversies ! "

# CHAPTER XIX.

THE "TRACTS FOR THE TIMES"—CHRISTIAN KNOWLEDGE
SOCIETY—PASTORAL-AID SOCIETY.

A. D. 1836—1837.

THE new year found Mr. Bickersteth employed on a work which, even now, after more than fifteen years have passed, is perhaps more important and seasonable than ever. As Editor of the " Christian's Family Library," he had compiled a volume of extracts, called, " The Testimony of the Reformers," and he seized the occasion thus offered, to direct the minds of Christians to " The Progress of Popery." His remarks on this subject, which formed the introduction to the volume, were published separately as a tract, and were felt to be of such value, that they passed, in a few weeks, through six editions. The first publication of them was in January 30 ; and in a letter of February 23 he notices that the third edition was already on sale. Hardly any of his works produced so deep a sensation at its first appearance, or contains, in the same compass, more important information, or a clearer exhibition of gospel truth. Recent events have proved the wisdom and foresight of the alarm thus sounded in the ears of a too careless and lukewarm generation ; though it awoke, even at the time, a full echo in the hearts of many Christians.

The Tract begins with a direct and simple statement of the Gospel of Christ. After an allusion to infidelity, as its most open, but not its most insidious adversary, he passes on to the direct subject of his remarks. He notices briefly the progress of Popery, on the continent, in North America, in the British colonies, and lastly in Great Britain itself, where its chapels had increased twenty-fold within forty years, and where, since the peace of 1815, half a million of money at least, remitted from the continent, had been employed to help its dissemination. He distinguishes the system from the persons by whom it is professed ; among whom there have been some bright and holy examples of devotion, and are still " thousands of amiable and moral men, who abhor from their hearts cruelty and tyranny." The system itself is then denounced, on the evidence of extracts from the Roman Missal, the Decrees of the Council of Trent, the Trent Catechism, and the Creed of Pope Pius, with an especial reference to the doctrine of justification, in contrast to the merit of human works. Its character is unfolded as the Mystery of Iniquity, the Man of Sin, the Antichrist, and the Apocalyptic Babylon, with an allusion to the grounds of separation, held by the Reformers, and the cruelties of the Romish persecutions. An inquiry follows into the causes of its progress, and the first place is assigned to " a great decay of Protestant principles." Here he digresses, to touch on an important and delicate subject, the doctrine taught in several tracts of the Christian Knowledge Society, wherein, in his judgment, there was a great departure from the standard of the Articles and Homilies, and from the vital principles of the Reformation. Other causes, related closely to the first, are mentioned, " our departure from the Bible, as

the only standard of Divine truth ; the state of many of
the public journals, and the general abandonment of the
Reformation-testimony against the Church of Rome, as
the Apocalyptic Babylon." The difficulties of the conflict are next unfolded, with the helps for carrying it on,
and the duties incumbent on faithful Christians in the
presence of such an enemy. Among these are specified,
prayer and watchfulness, entire devotedness to God, acquaintance with Romish arguments and doctrines, and
the Scriptural answers ; confession of Christ ; the instruction of the ignorant ; attention to the prophecies ;
and the preaching of the everlasting Gospel, with its
warnings of Babylon's approaching fall. The whole is
closed by several prayers,—for the Irish Church, for infidels, for Roman Catholics, and for grace to be faithful in
perilous times.

Mr. Bickersteth here gave expression to his judgment
on the Tracts for the Times, which had now been publishing for more than two years, and in which discerning
men saw, from the first, the germ of all those Papal
doctrines, which have since yielded their ripe and bitter
fruit to our church and nation.

"A highly respectable, learned, and devout class of
men have risen up at one of our Universities, the tendency of whose writings is departure from Protestantism
and a return to Papal doctrines. They publish ' Tracts
for the Times ; ' and while they oppose the more glaring
parts of Popery, the infallibility of the Pope, the worship
of images, transubstantiation, and the like ; the very
principles of Popery are brought forward by them ; undue
deference to human authority, especially that of the Fathers, overvaluing the Christian ministry and sacraments,
and undervaluing (rejecting ?) justification by faith. With

much learning and study of the Fathers, with great apparent, and doubtless in some cases, real devotion, and a
devotedness ascetic and peculiar, they seem to the author,
as far as he has seen and known their course, to open
another door to that land of darkness and shadow of
death, where the Man of Sin reigns."

This opinion on the true character, and probable issue
of the Oxford Tracts, which Mr. Bickersteth thus expressed, with equal gentleness and faithfulness, fifteen
years ago, has been fully and painfully justified by later
events.   Several of the writers of these Tracts, and a
large number of their enthusiastic disciples and admirers,
have already reached, in their steady progress, that
" land of darkness and the shadow of death," to which
their steps, from the first, were secretly tending,—the
idolatrous communion of Papal Rome.

The observations in the Tract, on the foolish unconcern
of Protestants, and its probable consequences, have been
not less fully verified.

" The false security in which the Protestant Church
has been resting, is a most serious difficulty, to which we
are by no means yet awake.   The victories over Popery
at the Reformation and the Revolution, the complete
exposure of its idolatry, and display of it as the Antichrist, at the Reformation, and of its contradiction to
Scripture and to all just reason, at the Revolution, and a
century's quiet since, have occasioned this security.   Our
various legislative protections, one after another, have
been removed, and still we have not yet awakened.   And
on what does this fancied security rest ?   On the enlightened spirit of the age ?   Surely we have not yet to
learn that ' the world by wisdom knew not God.'   On the
substantial good sense of the mass of the nation ?   Surely

we have not forgotten the lesson—' Cease ye from man ;
put not your trust in the son of man, in whom there is
no help.' But if we think our security rests on the word
of God deposited with us, and his people residing among
us, let the history of Israel speak volumes. When were
there holier men than when Jeremiah, Ezekiel, Daniel
lived ? Yet were the Jews carried captive to Babylon.
When had the Church a greater revival than on the first
spread of the Gospel from Jerusalem ? Yet was Jerusalem destroyed by the Romans, because, in both cases, of
the abounding iniquity of the mass of the people.

" Our difficulties from Papists will most probably very
greatly increase. As the Papists increase they will get
more political power, and they are very subtle to use it.
Already they very extensively hamper and restrain the
efforts of true Protestants, and, where they can, injure
and annoy them. How easily, if the Lord permit, may
this spirit of persecution rise and grow, and bring on all
the sufferings through which the Church may have to
pass in these last days."

" . . . . A conflict more arduous than the Church of
Christ has yet passed through, seems then to be rapidly
hastening on. Our advantages may hasten the last
struggle. May we remember that we conquer by suffering. Bad men's minds are too excited by evil principles on every side, to rest ; and God forbid that there
should ever cease to be, among good men, those who will,
at the extremest hazard, yea, at the loss of fortune,
worldly reputation, ease, and life itself, proclaim the only
name of Jesus to dying men, and the vanity of every other
foundation."

A letter to Lady Lucy Whitmore, of this date, exhibits
the spirit in which the Tract was composed, and the

chief subjects which now occupied Mr. Bickersteth's thoughts and labours.

*Jan.* 22, 1836.

MY DEAR LADY LUCY,

Your welcome letter reached me safely.  Very many thanks to you for all your kind remembrances of us.  It was particularly kind, making the corrections in the " Guide to Prophecy," and sending them ; and they are quite in time for a new edition, which will probably be called for.  I have been very busily occupied, the last two or three weeks, with a pamphlet on the " Progress of Popery," which seems now to call for a firm protest from all faithful ministers.  I shall be glad to send you a copy, when it is out of the press.

The two books on " Affliction " are peculiarly sweet and profitable, as far as I have looked into them.  My wife begs me to thank you most heartily for them, and as she is a constant sufferer from increasing deafness, it comes very seasonably to her.  The selection —" What must I do to be saved ? " is of very precious texts ; but may I suggest that the title is inappropriate?  The question itself was one answered simply—" Believe on the Lord Jesus Christ, and thou shalt be saved ; " and that answer should ever stand out prominent and distinct, as it does in the word of God.  Many of the texts rather describe what is a part of salvation, than the means of receiving it, which is simply, crediting God's word, and so obtaining joy, peace, love, and holiness.  My own spiritual experience has led me to be very jealous on this point.  " Bible Truths " might be a title that would not mislead.

My dear boy gives me much comfort ; I trust that we shall all receive (I include yourself) a rich revenue for all the seed of prayer sown for him.

I have been latterly preaching much on the love of God, as displayed in Christ Jesus, and in giving Him to be the Saviour of the world, and the necessity of really believing this truth, as the turning-point of happiness here, and happiness for ever ; with the great guilt of unbelief, as counting God a liar, and leaving the soul in darkness and misery.  I have found John iii. 16, and 1 John v. 9—12, eminently profitable, and have preached a course of sermons upon them. Our grand enemy is our own evil heart of unbelief. It gives Satan and the world and sin their chief advantage over us, and must be resisted at every point with the power of the Holy Ghost, who alone works faith in our hearts.

I have been occupied in preparing what I call the " Cottager's Guide to Christian Truth," a quarterly publication, with short meditations for the poor. The four first numbers were on the Scriptures, the Great God, Creation, and Providence. The next will be on Redemption, a glorious theme, especially as the Church of England so scripturally views it—a redemption of all mankind. There is a vast body of divinity in the explanation of the Creed in our Catechism.

On prophecy, my mind, with increasing strength and clearness, holds the Premillennial Advent and its approach, as the most blessed era for the people of God. I think we are living under the sixth Vial, and the first Angel preaching the Gospel; but I see not my way clear to particular dates. I feel thankful that the Lord led me to publish the " Practical Guide to the Prophecies," and still hold the truths there stated.

Pilate's turning away is just the picture of the world. God gives us truth in the Bible, and we all by nature turn rather to man speaking than to God : but Oh! how important truth is ; it is the light in which we see God. It is coming out of a dark, solitary dungeon, to the bright atmosphere of God himself,—as light, love, holiness, happiness; and all ours, to make us happy for ever in Him.

How affecting the history of the ——— family. What a lesson to us parents ! but dead in Christ, and O what glory awaits them ! Jesus it is, Jesus alone, that makes every thing sunshine, happy, and glorious, all working for good. Your own afflictions touched me greatly, especially the note on the word *scourge*. Well, there is nothing but wisdom and love in it ; and so we shall tell each other, when we meet in the coming kingdom of glory. O how different then—the sight of God as He is, the likeness to Him, the entering into His character, beauty, goodness, holiness, and glory—the be-

holding Him face to face, and that for ever! Is it possible this is
before us? Yes, it is sure unto us, for God hath given unto us eternal life, and we believe his testimony concerning his Son; and He
who has begun the good work in us, will perform it until the day
of Christ. Therefore will we love Him, and serve Him, and glorify
Him, while we live here, and spend a blessed eternity in the same
happy service. "His servants shall serve Him, and they shall see
his face, and his name shall be on their foreheads." Struggle, my
dear friend, against unbelief, so insulting to God, so wronging to
our own souls, so marring to our happiness! "Fight the good
fight of faith." Oh! what a daily battle!—"Lay hold on eternal
life." Oh! what a grasp it calls for! Be of good comfort; God
is for us, Christ is for us, the Spirit is for us, the promises are for
us; and if trials meet us here, they too are for us, to ripen us for
the coming glory.

Most truly yours,<br>E. BICKERSTETH.

The reference, in Mr. Bickersteth's pamphlet, to the
Tracts of the Christian Knowledge Society, was caused by
no sudden impulse of feeling, but a deep conviction of
duty, after much prayer and deliberation. His attention
had been drawn strongly to the subject, some years before, and he had carefully examined some of the Tracts
which were most faulty in doctrine, with a view to obtain their removal. It was only when the difficulties
were found to be such, as to delay indefinitely the hope
of a decisive improvement, that he felt bound, in Christian honesty, to bear witness against a serious evil, which
tended to neutralize all the benefits of so valuable an institution. The tone of his strictures was equally marked
by faithfulness to the truth of God, and a sincere love to
the Society. He was involved by them, for several
months, in a large correspondence. Those who knew and

loved the doctrine of the Articles and Homilies, and had
learned the nature of true wisdom, which is first pure,
and then peaceable, were very thankful for this honest
appeal, and were encouraged in renewed efforts to clear
away some Tracts that were peculiarly offensive, and to
raise the doctrinal tone of the Society's publications.

A proposal seems to have been made soon after, in a
high ecclesiastical quarter, for a kind of compromise ; so
that evangelical clergymen, and those of diametrically
opposite views, might each have Tracts representing their
sentiments, admitted and retained on the Society's list.
Some extracts from a letter to a private friend, through
whom the suggestion had been communicated, will show
the principles which guided Mr. Bickersteth, not only on
this question, but on several others of the same kind,
which arose in his later years.

*May* 23.

MY DEAR ——,

Though I am but just returned from the North, and find a great
pressure of work, your letter about the Christian Knowledge Society is of primary importance, and demands immediate attention.
. . . . The first thing is to ascertain the path of duty. Evil consequences, like a dark cloud, always seem to hang over us, when we
seek to go in that path ; but even if they arrive, present suffering
and loss, for Christ's sake, are infinitely to be preferred to present
ease and prosperity in any other course. . . .

You speak of a latitude of tracts and opinions being allowed. In
an important sense I fully agree with this. I mean, as it proposes
including the whole of Divine truth, the Law as well as the Gospel.
The Bible is full of contrast truths, and we are in great danger of
getting one-sided views of truth, or confounding them together.
Obedience to the whole law, practical godliness, devotion, honour
of all constituted authorities, careful avoidance of schisms and
divisions, I consider not only necessary parts of truth, but peculiarly

seasonable for these times : yet to be pressed, as the Scriptures and as the Church do, not to disparage the Gospel, but to show its necessity, the result of its grace, and the meetness for the promised glory, establishing the Law by the Gospel.  Now I am quite willing to admit that evangelical brethren have sometimes failed in this full statement of the Law, and I should rejoice to see these things more brought out in the Christian Knowledge Society.

But if by a latitude be meant an allowance of unscriptural state-ments of the way of salvation, O my dear brother, we must not give place by subjection, no, not for an hour !   It is not a point on which we can compromise any thing.  We had better die than do it, when we consider the awful anathema, Gal. i. 8, 9.   This would but multiply confusion.  And where is the use at all of a Christian Knowledge Society, if the views of truth are to be so latitudinarian as to embrace opposite opinions of this kind ?  It becomes Babylon, and not Jerusalem : the mother of confusion, and not the unity of truth.  We are dark enough, without any thing to increase our darkness.

We know that, in the present state of things, the majority, even of professing Christians, are against the truth.  The world is still the world, and we are called out of it to testify the truth, to suffer for it, and to receive our reward hereafter.  Whatever majority there may be against God's truth, our course is straightforward and plain.  God will uphold us, and if we suffer in meekness and love, will make us triumphant to the end.

I cordially rejoice in the list of valuable tracts which have been added to the Society, and doubt not their circulation will be attended with much good.  But surely, when we have such helps as the Liturgy, Articles, and Homilies, to a right view of Divine truth, we may at least hope to attain a standing as free from anti-evan-gelical tracts as the Religious Tract Society, which has no such helps.  I cannot but hope, that by a meek, humble, and affection-ate, but firm testimony to Reformation-truth, the Society may yet come to unity of faith and of the knowledge of the Son of God, and be a full blessing to our country.

Most cordially do I dislike any party feelings, as a party, and de-

sire only to be the Lord's. I see that we have all erred and strayed
from God's ways. We have all got partial views. All who have
the Spirit of God may help each other, and should watch against
partiality of judgment. But peace is not the first part of wisdom,
—the beginning is the fear of the Lord. The first part is *purity*,
the second only is *peace*. May our God give us grace to be very
zealous, first for the purity of His truth—and then, to speak it in
love, and follow peace with all men. . . .

. . . The Society's office is to hold up the truth, the whole truth,
welcome or unwelcome, and to take its judgment of acting rightly,
simply from the word of God, and the standards of the Church.
But I see in dear Dodsworth's tracts how difficult it is to maintain
the armour of righteousness on the right hand and on the left. The
great danger of the day is lawlessness ; we see it on all sides. But
here is a brother holding the truth, seeing the danger, and yet, in
his zeal against it, fighting against the grand Protestant principle of
the word of God, as a light to our feet, and a lamp to our paths,
—and thus returning by another devious path to Papal darkness.

How earnestly, then, should we pray for wisdom from above,
lest we fight in the dark, and contend unwarily for error, and not for
truth ; and how close should we keep to the written word, that we
may be guarded by that fulness of truth which God has there provided us !

I have thus given my views, as you wished, candidly and fully.
Greatly should I rejoice to see this Society an honour to the Church,
by a free and full confession of the glorious Gospel, and thus a blessing to our country and to the whole world. The Lord grant that
all who act in it may have faithfulness, wisdom, and energy, to aid
in the accomplishment of a result so desirable.

The description of Mr. Dodsworth's Tracts, toward the
close of this letter, was only too faithfully prophetic, and
subsequent events, after thirteen years, have been a
mournful confirmation of Mr. Bickersteth's spiritual discernment, which perceived so early the sure result, where
human authority is preferred to the word of God.

A letter, at the close of January, to his eldest child, shows the practical turn which he knew how to give, in private, to his public labours.

*Watton, Jan.* 28, 1836.

MY BELOVED CHILD,

I take the cover as my portion in letters for Clifton, and glad shall I be, if in a few spare moments I can say anything for your real good.

I am now full of work, with a tract against Popery, which has taken me longer than I expected, as I felt it an important opportunity to disclose Protestant Popery, of which there is a great abundance,—first, in every carnal heart, and therefore in our own,—and then, in all religious writings. Popery is, to be looking to ourselves and our own doings for salvation. Real Protestantism is, to be looking simply to Jesus for every thing. All things pertaining to life and godliness are in Him, and to be received by faith from Him. Now you will see, my dear, how you and I, though we hate the Pope, may have plenty of self-popery. O it is hard and impossible to flesh and blood, to live by faith in Jesus ; and to see, if we pray, it can only be by His Spirit freely given ; if we love, it can only be as his Spirit first discloses to us God's amazing love to us rebels in the death of Jesus ; if we have the same mind as Christ, it can only be as, beholding in the glass of the Gospel the glory of the Lord, we are changed into the same image. But Jesus has the Spirit, to enable you to do this. My dear child, you must every day, to your last gasp, live by faith in Jesus ; and come, as you first came, an empty vessel, to take all out of His fulness. O do not be content to live without Him, on the husks of this empty world ! In all your lessons, look through them to Jesus, and feel this,—" I do them, because Jesus bids me honour my parents and obey my teachers, and I delight in them, because they are His will." I will be loving to my companions, because my heavenly Father calls me to it. I will go to family prayer and public worship, in faith, that I may get a glimpse of my Saviour. He loves me :—O never give the Devil such an advantage as to doubt this—He washed me from my sins in His blood; and I may delight myself in my God, as my most holy and most loving Father. This will be a fresh spring of living waters, to refresh you in your spiritual warfare.

We almost long as much for March 22 as you seem to do; but O that we could always bask in the sunshine of our heavenly Father's greater love, and have *no idols whatever*, and delight in these as *His* gifts, that shew us His love, and are to be used for Him. Dearest children, keep these things in mind.

Your ever affectionate Father,

E. BICKERSTETH.

Another letter, in February, shews the pressure of his work, as well as the fidelity of the Christian parent.

*Watton Rectory, February* 24.

MY DEAREST CHILDREN,

My fingers ache with writing, before I begin to you, but I am glad to send the hymns for the next three months, and to add a few lines of a father's love.

While you are rejoicing in the short time between this and March 21, I am trembling, almost, at the quantity of work to be done between this and then. But our happiness is much nearer than in outward things; even in the present love of our Father, and in doing His will. All else is a broken cistern. Make not your parents your idols, for idols are to be broken.

I have been incessantly engaged, since I wrote my "Treatise on Popery," with all kinds of correspondence, partly on that, and partly on other things; and I have to be very thankful to God, for being called to testify to His truth.

O my dear children, get hold, fast hold, of God's truth, by weighing, praying over, searching, and meditating upon, His word. It is full of light and love. . . . . .

Tell Mrs. F——, that Dr. Chalmers, after reading my work on "Prophecy," is entering into the views there brought out. I know it is substantially God's truth, if no man on earth agreed in it; but it is a great comfort to see God bringing such minds as his to concur in it. But let our faith be only on God's word; I do not want anybody to think it, because I think it. What is my chaff to the wheat—the pure truth of the word? Rest there, my children, and walk in God's own light.

From your own dear father,<br>
E. BICKERSTETH.

The letter of Dr. Chalmers, to which allusion is here made, is interesting in itself, and still more for the sympathy it discovers between two men, so variously gifted, and honoured, above most in their own day, in the diffusion of Divine truth. In the width and range of his intellectual acquirements, in eloquence of the highest order, and those popular talents, applied to general subjects, which earned for him an European reputation, even among worldly men, Dr. Chalmers had a great superiority; and no one rejoiced, more than Mr. Bickersteth, to honour gifts so excellent, devoted so earnestly and effectually to the furtherance of the Gospel. And yet it may be doubted whether his own early concentration of all his powers on the one great object of life, the glory of Christ in the salvation of souls; the spirituality of his mind, which led him to labour, by choice, in "the best and richest part of the field;" the simple earnestness of his zeal, and the perpetual glow of love, which breathed in his words, and beamed in his countenance, did not render him an equal blessing to the Church of Christ as his more gifted and more celebrated friend. They have now met in the presence of their common Saviour, where they will both delight to render the full tribute of their praise to Him who blessed them in their labours, and made them vessels of mercy to their fellow men.

*February* 17, 1836.

My dear Sir,

I should have acknowledged much sooner the receipt of your kind note, and of the precious volume which accompanied it.   I am now reading it with great interest, and think I shall accord more fully with its views than with those of any author I have yet read, who has ventured on the field of unfulfilled prophecy.   I lately finished the perusal of all Mede's, and of all Cuninghame's prophetical works, and certainly have been much impressed by them. I sympathise, however, far more with your doubts, than I do with his decision, on the subject of a personal reign.   But of this, on the general, I am well satisfied, that the next coming, (whether in person, or not, I forbear to say) will be a coming, not to the final judgment, but to precede and usher in the Millennium.   I utterly despair of the universal prevalence of Christianity, as the result of a pacific missionary process, under the guidance of human wisdom and principle.   But without slackening in the least our obligation to help forward this great cause, I look for its conclusive establishment through a widening passage of desolating judgments, with the utter demolition of our present civil and ecclesiastical structures.

Let me advert to the practical character and unction of your work, as stamping an additional virtue upon it ; being throughout, a powerful address to the conscience, instead of a mere entertainment, which too many of our works on prophecy are, to the curiosity of men.

> I am my dear Sir,
>      Yours, most gratefully and respectfully,
>           Thomas Chalmers.

The views of Mr. Bickersteth on the duty here adverted to, of zeal in the cause of missions, will be seen in his reply to a brother-clergyman, who had asked his advice on the best means of awakening an interest in missionary labours.

*March* 10, 1836.

MY DEAR FRIEND,

I can only write in minutes broken, from incessant occupation.

The first great thing is, to get the missionary principle deeply seated in our heart. Nothing does this, but the tasted love of our God, fully enjoyed through faith in His own word. We then long to tell others of that love. Next, we have to credit His gracious mind, as set before us in such a passage as 1 Tim. ii. 1—8, taking His words to be true, that He will have all men to be saved, and come to the knowledge of the truth ; and not letting our faith be cramped and fettered by any false human system, God's oath is decisive : Ez. xxxiii. 11, and it is very wicked to set it aside. Then come His positive commands in rich abundance, as Mark xvi. 15.

The next thing is, to look at His gracious purposes. He means to gather a people out of the Gentiles, to show His abounding love in electing grace to them. He means to do this before He returns. Rev. vii. is to me decisive, as are several of the parables. My mind is clear, that a blessed harvest is to be gathered, before the Lord come, in the last tribulation, near at hand. When we see these things, we see the proper foundation of Missionary labours. Not to bring in the Millennium—the Lord will do that at His coming—but to gather a rich harvest of souls before He comes, by spreading far and wide the glorious Gospel.

I write shortly, but I write the results of lengthened study, and deliberate conviction. Part of my mind may be seen in my "Guide to the Prophecies," but I trust that I see things more clearly now than I did then.

The hope of our Lord's coming is a grand animating spring of liberality. Only the other day I had £100 sent me for the Jews' Society, by one who felt this from my work on "Prophecy." Nothing can be more unworthy of our cause, and of our Master, than the scanty contributions which professing Christians have yet given, because not yet raised to the blessed hope and prospect of the latter day, and the sweet enjoyment of God's love by faith in His word.

Here are the principles of true missionary zeal.  As to working with them, it must greatly depend on our circumstances.  Our people, brought to these principles, will be dead to the world, and will rejoice to give as they can.  Money given from false principle does mischief to the giver, and profits not the cause ;—but money given in faith and love,—oh how it blesses all !  How sweet the posthumous saying ;—It is more blessed to give than to receive !  I doubt not, you have tasted its sweetness, and can heartily recommend it from your own enjoyment.  The Lord bless you in the immense sphere where He has placed you, and ever enable you to testify the gospel of His grace, prays,

Yours affectionately,

E. BICKERSTETH.

It was in February of this year that the writer paid his first visit to Watton Rectory.  A very brief interview at Cambridge, in October 1834, led to a kind and pressing invitation.  After more than a year had passed, it was accepted in a time of heavy affliction, when the heart often divines, by a secret instinct, where deep and loving sympathy is to be found.  The intended visit of a few days was prolonged to some weeks, and issued, after a short interval, in the continued and almost unbroken intercourse of many years ; a privilege of which those, who have spent even a few days only under Mr. Bickersteth's roof, will best understand the full value.  It was in the domestic circle that his Christian graces had, perhaps, their most beautiful exhibition.  The glow of love, which gave a charm to his public addresses, and made his voice the signal of bright and happy looks in a thousand missionary meetings, shone with a quiet and steady lustre in the bosom of his family.  His expositions had a peculiar charm, rarely equalled ; they were so simple, earnest, and loving.  His prayers, in domestic

worship, were the outpouring of a full and joyful heart
in the presence of God.　His conversation, while often
playfully familiar, was always instructive, flowing from
a heart continually occupied with the cause of Christ.
And hence the friends, who paid a visit to Watton Rectory, always looked back upon it as a sunny spot in
their pilgrimage : and, to borrow the words of a young
missionary, in which he expressed his own feelings—it
seemed as if a breeze of the eternal summer had been
passing over them.

Amidst these public and private employments, Mr.
Bickersteth's journal discloses the inner springs of his
activity.

"*February* 28. . . . . O my Lord, though Thou art
teaching me more of Thy glory, and Thy grace, yet how
slow and dull a scholar am I !　O change me by Thy
almighty grace !

" I have been reading, I trust, with great spiritual
profit, ' Campbell of Row's Sermons ; ' and though not
seeing with him in every thing, the flame of love is so
beautiful and bright, that I long indeed to attain it. The
Lord give me His grace for this end. . . .

"*March* 19.　Through God's mercy I am now brought
to be fifty years of age.　A humbling and a grateful day.
Humbling in my innumerable inconsistencies, short-
comings, outside religion, love of human praise, disregard of God and His word, worldliness and unbelief.　O
the deluge of sin, from which I can find no clearance
but God's mercy in Christ, and looking constantly to
Him.

" A grateful day also, in the blessed hope that the
Lord is making the glorious light of His Gospel shine
more on my soul, and leading me to a clearer view, that

holiness and obedience are my happiness, suffering for
Christ my privilege, and daily dying to sin, my perfection
and true blessedness ; and that only the free salvation of
Jesus can accomplish this. I do see how good the Lord
is, in commanding me to love Him with all my heart ;
and that it is just the same as if He commanded me to
be happy, and to have no care, no fear, no anxiety, but
ever to rejoice in Him.

" Grateful also I ought to be, if the Lord has in any
way used my writings for good to others. As to myself,
there is so much defect in them, and so many unworthy
motives mixed up with them, that I see cause for deep
humiliation in them all.

" Two great things I desire to bend my strength to
from this day ;— prayer, and the word. O that these
were more in every thing that I do !

" *Prayer.* How far am I here from my real privilege
and happiness ! O that I spent hours in prayer ! Nothing
but my own sluggishness and love of sin prevents it. I
might thus be in the presence of God, when he is far out
of my thoughts. I might be gaining light, joy, and
strength, that would a thousand-fold increase my usefulness. O Thou blessed Father of my mercies, give me this,
I entreat Thee !

" *The Word.* I by no means study it as I should. It
is not so much in my reading, as in my reference ; now it
should be in my constant reading, to get food from the
store-house, and not food minced out by others. To get,
not merely bread, but seed-corn. O give me this grace,
that the word of Christ may dwell in me richly, in all
spiritual wisdom ! Keep me from vain books, lead me to
those which are useful—but especially lead me to Thy
word !

"*April* 2. *Before Easter Sunday.* I have, through mercy, been carried safely through a journey to Bath and Bristol, and have seen my three dear eldest children, who are at school at Clifton. The Lord is good to us.

" But these changes, and the occupations they bring, distract my mind from its immediate work,—waiting upon the Lord. Lord, let Thy table on the morrow be my refreshment and revival. Let me eat the flesh and drink the blood of Christ, spiritually feeding on Him in my heart, by faith with thanksgiving. O how weak I am always in myself! Lord, strengthen me out of Zion, to love Thee, to seek Thee, to labour for Thee.

" A long journey is before me to Ireland, and then another to Hull, York, and Sheffield. The Lord strengthen me for all, and bless me in all to His glory, and the good of souls.

" A new Edition of my 'Practical Guide' demands my attention. I pray for heavenly wisdom in it."

The journey to Ireland, here alluded to, had circumstances of peculiar interest. The previous year had been one of great distress to the Irish clergy. O'Connell was then in the height of his influence, the weight of Government was thrown very much into the same scale ; and an organized conspiracy was in operation through the island, to starve or terrify into submission the ministers of a heretic establishment. Resolutions, expressive of sympathy with their suffering brethren, had been largely signed by members of the English Church, and Ireland seemed to be, once more, the special battle-field in the conflict between Popery and the gospel of Christ. At such a time Mr. Bickersteth's presence and counsels were felt, by many of the Irish clergy, to be very desirable for themselves and their brethren, and he was urged to attend at their annual April meeting in Dublin, as the representative of the Church Missionary Society. The invitation was earnest and affectionate, but somewhat quaint and Irish in its style.

*February* 25, 1836.

DEAR FRIEND,

Did you not shake your hand, and look kindly on me, when I entreated you last year in Liverpool, to let us see your face once more in our island? and did you not give me a hope that, God willing, you would venture over the sea, and visit our metropolis once more? And do you not know, or guess, that we never more wanted your assistance, or more needed the kind exertions of a Christian friend, well acquainted with our Society? And do you not know, or guess, that I have a house and bed, and all the &cs., to make you forget your own land, in the comforts of this? Now surely, friend, you will undertake for us—'tis very easy. . . . .

You would be wanted to address our clergy on the morning of the Missionary meeting—there may be three hundred and more (if they are not shot between now and then,) and you would have to preach a sermon or two for us—to meet some parochial associations, and one or two Committee-meetings. . . . . . . . Now do not let me entreat you in vain; it is not for myself, it is for a Society which you love. . . . . . We would pardon you all past omissions. May the Lord send you, if Edward Bickersteth will not. . . . . . O may the Spirit of our gracious Master be with you, and direct each word and thought to His glory. Amen, and Amen.

Mr. Bickersteth gladly complied with the wish of his Irish friends, and spent about a week in Dublin at the Missionary Anniversaries. His address to the clergy at the Missionary breakfast, when about 260 of them were present, were soon afterwards printed, and may be seen in his "Occasional Works." It contains a great variety of wise cautions, and affectionate admonitions, well suited to impress the consciences, and reach the hearts of his beloved brethren. The appeal, with which it ends, embodies the spirit of the whole.

" We feel in England intimately united with you, as members of one outward, as well as one spiritual Church, members of the body, of which Christ is the head. If you suffer, we shall suffer with you ; if you are tried in the furnace of affliction, we are exposed to the same enemies. We stand together in the same conflict, the same struggle is before us both, the same Master is looking upon us, the same glorious crown is set before us. O may we together endure present sufferings for Christ, and all that further suffering which our God may, for His own glory, our good here, and our brighter reward hereafter, yet bring upon us ! Cheering as is our present meeting, O how much more blessed will be that swiftly-coming day, when we shall be gathered with the glorious company of the Apostles, the goodly fellowship of the prophets, the noble army of martyrs, the general assembly and Church of the first-born, around the throne of God and the Lamb, and for ever sing ;—'Blessing, and honour, and glory, and power, be unto Him that sitteth on the throne, and to the Lamb for ever.' "

A letter from Dublin, on this journey, gives some account of his engagements, and shews how a concern for the honour of the gospel mingled with and deepened his love to his children.

*Dublin, April* 13.

My dearest Children,

Mamma promised for me that I should write to you, or so much am I engaged with important duties, that I do not think I should have attempted it, though I need not tell you that I dearly love you. But what do I find around me ? a circle of immensely-

important duties, all of them calling for reflection and exertion.
The Lord Himself be my wisdom, and my strength!—my little
dears at Clifton will say, Amen.

I left home on Monday night.   Mamma and the four children
accompanied me to Welwyn, and I then pursued my solitary way to
the mail at Redbourn.   I had not interesting companions—so I
partly slept, partly read, and partly rode outside to see the country.
The road through North Wales is often very striking : Snowdon and
many of the hills are still covered with snow, and the iron suspen-
sion-bridge at Menai is one of the wonders of the world.   I rode
over it outside of the mail, as it was getting dusk.   We reached
the sea-side about a quarter past eleven, and embarked soon after,
and were eight hours in crossing.   As usual, the night also being
stormy,—I suffered much from sickness, but through mercy was
brought safely here, found my friends at the shore, and received all
kindness and attention.

I have since been, among others, to call on the Archbishop, and
met with a very kind and cordial reception.   He is to be in the
Chair, on Friday, when our Church Missionary Meeting is to be
held.   I am also to speak at the Bible Meeting to-morrow, preach
in the evening—have three services next day, two the following,
two on Sunday, and hope to return home on Monday.   O may our
God make every service acceptable and blessed to His people, and
raise me above the fear of man !

I trust that you are now again diligently, as God enables you, at
your appointed duties.   My anxiety is to give you the best Christian education in my power, that, with the Lord's blessing, you may
be more happy, and more useful, and glorify Him, and benefit others
more.   Do not, my dearest children, let these good hopes be disappointed.   Oh remember, the sacrifice of our grand idol, Self, is the
one great work, to which the grace and love of the gospel constantly
leads, and for which it gives power, by the Holy Ghost dwelling
in us.

Then think, my dearest children, of this.   People everywhere
hear me talking of the love of God in Christ, and everywhere read
my books, which have been more circulated than any other religious

books, perhaps, of our day, through our whole country. O how sad it would be, if they could turn to my children and say—See, they do not love Christ, they are as fond of vanity and folly, as if they had no such instruction; their father cannot have been consistent at home, or God's promise has failed. O let neither of these reproaches be raised, my sweetest children, by anything others may see in you. " What do ye more than others? " is a question that may be put with special meaning to my dearest little ones.

But indeed you have given me comfort already, and will do so, I trust, more and more, by seeking to commend the gospel of Him who loved you, and bought you with His blood. The sweetest life is, to be ever making sacrifices for Him ; the hardest life a man can lead on earth, the most full of misery, is to be always doing his own will, and seeking to please himself.

The Church of Christ here, as almost everywhere, is greatly broken up and divided. The harrow of Providence seems breaking all the clods of earth, that there may be more room for the good seed. It is the seed-time, and we must sow as much good seed as we can. . . . . .

I hope that Rom. xii. sometimes recurs to you all. Let us watch and pray, as those waiting for their Lord.

Ever affectionately yours,<br>E. BICKERSTETH.

Within a fortnight after his return from his Irish visit, he was called to preach the Annual Sermon of the European Society, which succeeded the Continental, and, with some change in its constitution, has since been merged in the Foreign Aid Society. The occasion led him to dwell on the prospects of the Church of Christ, and the spiritual condition of the continent of Europe. In the early part of the Sermon, he gave a brief, but full outline of his own expectations, with the Scripture passages on which they were founded, and afterwards brought together much information on the actual state of the foreign churches and kingdoms. Indeed the peculiar character of his anniversary discourses was the union of full information, collected diligently from various sources, with a simple, glowing exhibition of gospel truth, enriched ever by the glorious hope ot good things to come. The effect of this was, to give most of them a permanent value, for historical reference, when the immediate occasion was gone by. The fact, for instance, mentioned in this sermon, that from 1817 to 1829 there were circulated in France 4,768,900 volumes of the four chief Infidels, Voltaire, &c. and only 61,794 Bibles and Testaments, retains to this hour its practical significance. The description of the Continent, which follows, has found a signal illustration in the four last years.

" The people of the Continent, wearied with Popery and abstract Protestantism, tried Infidelity as a remedy ; it disappointed them. Groaning under despotism, they tried revolution again and again ; it also has failed them. Out of the serpent's root has come a cockatrice, and the fruit hath been a fiery flying serpent. Everywhere there is the expression of *want :* the cry is, ' Who will shew us any good ?' The delusion of St. Simonianism seemed to promise it ; it was taken up warmly and largely, and found to be vanity. Worn-out Popery, decayed Protestantism, cold infidelity, scientific attainments, national reputation, revolutionary movements, sensuality—these meet not the want. There is a void in the human soul which God alone can fill. How can the creature be happy, sundered from the Creator, or the sinner without a Saviour ? "

The following letter was written to his children in the month of May, during another journey.

*Hull, May* 12, 1836.

MY DEAREST CHILDREN,

. . . . I attended the public meetings, Bible, Missionary, Prayer-book, and Jews, and spoke at all—at the second meetings of the two first, for there were two meetings, and preached also for the European Missionary Society. I have since been travelling, after stopping four hours at Watton, and preaching and speaking continually for our heavenly Master. O how needful is grace within, that all this bustle and testimony without, may be from a real spring of living waters!

*York, May* 13.

I was interrupted at Hull, and resume my letter here. God was pleased much to prosper our efforts there, and greatly increased contributions were raised. I came on here by the mail yesterday, arrived at four, and was heartily welcomed by our dear old friends, Mr. Gray and his son. I had not been here long, when I was summoned to an evening meeting, and find, that though I came for relaxation, work is fully laid out for me. Well, we must not be idle and silent in these days, but work heartily while it is day.

My friend Mr. Gray, is one of the most venerable, devout, simple-hearted, evangelical Christians that England contains. In his 87th year he is glorifying God, and a blessing to others, by still doing much for Christ, and by a consistent example, now prolonged for nearly seventy years, during which he has been walking with God. Who can but see the blessing of a life of godliness, even in this world, in such a sweet example? . . . . But, my beloved children, this was not obtained without many a struggle, in youth, with the corruptions of his heart, many a loss, sacrifice, and disappointment in his early days. He was content to bear the yoke in his youth, and now the Lord has richly rewarded him here, and there is waiting for him the great reward at His coming. I mention it as a quickening motive to all of you, to sacrifice present inclination, and patiently wait on the Lord for His recompense. . . .

. . . . What I want for my beloved children, is real joy and happiness in the knowledge of God, and then to seek to spread that happiness all around. God is light, and in His light we see light. God is love, and in His love we feel love : and light and love are happiness. The Gospel is to bring us to this, and the door of faith opens all the treasures of the Gospel for our daily use and enjoyment.

Well, my dear children, I suppose that your thoughts are constantly turning homeward. But O remember, home will be but a place of misery, if you do not make God your portion and your dwelling-place. In Him only is rest, in Him only is happiness. If parents are dear, if brother and sisters are dear, He who gave us them, and continues them, should be our confidence, and our joy, and infinitely dearer. . . .

From your own affectionate Father,<br>E. BICKERSTETH.

In the course of the previous summer, Lord Ashley, (now the Earl of Shaftesbury) had called at Watton Rectory,—his regard for Mr. Bickersteth's character and writings having led him to desire a personal acquaintance ; and the foundation was thus laid of a friendship, which continued, with growing attachment, till Mr. Bickersteth's death, and was maintained by a copious and interesting correspondence. A visit of a few days at the close of August in this year, was a season of peculiar privilege to all who were present. The diversity of gifts, of station, and of character, only rendered more striking the deep harmony of feeling and judgment, between the devoted minister of Christ, who had now laboured twenty years in the cause of missions, and the rising statesman, the advocate of Christian mercy and Protestant truth in the high places of the land. The mutual pleasure experienced appears in a note of his Lordship, written about a month later. " I am much gratified," he says, " to learn from you that I have left a favourable and lasting impression among you. Few things have ever given me more pleasure than my visit to Watton, and I hope and trust that, by God's blessing, I shall ever find consolation and delight in such relaxations as these."

One or two extracts from the private journal show some of Mr. Bickersteth's employments in the latter part of the year.

"*September* 25. My new Edition of the 'Practical Guide to the Prophecies,' is now publishing. I have been spending some days at Walton by the sea-side. . . .

"O that I could realize more the crisis of the Church's history in which we live, and the great work resting upon ministers now, of warning men of the coming day of tribulation, and the Bridegroom's approach! Lord, help me to be a wise and faithful steward of Thy mysteries.

"*October* 30. . . . . . I have been to Norwich, Yarmouth, Bury, and Sudbury for the Jews, where the Lord was graciously pleased to use me for good. . . .

"O Lord, I cannot have rejoicing in myself, for all is most defective and defiled. Yet such Thou receivest,—O wonderful grace! 'Good and upright is the Lord, therefore will He lead sinners in the way.' I cry to Thee, O my Father, for bread, the bread of life—Christ for me and Christ in me ; Christ for me, in all He has done, is doing, and will do ; Christ in me, by His Spirit, every day, every hour.

"What a description of Asa ! he did that which was right in the eyes of the Lord ; but he was diseased *in his feet* in his old age. O let not that be my state spiritually.

"*November* 27. In the last month I have published No. 8 of the 'Cottager's Guide.' (No. 7 in August.) O bless it for much good. I have had much impressed on

F 5

my mind the great sinfulness of my heart, in the low
state of intercessory prayer that marks my own devotions,
both social, family, and private.  My own exposition of
2 Cor. i. 11 in the family, was, I trust, profitable, in leading me to see this.  O Lord, let thine own Spirit admit
me into the liberty of prayer to Thee."

Early in 1837, Mr. Greig, who had been his valued
curate nearly three years, was called to a wider sphere
of duty at Barford, near Leamington.  An engagement
was then made with Spencer Thornton, the nephew of
his patron, Abel Smith, Esq., to supply the vacant post.
Mr. Thornton came to Watton soon after his ordination,
about the end of February, and continued there till the
close of the year ; and was then presented by his uncle
to the living of Wendover, near Aylesbury, where he
laboured for twelve years, till his sudden and lamented
death.

The connexion was one of unmingled affection, and of
mutual benefit.  Early consecrated to the service of Christ,
Mr. Thornton possessed, in a peculiar measure, the gifts
and the grace, which qualify for the work of pastoral
visitation.  With a deep love to immortal souls, he joined
a very practical turn of mind, and an instinctive aptitude
for the details of parochial management.   His stay at
Watton, though short, was eminently useful to the parish,
while he always retained a deep sense of the benefits he
derived from Mr. Bickersteth's ripened judgment, and
regarded him with a filial esteem and reverence.   The
very day before his sudden death, he had called at Watton
Rectory, to confer on several points connected with the
welfare of his own parish ; and the last published writing
of Mr. Bickersteth was a brief obituary of his beloved son
in the ministry, which he had drawn up only a few days

before he was himself seized with his mortal illness. The words of the sweet Psalmist might be applied to them both, even with a fuller emphasis than in its original reference. They were lovely and pleasant in their lives, and in their death they were not divided.

Difficulties arose at this time in the Church Pastoral Aid Society, which had been only lately formed, from the reluctance of many of the bishops to sanction the employment of lay-agents ; an error of judgment much to be deplored, and which has since, in most cases, been happily corrected by experience. On this subject Mr. Bickersteth wrote two letters, which show his distinctness in asserting the great principles of the gospel, and his regard to the authority of superiors, up to the furthest limit which conscience will allow. In one of them he advised that the Society should cede the point in its practice, while asserting the principle, because there was already another institution which had that object specially in view; while the second letter, addressed to a friend of one of the bishops, as the best and most respectful means of communication, urged the duty and necessity of laymen co-operating in the spread of Divine truth. His advice was not adopted by the Committee ; and indeed the event seems to have proved that the retention of lay agency, as one branch of the Society's operations, was the wiser course. If he erred, however, it was from no backwardness to encounter reproach where Scriptural principles were at stake, but simply from not observing, at the moment, how seriously the true unity of the Church would be obscured, if lay and clerical agency were reckoned so distinct in kind, and so independent in their nature, as to be best administered by two independent Societies. The danger would thus be increased, on the one side, of clerical formalism and superstition ; and on the other, of growing irregularity, and a lawless disparagement of the ordinances of Christ. When once the decision was made, Mr. Bickersteth fully acquiesced in it, and gave the Society his zealous support and co-operation.

*February* 7, 183 7

MY DEAR LORD ASHLEY,

Feeling anxious about the present position of the Pastoral Aid Society, from having been informed that several of the Bishops refuse to sanction lay agency, and that this has occasioned much perplexity and discussion, I venture to write to your Lordship such views as have occurred to me on the subject.

I can have no question in my own judgment, from statements in the New Testament, that lay agency is a most scriptural and important means of diffusing Divine truth among men. We clearly see in Rom. xvi. and Phil. iv., as well as in other parts, that women, and I doubt not in the list of names, laymen also, laboured in the Gospel. The principle is scriptural.

In the present day it surely would be the part of wisdom in the Governors of our Church, to secure, in every scriptural way, all the lay co-operation that is practicable. Attacked as the Church is on every side, how could it be more strengthened than by a full, scriptural use of the laity in connection with it?

Fully, however, seeing and insisting on these principles, there are two or three weighty reasons, which lead me to think that the Society will follow a wise and Christian course, in conceding, for the present at least, the direct employment of lay agents.

We know that lawlessness is the peculiar character of·these days ; to speak evil of dignities, to cast off the yoke of restraint, to be self-willed and highminded, are the special temptations of the times. An opposite course to this, a giving up of our own plans, in submission to authorities over us, where not contrary to God's word, is likely, then, I think, to obtain the special blessing of God, and to commend itself to the consciences of our rulers.

Simplicity of object is a great point towards the attainment of enlarged and full support, as it shuts out a variety of scruples of conscience, which more diversified objects let in.  In this view the simplicity of the object,—additional clergymen for parishes needing them,—would commend itself very extensively to the Church of England.

But would I then abandon the principle of lay agency ?  By no means, as churchmen individually ; and happily there is another Society, already in efficient and extensive operation, which takes this object up explicitly.  I mean that excellent institution, the District Visiting Society.  Let the Pastoral Aid Society leave direct lay agency to that Society, and occupy itself in furnishing assistant pastors to overgrown parishes, and such other aid as may be approved in connection with it.

We must give up God's truth and will to no man ; but wisely to discern things that differ, and choose the best plans for attaining the best end, is unspeakably important ; and it is my hearty prayer that this wisdom may be given to our friends meeting together.

I see, all through the history of the revival of religion in our country, that those have been specially honoured of God, who respected authorities over them, and, while full of zeal for the truth, walked orderly in maintaining and diffusing it.

There are other material points, which cannot be conceded, and will not, I hope, be asked of the Society.  The nomination of those persons whom it supports is so clear a matter of equity, and so analogous to private patronage, and to the established practice with Government and in Missionary Societies, that as, on the one hand, the Society could never relinquish it without relinquishing all its usefulness, and its claims on the more zealous members of our church, —so, on the other hand, I trust it will never be required to give up this right ; the due qualification of candidates being always finally determined by the bishops, in the discharge of their high and most responsible office.

It might be desirable, I would suggest, in giving up lay agency, to testify the scriptural value and importance of that aid to the ministry ; and in confining yourselves to maintaining assistant-pas-

tors, to suggest, in the present exigency of the Church, the importance of not confining ordination to those who have had an university
education, so as to make that the main, which is really only a subordinate qualification; while the more important requisites, fulness
of scriptural knowledge, maturity of Christian judgment, depth of
experience, and warmth of zeal and love, are disregarded.

My great love to the object of the Pastoral Aid Society has led
me to make these remarks; but I gladly leave the subject with the
brethren whose immediate duty it will be to decide the important
question submitted to them, and have the honour to be,

Your Lordship's obliged and faithful Servant,

E. BICKERSTETH.

*February* 13, 1837.

My dearest B——,

I thank you for your note. I had not received tidings from any
other quarter previously, about the meeting, and your account was
the more interesting. Having already made a statement to Lord
Ashley of the judgment to which my mind had come, I do not feel
called upon to interfere personally at the adjourned meeting.

For the reasons I have stated, subjection to authorities, simplicity
of object, and the fact that lay agency is provided for by another
Society, I feel satisfied that the Pastoral Aid Society would act
wisely in giving way to the expressed wishes of the Bishops, while
they firmly maintained the scriptural principle itself.

Admitting this, I cannot, however, but be very anxious about the
judgment which our respected superiors, the Bishops, seem in part
to have formed, not to sanction lay agency in the present day.
Surrounded as the Church is with most able, bitter, and yet apparently conscientious opponents (acting at least professedly from
conscience), tottering as its position is, with regard to the support
of Government, and feeble as its hold is on even the conservative
classes themselves, I cannot but have great fears for the continuance of the *national* maintenance of our Establishment. With its
fall from that great and high position, what Christian member of
it can but see—however the spiritual part of the Church may be

quickened, revived, and purified—great, wide-spread, and fearful
evils to our beloved country ?   The rejection of God's true church
by the nation, would be a national crime, to be visited by awful
national judgments.

We see, in the case of Popery, how the aggrandizement of the
clergy, beyond the scriptural limit, everywhere weakened it in the
result, and has been the great occasion of its fall ; and I fear much
lest the radical spirit abroad, causing a powerful reaction, should
throw us in the ministry into that false position.

Instead of seeking, by being an extended blessing, to meet all
.the spiritual wants of the people, if we are standing upon a system
of exclusiveness and self-exaltation, as I cannot but see some are
doing, we shall precipitate our fall, and give our watchful enemies
special advantage over us.

Dissent is not to be met and overcome by such a system; it will
rather be exceedingly strengthened.   For though the principles of
our Establishment are most scriptural,—though it is the plainest
duty of a Christian nation to support nationally the Gospel,—yet
never, on the one hand, shall we have the consciences and hearts of
our country with us, but as we are a real spiritual blessing to them ;
nor on the other hand, shall we have the Divine protection, but as
we are fulfilling that high office.   The Jewish Church itself, ceasing
to fulfil it, was laid aside.

To have the consciences and hearts of the people with us, it must
be seen that we are not backward, but forward, in promoting their
spiritual welfare—the great end, as respects them, of our Establishment.   If they see us earnest about the temporalities, and cold about
their spiritual state, they will be careless of the temporalities, and
seek spiritual blessings in other quarters.

How important also is it to increase in every way, not inconsistent
with, but according to the Scriptures and primitive custom, that
interest which the pious laity are beginning to feel in the Church.
I cannot conceive how it is possible to get over many plain statements in the New Testament, that those not in the ministry were
helpers in Christ Jesus, and laboured in the Gospel; or the statements given by Bingham respecting the primitive catechists.   The

laity must see and feel this. They are willing to assist us. The Dissenters are open to their exertions, and use them to the utmost, and draw off from the Church its resources. What could deepen more the interest of the laity in our Church, or more increase their affection to it, than to use them as instruments to diffuse vital truth in our parishes? But if this be checked, all their zeal will naturally flow into sectarian channels, to the continued weakening, and in the end, to the certain and righteous destruction of our Establishment. On the other hand, let their employment be wisely regulated by the sanction, suggestions, and controul of our superiors; and it will infinitely more endear our Church to the whole country than even those valuable improvements in secular things, which the Church Commission is now effecting. Nothing but that which is single-eyed to God's glory, and the salvation of man, by the free circulation of the unadulterated "good tidings of great joy," in every scriptural method, will at all meet the present exigencies of the Church of England, that sacred deposit of three centuries, now entrusted to us in a season of peculiar peril.

You see then, my dear B——, how, though I think the Society, as a society, ought to concede its just and lawful objects to the expressed wishes of our superiors, I feel also, judging on a large scale, that the principle sought to be established, of rejecting lay agency in the instruction of the poor, is really prejudicial, as it regards the enlarged interests of the Church of England, as well as the cause of Divine truth. . . . . .

The Lord guide the minds of all concerned, to His glory, and the good of our Church, prays

Yours most truly,<br>E. BICKERSTETH.

" *February* 26, 1837. My dear brother, Spencer Thornton, has now joined me as a fellow-labourer. The Lord himself abundantly bless us in our union, making us a large blessing to each other, the parish, the country, and His church.

" My sermons entitled the 'Apostolic Benediction' are now printed : may it be for good.  I am called to preach a sermon to the Jews.  Lord, bless me in doing this.

" Lord, I ask of Thee this day at thy table these seven things—grace for early rising, full private morning prayer, constant mid-day prayer, diligent evening prayer, self-denial in things pleasant to the flesh, intercession for the people committed to me, enlarged liberality.

" May my intercourse with Spencer Thornton be really a blessing to him, so that his whole ministry may be prospered through the good he gets here.  Lord, do this. for me."

Two short notes to Mrs. Abel Smith, at this time, allude to Mr. Thornton's labours, as well as to his own engagements.

*March* 28, 1837.

. . . . . . . I feel very thankful to God, who has given me such a fellow-labourer as dear Spencer, who with unwearied zeal and perseverance visits the poor, and attends to all his duties.  The Lord Himself smile on our joint efforts for the good of dear Watton.

I leave here on Monday for a fortnight, if God will, to go to Bristol, Bath, and Birmingham.  It is an important journey, for many large meetings and congregations are to be addressed.  The Lord make me faithful, and a blessing.  You must say ' Amen ' to this.  I am engaged also to preach the Annual Sermon for the Reformation Society, on the first week in May.  It is a weighty duty, for which I ask the prayers of my friends.

O that the fulness of the blessing of Christ's Gospel may give us present and personal joy, and, in the experience of that joy, constrain us to seek to impart the same blessedness to others !

*May,* 1837.

. . . I hope that we may soon see you among us.  The country is so exquisitely rich, that we heartily desire our kind friends should enjoy it with us. It so naturally (if I may use the term, which is only true spiritually) leads the heart to the bounteous Giver of all our mercies; and the delay so enhances the goodness when it does come, that the whole face of creation is full now of lessons of grace, leading us to joy in our heavenly Parent.

I have been writing another number of the " Cottager's Guide," on Christian Privileges. It is a sweet subject, in the light and blessedness of which we might live, with more faith, in much more love and happiness. God grant that it may help some of my dear flock to do so.

I have increasing hope and comfort among the people. A spirit of hearing is spreading, and it is a token for good that some manifest their dislike to what is going on. Dear Thornton's aid is most precious to me, and he quite wins his way among all.

Our dear C——has been our chief domestic cross the last seven weeks. I pray God it may be sanctified; for oh I find how much that is hard wants softening, what is high wants bringing down, and what is worldly wants removing, in my own heart; and that only two things do this—the warm sunshine of God's love—and the sharp, but really kind strokes of affliction. . . . We doubt not that sweet end of the Lord's dealings, that He is very pitiful and of tender mercy.

" *March* 19, 1837. I am now fifty-one years of age. And, O how graciously has the God of all grace and mercy dealt with one who has made such unworthy returns to Him ! The mercies that surround me now are great, and beyond my enumeration. What full provision has He made for all my wants, and for my usefulness to others ! Near our Metropolis, so that it is accessible ; far enough from it, to be free from its distractions ; a full competency for my family, and power to help others : a friend to confer with in my studies, and another, like Thornton, to labour in my parish ; the joy of ——'s steadiness in the Lord ; the circulation of my religious

works, the good measure of health I enjoy ; the valuable
library the Lord has enabled me to gather ; some usefulness, I trust, in my parish, and yet more in my country :
the glorious gospel of the grace of God, committed to my
trust, and opportunity to testify of its blessed truths to
my fellow-sinners.

" Under these many mercies may I at length be constrained to devote myself, and all I am, to the Lord, far
more unreservedly than I have hitherto done.

" I have been struck with the original of that text ;—
' If therefore thine eye be single, &c,' as implying rather,
if thine eye be bountiful (ἁπλοῦς See 2 Cor. viii. 2 ; ix.
11, 13. ; James i. 5, ; Rom. xii. 8.) or at least bearing
that sense, which the context seems to favour. The Lord
give me this bountiful eye.

" In considering the law of Moses, it appears to me
that the Jews gave one-fifth of their property in tithes
to the Lord, in three kinds of tithes, and that I might
more systematically and largely enjoy the blessedness of
giving for the Lord's sake. May my God give me grace,
from this day, to practise it with all sums which I hereafter receive.

" First Tithe. One-tenth of my income, Lev. xxvii. 30.
Mal. iii. 10. This for *everything relating to God's truth,
worship, and immediate service.*

" Second Tithe. Two-thirds of a tenth. Deut. xiv.
22—27 ; xvi. 16. This for the social happiness of others,
and their enjoyment in God's worship.

" Third Tithe. One-third of a tenth. Deut. xiv. 28,
29.; Lev. xix. 9, 10. FOR THE POOR.

" *March* 25. Easter-Eve. To-morrow, I hope to receive
and administer the Lord's Supper. May it be blessed to
me, and to many. O how plain it is I have to go, not as

holy, but as sinful; not as righteous, but as unrighteous. May the Lord Himself shine on me, that I may be a blessing to others.

" . . . My only hope is in judging and condemning myself, that I be not condemned with the world. O Lord, may I be healed by Thy stripes. Apply, by thy Spirit, Thy wounds to my heart and conscience, that, like Job, I may hate and abhor myself.

" I wish to get a much fuller reading, daily, of God's word. Lord, enable me, from this time, to practise more this precious duty.

" *April* 30. Brought through my journey, in God's mercy, I erect a fresh Ebenezer to his name. What results do I come to, in looking at my own doings. Sin mars all I do—vile, vile, vile ! What results do I come to, in looking at God's dealings ? Mercy always helps me. ' Good and upright is the Lord, therefore will He lead sinners in the way.'

" *May* 21. I attended several of the meetings in London, and preached for the Reformation Society. The Lord pardon and bless. We have since had two meetings at Hertford and Watton for building the Hebrew church at Jerusalem, and more than £50 was contributed. To God be all the praise."

The sermon before the Reformation Society was founded on the address to the Church of Sardis, as a rebuke to the actual decay of faith and zeal in the Protestant Churches. It is marked by energy, boldness, and simplicity, and recent events have only given fresh interest to its voice of warning and admonition. One paragraph is like an anticipation of our actual state.

" While we slept, the enemy has been busy sowing tares, and the tares are rapidly multiplying. The plague

of Popery is spreading through the camp, and it is needless to make haste and withstand it.   Statistical returns
show abundantly the increase of Papal efforts among us,
and the records of this Society furnish fearful evidence
of their success.   Though, outwardly in its revenues,
Popery is wasting away in the chief countries of its riches
and influence, the zeal and energy of its expiring efforts
are worthy of a better cause.  It is said that ' the Romish
bishops in this country have resolved to reconstruct their
Church in England exactly on the same plan as before
the Reformation, throwing off the titles of Vicars Aposto-
lical, and reviving the dignities of territorial bishoprics.'
Thus does Rome, while she still adheres to all her abominations, identify herself with the spirit of Edom of old,
which said—' We are impoverished, but we will return
and build the desolate places.'  And what was the result ?
' Thus saith the Lord, They shall build, but I will pull
down ; and they shall call them, ' The border of wickedness, and, The people against whom the Lord hath indignation for ever.' "

The plain and faithful warning of this discourse served
to detect, in some cases, like the spear of Ithuriel, the
secret tendency to Papal doctrines, in those who were
themselves little aware on what slippery ground they
already stood.   One clergyman, deeply tinged with " An-
glo-Catholic " sentiments, wrote to Mr. Bickersteth at the
time, expressing his strong disapprobation of the Society,
and his regret at several statements in the discourse, as
adapted to give a great advantage to the Romanists in
argument.   After the lapse of fifteen years he is unhappily himself numbered among the open deserters to the
Church of Rome.

Amidst his public labours, Mr. Bickersteth was not

forgetful of his duty as a parent.  One of his children,
now at school, was always very delicate, and another was
suffering from a complaint, which seemed not unlikely
to occasion loss of sight.  The following notes were
written to them at this time.

*March* 1, 1837.

MY DEAREST F——,

Papa has a great many sheep scattered far and wide to take care
of, but he has one little pet lamb, to whom he must try to send one
little cup of milk for nourishment—not of the body, that, I know,
is full well taken care of—but of the spirit, which requires constantly
" the sincere milk of the word."

What think you, love, is the meaning of *waiting ?*  It is not the
same as obtaining : it is not the same as having, nor is it just the
same as hoping, though hope be the ground of waiting.  It is staying for something, till it arrive, or be given.  Some things come at
a certain time, as servants' wages when due.  Other things come
quite unexpectedly and suddenly ; both sad things, as your falls,
and good things, as when mamma came to Clifton.  For these
things we can hardly be said to wait.

But the Lord gives us His grace in every way, and our right
posture is, always to be waiting and expecting very great things
from our gracious God.  I will give you some passages that shew
this ; Psalms lxii. and cxxx., are full of the duty, and Isaiah xl. 28
—-31 is very plain ; and then think of,—yes, and get by heart those
precious verses, Lam. iii. 22—33.

Now while you are always waiting, you will be always receiving.
God never disappoints those who look to Him, and He delights to
give more in prayer than we think of.  How full and rich is that
promise—" Call unto me, and I will answer thee, and shew thee
great and mighty things which thou knowest not, Jer. xxxiii. 3."

Only see to it, love, that you are really delighting in the Lord—
that you have such a Father, so glorious and so good, so holy and
so gracious, so rich, and yet so tender, so near, and yet only to be

seen by faith, so unsearchable, and yet so beautifully manifest in all
that Jesus was, and Jesus did—in whose life you have the very
inward heart of God, as full of holy love, laid open to you, and to
all sinners whatsoever. It is its being *love to sinners*, that makes
it such precious love *to us*.

When you see this, you get to hate sin, which is nothing else than
rebellion against this good God; and you get that state of mind,
in which our God can wisely, holily, and graciously, give you the
desires, yes, all the desires, of your heart. See how these things
are joined together, Psalm xxxvii. 4, delighting in God, and having
all our wishes gratified. The Lord give you this happy mind, and
this perfect satisfaction.

This is my cup of milk—so good bye, my dearest.

Your own Papa,<br>
E. BICKERSTETH.

*June 9*, 1837.

MY DEAREST C——,

. . . . . We fully hope, if it please God our heavenly Father, that
you will be well enough to get home by the 28th. . . . . . . Watton
Rectory never looked more beautiful than it does now, and we shall
be glad to have the house well filled with all our beloved children.

In considering the dangers to which my dear child is exposed in
her present situation, my mind is chiefly directed to her spiritual
temptations. It has occurred to me as no slight one, that you are
by your illness made an object of sympathy and interest to many.
Sympathy is so delightful, that we are glad to get it increased in
any way. I entreat you, then, to watch against this great spiritual
danger. Remember how our Saviour acted, when going through
His most painful crucifixion. When a great company of people and
women bewailed Him, He did not indulge himself in their sympathy ;
but, with noble disinterestedness, disregarding His own sufferings,
turned His holy, heavenly, loving heart to *their* situation, and how
He might lead them to their best interest. " Weep not for me,
daughters of Jerusalem, but weep for yourselves." I find continually, my love, in my own heart, how great and constant a temptation

is the love of men's admiration, and the desire to be much thought
of, and be an object of interest to others.   It is only weakened by
contemplating Jesus, despised for our sake, and His follower, Paul,
made an offscouring of all things, that we might have the gospel.
The Lord give us this spirit, of living to others, and not to ourselves,
now, and always.

Your affectionate father,

E. BICKERSTETH.

# CHAPTER XX.

ACCESSION OF THE QUEEN—VARIOUS WRITINGS.

A. D. 1837—1839.

THE session of 1837, which had been one of great national interest, from the balanced state of political parties,
and the important questions of which the decision seemed
to hang in suspense, was closed abruptly by the illness
and death of the king. It was a period of deep excitement and much anxiety to every thoughtful mind. On
June 19, Lord Ashley wrote to Mr. Bickersteth—" We
are in much anxiety ; the King is given over, and we are
all awaiting the first act of the new reign. It is a trying
season, for, turn which way you will, there is nothing but
distress of nations, and perplexity, men's hearts failing
them for fear. This is literally true, for except the radical
party, 'quibus quieta movere, magna merces videtur,' I
meet no one who is not full of misgivings. The intrigues
of the courts of Elizabeth and Anne, disgusting and injurious then, would be destructive now. We play at a
higher game, and in more perilous circumstances. The
greatest empire of civilized men that the sun ever shone
upon, is to stand or fall, humanly speaking, on the will
of a woman barely eighteen. But I cannot forget that
the grace of God has been wonderfully exhibited in young
and royal hearts. I love to think of the good Josiah, and

our own Edward VI., whose hearts were indeed disposed
and turned as seemed best to His godly wisdom."

Mr. Bickersteth shared fully in these natural anxieties
and hopes, connected with the opening of a new reign.
On Sunday, June 25, he preached a sermon on the Queen's
Accession, from Proverbs viii. 14—17, which was afterwards printed, and contains a simple exposition of his
own principles, with regard to the great outlines of Christian politics.   It was a seasonable testimony to the great
lessons of Divine truth, in their bearing on the duty of
rulers, and the prosperity of nations, and closed with an
earnest and solemn invitation to united prayer for the
new sovereign, who had been placed, at such an early
age, at the head of so vast and mighty an empire.

The personal views of Mr. Bickersteth might be called
moderately conservative.   Occupied with the great and
lasting concerns of the kingdom of God, he took no interest in questions of mere party strife.   But he had a deep
sense of the true dignity of government as a Divine ordinance, and of the obligation of rulers to honour Christ,
the true fountain of all power, in their public actions, to
make the word of God the primary law of all their legislation, and to study the advancement of the people, not
only in wealth and peace, but in true godliness.   He deplored the divisions of Protestant Christians, not only
because of their direct evil, in strife and bitterness, and
the hindering of works of love, but because they had so
powerful a tendency to help forward a national apostasy
from the faith of Christ, and to render the practical recognition of Christianity in all public measures, difficult,
if not impossible.   These views, which he derived, at an
early period of his religious experience, from the direct
study of the word of God, continued unchanged through

all the stirring changes of his later years, when many
were drifting into the furthest extremes of political radi-
calism, or were recoiling from its dangers into the pretended peace, and artificial unity, of the Church of Rome.
He believed that the word of God, in its main outlines of
doctrine and practice, was a clear and sufficient guide to
statesmen in their public duties, as well as to the private
Christian in every walk of domestic and social life.

The following letter, during a journey to Surrey for the
Church Missionary Society, alludes to some of his multiplied engagements at this time.

*Godalming, July* 18, 1837.

MY DEAREST BIRKS,

. . . . . I have been, as usual, fully employed. I preached three
times on Sunday, at Godalming and Guildford, from 2 Cor. iv. 15,
and Isa. xlii. 4., and they seemed to impress many. I have every
morning here a congregation at family prayers, and every evening
attend a meeting for the Church Missionary Society, besides meeting all day long with one and another, to converse of the things of
Christ.

My sermon on the Queen's Accession is now circulating, and that
for the Reformation Society is just printed, after being lost for two
months. May its temporary death, and then its recovery, be a
token for lasting good.

I had an interesting and important meeting in London, when
Mr. Wybrow, an eminent clergyman, was sent to Calcutta from the
Church Missionary Society, as Secretary of its mission there. I
had to commend him in prayer to the God of missions, even the
God and Father of our Lord Jesus Christ, and I doubt not He was
with us of a truth . . . . May He far more abundantly use us, however weak and unworthy we really be, to the good of His Church
and of our fellow men, and to the glory of His own great name. O
that we may diffuse the cheering, holy, and happy light of His own
precious and saving truth, and so rescue many souls from darkness

G 2

and misery! I trust He has led me more and more to see that this is the great end of the grace given to us, that we may have the fuller glory in His own likeness, here and for ever.

"*July* 20. I greatly enjoyed, in a solitary ride, communion with my God. It was a season of spiritual joy and peace which I shall not, I trust, soon forget. O that I lived more with God! but soon I fall away, and all is greatly mixed with my own sinfulness.

" O that I may, in eating the flesh and drinking the blood of Christ at the communion, find my soul strengthened against my besetting sins! Lord, give me a broken spirit, and a contrite heart, for Christ's sake."

"*August* 27. I have been to Dover and Canterbury, and was much interested in going over Hooker's Church and residence at Bishop's-bourne. I admire the holiness and comprehensiveness of that devoted Christian.

" *October* 1. In the last fortnight I have been to Burslem, Derby, Newark, Retford, Tuxford, Chesterfield, Liverpool, and Sapcote for the Church Missionary and Jewish Societies, mercies having followed me all the way. How gracious the Lord has been! full of mercy, grace, and truth, are all His ways.

" And yet how contrary I walk to Him! O Divine Purifier and Redeemer, what a work I give Thee to do! Fail not, faint not, in purifying my soul."

The following note was written about this time to one of his children, who had lately left school, and was visiting some friends.

MY BELOVED CHILD,

....... We were very glad to hear from you, and to learn how you employed your time. You must consider that you are still *at school,* only in another class : till we get to heaven we are all pupils and scholars. . . . . . . There is the school of *Providence*, which includes all the varied events of life. There is the *school of the family circle*, where we learn duties to parents, brothers, sisters, servants. There is the *school of society*, where we learn the duties of the social circle. There is the *school of temptation*, in which we discover our own weakness, and our Saviour's strength. Now, my dear child, be a humble, diligent, and prayerful learner in all these schools, and so you will be fitted for higher usefulness and enjoyment, here and hereafter. . . . .

I do not wonder that you sometimes find prayer a burden, and if Satan can fill your mind with the new scenes you pass through, he will thus turn your affections elsewhere than to God. This is the school of temptation. Now you must learn your Saviour's strength, as well as your own weakness. Look much to Him. See Him pleading and interceding for you, when you kneel to pray, and this will be a great help to the feeling of prayer, and will enable you to pray with confidence, feeling, and affection.

Your ever affectionate Father,<br>E. BICKERSTETH.

"*November* 22. I have been interested, and I trust, profited, by reading the new volumes of Henry Martyn's journals and letters. Many things here have shown me how low my state is. I was particularly struck with his seizing all opportunities of doing good in journeys, his time given to private prayer, his manifest habit of constant prayer in all things, his great deadness to worldly ease and pleasure, his eminent spirit of holy devotedness ; and especially, his prizing Scripture above every thing, and his enlarged study of it.

"O Lord my God, enable me, thy most sinful creature, to follow him in these things, as he followed Christ, and to abhor myself for the things in me, opposite to this bright example, or falling so short of it.

"Yet I cannot but think there was a spirit of bondage,

in some degree, in Martyn's service of God. Comparatively but little is manifested of the grace of the Gospel ; and where there is set forth the happiness of holiness, and the true spirituality of a Christian, there is, perhaps from natural constitution, despondency and depression, hardly rising to the standard—' as sorrowful, yet alway rejoicing.' A fuller view of Divine truth would have raised him to a *happier* mind."

" *December* 25. . . . I have been publishing a sermon, preached at Brighton, on the ' Overflow of Grace,' an ' Address to the Jews at Liverpool,' a ' Calendar of Lessons,' and No. 12, of ' The Cottager's Guide.' My Volume of the ' Christian Fathers' is passing through the press, with a new and enlarged edition of the ' Scripture Help.' O let me remember the words. ' Thou that teachest another, teachest thou not thyself?' Thy books thy condemnation—what a sentence that would be ! O Lord Jesus, my only hope is my self-condemnation, that I may win Thy righteousness and Thy grace. Thou must approve the just acknowledgment of my sin. But when shall I rise out of it, into holy love, and self-sacrifice, and painful labour ?

" O how great is the goodness, long-suffering, and tender mercy, of Him on whom I depend ! O that I may loathe myself for the abuse of so much grace ! "

" *January* 27, 1838. We have been passing through an affecting season of death, about fourteen in two months, several in the higher classes, and several very sudden ones among the lower—two children burned to death. The Lord sanctify it to the people here. . . . . I have been writing important letters to Paris, a Preface to Hannah More's Life, and a letter about the ' Factory Children.' "

" *February* 24.   My ' Christian Fathers,' and the new edition of the ' Scripture Help' have just been published. I have been deeply engaged, the last three weeks, in preparing a ' Treatise on Baptism,' which it appears to me important at this time to bring before the Church.   May the Lord himself assist me in it, for the edification, awakening, and conversion of men."

" *March* 25.   I have in the last month been preparing six fresh chapters of my ' Cottager's Guide,' No. XIII.— XVIII, and am concluding with some forms of prayer. The Lord make it a blessing.

" I set off to-morrow, if it be His will, on a long journey, to Durham, Newcastle, Edinburgh, Paisley, Greenock, and Glasgow.   O for grace to go in the spirit of Christ, and have a real blessing.

" But, Lord, help me, that I may in nothing neglect my own vineyard—that I may be sincere and without offence unto the day of Christ.   Keep me from dishonouring Thy name, even to the end ; and let me, with increasing confidence, patience, hope, and love, be waiting for Thy coming ! "

This journey to the North is described in the following letter to one of his children.

*Greenock, April* 5, 1838.

My dearest C——,

Dear Mamma having commissioned you to write, I suppose I must write next to you, and I begin a letter here, which I hope to close to-morrow at Glasgow, and to find there, perhaps, another from home.

My time at Edinburgh was occupied with the Society's work from hour to hour, and the last day we had three meetings, morning, afternoon, and evening ; and they wanted me to promise to come a month in the summer, for there is a great desire to hear of the things of Christ, and promote His kingdom. The collections came to near £250, greatly exceeding any former year.

Nothing could be more kind than the Murrays : my comfort was studied in every way, and I had every possible convenience for my wants. When we came to Paisley yesterday, things were in a different state. The Clergyman was ill and away. My fellow-traveller and myself had to sleep at a dirty-looking Inn, in the middle of the town. We had to grope our way to the Clergyman's house, to learn what we had to do, and there took tea, and I preached in a chapel only half full. All this was very good to those bad old gentlemen, Pride and Self-sufficiency, that sometimes take a liking to be in your Papa's heart, though he would gladly turn them out ;—for this helped to do a little damage to those bad old gentlemen. After the sermon, no one invited us to their house, so we went back to the Inn, and breakfasted this morning ; and then came off, first by a rail-road, three miles to Renfrew, and then by a steam-boat twelve miles hither, where we find a much warmer and more hopeful state of things. So we have ups and downs in our journeying.

I addressed, on Wednesday, six hundred young persons, eighty-five of whom, from the Address, became Collectors of the Church Missionary Society, and others were to ask their mammas if they might. They listened for a whole hour, and seemed quite interested with Missions. I thought—what are my own dear children doing at home ? Won't it be sad, if these young people go beyond my own ?

But I shall have plenty to tell you of, on my return, should it please God to bring me back in safety ; and hitherto, all the way has been one unbroken journey of mercies, and my cup has run over with blessings.

I was amused to-day, by hearing that one who had been deeply interested in my books, when he heard I was coming to Edinburgh, said,—Oh ! I thought he had been dead long ago ! I read his books twenty years since, and numbered him with the old Fathers of the Church that had passed away.—I have, however, to be very thankful to the Father of mercies, for being informed of several instances of conversion to God, through reading the " Scripture Help." To God alone be praise, for any good done through us.

I was stopped in one of the principal streets of Edinburgh, by a nice-looking elderly woman, who said she must speak to me. The last time she had seen me, was in the riding house at Clonmell, when 1 addressed a regiment of soldiers, with Peter Roe. I remember it well: it was fifteen years ago, and she had never forgotten it.

We were surprized, in passing through Glasgow yesterday, to find all the shops shut, like Sunday. It is the case twice a year, being their half-yearly fasts before the Sacrament. The churches were open, and ministers came from different parts to preach. It happens unfavourably for the Missionary Society, as the Presbyterians cannot leave their own Church to attend the sermons; and some other things are trying to our friends at Glasgow, but all will work for good.

. . . . I shall not reach home till late on Thursday—if it shall please the Lord, on whom we depend for life and breath, and every movement we make, to bring me to you at that time. My heart thirsts for home, and yet God has so prospered the journey, that I have room for nothing but thanksgiving. . . . Love to all around you. The Lord, in His goodness, bring us together in peace.

Most truly, your own Papa,
E. BICKERSTETH.

" *April* 15. Through the Lord's mercy I have been carried through a journey of nine hundred miles, and have preached sermons, or attended meetings, at all the places mentioned above. To God be all praise for innumerable mercies.

" *May* 27. I have again been for the Church Missionary Society to Cambridge, for the London Association of the United Brethren, to London, and for the Jews' Society to Ipswich, Woodbridge, Saxmundham, and Lowestoft. I returned last night. The Lord has been very gracious to me, a sinner.

" The Sermon for the Moravian Missions is printing, and the last part of the ' Cottager's or Family Guide.' How good is the Lord, to permit me to do any thing for bringing others to the knowledge and enjoyment of His love ! The Lord give me delight and joy in His holy will and service ; that, as it is my only real and proper happiness, so I may rise to partake of its blessedness day by day.

" I have just been thinking on that important principle,—' Look not every man on his own things, but every man also on the things of others.' May I know that this is happiness, as well as usefulness. I want to find my true joy in my most self-denying duties. Lord, give me this, that the joy of the Lord may be my strength in them.

" *July* 1. . . I have found much comfort latterly from Bishop Andrews's Devotions, in the original Greek and Latin copy, and think that an exact translation may be useful to the Church. O make me in any way an instrument of good to my fellow-men !

" The next week is to be engaged in Missionary Associations ; the Lord use me and bless me. Oh I feel it is our privilege to be kings and priests unto God. May I rise to the fulness of this blessing, and for this end wait more closely on God. All good must begin in closer and more lengthened communion with God—solid time given to it, and this as time redeemed.

" *July* 28, 1838. It pleased God, on this day week, to give me a merciful deliverance. I was thrown off my horse, over its head, and fell on my back, by its stumbling, and yet He preserved me. I have indeed been much bruised and weakened, and kept from walking, but I was able to preach on Sunday last, and to journey this

week for the Jews' and Church Missionary Society, to
Aylesbury, Wendover, and Chesham. All praise be to
my heavenly Father, for protecting, preserving, and
sparing grace. . . .

"Before me is the confirmation of the young of my
parish. O that it may indeed be a blessed season to their
souls, and to my own dear children."

The season of confirmation was one which Mr. Bickersteth greatly prized, and was very diligent to improve,
for the awakening and deepening of religious impressions
in the hearts of the younger members of his flock. Aware
of its dangers and evils, when viewed as a superstitious
charm, or perverted into a youthful holiday, he was thoroughly alive to its great importance, as the frequent
turning-point between a careless, worldly course, and a
life of real devotedness to Christ and his blessed service.
His addresses to the young of his parish, in his private
catechetical Lectures at such times, were very plain and
earnest, and though he had to deplore, like other faithful
clergymen, too many cases of fruitless labour, he was
also cheered by not a few instances of deep and lasting
impression, when living stones were added to the temple
of the Lord. Every confirmation, for twenty years, was
usually followed by some permanent increase in the
number of the communicants, over whom he could rejoice
that his labours had not been in vain. He could
thus, from his own experience, remark in his Treatise
on Baptism, p. 286 : "I am persuaded that I speak
the universal voice of all my brethren in the ministry,
who have earnestly and patiently sought to improve
this rite, that in no part of their ministry have they had
more delightful tokens of the Divine blessing on their
labours for the abundant good of those committed to

their charge, than in confirmation. O how many thousands will for ever thank God for leading them thus to decision of character, and entire devotedness to the Lord ! "

" *August* 25. Through the mercy of God, I am recovered from the effects of my fall, and as well as usual. O may all my recovered strength be used for God. When I look at my standing in the sight of God, and His purity, and my own formality, I can enter into Job's words, and say from the heart, ' I abhor myself.' Truly I have reason so to do. . . .

" I preached for the Hertford Infirmary last Sunday morning, and the sermon is now printing. The Jews' Annual Meeting is to be held on Monday, which -closes our annual Herts Meetings, for the Bible, Church Missionary, Jews', and Tract Societies.

" I hope to admit several of my young, who were confirmed, to the Lord's Table, and among them two of my own children.

" My correspondence is so heavy, that I am quite hindered in getting on with works which I have in hand. But let me serve the Lord in that way in which His providence calls me, knowing, that His workmanship is unto good works."

" *September* 29, 1838. Through mercy I have been preserved and blessed in a long journey to York, for the Jews' Society, and am brought home in peace. To God be all the praise.

" I preached twice at Brighton, before my journey to York, and attended several meetings."

During the same journey he wrote the following letter to his children.

*York, Sept.* 22, 1838.

MY DEAREST CHILDREN,

. . . . Through God's mercy I reached Ware before the mail arrived, and had a prosperous journey here in nineteen hours. My companions were rather of the hunting and racing class, so that I was left to my resource of reading, for which I got a much longer day than I can at home.

I reached here about five, dined, and went to the evening meeting, and much enjoyed seeing the many valuable friends, whom God has brought me to know here. Mr. Gray is quite a monument of the goodness of God. He hears nearly as well as when he was a child, and is full of all the sprightliness and cheerfulness of youth ; he is a perfect patriarch, presiding still over all that is good in York, as well as over his own spreading family.

But oh! what is even this to the brighter and better hope the gospel has given him—of having to say, of a glorious company in the last day—" Behold I, and the children whom God hath given me! " May this too, be my happy portion, my dear children! Of all the joys God gives a parent, this is indeed one of the very highest. " I have no greater joy than to hear that my children walk in the truth."

Our meeting last night was of a more private and social kind— about fifty at the house of one of the Secretaries of the Jews' Society. I had a little friendly discussion with Mr. ——, who would not see that Isaiah xi. 11, belongs to the future restoration of the Jews. . . . My children will have some advantage in not having to contend with old opinions, through which their father had to fight his own way to the truth in this matter. . . . I long that they should be looking for that great day, and preparing for it, that it may be to them a day of unspeakable blessedness.

I could not look around on our friends, and see how many had been removed since I first came here, without a new impression of the transitoriness of earthly things, and the infinite importance of redeeming the time for God, and laying up now in store a good foundation against the time to come. Let us plan each day's work wisely, sow seed widely, keep to our Master's will and work steadily, and rejoice all the day in His grace and loving-kindness.

I see nothing to hinder my return to you at the time we expected. May our God be glorified, and a lively zeal for His kingdom, and the house of Israel, be excited here between this and then, by your father and his fellow-labourers. My love to you all, and remembrances to the servants.

Your own affectionate father,<br>E. BICKERSTETH.

" *October* 27. . . . . I trust that the Lord has been effectually working in the hearts of two of my children, and leading them back to Himself. O may He maintain this work of grace, and increase it continually, by fresh supplies of His own Spirit."

This autumn the illness of one of his daughters, who had symptoms of decline, rendered the sea-air desirable, and Mrs. Bickersteth and one of her sisters accompanied her to Brighton. They were hospitably entertained by General and Mrs. Marshall, who had lately removed from Watton, after a residence there of about three years, in which the two families had been in the closest intimacy. Some notes, occasioned by this visit, illustrate Mr. Bickersteth's private intercourse, as a pastor and a friend.

*Watton, Oct.* 5.

MY DEAR GENERAL,

How can I thank you enough for all your kindness to my dear wife and children, and the love with which you received us to your dwelling! May multiplied spiritual blessings be imparted to you both, and all your anxieties be relieved, and turned into blessings, according to the fulness of love in Him, who is the Father of mercies, and God of all comfort. I am joyful in the thought that you both love God, and therefore all things must infallibly and omnipotently work together for your good. May you ever, in this precious life-boat, ride above the stormy waves of this transient and tumultuous scene, through which we must pass to the heavenly kingdom. . . .

I rejoice in the great plainness of your circular. God honours simple truth. Perhaps for the sake of others, ———'s name was not the best; but I never did any good without making some blunders, to keep me in my proper place, as a poor, sinful, dependent creature. I doubt not that you have found this.

Hearty love to Mrs. M. We had that passage this morning— " Let the peace of God rule in your hearts." That queen of graces is ours in Christ.

Ever most affectionately yours,<br>E. BICKERSTETH.

*October* 20.

I must write you a few lines, to express my own very cordial thanks for all your kindness to my dear children. . . . . To God, our own God, be praise for every fresh act of love and goodness, in addition to myriads on myriads that we have already received. The chief joy, indeed, to a parent's heart, is the spiritual health of his children, and of this our God is giving us some sweet tokens. But we must rejoice with trembling, that we may rejoice for ever.

Again and again I mention you at the throne of grace, and this has been much strengthened by your kindness to ourselves and our children.

*October* 27.

. . . I send you the enclosed, only to show that I had written, when we were disappointed of a frank by our noble-minded Lord Ashley's removal to Shropshire. I hope you pray for him, that he may be a blessing to our country.

Tell Mrs. M. I have got the first edition of " McNeile's Lectures on the Advent," and was both pleased and struck with the points she has noticed. My heart goes very much with dear McNeile in his views, greatly as he soars above me in the noble powers God has given him, and his use of them for the Master's glory. But to be anything for Christ's service is a privilege indeed.

*November* 17.

MY DEAR GENERAL,

I must thank you for your kind letter. . . . We trust that our dear child may yet be spared to be a blessing. Our other children also give us increasing comfort. How can we be thankful enough to the Father of all our mercies?

. . . There is a blessed opening, through the Societés Evang. of Paris and Geneva, for good on the continent. I am busy preparing a work to be called " A Voice from the Alps," showing this. It is now in the press, and I think will interest you.

O that we had you here again! We want to form a Protestant Association, but we want *hearts* as well as *Herts;* for we are at a very low ebb in Protestantism in this county. . . . McNeile's speeches and sermons at Hereford were most admirable. I quite agree in his views of Antichrist applied to Popery, and believe that to be our stronghold in this day of battle. . . .

How often we think of you with affection, I need not say. Actually having been with you gives us an insight into your plans each day, its trials as well as its joys. All, all is ordered by the wisest, the fullest, the most comprehensive, and the most enduring love; the furnace, to destroy the dross; the green pastures and the still waters, to nourish and refresh the soul; the wilderness, that you may prize the pillar of fire by night; and goodness and mercy marking all the way to the very end. Nothing shall happen to you but what is best in the eyes of infinite wisdom and boundless grace. Only trust in the Lord with all your heart: this is your late Pastor's instruction, dear friends, and God Almighty bless you both, and make you an increasing blessing to all around you.

Ever affectionately yours,

E. BICKERSTETH.

" *November* 25, 1838. The Lord has been very good in enabling me to complete works for Him, either now printed, or in the press. A second edition of my ' Christian Truth,' is printed ; the ' Voice from the Alps,' and the book of ' Private Devotions,' are in the press, and the ' Treatise on Baptism,' nearly ready. To my God be all praise and glory for all His goodness. May these things be profitable to His church.

"O Lord, what a debtor I am to sovereign mercy—that one so very dead and formal should be used in any way for Thee—what grace is here ! What treasures in an earthen, most earthen vessel ! I praise Thy name alone for ever. Only add this grace, to raise me out of the form into the power, out of condemning others into condemning myself, out of selfishness into love. Amen and Amen."

The " Voice from the Alps," to which allusion is here made, was a collection of several discourses of Merle D'Aubigné, at the Theological School of Geneva, with reports, and a variety of information respecting the progress of the Gospel in France and Switzerland. It was one important means of drawing attention to the work of God on the continent of Europe, and of stimulating that zeal for its advancement, which issued, not long after, in the union of the European Society with the Central Committee for French Evangelization, and the consequent formation of the Foreign Aid Society.

The following year (1839) saw Mr. Bickersteth involved in a growing pressure, both of public and private duties. Their general character, however, was much the same as before. Early in January he was called to address a number of his brother clergymen, at Islington, on the dangers of the Church of Christ, and his remarks were soon afterwards published, in an enlarged form, and had a rapid and extensive sale. In March he journeyed for the Church Missionary Society, to Manchester and many

other towns in the north, and for the Jews to Reading,
Wallingford, and Abingdon. In April he took part in
opening a Temporal Relief Fund for the Jews, and in
labours for the Foreign Churches. In May he preached
two Anniversary Sermons, for the London City Mission
and the Colonial Church Society, attended and spoke, as
usual, at several of the other meetings, journeyed to Edinburgh for the Jews, and set on foot a Herts Protestant
Association, preaching a sermon on its behalf, and sustaining nearly all the labour of its practical organization.
In July he was occupied with a variety of local anniversaries in his own country. In August he again journeyed,
along with his two eldest children, to the Isle of Wight,
for the Church Missionary Society, renewing his intercourse with some of his old friends. In October he went
to Cheltenham, Worcester, and Gloucester for the Jews,
and to St. Alban's for the Church Missions. In the interval
of these journeys he was occupied, as usual, with various
publications. Besides the " Dangers of the Church," and
his three Anniversary Sermons, he was much occupied in
revising and enlarging his " Guide to the Prophecies," of
which the seventh Edition was published in August, and
his " Treatise on Baptism " was also finished before the
close of the same year. A few of his private letters, how·
ever, will give the best view of that under-current of
Christian love, by which he was sustained in his public
labours.

*February* 14, 1839.

MY DEAR MRS. SMITH,

Thanks be to our gracious God, who has heard our prayers, and
given you another pledge of His confidence and love, another immortal plant to rear for His heavenly paradise. . . . . .

The spiritual state of my own dear children is to me now a full fountain of grateful emotions and daily joy. To God, my God, be all glory! It is a joy so much above all earthly good, that words fail to describe the comparison. O may you, whom God has enriched with so many temporal blessings, have the far higher joys, which only His grace gives, in every member of your family!

And it will be so, if the main principle be constantly aimed at in practice, to seek for them first the kingdom of God and his righteousness, and sacrifice other things to this; which indeed is soon found, as St. Paul shows, to be no sacrifice, but only parting with a loss, and worse than loss. Phil. ii.

We opened the Church last evening, being Ash-Wednesday, and had a large congregation. I preached on Luke xii. 56—the Signs of the Times. I deeply feel the responsibility of the office of a watchman, in such days as these, lest the Church suffer damage by his ignorance, and neglect of warning with that earnestness to which God's word, and the events of these days call us; and yet the great blessedness of seeing and testifying His truth, as a faithful steward. . . . . .

Most truly yours,<br>E. BICKERSTETH.

*Liverpool, March* 14.

MY DEAREST BIRKS,

Thanks for your useful remarks on W.'s letter, and Sir F. Head's narrative. My mind and heart go along with you in both. Oh! may we have wisdom and grace clearly to discern the Lord's will, and faithfully to act on our convictions, amidst all the darkness and difficulties of the days in which we live.

God opened great doors of usefulness before me at Manchester, so as to make it clear to me that He was with me in the journey; gave me acceptance in the sight of His people, and a great opportunity of testifying to His truth amidst vast concourses of people in these large towns, Bolton, Burnley, Bury, Manchester, Oldham, and Rochdale. Everywhere I see faithful ministers multiplying, and doors of usefulness opened. . . . . .

I got to Liverpool this morning, and found my sister, and her son

Edward, very poorly, but in a Christian state of mind—so good is our God in affliction. My visit was treated as that of a messenger of mercy, and I hope has been found a real refreshment.

I have since called on M'Neile, and as he can come in May, I feel disposed to wait for him. The Lord himself guide and direct. He compelled me by earnest entreaty, sore against my will, to preach for him to-night; perhaps, however, the Lord may have a message through me to His people. Our only comfort is entire union with the will of God. . . .

. . . . My heart is much with my dear wife and children, and parishioners. May spiritual and heavenly blessings without number be given to you all, prays

Yours most affectionately,

E. BICKERSTETH.

The illness of his nephew continued, and led, after his return home, to the following letter.

Watton, April 1, 1839.

MY BELOVED K——,

Much have I thought of your afflicted chamber, and the prayer on the other side will show I have not been unmindful of my promise; amidst multiplied occupations, attending a journey to Berkshire for the Jews', and the important parish duties of Easter, as well as the many things which are now before me. If we can by love serve one another, we are truly happy in a work our heavenly Master delights in. I was pressed to go to Edinburgh, to form a Jews' Society, but could not, and have engaged to preach two of the annual sermons, for the London City Mission, and the Colonial Church Society.

*A Prayer for my dear sick Nephew.*—Almighty Father, my heavenly Parent, help me to believe that Thou dost love me, far beyond mother or father, or brother or sister; for Thou didst not spare Thine own Son, but didst deliver Him up for us all, and Jesus died on the cross, to put away all my sins. Help me also to see and feel that this sickness is sent, not only because I am a sinful child, and need it, but also because Thou dost love me so much, as to chastise and correct me for my good. O may I believe this Thy real goodness for me, and so neither despise Thy chastening, nor faint and be weary under it; but give glory to Thee my Father by saying from the heart, and at all times—I delight to do and to suffer Thy will, O my God. If it be Thy will, make me and my dear sick mother quite well again, that we may joyfully praise Thee, and be made useful by telling others how good Thou art, our God; that they also may know and rejoice in Thy loving-kindness. Thus may we be accepted of Thee now, and finally meet all Thy true servants, in the glory of our Lord Jesus Christ, when He shall come again, and receive us to Himself. Hear me, for His great name's sake.

The following note alludes to a liberal donation received for the building of a Church on Mount Zion, an object in which Mr. Bickersteth took, as was natural, a most lively interest.

*Watton Rectory, April 17.*

My dear General Marshall,

Many thanks, first to the Lord, and then to you, for your bounty for the poor Jews. That letter has stirred up many. I received £20 yesterday for the same object. To God be glory! It will be a new day to Jerusalem, and I long for wings like a dove, to fly and tell Nicolayson and Young. God has done it beyond all my thoughts.

How I wish I could write fully to you, but the pressure on me now is prodigious. I was at Bristol and Bath last week, I have a Protestant Association before me, and continual meetings, public sermons, &c., till May 14, when I expect to go to Edinburgh for the Jews. Only, dear friends, ask for me that the Lord may be glorified in me and by me, the souls of others blessed, and my own soul preserved, and sin destroyed. The Lord himself give to you both richly the same blessings. I do indeed sympathize with you. Love from all here.

Affectionately yours,

E. Bickersteth.

"*March* 31, *Easter Sunday.* The Lord carried me safely and with a blessing through my journeys—all glory be to His name. How sweet it is to give glory to my God, and my emptiness and vileness may well make me glory in Him alone.

" My dearest E. goes this day, for the first time, to the Lord's table. O may it be a season of great grace, help, light, and love to his soul ! What thanks above measure I owe to my God for His grace to my dear children, seeing it is wholly His work, beyond all my thoughts, and any means I have used.

" I do earnestly seek of my God grace for—more fervent and full private prayer and intercession—more diligent, constant, and extensive visiting in my parish—more daily habits of self-denial in ordinary things—more real communion with God in all my duties and occupations—more enlarged blessedness in my talents, for the good of others. . . . I fly to Christ. O now give me resurrection-blessings, (Col. iii. 1—4,) this day, I entreat thee."

" *April* 28. I went to town this week, to assist in opening a Temporal Relief Fund for the Jews, and in the Central Committee of the Evangelical Societies. The Lord assisted me, blessed me, and humbled me. It is good to lie in His hands altogether.

" Another week's arduous duties are before me. O Lord, direct, strengthen and bless ! I am feebleness itself—I am full of sinfulness—I am nothing. Be all in all, O Christ, that by Thee such a worm may be blessed and a blessing.

" The love to me of Christian friends, of varied and opposing sentiments, is wonderful. Little do they know the inward defects under which I groan. O Lord, I am oppressed, undertake for me."

The sermon for the City Mission was undertaken under circumstances which involved some self-denial and moral courage. The Society was still in its infancy ; and its mixed constitution, with a Committee half of Churchmen, and half of Dissenters, exposed it to much odium from high-churchmen, and considerable suspicion and fear, even from many of the evangelical clergy. It added much to the difficulty of the task, that the Bishop of London, since the last Anniversary, had forbidden sermons to be preached for it in any of the parochial churches of his diocese ; following, no doubt, his own sincere conviction respecting his official duty. Mr. Bickersteth was fully alive to the weight of these reasons, which might have deterred him from pleading its cause. He had a deep and habitual respect for episcopal authority ; not the less sincere and practical, because it was ever made subordinate to the claims of Divine truth, and never prompted him to speak of bishops, with flattering words, as inspired apostles, with a miraculous halo around their brows. He was also aware of the influence he had gained among his brethren, and the great duty of not sacrificing lightly so precious a talent. But he had an eminent measure of straightforward singleness of purpose, where the path of duty seemed to him to be plain. In writing on " the Dangers of the Church," his attention had lately been drawn to the spiritual destitution of London, and his soul had been stirred within him, like St. Paul's at Athens, by the view of nearly a million of habitual sabbath-breakers, in the metropolis of a nominally Christian land. He felt it the clear duty of all who loved the Lord Jesus in sincerity, to grapple with this fearful evil, and so far as was practicable, to unite in labouring against it, and to tread under foot their mutual jealousies in the presence of this appalling mass of iniquity, so ruinous to souls, and so dishonouring to their common Saviour. As a Churchman, he felt persuaded that the more the Church of England, its bishops and its clergy, cared simply for the things of Christ, and the salvation of dying sinners, the more surely would Christ himself espouse their cause as His own. The means employed by the Society, in his opinion, were scriptural and lawful, the object unspeakably important, and the union of Christians in the work, so far as it was practicable without direct collision or compromise, highly desirable. With these convictions he complied with the earnest wish of the Committee, and preached on May 2, at St. John's Chapel, Bedford Row, their Annual Sermon, from the closing verses of Jonah's prophecy. One or two notes written at the time will throw light on his feelings and motives.

*Watton Rectory, Feb.* 20.

My dear Garwood,

Though it is not a situation that I should have voluntarily chosen, (and I feel the deep responsibility of it before the Church of God,) I dare not, in the present state of London, refuse to use any powers that the Lord may have given me in his Church, to promote the salvation, in a truly Christian way, of so many destitute souls, so very near to us, and with such affecting claims upon us.

Expecting, therefore, much blame and reproach from man, and diminished usefulness in some quarters, where another course might have given me access, I will, God helping me, yet preach your Annual Sermon. It appears to me that if I can, as a minister of the Established Church, conscientiously support you, now is especially the time in which that support is due to the Society.

I trust to have the united prayers of the friends, who conduct your proceedings, that the Lord may guide me to that view and statement of his truth, which may be a real blessing to His Church, and help forward the great work which the Society has been established to accomplish.

Any statements that you can give me, I shall be thankful to receive. I have to journey nearly a thousand miles for the Church Missionary and Jews' Societies, with a vast weight of work besides, before the May meetings, but the Lord will strengthen and provide.

Affectionately yours,

E. BICKERSTETH.

*April,* 1839.

MY DEAR GARWOOD,

I am getting on as well as I can amidst a mass of other work, but a good deal of information is yet wanting. A fuller account of Socialism than in my Tract, "The Dangers, &c.," would be important. Also some idea of the neglect of God in *the higher classes.*

Has the Society a copy of "The Great Metropolis," and could they lend it me, or if not, where can it be bought?

Very much of London has yet to be brought out into full view. I want to learn its *wealth,* if there be any means of getting at it, which I suppose there are. We must, if possible, make a great impression, that will swallow up all these little cavils, that come round about me like bees on every side, just as if I had committed some great crime; suffering trouble (though not as the Apostle, to bonds) as an *evil-doer;* on which I was preaching yesterday. 2 Tim. ii. 8—10.

Affectionately yours,

E. BICKERSTETH.

*Edinburgh, May* 19.

MY DEAR GARWOOD,

Thanks for your kind attention in sending me the sermon; it enabled me to put it into several influential hands on my way here. Remember who went through evil report and through good report, and let us be thankful for our portion of both.

I by no means meant to condemn only the present Government at the public meeting of the Tract Society, and much regret not

stating the decided ground I took, whoever governed. Though, on
the whole, I go nearer the conservatives, as believing their views
of politics nearer the Scriptures ; I am deeply aware how much is
to be condemned on their side also.   I would stand on the word of
God only, and in condemning any government act, would do it only
in the spirit of faithfulness which has ever marked the servants of
the Most High, like Elijah, Daniel, John the Baptist, and Paul—
but, oh ! how far short we fall !

I am glad you sent the sermons as "from the author."   I am
not ashamed of the path in which I trust the Lord has led us. . . .
God strengthen us and bless us in His work.   Much to be done,
while here, for Him in the Jews' Society.

Ever affectionately yours,<br>
E. BICKERSTETH.

" *May* 26.  Of what mercies have I to sing !  How
good has my God been in using me for His glory, and for
benefit to my fellow-men !  I cannot be too grateful for
His love in carrying me through duties, and blessing me
and others in them.  Notwithstanding all my sinfulness,
I have been blessed in my sermons—carried through my
work in Scotland, and brought back, encompassed with
blessings, to my own beloved home.  O make me faithful, under so much love, to Him who hath so loved us !

*Cheltenham, Oct.* 8.

MY BELOVED CHILD,

, . . I left home on Friday evening, slept in London, and came
on the next day through Oxford, and Cheltenham, to Worcester
late at night.   I preached for the Jews in two of the principal
churches to large congregations, and on Monday we had two important meetings.   It was very pleasant to meet many old friends.
I believe it is ten or twelve years since I have been at Worcester,
and there have been great changes.   Some devoted servants of
Christ have been removed by death, and others by Providence ; but

God has more than made up by a large accession of fresh labourers; and though I see many new faces, some of the older friends remain, as links of interest and affection.

It is so here at Cheltenham : through mercy I find old friends, and many a fresh one beside.   Two or three Wheler Chapel associations are here revived.   How can we be grateful enough to God, my child, for being called early to Christ, and enabled early to testify His truth !   there is such a growing blessedness in His ways. Two of my Wheler congregation are fixed here, who trace their spiritual blessedness to the Lord's grace on my ministry there. Glory to God alone for the least good that has been done.   But let us learn to be diligent in seizing opportunities, and zealous to bring souls to Jesus, while we have time.

. . . I should wish to be quiet and hidden, but I am perpetually brought before the public.   There is a strong letter to me in the Peace Herald, about my remarks in the Dangers of the Church, on the Peace Society, in which the writer says, he could weep over me for my sad change since writing the Christian Student, Treatise on Prayer, &c., and that because, in truth, I have justified the word of God against the perversion of men, who deny defensive war to be according to the will of God.   But if we would maintain all God's truth, we cannot fail of provoking the enmity, not only of the wicked, but also of some of God's children, who do not see this or that truth in particular.   I shall get as little into controversy as possible, that I may pursue more practical and profitable work. I long, like my dearest brother, to be more thoroughly a parochial minister, seeking continually the spiritual good of those specially committed to my charge, and I trust you will bring back many a useful hint for the good of Watton.

Your affectionate Father,<br>E. BICKERSTETH.

" *October* 26.   The impediment I find in journeying is this—it makes it exceedingly difficult to keep up constant visitation in my parish ; the links are broken, and it is difficult to re-unite them.

H 2

" O Lord, forgive me my great neglects, and direct my
conscience always aright, in discerning things that differ,
and following that which is pleasing to Thee ! Let not
the devil keep me in doubt and darkness about the path
of duty ; but may I ever do that which, I am fully persuaded, Thou wouldest have me to do.

" I have sent seven chapters of the ' Treatise on Baptism ' to the press. O Lord, help me to clear away mists
from men's minds, that hinder the bright shining of the
Sun of righteousness, and the sweet descent of Thy heavenly grace.

" When I look around, I am ready to exclaim—Never
was any one so great a debtor to God's mercy and love
as I am. My sweet family, full of love to me and to
each other, and all springing from the grace of Christ ;
my dear wife heading them, and helping them in the
best things ; and my four eldest—as well as my three
servants—going to the table of the Lord, and others, I
trust, preparing for it ; my beloved fellow-labourer, a
constant help and comfort, and the two pupils coming on
in the best things ; the number of attendants and communicants in my parish multiplying ; my patron supporting two, and nearly supporting a third school in my
parish. O my God, what do I owe Thee for such holy
and undeserved blessings here, as well as for using me in
any way to do more extensive good ! Thy mercies can
never be numbered ; and it is Thy delight, as well as
our blessedness, that we should correspond, and rise to
the fulness of Thy love, in seeking to be a blessing to
others.

" I beseech Thee, quicken me now according to thy
loving-kindness. Lord, I covet the joy of being a large
blessing to others. Make me willing and glad to give

the cost for so great a prize, as bringing others with me
to Thy heavenly kingdom ! "

The " Treatise on Baptism " was published early in the
next year, and was the fruit of much thought and labour.
Shortly before Mr. Bickersteth's death, when controversy
on this subject was agitating the Church of England, his
sentiments were further unfolded in a series of letters.
In his construction of the services for Infant Baptism, he
preferred the view of Bishop Bradford, as justified by
many examples of Scripture, where the same titles of
privilege are used both in a lower and a higher sense.
But he felt strongly that a difference in the precise meaning attached to a human formulary of devotion, was of
little moment, compared with a firm adherence to the
doctrine that spiritual regeneration, the new creation of
the soul in Christ, is a vital and abiding change, and that
while the means of grace are to be used with prayer and
faith, the Spirit of God remains a sovereign, in the time
and manner in which He bestows His blessings.    The
following passages explain his views, which were the ripe
fruits of his own experience.

" It is no fancy, no deluded imagination, no mere outward reformation, when one, who has been baptized in
the name of Jesus, and lived only to the flesh, first
receives the word of God, not as the word of men, but
as it is in truth, the word of God, which effectually
worketh on them that believe.    It produces no mere
temporary, fictitious change, but an entire moral revolution in the inward man.    It turns the whole bent of his
will, and the whole course of his affections, from earthly
things to heavenly.    It changes the whole character from
selfishness to love, from high-mindedness to humility,
from self-righteousness to contrition, from pleasure-loving

to self-sacrifice, from grovelling on earth, to setting the
affections on things above, from looking at things seen to
looking at things unseen.   It fills the mind with peace,
the heart with joy, the lips with useful and holy and
edifying words, and makes the whole life one course of
blessing to all around us, bringing glory in all to our
Father which is in heaven.   The world is never left without remarkable instances of this mighty change, to illus
trate the sovereignty and riches of Divine grace.   The
same blessed result, indeed, in many cases, more gradually
follows a right improvement of Christian baptism, through
the faith, prayers, and careful discipline of Christian
parents in a consistent education ; but without such a
real change from nature to grace, manifested in a really
Christian and holy life, baptism, however rightly administered, leaves the baptized only under heavier guilt."

" Notwithstanding the solemn and repeated testimonies
of the scriptures, how unavailable the outward act is,
without the inward change, (Rom. ii. 28, 29 ; ix. 1—5 ;
1 Cor. vii. 19 ; Gal. v. 6 ; vi. 15.) and the express testimony of the Church of England, that ' it is a sign of
regeneration, whereby, as by an instrument, they that
receive baptism *rightly* are grafted into the Church,'
some persons view baptism almost wholly as the thing
signified, and dwell little on its right reception.   Thus
baptism becomes a cover for delusion, a rest in an outside
service, a charm to ensure our salvation, and a putting
off anxiety about the new heart, instead of an encouragement to seek and attain it."   Pp. 156, 293.

The remark, with which he resumes his journal, throws
light on the motives which guided his own conduct for
many years.

" *November* 24.   In explaining Phil. ii. 15—23, I have

been led to see that much of "not seeking our own but
the things of the Lord Jesus," may lie in giving up home
comforts, and being willing, from a view of the larger
interests of Christ, to leave an immediate and more con-
tracted circle of duties, for the wider and fuller service
of the Lord, when He calls us to it ; and to go through
the self-denying work of journeying. Oh, Lord, make
me one entire self-surrender and consecration to Thyself! Give me this happiness—Thy will wholly mine.

"Yet must not home duties be neglected. Here is my
snare—self-indulgence in drinking in new thoughts from
books, instead of pouring out acquired truths into the
hearts and minds of my people. I do not, in spiritual
things, act on that promise.—'Give, and it shall be given
unto you.' O had I not a most compassionate High
Priest, what would become of me? Blessed Jesus, be
my refiner and purifier ; give me new refreshment and
strength in a believing view of Thy death for my sins.

"*December* 25. Another year nearly closes—a year of
many mercies. The printing of my work on Baptism
is now completed. The Lord bless it to the peace, holiness, and comfort of His Church, and the enlargement
of His kingdom. O that it may also be personally
blessed in raising my own soul to higher, holier, and
fuller views of that blessed ordinance ! . . . .

" The new postage has greatly increased my correspondence, and the applications for help ; and I cannot tell,
in many a case, whether I am justified in my course.
O Lord, make me a large blessing to my fellow-men !
Make me willing, for this, to sacrifice joyfully what Thou
hast given me ; and give me discernment to know what
I ought to do, so as most effectually to advance Thy

blessed kingdom, of righteousness, peace, and joy in the Holy Ghost ! "

With this prayer ends the private Diary of 1839. It was graciously heard and abundantly answered, until the hour of his removal to the heavenly kingdom.

# CHAPTER XXI.

The reduction of the postage, in January, 1840, amidst its many results, affected in some measure the character of Mr. Bickersteth's employments, and limited his time for direct study and composition, while it enlarged the sphere of his correspondence. The confidence so widely reposed in him, and the publicity resulting from his journeys and publications, led to daily applications for advice in difficulty, or for aid in various works of Christian benevolence. In a note to two of his children he thus alludes to the change :—

*January* 1, 1840.

My beloved Children,

The fruit of the penny postage, on its first day, must come to my children, if only to express a father's love. . . .

This is the twelfth letter sent off to-day. This change will, at any rate, increase my correspondence. God grant it may equally increase my usefulness ; but there is great danger of work thrusting out God, instead of being *for* God, and leading the heart more *to* Him.

Well, children, be happy all the day long in God's love, and then spread it as far and as wide as you can. God bless you.

H 5

In a note written a few days later, he observes :—
" As to poor Bythner, it is, as you say, buried in letters.
An hour goes in reading, and at least three in answering
them. Then the afternoon visiting, and evening meetings, leave hardly any time for study, or anything but
what is necessary to be done. I had no idea that the
new post would so alter my duties. Yet a great sphere
of usefulness is thus opened."

" *January* 26. The penny postage since Jan. 1, has so
increased my work that a considerable part of each day
has now to be given to correspondence ; only, O Lord,
let it be to Thy glory !

" I trust that there has been a little revival in attention to my primary duties, since the beginning of this year.
O Lord, increase it ! O Lord, carry it forward in every
thing—in my own body and soul, studies and labours,
wife and children, parish, relatives, friends, church and
country, to Jews and Gentiles, and all over the earth.
May God be glorified in everything ! "

The labours of the year, as usual, were abundant. In
February he preached twice at Clapham for the French
Protestants, and once for the Church Missions—and the
first of these discourses was published soon after. Early
in March, he visited Oxford for the Jews' Society. On
April 21, he preached the annual sermon for the Pro-
testant Association ; and about the same time prepared
a long article for the " Protestant Annual," on the
" Church's Trials and Deliverance," which was enlarged
for separate publication. In May, he travelled for the
Church Missionary Society to Liverpool, Preston, and
Wigan ; and on his return, preached in London for the
Home and Colonial Infant School Society. On June 8,
he set out for Ireland, where he preached and attended

meetings for the Jews at Dublin, Cork, and Limerick. In July, besides taking part in three or four local auxiliaries, which he had set on foot in his own county, he had another missionary journey to Dover and Canterbury. In August, he set out with his whole family on a long deferred visit to Westmoreland, his native county. But this could hardly be called a time of relaxation. During his absence of six or seven weeks, he visited Carlisle, Penrith, Keswick, Durham, Lancaster, and Settle ; and preached in all these places, as well as several others, for Jews and Gentiles, and the Pastoral Aid Society. In October, soon after his return, he was engaged at the same time in the publication of three works, a volume on the " Restoration of the Jews," another of " Devotions," compiled from his own practical writings, and a new edition of a " Harmony of the Gospels." Till the close of the year, he was occupied with these works and his parochial duties, with attendance on several very important committees in London, when the Foreign Aid Society was constituted, and also carried on a laborious and very discursive correspondence. Application was made for his help this year from the London City Mission, the Protestant Association, the Colonial Church, the British Reformation, the National, the Prayer Book and Homily, the Religious Tract, the Home and Colonial Infant School, the Shipwrecked Fishermen's, the African Civilization, the Indigent Blind, the Church Pastoral Aid, and the Clerical Aid Societies ; and by the editors of five or six religious publications. Communications reached him, bearing on the progress of the gospel, from Scotland and Ireland, from France and Geneva, from North America, from North and South India, from South Australia, from Con-

stantinople and Jerusalem.  He exchanged letters with
Merle d'Aubigné on the authors to be consulted in the
history of the English Reformation, and with Alison, on
the illustration of prophecy in the events of the French
Revolution.  These are specimens of work, unnoticed in
his brief journal, which occupied much of his time, and
made him almost realize the description of the Apostle—
" that which cometh upon me daily, the care of all tho
churches."

Few of his more public letters at this time are preserved ; but his notes to his children, even amidst the
pressure of his other engagements, show his watchful
attention, during his journeys, to their spiritual welfare.

*Liverpool, May* 21.

DEAREST F.

I was glad to receive my dear child's letter this morning.  It is
very pleasant to have daily intercourse with home.

If we are to be true followers of Christ, a thing to be desired
above life itself, we shall have difficulties on every side, as your
Papa daily finds.  First, we have not to please *ourselves* at all, and
that it is a sad daily conflict, and then, we have *not to please our
fellow-men,* but often to offend them, and walk only according to
the light of God's word, and this is often painful.  But then, we
have *to please our dear Master Jesus,* who loved us even to death,
and this is happiness itself, peace and safety, holiness and joy.

I am full of work here each hour through the day—what with
public services and committees and meetings—but our gracious
God prospers all. . . . God bless you all.

*Liverpool, May* 20.

MY BELOVED C.

As you are the one from home, I must write a short letter to you
first.  I have six to answer, amidst all the bustle of two public
meetings this day. . . .

The most needful of all lessons is to know our inward sinfulness ; and humbling as this lesson is, without it we cannot welcome His grace, and rejoice in His free salvation. O the boundless love of the Lord Jesus to those who are so entirely empty of all good, and so constantly prone to all evil, as we are in ourselves, at our best estate ! And O the mighty grace of His own Spirit, that can, at more favoured times, raise in our hearts thirstings after better things, and some little faith and hope and love ! . . .

God has blessed us much here. About £700 will be raised by to-night, since we came, and £2500 have been given in the year. I was speaking in the vast amphitheatre last night, to, I suppose, between four and five thousand people. Blessed be God for all success.

*Dublin, June* 15, 1840.

My beloved C.

I must write to thee in the midst of the crowd and pressure of duties, hoping this may reach thee on thy birth-day. The Lord himself give my child abundant birth-day blessings, more even than her earthly father can think of, or pray for. Especially may He give her patient perseverance in well-doing, meekness of wisdom, contrition and lowliness, humility and love, strong faith, lively hope, and full charity. Glad should I be to write at length, but I am pulled on every side, and you must therefore be content with a few words of love. Surely my highest joy is to see my own dear children walking in the truth.

The visit in August, to Casterton and Kirby Lonsdale, was a season of deep enjoyment to Mr. Bickersteth and his whole family. None of his children had ever before seen the place where their beloved father had spent his own childhood ; and the pleasures of association, great in themselves, were heightened by the beauties of the scenery along the banks of the Lune, and among the lakes of Cumberland. Visits were paid, on the way, to the families of Mr. Bickersteth's brother and two sisters, at Coppenhall, Acton, and Liverpool; while the kindness and hospitality of his old friend, the Rev. W. C. Wilson, of Casterton Hall, and the society of Sir Jahleel Brenton, who was residing there at the time, added fresh interest and variety to the journey. The following notes were written, shortly before, to his daughter who had accompanied him to Ireland, and was now staying with his brother at Liverpool, till the arrival of the whole party from Watton.

*July* 4, 1840.

My beloved Child,

You are much in our hearts, as well as on our lips, and your vacant seat leaves us short of one we dearly love. But all these separations are good, and I am glad you are on this side of the rolling ocean.

You know how each hour brings its work, and this month is specially busy, to get in the claims of the two next; but the Lord gives me health, and strength, and usefulness, and hope and joy in His service, so that my cup runs over.

As to your movements, . . . the great thing is to do what shall be most pleasant to my dear brother and sister first, and then to be sure the path of duty will be the path of happiness to yourself. Any kind of intellectual improvement for their good, I wish my children to have as far as I am able. God bless you, my dear child; live in prayer and active duty each hour of each day.

*July* 18.

My beloved Child,

I must give you again the treat of a letter from home, though every day is full of work.

We had eighteen at our clerical meeting on Thursday, and should have had more, but for unexpected casualties—a very profitable meeting, thanks be to God.

Yesterday I took E. and H. to Buntingford, where we formed a new Church Missionary Society.

Next week we are all to be busy.  Monday, Religious Tract Society, and your uncle comes.  Tuesday, the school-children's tea. Wednesday, the lecture.  Thursday, feast for the poor at Wempstead. O may the eye be single, or all is vain toil and labour.  Let us, in everything, simply aim to be accepted of our Lord.

. . . . The Lord graciously watch over us in these many journeys.  I feel as if all my earthly jewels were being set afloat—but what is fixed, except as united to Jesus, the same yesterday, to-day, and for ever.

*July* 23.

One word thou shalt have from thy Papa, because he loves thee —so saying I snatched up this bit of paper.

We are enjoying my beloved brother John's society here.  It is no small treat to me to have my earliest friend thus with me.  We went to Amwell, where we went forty years ago together.  O how great the change since then!  The greatest was when we were brought together to know the blessed Saviour, and for this we shall have to be most thankful through eternity.  Serve Him, heartily, my child, from the beginning :—that is bliss to us, and a blessing to others.  Love to all.  Your own Papa—guess his name.

*July* 27.

MY BELOVED CHILD,

Your frequent letters deserve frequent answers ; but we are in whirlpools and eddies of work, that make straightforward sailing difficult.

I yesterday preached from Gal. vi. 9, and thanks be to God, our collections were more than £20 for the Church Missionary Society. To-day I go to Cheshunt for their Church Missionary, and to-morrow is our own Hertford Bible Meeting.

You must pray for us, that we may have a prosperous journey by the will of God.  I feel the responsibility and anxiety of taking my family such a journey. . . . . . .In the meanwhile may we all be redeeming time, and occupying talents, and looking for the Lord's coming, and waiting for Him. Give our kindest love to C. and M. A., and our sympathy with the suffering child. It is well for all that the frailty of our earthly treasures should be made clear in our eyes.

"*August* 1. How enduring is the goodness and long-suffering of the Lord! I am carried through my duties with many a blessing, yet humbled continually by my inconsistencies and sinfulness. Where I am most blessed, I have sometimes most reason to groan under my corruption. I have seen this in my late journeys.

"And now there is before me a most important step, —taking my whole family to Westmoreland. I left my native county forty years since, and how graciously has the Lord dealt with me since then, giving me such a family as He has given me, and using me, as He has used me, to His glory. I now propose taking all to see the scenes of my childhood, in the hope of communicating, as well as of obtaining, a blessing there. Lord, I commit all my family, and all this journey, in all its stages, unto Thee! Let no evil befal us by the way! May Thy name be glorified in us! Bring us back, with a full blessing, to our own home at the appointed time."

The visit was one of unmingled pleasure to the younger members of Mr. Bickersteth's family. They took up their home at Casterton in an old, tapestried mansion, then unoccupied, close to the Clergy and Servants' Schools, and within a short walk of Casterton Hall, the residence of their hospitable friends, to which the whole party removed before their return. Excursions to the caves at Clapham, to the sea-side, to Keswick, Derwentwater, Grassmere, and Windermere, varied their quiet rambles along the beautiful borders of the Lune. Their

father took them to see the grammar-school where he had
been educated, and pointed out to them all the familiar
scenes of his boyhood, ever leading their thoughts to the
love of their heavenly Father, who had guarded and
blessed him through so many years of his earthly pilgrimage. Yet his customary zeal shewed itself in this
journey of relaxation. Every sabbath, and several times
in the week, he was occupied in pleading the cause of
missions, and after escorting his children on a party to
Keswick, he left them to enjoy the scenery, while he
started off to attend a missionary meeting, which he
had planned for himself, in the middle of their day of
pleasure.

In a letter to one of his flock at the time, Mr. Bickersteth wrote—" Our visit here has been full of mercies
and blessings, and many delightful spheres of usefulness
have opened before me, in scenes with which I have been
familiar from my youth. The enclosed account of Queen
Adelaide's visit will shew a little of what my beloved
friend W. Wilson has been honoured of God in effecting
here. . . . . . May we mutually help in the communication
of gifts which God has bestowed on each, that they may
be imparting to others, and be helpful in maturing and
ripening our souls for His eternal kingdom. All besides
this is such a vanity, when compared with it, that in our
best movements we cannot but trample it under foot and
despise it. Soon, I believe very soon, we shall have to
give account to the coming Saviour of all the talents
which He has entrusted to us, and the opportunities we
have had of glorifying His name. May our one object
be to be accepted of Him on that day ! "

" September 26. Through God's mercy I have been
carried with my whole family, ten in all, to the north

and back again.  We left home, Tuesday, August 4, and
returned September 24, after a journey full of mercies. . .
We saw together the lakes in Cumberland, as well as the
place of my birth.  I preached every Sunday for either
Jews or Gentiles, and trust that many blessings have
flowed to us in each part of the journey.  To God be all
the glory.  It was the greater mercy, as only the Sunday
before I left home, August 2, I fainted in the pulpit at
Tewin, from serious illness.

" The blessings have been innumerable, in the great
and costly kindness of relatives and friends, the opportunities of usefulness afforded to me, the advantage of seeing
the good done by others, the recalling of early scenes,
days, and persons, to my recollection, the introducing of
my dear children to Christian relatives and their children,
the increased facilities given by railways for accomplishing
the journey, and the preservation from any accident in
travelling above 600 miles with so large a family.

" Would that my conduct and usefulness corresponded
to my opportunities.  Oh, when shall it once be !  The
great secret is in much retired communion with God.  O
my God, pour upon me the spirit of grace and supplication ! "

The close of the year was marked in the political
world, by the breaking out of war in Syria, and the intervention of the four powers to restore that province to the
Sultan, which Mehemet Ali had just wrested from him.
Allusions to these changes appear in Mr. Bickersteth's
journal.

" October 24. . . All the nations of the earth are shaking
with rumours of wars, and commencing wars.  O Lord,
yet prolong the day of grace, and enable us Britons to use
it more to Thy glory.

"*November* 29. I will sing of mercy and judgment; unto Thee, O Lord, will I sing ! Thy mercies are many, Thy judgments are few. At present, my wife and one of my children are unwell, and I have myself been suffering —but mercies so abound over trials, that I have innumerable causes of thanksgiving.

"*December* 25. O what thanks I owe to God for another year's full cup of mercies ! The printing of my .work on the Jews is advancing rapidly—The Lord himself prosper it to the enlarging of the faith and hope of His people, and their preparation for things to come, as well as the awakening of careless sinners.

" I feel much of the infirmities of growing years—but how few are my afflictions, and how innumerable my blessings.

" The state of my parish affords me much anxiety. . . . there are painful features on the dark side. And yet there is much that is pleasing and hopeful. The rich do contribute to the wants of the poor ; some of the poor do trust in the Lord ; some of the young are teachable, and some of the old awakened and converted—but there is no general concern and awakening. Come down, O our God, with great might, and succour us ! "

The year 1841 was very fruitful in important events, and brought on Mr. Bickersteth a great variety of special engagements, connected with the progress of Divine truth, and the kingdom of God.

In 1835 he had preached the Annual Sermon of the European Society, which was then newly re-organized, after serious difficulties ; and had felt, ever since, a very deep interest in the spread of the Gospel among the continental churches. The Evangelical Societies of Geneva and Paris had been formed abroad a little earlier, in 1831

and 1833, and an English Committee had undertaken to
procure aid for them from British Christians. The visit
of Merle d'Aubigné to England, in 1838, gave this work
a new impulse. In May of that year, he met Mr. Bickersteth at Cambridge, and the fruit of their intercourse was
the publication of the " Voice from the Alps," alluded
to before, which was extensively circulated among the
friends of the cause. It was soon found more convenient
that the two English Societies, as they had a similar ob-.
ject, should be merged into one ; and that an important
source of jealous opposition would be removed, if the
actual management of the work were devolved upon the
foreign brethren. A meeting for this purpose, in which
Mr. Bickersteth took a leading part, was held in November 1840, and the European Mission and the Central
Committee were both merged in the Foreign Aid Society.
This institution had ever afterwards a large share in his
affectionate sympathy and willing labours. His last
journey, before his mortal illness, was to plead its cause ;
and a message from his dying bed to the faithful brethren
at Geneva, proved how dear it was to his heart. A
journey to Shrewsbury, early in this year, was the first
of many similar labours in its cause, and its business,
throughout the whole year, had a large place in his correspondence.

Another work began at the same time, which had a
deep interest for himself and many of his fellow-christians. Ever since his own attention had been given,
prayerfully, to the word of prophecy, he had been very
desirous to arouse the Church from a neglect, which he
believed to be alike sinful and dangerous. He made repeated attempts, therefore, to persuade one or other of
his brethren in London to open their church for a series

of lectures, having this object especially in view. It was
not until this spring, however, that the desired opportunity was given. His friend, Mr. Fremantle, had just
returned from a visit to Palestine, and taken the charge
of West Street Episcopal Chapel. He gladly concurred
in a plan, which the general interest awakened by the
Syrian campaign rendered more than ever seasonable,
and which harmonized so thoroughly with the deep impressions, produced by his own travels in the land of promise. Accordingly, in the spring of this year, a course of
twelve lectures on the Restoration of Israel were preached
there by twelve different clergymen. The congregations
were numerous; and the large sale of the lectures, when
published, showed how deep an interest on the subject
had been aroused. After an interruption, occasioned by
Mr. Fremantle's removal to Claydon, the Lectures were
resumed in Lent 1843, at St. George's Church, Bloomsbury, and have since been continued annually for nine
years. Mr. Bickersteth took a main part in this united
testimony to those views, respecting the character of the
times, and the hopes of the Church of Christ, which he
felt to be highly seasonable and important. It was
while preparing a lecture for the course of Lent 1850, on
" The Goodness of God in his dealings with Israel," that
he was called to rest from his labours, and himself to
enjoy the goodness of the Lord, in more immediate vision.

Another work of this year, which occupied much of
his time and thoughts, was the formation of the Parker
Society, for republishing the writings of the British Reformers. The idea was one which had been long present
to his mind, from a strong conviction of its practical importance. When the select works of the Fathers began
to be published at Oxford, he publicly expressed an ear-

nest hope that the example would be rivalled by the sister university, in a similar selection from the writings of the Reformation, and bent his efforts, in private, to the attainment of his desire.  Attempts were being made, at that time, to procure a republication of Foxe's Acts and Monuments by the Christian Knowledge Society.  When these had failed, and the work was taken up in 1837 by his own publishers, he lent all his influence to ensure its success.  In the course of the same year, he republished Coverdale's "Godly Letters of the Martyrs," with a Dedication to Queen Adelaide, and some Introductory Remarks ; while, as Editor of the "Christian Family Library," he engaged the vigorous pen of Charlotte Elizabeth in a smaller work of "English Martyrology."  But the larger design was not forgotten ; and the concurrent efforts of Mr. Stokes of Colchester, of Mr. Bickersteth himself, and a few others, led, in the close of 1840, to the formation of the Parker Society.  Its object was to republish the chief works of the English Reformers, down to the reign of Elizabeth, on a plan which secured cheapness, accuracy, and elegance.  The number of subscribers soon reached and surpassed seven thousand.  The works of Ridley, Cranmer, and Latimer, of Tyndale, Becon, Philpot, Grindal, Bradford, and Whitaker, were cleared from the dust of centuries ; and obtained so extensive a circulation, under patronage so distinguished, that the Society might almost claim for itself the character of a great national work.  Mr. Bickersteth, from the pressure of other duties, took no direct part in editing the volumes ; but scarcely any one, except his friend Mr. Stokes, had so large a share in originating the design, or lent it in its progress a more effectual advocacy.  Amidst the growth of formalism and semi-popery, he always rejoiced in its

continued prosperity, as one proof that the candle, lighted
by our martyrs at the stake, was not yet to go out in
utter darkness.

The following summer witnessed another event, in
which he felt the most lively interest;—the establishment
of the Protestant Bishopric at Jerusalem. The maintenance of Reformation-truth was indeed always very
closely connected, both in his judgment and his affections,
with the work of mercy towards the house of Israel.
When, in 1838, Mr. Young was appointed British Vice-
Consul at Jerusalem, he embraced an early opportunity
of spending a few days under Mr. Bickersteth's roof, and
conferring with him on the hopes of Israel, before he set
out, as the first British Representative who had ever been
sent to the Holy City. In 1840, when Mr. Nicolayson
returned to England from Jerusalem for a short time, he
also paid a visit to Watton, that he might confer fully
with so warm a friend of the Jewish cause, on the progress and future prospects of the church then building
on Mount Zion. The appointment of Dr. Alexander, as a
Protestant Bishop at Jerusalem, gave Mr. Bickersteth still
deeper pleasure. He had known him intimately for
several years, and had welcomed him, not long before,
at the Rectory, as a fellow-helper in advocating the
claims of Israel. The co-operation of Great Britain and
Prussia, the two great Protestant kingdoms, and the
brotherhood shown to the Lutheran Church, the first-born
of the Reformation, were highly grateful to his truly
catholic spirit, which longed for closer union among all
who maintained the purity and truth of the Gospel.
Every step in the progress of the work was made known
to him, as it occurred, by his noble friend, Lord Ashley,
who had so main a part in its promotion ; and their

correspondence was an illustration of the promise to
Zion ;—" It is time to favour her, yea the time is come ;
for thy servants take pleasure in her stones, and favour
the dust thereof."

The journal of Mr. Bickersteth, throughout the year,
shows the number and variety of his public engagements.

"*January* 30.    I have this day corrected the last proof
of the 'Restoration of the Jews.' On Tuesday, Feb. 2,
I go to London for the meeting at Islington, our subject
being, the Preaching of the Reformation.

"*February* 27.    I am busily occupied with preparing
an enlarged edition of my Hymn-book, and have important sermons before me, a public Lecture on the Jews,
March 23, a visit to Bristol, and on the following week
to Bath, and then to Chester and Shrewsbury.

"*March* 19.    My 'Treatise on the Lord's Supper,' is
required for the eleventh Edition.    I am appointed to
preach a second Visitation Sermon on May 25, and for
the District Visiting Society the same month.

"*April* 10. I was preaching last night in London for
the Jews.    I go to Bath next Saturday.    We have our
Protestant Association next Thursday. . . .

" O for more of a spirit of prayer.    O Lord, draw me
to Jesus effectually, constantly, with earnest thirstings
and longings.

"*May* 29. . . . I was carried mercifully through my
duties in London, speaking at the Church Missionary,
Prayer-Book and Homily, Jews', and Religious Tract Societies, and preaching for the District Visiting Society.
I was also mercifully assisted on Tuesday the 25th, in
preaching the Visitation Sermon, which is now printing.
God bless it to my own good, and that of many. . . . O
for quickening grace, that I may not teach others, and

remain myself untaught. I want wisdom in all the work of the Lord.

" *June* 27. I have been on a journey to Shrewsbury, Chester, Liverpool, Acton, and Coppenhall, and am brought home in peace. Forty-four young persons have been confirmed. My sermon before the District Visiting Society is now printed. All glory be to God.

" We have had the Church Missionary, and Religious Tract Anniversaries, and are to have the Bible Anniversary next Monday, and I am to preach at Stotfold on Sunday evening. O Lord, give me grace, that in all these works of love, my heart may be right with Thee!

" *August* 28. God has most graciously carried me and mine in peace and safety to Acton, Old Newton, Norwich, Yarmouth, and Cambridge. We had a journey full of mercies, and many opportunities of usefulness were opened to me.

" O my God, give me special grace to walk more closely with God, to live more in prayer and communion with Thee all the day, and in every duty.

" I had much joy in seeing a larger meeting than usual of my communicants last night at our preparatory meeting. I trust a good work is going on among them."

The work on the Restoration of the Jews, published early in this year, was composed mainly of various sermons, preached on behalf of the Jews' Society, with an introduction of nearly a hundred pages, on the Scriptural evidence for the recovery of God's ancient people, their national restoration, and the practical lessons to be drawn from these hopes of the Church; and an appendix, containing suggestions for the study of the subject, and remarks on the duty of preparation for times of suffering. The whole is marked by the same unction and earnest-

ness of tone, which had struck the mind of Dr. Chalmers
in the Guide to the Prophecies. One or two passages
from the practical lessons at the close of the work will
give some imperfect impression of its general character.
The work itself must be consulted by those who wish to
see his mature judgment on various questions of prophetic
interpretation, connected with the last times of the
Church, and the promised redemption and recovery of
Israel.

" Let us for a moment glance at the glories of the risen church
of Christ. Who can describe this ? If *eye hath not seen, nor ear
heard, neither have entered into the heart of man, the things which
God hath prepared for them that love him,* or *them that wait for
him,* and they are only *revealed to us by His Spirit,* what must be
the blessedness and glory of a resurrection body, and a perfectly
purified soul ! What the blessedness of associating for ever, only
with those who are thus glorious ; of sharing all their joys, and living
with them always in the presence of our one Lord, where there is
fulness of joy ! Who can tell what royalties we partake of in the
heavenly kingdom, what priestly offices we are honoured with, what
the beauteous splendour of the heavenly Jerusalem ! Who can
reach the height, or fathom the depth, or measure the length and
breadth of the love of our Immanuel, and the glories of the mansions he is preparing for his followers ! See the promises made to
the overcomers in the seven churches, how they are added one to
another, till they are raised to the highest throne of Immanuel's
glory. ' To him that overcometh will I grant to sit with me on
my throne, even as I also overcame, and am set down with my
Father on his throne.' . . .

" Arm yourselves with the mind of Christ. To be like him is the
glory of a Christian. He foresaw with perfect distinctness all the
bitter cup He had to taste ; yet He withheld not himself from His
overwhelming baptism, and was only straitened till it was accomplished. Amidst all temptation, from friends and from foes, from

the world and the devil, and from those infirmities of our nature, with the feeling of which He was touched, look at the invincible firmness, patience, meekness, gentleness, love and faithfulness of our Divine Lord.   Truly we must look much to Jesus, if we would be armed with His mind.   He will give us His Spirit; He will strengthen us with His grace. . . .

" Cheerfully endure the present cross, to be taken up for the truth. There is each day some sacrifice of ease and inclination to be made, some restraint to be put on appetite and the love of pleasure, some mortification of highmindedness, something disagreeable to flesh and blood to be endured, something laborious and toilsome to be effected, by acting on Christian principles.   By faithfulness in these things, we shall be inured to greater trials, and so be meet for a larger blessing.   I *die daily*, was the experience of one of the noblest sufferers in the school of Christ.   It is easy to think we may be firm and valiant for the truth in a great trial, and yet to neglect present self-sacrifice ; but the best means of being firm then, is now to begin a course of self-restraint.   Observe how the self-denial of Daniel and his companions in private preceded their public boldness, in standing for the truth. . . .

" Be animated by the bright hope of a glorious and everlasting redemption.   This is what the whole creation is waiting for.   All the exhibitions of evil in our world, will, through the mercy of our God, be overruled for this end.   O how well was it for Enoch that he walked with God, and for Noah that he was a preacher of righteousness ; for Abraham, that he went into a strange land, and withheld not his only son ; for David, that he was bold, trusting only in the name of Jehovah, to contend with Goliah, and became the man after God's own heart ; for Daniel, that he was cast into the lion's den ; for Peter, that he followed the Lord in his sufferings ; for Paul, that he went through unequalled afflictions for the truth ; and for John, that he was the companion of the faithful in their tribulation.   O happy confessors, martyrs, fathers, reformers, and sufferers in every age, who, enduring all evils for Christ, through much tribulation have entered the kingdom of heaven !   How much better all their momentary sufferings, issuing in such an everlasting

glory, than this world's highest gains, pleasures and honours, that
do but end in shame and everlasting contempt. Let us follow our
Protestant fathers in the part of the war now left to us; and if need
be, by suffering, let us achieve the victory both for our church, our
country, and the world; the full blessedness of which will only be
known and enjoyed in the new heavens and the new earth, wherein
dwelleth righteousness."

In the course of August, an event occurred, in which
Mr. Bickersteth took a most lively interest, (and for
which his own labours, in previous years, had contributed to prepare the way) the accession of the two Archbishops, and of all the Bishops who were not members
already, to the Church Missionary and Jews' Societies.
He rejoiced in this change, partly for the sake of the
Societies themselves, but still more for the sake of the
Church of England. He had a sincere and deep respect for
his ecclesiastical superiors, and a feeling of especial regard
to his own beloved diocesan, the Bishop of Lincoln, from
whom he had received invariable kindness, and frequent
marks of genuine esteem. He had, however, a still deeper
sense of the supreme authority of Christ, and of the plain
duty, incumbent on all Christians, to fulfil the great
command of their Lord, and spread the gospel both to
the Jews and to the heathen. The work of the Societies,
in his view, was so good and holy, so plainly imperative on the whole Church, that the bishops themselves
received, rather than conferred honour, by a patronage
and co-operation, which had been perhaps too long delayed. Yet he rejoiced very greatly in this proof that
the rulers of the Church were rising to a just view of its
real interests, and of their own privilege, and in the new
talent which was thus entrusted to the friends of the
Societies, to help in the wider diffusion of a missionary

spirit through the land. Influenced by these feelings, as he had a journey in prospect for the Jews the following month, to Derbyshire and Liverpool, he planned for himself an unusual amount of work. One of his friends, in a playful reply, sought to temper his zeal by a friendly caution, and reminded him that all were not so ardent as himself in the cause of Israel, nor likely to be so much impressed by this new accession of patronage to the Society. "It is very delightful," he wrote, "that you are coming here for the Jews; and I trust that an advance will be made under the blessing of God; but your note seems to go at a high-pressure speed, which the Derby train, being heavily laden, cannot keep up with. We have two or three other public matters to attend to at this juncture. . . . It is a very good thing that we have got the Archbishop, but it does not follow that all Derbyshire will rise up at a moment's notice, as if the Archbishop were an archangel. . . . . You will move them, I have no doubt, much more."

In Mr. Bickersteth's own journal, he expresses his thankfulness for the recent change.

"*September* 25. By God's great mercy I have been blessed and preserved in journeys to Sapcote, Derby, Melton, Ashbourne, Matlock, and Liverpool, for the Jews' Society, and brought back in safety to my happy home; much gracious feeling, I trust, having been produced in many hearts. All glory be to Thee, O Lord.

"The two Archbishops and fourteen Bishops have joined the Society. Glory be to God alone!

"But now I come home,—home to my parish, my family, my heart. Here is my primary duty, and greatly ought my watchfulness, prayer, and diligence, to be here exercised. O Lord, forgive all my sins—renew a right spirit within me! O may I walk closely with Thee, and never mistake " zeal for the Lord of hosts " like Jehu's, for that inward holiness, whose praise is of Thee, and not of men.

" Gracious Father, draw me to Jesus! O draw me to Jesus, that my whole soul may cling to Him, and in His strength I may go forward!

" As usual, the great failing is the want of close, fervent, continued prayer. Therefore turn thou to thy God, keep mercy and judgment, and wait on thy God continually, Hos. xii. 6. This is what I want. O write this Thy law on my heart, and in my life! With this failing the other corresponds, of close, searching, patient, self-applying reading of the Bible. O how sad it is that I, who have called others to these duties, and have myself so experienced their blessedness, should yet so often be negligent of them! Precious Jesus! what should I do without Thee?

" I feel greatly the danger of our Church from the progress of the apostate principles of Rome in the new Oxford school. What a dreadful host is gathering for judgment in the day of the Lord! "

The gentle remonstrance of his friend, on the amount of work he had planned for this journey, was not without cause. The very day after the last entry in his journal, Mr. Bickersteth was seized with an attack of paralysis, brought on by excessive exertion, which laid him aside for several months, and threatened at first to supersede entirely his public labours.

" *October* 3. I did not know, when I was writing the above, that I was preparing for the trial of a slight attack of paralysis on the right side of my face. I came home from Liverpool unusually fatigued; and at Birmingham on the 22nd, was detained several hours unexpectedly,

by missing the regular train a single moment.　This prevented my fulfilling engagements in London, and acting
on my mind, distressed me more than usual.　Some
symptoms of paralysis affected my speech in Sunday's
duties, which are heavy,—the Bible class, two sermons,
and the evening lecture.　But the cause was hidden till
the Tuesday, when my medical adviser stated what it
was, and the absolute importance of entire rest from all
public duties.　Thus I am for the present laid aside.
The name of the Lord be glorified.　The will of the Lord
be done !

" I doubt not it is the best thing that infinite wisdom,
righteousness, and love, could do for a poor sinful creature, so greatly needing all heavenly aid, for my soul's
welfare, and the good of my family and my flock.　Most
slight has the stroke been as yet ; but most solemn and
instructive the voice.　O that I may listen to this correction of God's own hand, and be effectually drawn to
Christ, and then help to bring others to Him !

" The kindness of friends has been almost overwhelming !　What, then, must the kindness of the Lord be, from
which all other kindness springs ! "

This alarming seizure called forth many letters of deep
Christian sympathy.　Those of Mr. Grimshawe and Mr.
Pratt—two of his most honoured friends—express the
thoughts which were passing in many minds.　Both have
since been called to their rest, the former only a few
weeks before Mr. Bickersteth's own removal.

*Biddenham, October 7.*

MY DEAR FRIEND,

I have heard, with very sincere concern, that your health has met
with a severe check.　I am not surprised, though I am afflicted, at
this intelligence ; for I have long been convinced that your labours

were too abundant, far beyond what the ordinary degree of strength, allotted to most men, could justly authorize. You have not only done much, but too much. The cause of God has been benefited, but you have suffered. And therefore for your own sake, that of your family, and the interests of the Church of Christ, let us all beg of you to relax the measure of your exertions for the time to come, and for the present shut the door of *thought*, as well as of *action*. By such means your valuable life may still be preserved for many years, through the Divine mercy. May the transition from active exertion to calm retirement, and much inward communion with God, be beneficial both to body and to mind. May you enjoy a large measure of the manifestation of His love and presence; and be so strengthened, in His own good time, with renewed health, and facilities for resuming your usefulness, as to be long an instrument of enlarged benefit to the cause of Christ. With kindest Christian regard and love,

Very affectionately and truly yours,

T. S. GRIMSHAWE.

The letter of Mr. Pratt is beautifully characteristic of both parties, who had so long been associated in the blessed work of missions.

MY DEAR FRIEND,

Some rumours reached me a few days since, that you were indisposed. I did not understand to what degree, till I called on Mr. Bunyon yesterday for the purpose of inquiring. You meet the will of our Heavenly Master, I doubt not, with submission. It is ground of wonder and thanksgiving to me, that you have been so long upheld, with scarcely any interruption, in your course of varied toil. I am jealous over you and myself with, I hope, a godly jealousy, that I may not so speak as to give occasion to the working of infirmity. That indeed can hardly be avoided, but we both of us know full well, that whatever may have been wrought in us, and done by us, it is so far short of what our Lord was ready and willing to work in us and by us, if we had had the faith to desire, and to seek more grace out of its fulness, that we must fall before Him as unprofitable servants. I cannot express to you a higher sense of my judgment and my love, than breathing out the fervent wish and prayer—sit anima mea tecum!

May the light of our Saviour's countenance be lifted up upon you! May he speedily restore you to vigour and usefulness again! But whatever may be His will, may He graciously prepare you for it! This is plainly, my dear friend, a transition and a warning. You are nearly twenty years younger than I am, and may yet survive me; but this *may* be the entrance on a course of passive submission to a chastening hand. You have been enabled to make known the Saviour's name to multitudes, and He has doubtless made your labours savingly profitable to the winning of many souls. But He *will* be on the throne, and *must* have all the glory. . . . You are in all our hearts, as an old friend, and a fellow-servant of God our Saviour. I am ever, my dear friend,

Very affectionately yours,

JOSIAH PRATT.

After a few weeks, Mr. Bickersteth was so far recovered, that his medical attendant advised a change of air, by the sea-side, as the most likely means of his complete restoration. He accordingly set out with Mrs. Bickersteth for Brighton, early in November, and was entertained some weeks, most kindly and hospitably, by General and Mrs. Marshall. The following were his reflections on the trial.

" *October* 30. . . . This dispensation of God is speaking to me powerfully. May I understand the warning, and what all the gracious lessons are, which God is thus teaching me.

" 1. That I may know what my days are, as an hand-breadth—how frail I am. That all here is transitory, fading, and perishing.

I 5

" 2. To redeem time for the great ends of life—to
glorify God, spread His truth, and do His will.

" 3. To aim especially at attaining *holiness* and usefulness.  I have been coveting too much,—learning, knowledge, insight into new truths, and neglecting too much
the things which will be most valuable hereafter.

" 4. To attend to home and parish duties—so as to give
my strength to that, to which God has thus, by His providence, now more directly called me.

" The scene of usefulness abroad was so great, and the
calls so urgent, I did not see my way clear to refuse.
God has now made it much more clear, and with that
voice tells me ;—Pray more for, think more of, plan more
for, your own flock.  Go among them more abundantly—
become more acquainted with all.  Lay aside all studies
that would turn your mind from this.  Think more of the
state of your own soul—of its preparation for the day of
Christ.  Strive more for that conformity to God's will,
which is the only happy state of man.

" O write all these lessons of Thy providence, by the
effectual working of Thine own Spirit, on my poor, weak,
frail soul !

" Another especial trial has befallen us, in the more
confirmed tendency of my child's cough towards consump-
tion.  But I trust that the Lord is thus working good for
her, and for us all.  Lord, let it be so, abundantly ! "

The nature of Mr. Bickersteth's illness, and the entire
and sudden cessation of those employments which had
become habitual, but were now forbidden as dangerous
to his life, conspired, for a few days, to produce an air of
unwonted languor and depression.  But while the outward man was apparently smitten with decay, the inward
man was renewed the more powerfully by the secret grace

of God. In a very short time, the seeming depression passed away, and was followed by an evident growth and ripeness in Christian patience, hope, and experience, those rich fruits of sanctified affliction. His notes at this time to his children, and other friends, breathe a peculiar fragrance of gentle and holy love.

*Watton Rectory, Oct. 5.*

My dear Mrs. Smith,

How kind you are in your remembrances of your disabled Pastor! I write a line to shew you my hand is not affected, and to assure you that never did I more enjoy the sweet truths—God is light, and God is love. I am not walking in darkness, but rejoicing in the light. I see his peculiar goodness in giving me tokens for good on every side. His name be glorified only, and my dear flock profited by this dispensation.

May you be a comfort to dear Blunt, whom I have long loved as a faithful brother. God bless you and Mr. Smith, and all your children, prays,

Gratefully yours,

E. Bickersteth.

The following letters were written during his stay at Brighton, where his strength was slowly and gradually being restored.

*Sussex Square, Brighton, Nov. 6.*

My beloved F.

. . . . We are living in splendid idleness and luxury, some would perhaps say; but I hope I could reply, we are yielding ourselves simply to the Divine will, and enjoying what He ordains and sends. This is true happiness, God's will our will, for sorrow or joy, for labour or rest, for time or for eternity, for life or for death. I hope you are often praying. "Teach me to do thy will, O my God; thy Spirit is good—lead me into the land of uprightness." When we delight in God's will, nothing can come amiss; and the only way to this is to see Jesus, God's gift of love for our sins. Then, we know, God must love us, and sends every thing for our good.

I hope my precious child will more and more realize what a vapour life is, what a full salvation we have in Jesus, and how complete its deliverance of our souls from sin, death, hell, the grave, and all that is terrible to nature. Then, be her illness what it may, it can bring nothing but good.

Your own affectionate Father,<br>E. BICKERSTETH.

Nov. 9.

MY BELOVED C.

. . . . . . . My dear child must make a point of getting into the open air daily, and of learning to cast *all* her cares on Him—it is really true what I am going to write—who *careth for her.* Wonderful words ! The great God careth for you individually, loves you individually, with an intense love, and desires your happiness for time and eternity, and Himself orders every minute thing, so as to promote it most effectually, completely, and permanently.

Now honour Him, my child, by *entire* confidence, by making all your requests known to Him, and by being sure that He loves you, and rejoices in your joy. . . . . Rejoice then, in His love, whatever else disappoints you ; for all is ordered by Him, rightly, and wisely, and graciously. . . . .

Your own Papa,<br>E. BICKERSTETH.

November 16.

MY DEAR MRS. SMITH,

My heart is yearning after my dear flock at Watton, and I long to return to them. God graciously grant that this constrained silence and absence may render me a more willing and active labourer among them, when my health is restored. About the first week in December, at latest, I hope to return.

I have just seen dear C., and your little ones at German Place. . . . . . I know by my own feelings how much you must sacrifice in being separated from them.   But their real good is a full recompence, and if we feel so as parents, what must be our Heavenly Father's full heart of love toward us!   O that we may dwell more in the light and joy of that *intense* love !

We are enjoying here every thing that the most bountiful hospitality and continually watchful kindness can give us.   In Christian friendship there are indeed unpurchasable benefits, far beyond any that this world's prosperity, merely, can bestow.   The sweet interchange of social kindness day by day, the mutual fellowship of Christian feelings, the communion of saints, all that the Apostle combines in "consolation in Christ, the comfort of love, and the fellowship of the Spirit," are joys fully understood only in Christian union ;—but, oh, how blessed they are, and what an earnest of that glory to come, when we shall sit down with Abraham, Isaac and Jacob, in the kingdom of heaven!

If I can but hereafter be a humble instrument, in helping to raise my beloved people to partake of this benefit in Christ Jesus, how thankful ought I to be ! . . . .

Thanks to you for all your kindness about F.   We have sought Divine guidance, and I trust, have been, and shall be, directed aright.   He does all well—well for her, for all the family, for the parish, for the Church, for all; and in Him I rest, and rejoice with joy unspeakable, trusting that not one of our children shall fail of a part in His heavenly kingdom, so speedily to be established.

Always, I trust, the Lord will keep us in the love of God, and in the patient waiting for Christ.

May our Lord ever watch over you, and bless you both, and make you a full blessing here, that you may inherit a full blessing hereafter,—so prays            Your affectionate Pastor,

E. BICKERSTETH.


*November* 16.

MY BELOVED B.

. . . . . I had this evening a very interesting and animating letter from Lord Ashley.   He gives me an account of the consecration of

Alexander, and a very curious dialogue W. C. had with Dr. Wiseman, who told him of his hopes as to the Puseyites.

I find more difficulty in being quiet, as my stay is prolonged. . . Do not trouble yourself about the work on Baptism. I write a family prayer each day now, and hope, if I can keep up the practice, in time to get a book of Family Prayers. God bless you all, prays with a full heart,

Your affectionate father,

E. BICKERSTETH,

The following is the account of the consecration, to which Mr. Bickersteth here alludes.

" *November* 15, 1841. The consecration of Bishop Alexander was most impressive. Perhaps a more solemn effect was never produced, than when the Bishop of New Zealand selected Acts xx, and read the passage. 'And now, behold, I go bound in the spirit unto Jerusalem, &c.' The Archbishop seemed quite inspired : his faint voice and timid manner were altogether changed : every one was struck by his feeling and dignity. The Bishop of London was afterwards in tears. . . . . . On Monday evening we had a service by way of thanksgiving (yet how weak ! ) at the Chapel on Bethnal Green. There was a positive throng of people ; they were as devout as they were numerous. Nothing could surpass the singing of the Hebrew children, a music, both in itself, and in its subject, so peculiar, that it stirred, while it softened, every feeling. The Bishop took for his text Acts xx. 22—24 ; the heart must have been hardened in the Devil's own furnace, which did not feel, and most fervently reply. His sermon was simple, pure, and inexpressibly touching : and I shall never forget the moment of his episcopal benediction, the first from a Jewish Bishop of Jerusalem for more than seventeen hundred years. *Non nobis Domine.* Charlotte Elizabeth said to me on Monday; ' Yesterday the fulness of the Gentiles was completed.' Even if not so, the remark must make one reflect. Something is at hand : you, and I, thank God, have a common and concurrent opinion, as a son of the Church, and a member of the British nation. I bless God that we have been called to this mighty office.'

" A ship has been obtained to land the Bishop at Jaffa, in his own Diocese : he will go out and disembark under the British flag. Hail to the ships of Tarshish ! we have here sanctified our national standard. May God prosper and bless you, and restore you to health, and that which you prize above all things, activity in His service."

Two of his daughters, then in town, consulted him at this time on the lawfulness of attending one of the Exeter Hall oratorios. The following was his reply.

*November* 22.

MY BELOVED CHILDREN,

The Lord preserve and bless you both, keep you from all evil, and watch over you for good.

I know too little about the Exeter Hall Oratorios, to form a Christian judgment ; but I have written the enclosed, for you to send to Mr. C——, and let his answer govern you.

I wish you to have all joy, and no sorrow, all good, and no evil, all holiness and no sin; and so you will by and bye, when you reach your heavenly home ; but not yet. For the way to this is through self-sacrifice and self-denial, taking your cross daily, following Christ, and suffering for well-doing.

By and bye, music and dancing, and every instrument of music, and every motion of joy, will all be redeemed and sanctified ; but the god of this world has now so got possession of the palace here, that we are continually tempted to walk in its territories, instead of walking in the narrow way of holiness, where no lion can come, nor any ravenous beast is found.

Write daily, for our hearts are with our children,

Your own affectionate Father,

E. BICKERSTETH.

*November* 20.

MY DEAREST B——,

As you will be left almost alone, I must write a line to the forsaken Rectory. Lord Ashley writes to me that the Prince of the Druses has arrived, to solicit religious protection.

Bishop Alexander has received his Diploma from King's College, with a most beautiful letter from the Bishop of London.

Five new Bishoprics have been founded,—Malta, Van Diemen, Ceylon, the Cape, New Brunswick.

Newman and his friends have sent a formal Protest to the Bishop of Oxford against the consecration of a Bishop, united with " the Lutheran and Calvinistic heresies," before they were reconciled to the Church !

O how much love I could send to Watton, going from the Rectory through the village, the hamlet, the farm-house, and the hall. Well, may I return to be a much greater blessing !

Your affectionate Father,

E. BICKERSTETH.

*Brighton, November* 29.

MY DEAREST CHILD,

I cannot let one of the lambs of my flock, and of the special enclosure of that flock, be at a distance, without following the Chief Shepherd's direction—" Feed my lambs."

And what food is best ? Why, truly, the sincere milk of the word ; so sweet, so simple, so nutritive, that it will not disagree with any lamb that desires it, and drinks it in, day by day.

Truly, the good tidings of great joy—that there is a Saviour, which is Christ the Lord, for our sinful souls—are most nourishing and wholesome at all times, and especially when we are sick and weak.

I do trust, my love, you have cast your whole soul, for life and for death, for judgment and for eternity, on the Lord Jesus, as able and willing to save you to the uttermost. Keep your eye steadily on His death, as the propitiation for all your sins, and keep fast hold of the sweet truth, that you are freely justified by faith in His blood. Nothing else will heal and bless, and sanctify your soul. Peace and holiness follow looking unto Jesus, and are the fruit of His Spirit, given to those who believe on Him.

Think of her who applied to Jesus, after trying all other physicians, and was healed by touching the very border of His garment. (Matt. v. 25—29.) Think of Asa, seeking to the physicians and not to the Lord, (2 Chron. xvi. 12,) and getting no good; and be sure, my dearest love, your heavenly Physician, caring for your eternal health, will do what is best for you, while you come to Him. O my dear child, give Him glory by entire confidence, being strong in faith! It is my hearty prayer for you.

The time also is very, very short, before the Lord shall return in His glory, and raise our souls far above all the fleeting cares and sorrows, or even the joys and glories, of this transient world. He has promised to come. I believe the time is near; and though many temptations and troubles are to be passed through, the end is the kingdom of light and glory for ever! All things in the way to it, whether health or sickness, life or death, are ours, and working for our good.

Your own Papa,<br>E. BICKERSTETH.

Watton, December 13.

MY DEAREST CHILDREN,

The enclosed are our Sunday sermons, as far as short sketches can go. O that all God's dealings with my dear F. may be so blessed that she may become very rich in grace and strong in faith. God can do great things for you, and will if you ask Him. . . . . .

I grieve that we have lost Mr. C.'s letter. But you can tell our friends, that, being full of anxiety lest my children should enter into worldly pleasures, or sanction the inconsistency of sacred music performed by persons of immoral character, I wrote to him ; and he replied, that the whole was conducted under the direction of pious persons, anxious to redeem music for its great end—the glory of God. No merely intellectual enjoyment of music would justify your going, but to get a help to the heavenly hope would be a real blessing, of which I would not deprive you. But, remember, the border lines are the scenes of danger, full of sharp-shooters, very quick to discern a straying soldier.

I hope now, through mercy, gradually to return to home duties.

I cannot tell you how greatly we feel the kindness of such friends as would be burdened with all the infirmities of a sick child. May our gracious God give them the joy of His love, and abundantly recompense them in blessings to their own children.

Such packets of love from all here ! Remember the first fountain.

Your own affectionate Father,

E. BICKERSTETH.

During the same visit he wrote a letter of affectionate sympathy to his friend Mr. Elliott of Brighton, whose beloved wife had been suddenly taken to her rest.

*Sussex Square, Brighton, Nov. 5, 1841.*

MY BELOVED ELLIOTT,

On my arrival here last night, I was grieved to the heart to hear of your bereavement. I do most tenderly sympathize with you in this heavy trial. I doubt not you have often said, " The Lord gave, and the Lord hath taken away ; blessed be the name of the Lord." But to weep is a Christ-like privilege ; and to weep with them that weep, a Christian duty, which I desire from the heart to enter upon with you. Her state is indeed one of true blessedness. Speedily carried to her Saviour's bosom, she is *with Christ,* which is far better ; resting from all her labours, and joying with the spirits of the just. We durst not wish to recal the departed, whom we love most. And then for you, and your children, and her relatives, my beloved Elliott, the Lord who loves you and them infinitely better than any other can, and has infinitely more and fuller wisdom in all His ways of love,—He saw what would be for your highest good, and had the faithful love, which would not be hindered by the pain it gave, from accomplishing that highest and eternal good. How surely we may rest in infinite wisdom, almighty power, and boundless love, engaged in Christ for our eternal benefit! The time is also short, as the blessed Apostle, on this very point, states. (1 Cor. vii. 25—31.) The Lord so quickly comes in His glory, and we are so soon to be with Him in the glories of the resurrection, that all that helps us to live in preparation for it, and in bringing others to share it with us, is really working for us, and not against us.

We are *ministers*, and the Lord would make us able, faithful, tender-hearted, experienced, and sympathizing ministers; and how can we become such, unless we be afflicted for the sake of our people? (2 Cor. i. 6.) My dear brother, you know all this better than I can tell you; but when stunned by an unlooked-for trial, I have found how sweet a common truth is from a fellow-Christian, and so I write to you.

God has dealt most gently with me : Though, for the present, entirely resting from all public duties, and forbidden the excitement of society, I am otherwise quite restored ; and, if it please God, have the hope of again returning to the blessed work of the ministry.

My dear wife, and our beloved friends the Marshalls, tenderly sympathize with you, and pray for you.

Most affectionately yours,

E. BICKERSTETH.

Upon the first abatement of his illness, and while close occupation of mind was pronounced to be dangerous, Mr. Bickersteth was very wishful to be employed in some work, which might benefit the souls of others, without the risk of too great excitement. He could only be happy while occupied in his Master's service. He had been urged by Christian friends, several years before, to publish a volume of " Family Prayers," and he began the work, soon after he reached Brighton, when all mental activity was still forbidden. In a note of November 18 to one of his children, he reports his daily progress, adding the weighty remark, suggested by a visit he had just paid to one in sickness.—"How blessed a thing it is to be an unequivocal Christian !" The volume was published in February, and dedicated to the kind friend, under whose roof it was begun. The following notes were also written to express his gratitude after his own return.

*December*, 1841.

MY DEAR GENERAL,

I cannot be content with the newspaper only coming, to assure you of our safe arrival. Our hearts are too full of the grateful feeling of all your kindness during the last five weeks, to allow my pen to be idle.

I know we both thank God for all His grace to us, whether we give of what He first gives us, or whether we receive—all is of God's full love, and to feel this is peace and joy, here and for ever. I know that it was love to our blessed Redeemer, that led you and Mrs. M. to shew love to us, and I doubt not, it is accepted of Him, and will be owned by Him, to whose name alone be all glory. May we be more knit to each other in Him, and more remember each other at His mercy-seat !

We were just three hours on the road in the railway, and had a journey of mercies, quiet from the fear of evil, which is often worse than evil itself. With our earnest prayers to the Father of mercies, that every spiritual and temporal blessing may be showered on you.

Very affectionately yours,

E. BICKERSTETH.

*December* 15.

MY DEAR GENERAL,

Through mercy I keep my Brighton health, and preached with comfort on Sunday.  The refreshment of my visit to you will not easily pass away.  Such is the love that our Lord delights to see, I doubt not, in us His children ; may it abound more and more in us to His glory.

I hope you will have seen Lord Ashley's admirable letter to Mr. Palmer.  Thanks be to God for such a nobleman.

I am getting on with my "Family Prayers," though not so easily as at Brighton, where half the volume was written.  You must allow me to dedicate it to you and Mrs. Marshall as a token of love.

Every blessing be with you both.  Realize the sweet truth, that our God does really love you, and is ordering all things, mental as well as bodily, future as well as present, for your highest good.

*December* 23.

Thanks to you for all your kind thoughts of us, and especially your last note.  Our joy, as believers before God and man is not in any thing in us.  I cannot stand a moment there ; for I too feel a sinfulness which only the Lord can discern—but our joy for here and eternity is in the righteousness of Jesus ; and that we know Him, and put all our trust in Him, and hope He will yet gain glory to Himself by us, from our love to Him, and His people, and all men.

I wrote to S—— about Lectures against Tractarianism.  Things are rapidly ripening for the day of Christ, and He will soon expel all these unclean spirits, be their name Legion, or however wonderful their increase, or prevailing the delusion. . . . God bless you both.  Our hearts are warm with grateful love to you.

Affectionately yours,

E. BICKERSTETH.

" *December* 12, 1841.  After staying nearly five weeks with my dear wife at Brighton, partaking of the bountiful hospitality of our beloved friends, the Marshalls, and being wholly free from all public duty, I am mercifully brought back, with much recruited health and strength, to my parish.

" I have now been in orders as a Minister just twenty-six years, having been ordained deacon, December 10, 1815, and never before reduced to silence in my ministry. The Lord grant that I and my people may profit by it. For ten Sundays I have been kept from preaching, as a matter of duty, and now this Sunday, for the first time, preached on 2 Cor. iv. 7. O Lord, my leanness and unprofitableness, my great sins, which often unexpectedly rise up in humbling recollection to my mind, all through my past days, may well make me lie very low before Thee. I desire to humble myself in Thy sight, as a most guilty creature, whose only dependence must be fixed on the Lord Jesus.

" I hope gradually to resume my duties in the parish, but journeying for Societies must, I apprehend, be relinquished. Lord, teach me, and lead me, that I may do Thy will and not mine ! "

# CHAPTER XXII.

THE nature of Mr. Bickersteth's illness made it his clear
duty to refrain for a season from those public and exciting labours, in which he had been so actively engaged.
The year which followed it was, therefore, passed in
comparative retirement. His home employments were
still varied and enlarged by an extensive and interesting
correspondence ; but, with the exception of one Annual
Sermon in May, for the Prayer-book and Homily Society,
and another, in November, for the Protestant Association, he engaged in hardly any public services, and entirely gave up his usual missionary journeys. None,
however, loved him so much, as those who saw him under
his own roof, surrounded by his family, and in the quiet
course of his home life. The fragrance of Christian love,
which breathed around him, lives still in their memory,
though it is impossible, in words, to convey the full impression of it to others. Yet a few recollections, however
imperfect, of his Watton life, as it appeared to visitors
from a distance, and to his own children, will find a
natural place in his biography, at this time of seclusion
and retirement.

When he first removed to Watton, the youngest of his

six children was a few weeks old, and the eldest only about ten years of age. But at the time of his illness, the lapse of more than eleven years had made a great change in his domestic circle. All his children had now been united, for four or five years, under his own roof. His three eldest received mainly, and the others exclusively, a home education. They had most of them reached an age, in which they could appreciate their father's position in the Church, and sympathize in his public labours. They were able now, more than in earlier years, to delight in the overflowing love, which marked his character as a parent, and by reflecting it from one to another, to multiply and diffuse its happy influence. His own incessant activity gave its tone to the whole family. It was a little hive of busy, happy workers. To get good, and to do good, was the double charge he impressed constantly on his children, as the great rule and object of a Christian life ; and as they rose successively into the knowledge and enjoyment of the gospel their father proclaimed and practised, they were taught that it was their highest privilege to help in diffusing its blessedness to others.

The notes of Mr. Bickersteth to his children, in the previous chapters, illustrate his general principle in their education. Religion was never exhibited to them as a system of arbitrary restraint, or as contracting for them that wider circle of pleasures, in which the children of worldly parents would be permitted to engage. They were taught to regard it as a system of privilege, a constant fountain of domestic joy and mutual love. Their father carefully excluded them, it is true, from worldly society. Novels were practically prohibited ; and vain and idle words in songs, even when they might happen to intrude in music-lessons, met his instant and decided disapprobation. He objected to dancing, and the ball-room was of course, entirely prohibited. But the home-circle was so happy—life was so rich with varied interest,—that his children were little tempted to desire amusements of which they felt no need, and which were habitually associated, in their minds, with the ideas of unhealthy dissipation, waste of time, and extreme spiritual danger. When they heard other Christian parents speak of the difficulty they found in restraining their children from worldly pleasures, they learned how great was their debt to the wise and tender love of their own father, which had left them no excuse for craving those dangerous amusements, by furnishing them with a rich variety of home enjoyments. He spared no expense in their education, provided them lessons, in music and drawing, from the best masters, supplied them liberally with books, and encouraged them in their own voluntary studies. He allowed his children, as indeed he pursued himself, a wide range of reading. His large library was well stored, not only with a very great number of theological writings, in which it was rivalled by few private collections, but with works of history, science, and general literature.* He cared little himself for works of imagination ; but, whenever there was nothing plainly objectionable in their tendency, he rejoiced to procure them for his children. There was a free liberality in all his gifts, which made them doubly welcome. Filial piety had eminently marked his early days, and God gave him, as in recompense, a large measure of parental wisdom, and an unusual share of domestic happiness. His authority,

* The number of volumes he had collected, before his death, amounted to nearly eleven thousand, including a large collection of old divinity, as well as the best modern authors.

it is true, was so gentle, that the father seemed almost merged in the companion, but his will was ever felt to be a spontaneous law to the whole household.

When his children, by the blessing of God, had learned to prize the truth, which was so powerfully commended to them by his daily instructions and example, this discipline of love produced its natural effect on their minds. It became their highest pleasure to help on his work—the Master's work, as he loved to call it. This was his own great object, which carried him cheerfully through every little sacrifice. " I don't much like leaving home," he would say often before a journey, " but it is for the Master." " You are overworking yourself," was the not unusual remonstrance of Mrs. Bickersteth, or of his children. " It is all the Master's work, my love," would be his reply. In this blessed work he delighted to have his children for helpers and companions. They were early accustomed to take part in the Sunday School, and to visit the cottages of the poor. When they grew older, he delighted to employ them in the village, and used playfully to call them his curates. " I am going into the village, can I do anything for you, Papa ?" was a frequent inquiry. " Yes, my love, all the good thou canst," would be his answer, whenever there was no special commission. If any good was done, they were cheered by his full and ready sympathy ; if any perplexities arose in their part of the parish work, his wise counsel was always at hand. At home he found them frequent employment, in copying important letters, translating passages for quotation, preparing indexes, and other tasks of a similar kind. Much of the work thus provided for them was very interesting in itself ; and the rest, which might have been rather irksome in its own nature, was so gratefully acknowledged,

that the little self-denial was found, in the result, to
yield them one of the purest and deepest pleasures.  At
such times it was their privilege to sit with him in his
quiet study, to watch his busy progress, to hear the ejacu-
lations often gently breathed for divine help, as matters
of weighty importance came before him ; and to feel that,
by taking some of the more mechanical parts of his work,
they were helping to redeem his precious time for more
abundant labours in the cause of Christ.  He contrived
to find some use for almost every thing they might have
learned in the school-room, in connexion with his own
work ; so that, although he took very little part in the
direct superintendence of their studies, all was instinctively connected with him in their thoughts, and seemed
to draw them closer and closer to him.

From an early age his children were admitted to share
all the various church-interests which daily clustered
around him.   He made them his intimate companions in
all his labours for promoting the Redeemer's kingdom.
His fears as to the dangers which threatened the Church
of Christ ; his perplexities as to his own course on particular occasions that might arise ; his impressions on the
character of public men, or the tendency of public measures in Church or State—all were discussed freely in
the family circle, and the youngest were not forbidden to
mingle in the conversation.  A conviction was thus
silently formed in their minds, that everything which interested their father, since it affected the cause of the
Saviour, ought to be also of deep interest to themselves.
Every morning, before breakfast was ended, or a little
later, the post came in, usually with a large variety of
letters.  Unless the contents required privacy, the various intelligence from every part of the kingdom, and

often from distant lands, became the subject of conversation to the whole family. It was his constant practice to walk before dinner ; and he would then often discuss with his wife and children, or Christian inmates and visitors, the duties which the morning's post had brought upon him ; and would sometimes leave the table at dinner, when the conversation turned on the same subjects, to fetch the answers he had written. It was his own principle, through life, to have for his main object the glory of God in the salvation of men. This he sought also to impress in every way on their minds. A great work was to be done ; and each one, according to their ability, was to take a part in it. Self-denial was to be expected as a needful means ; but the end was glorious, and wor-thy of every sacrifice. Life, they were thus taught to feel, was solemn and earnest, full of interest, full of hope ; and though beset with many dangers, and exposed to many trials, full also to a Christian of the richest blessings. A variety of quiet amusements were at hand, to fill up every hour not occupied with active and pressing duties ; and the only complaint often heard at the Rectory, was, that the day was not long enough for its numerous and interesting occupations.

For many years of his life, Mr. Bickersteth was a very early riser, and two or three of his most popular works were composed in these morning hours, before the business of a laborious day began. At Watton, latterly, he rose between six and seven, and then took a cold bath, which he found very beneficial to his health ; and in winter he would often break the ice with his own hands in severe weather, rather than omit the practice. After a short time spent in private in his study, he retired to a quiet walk in a field above the Rectory, where he

used to continue his morning devotions. Not far from one end of this private walk there were two or three cottages, and unknown to himself, his voice was sometimes overheard by the simple cottagers, as he poured out his earnest supplications before God. He was accustomed for years to meet his children a quarter of an hour before breakfast, to hear them repeat a few verses of Scripture. When they grew older, he encouraged them to learn larger portions of it, and to repeat them to him. The book of Revelation, and several of the Epistles, were thus committed to memory. He had a great desire to read the Old Testament in Hebrew, and made several attempts before breakfast with his eldest daughter ; but his occupations never allowed him to give a reasonable time to such a pursuit, especially as he had no special readiness for the acquisition of a language : but all the time spent with him in private by his children was so delightful, that these Hebrew lessons are still looked back upon with peculiar pleasure.

He always laid great stress on punctuality. At eight o'clock the bell rang for breakfast, which was ever at Watton Rectory a time of social enjoyment. Even when his children were young, he never consented to the rule that they should be forbidden to speak at table ; it was his chief opportunity of intercourse with them. Thus the habit was early formed of regarding meal-times chiefly as happy seasons for the interchange of thought, and the cultivation of domestic sympathy. At half-past eight the bell rang again for prayers, and he was very careful that every member of the household should be present, or at least that no light cause should be held to justify their absence. A hymn was sung, accompanied with the harp or piano, or occasionally with both instru-

ments.  Though gifted himself neither with a good voice
nor a very correct ear, he took peculiar delight in this
part of worship, which was so congenial to his thankful
spirit, and he might be said with truth to ' make melody
in his heart to the Lord.'  His expositions were simple,
earnest, homely, full of life and power.  Most of them
latterly were taken down, each day, by one or other of
his children ; and those on St. John's and St. Jude's
Epistles, after being revised by himself, have been published with the title of ' Family Expositions.'  In his
prayers it was his custom to introduce the mention of
each passing circumstance of domestic interest.  No servant left or joined the family—no one set out on a journey,
or returned from it, was laid aside with sickness or recovered, without a separate petition or thanksgiving in these
morning devotions of the household.

After prayers he returned to his study ; and three or
four hours were busily employed, first of all, in looking
over and answering the day's letters, or the arrears of correspondence during his journeys ; and then, if time
allowed, in carrying on whatever work he might be preparing for publication.  About an hour before dinner he
summoned his family for a walk.  He found this regular
exercise necessary for his health, and insisted on its importance, with his children and others, as a real economy
of time, and that it should not be a continuation of
study in the open air, but a thorough relaxation.  At
one time he rode frequently on horseback before breakfast with one or other of his children, and in this case he
expected a hymn to be repeated to him in the course of
their ride.  Such times of solitary intercourse were precious seasons for gaining spiritual counsel.  He would
listen tenderly to every doubt and anxiety, and could

enter thoroughly into every statement of spiritual conflict.  " I have felt just the same," he would affectionately answer, " I too have known the summer and winter
of the soul ! "

After dinner a few minutes were given to free, hearty
conversation by the fireside, and then a little time in
his study to lighter reading, or letters of less importance.
He then went down, usually about four o'clock, to the
schools, or the sick poor in the village, or took the afternoon cottage-lectures, when he had no curate.  An early
tea, about six or seven, was followed on Wednesday by a
lecture in the school-room, on Saturday by a weekly
prayer-meeting, and on the other evenings, by study or
composition.  A strip of paper was fastened on his desk,
with notes of the work he had to do ; and thus, amidst
the great diversity of his engagements, it was very rarely
that any thing was forgotten.  He read with great
rapidity.  In general he had some special object in view
in the books he took up; and he would run his eye
rapidly through many volumes, passing over all that did
not interest him, and fixing his attention on all those
parts which gave him the information of which he was
in quest.  It was probably this habit of rapid selection
which made him dislike being read to by others ; and
even in times of illness he always preferred to have a
book in his own hands.  A quiet study was found by him
essential to his progress in his work, and access to it in
working hours was a privilege very carefully limited.  In
this he owed very much, as he used often to say, to his
beloved wife, who took his share, as well as her own, of
little household interruptions, that he might be left entirely free for his more important employments.  The
day closed with family worship, and a few minutes of

pleasant social conversation. He was an advocate for
early hours of retirement. At ten o'clock the little
party, however fascinating the subject of conversation,
was invariably broken up, and any recusants had a
lighted candle put into their hands.

Next to his glowing love and untiring diligence, consistency was the most prominent feature in Mr. Bickersteth's domestic character. He was just the same in his
own family as he appeared to be abroad. It is the testimony of his children, in looking back upon all the past,
while they would not dare to claim for so beloved a parent
an exemption from all human frailty,—that they remember no instance in which he led them in a course inconsistent with the truths he ever inculcated on them. In
any little social perplexities that might arise, they often
observed how quickly he cut the knot, by pointing out
the law of Christian duty, and then following it, undisturbed by the fear of man's displeasure. In his arrangements for their welfare, it was always evident that
their soul's prosperity was viewed as the main object.
His whole life was a commentary to them on those words
of the Lord—" Seek first the kingdom of God, and his
righteousness." It was this fact, perhaps even more than
all his direct instructions, which made an uneffaceable
impression on their minds. They could not help feeling
that their father viewed the things of God—closet duties,
the means of grace, the growth of true religion in the
heart, as the things of chief importance. The impression
thus made, as it was never weakened by practical inconsistency, gathered strength from year to year, till his last
hours put their seal upon it, and gave it a still more
sacred character.

The same features which marked Mr. Bickersteth's do-

mestic life, were seen in all his intercourse with his own
flock. His daily visits to the people were short, because
he was always full of work; but they were frequent and
impressive, for his heart was full of love. His very presence in the street often shamed quarrellers into peace
and silence; and his cheerful happy look and friendly
greeting were so highly prized, that the poor of his flock
have frequently gone out of their way, to meet him in
his daily walks to the village. Every one was deeply
convinced that their pastor loved them, and sought earnestly the good of their souls. In times of affliction his
visits were especially valuable. He knew well how to
speak a word in season to the weary. One sick and in-
firm parishioner has mentioned that he never failed, for
years, to pay her a weekly visit; and the impression left
on their minds was seen by the crowds who assembled,
and the many tears that were shed by the poor, around
his grave.

It was not, however, merely to the partial eyes of his
own family, that the private life of Mr. Bickersteth was
thus peculiarly attractive. The same influence was felt
by every friend who partook of his hospitality, and by
the Christian strangers, who might come to him from a
distant country, attracted by their knowledge of his
writings and public labours. All these found a special
charm in their visits to Watton Rectory. His presence
diffused around him an atmosphere of warm affection
and holy love. The present year, in which he was with-
drawn from public work, was rich with these privileges
of Christian hospitality. In the previous summer his
friend, Bishop Meade of Virginia, had paid him a visit of
a few days, and preached in his church. In January,

Mr. Bickersteth received from him a most affectionate letter, in which he thus expressed his own feelings.

" Having got through the most pressing duties, awaiting me on my return, I enter on the most delightful task of writing to some of those Christian friends, with whom I held short, but blessed fellowship, while in England. I think and speak and write about them, with feelings which I number among the happiest and best that pass through my heart. . . .

" You have been stricken by the hand of God, my dear brother, and for a time even silenced from preaching the gospel. Well, it is the Lord, let Him do what seemeth Him good! He has other voices besides yours, to speak of his loving-kindness, and I doubt not, you rejoiced in the thought; but I trust that, long ere this, yours is as loud as ever, and will yet sound for many years as music to the sinner, because it speaks of Christ. O the glorious privilege of preaching and writing, as you have done, His great salvation. I thought we had all your works in America, but on opening your parcel, I was overjoyed at the thought of the pleasure laid up for some early day. Your hymns I have often used, since my return, in my family, and your heads for daily private prayer have their turn with Leighton and Andrews; and thus you are not only in my heart very often, but in the hearts of my family, and I shall freely lend your books, as they were freely given. . . .

" And now for your dear family—wife, daughters, son, so loving one to another. How often do I see you all around the table, conversing, singing, praying, in anticipation of heaven! God bless you all, especially your dear son, with double grace for the ministry. I shall see you and all of them together one day, yet more loving, in the presence of our blessed Lord in heaven. . . . And now may the Father of mercies and God of all consolation evermore be with you, and all yours, is the prayer of your affectionate brother, in Christ our gracious Redeemer,

                                        " W. MEADE."

In May of this year Mr. Bickersteth preached in London the Annual Sermon of the Prayer Book and Homily
Society, which he published, soon after, with the title,
" The Permanence and Progress of Divine Truth." It
was during this brief absence from home that he first
met with Dr. Tyng, then of Philadelphia, and since of
New York, and invited him to see him at Watton, where
he paid two short visits before his return to America.
These were a season, on both sides, of great enjoyment.
In those reminiscences of England, which Dr. Tyng afterwards wrote for his flock and friends in America, he gives
the following description of the impressions made on him,
as a Christian stranger, by Mr. Bickersteth's personal
appearance, and of his character and influence in the
more private sphere of parish duties and of domestic
life.

" With what delight I met my revered and excellent
friend, Mr. Bickersteth, you can readily conceive. Nor
was I disappointed in him. The sweetness and openness
of his manners, and the remarkable cheerfulness of his
countenance and conversation, would win the heart of
an entire stranger. To me they were peculiarly enchant-
ing. He was apparently in very feeble health, stooping
a little, perhaps from weakness, and indicating, in all his
aspect, that spiritual character, and separation from this
evil world, which so distinguish him as a minister of
Christ. . . . The influence of Mr. Bickersteth is most extensive. There is such universal confidence in his remarkable excellence of judgment and integrity of purpose
—such unfeigned respect for his real learning and holy
and exemplary ministry—that there are very few, if there
are any, among the clergy, who have at all an equal influence over the minds of others. He seems enshrined in

the affections of his brethren ; and I could not but feel
the worth of such a character as his, when I heard him
spoken of by them in private conversation, under the title
of ' dear Bickersteth.' . . . All that I saw of him continually increased my love for him ; and cheerfully would
I cross the Atlantic again, for the simple privilege of one
more visit to Watton. . . .

" When we descended into the quiet valley, in the
bosom of which this little village rests, every spot
awakened my increasing interest.   It is a single street
of cottages, with no houses of a higher character among
them, in a narrow vale, which is crossed and watered by
a beautiful stream.   On an eminence on the right, before
you reach the village, is Woodhall Park, the seat of Abel
Smith, Esq., a large, modern residence, looking more like
a public than a private edifice, encompassed with very
extensive grounds, in which are large numbers of deer.
On the hill opposite, before you reach the village, are the
church and parsonage.   The former is about 500 years
old, and built of parts erected apparently in different
ages ; and, with its ancient tower among the trees, it is a
striking object.   Just above it stands the residence of
Mr. Bickersteth, a large and commodious house, in the
midst of a neat and well-improved inclosure.   The exte-
rior, like all the country residences, is beautiful from the
extreme neatness of the grounds.   I walked up through
the lane and churchyard with peculiar interest.   It was
the home of a man whom I have venerated and loved for
years, and to whose writings I have been indebted for
much important instruction.   He was now to be seen by
me in private life, and all the feelings of regard, which I
had cherished at a distance, were confirmed and deepened
by nearer observation.   His manners are full of kindness

and love; and there is a spiritual character in his conversation, and a religious influence about all he says and
does, which is very impressive, and most delightful.  He
is also full of vivacity and life in his conversation, and
exhibits that most interesting combination of gentleness,
animation, and seriousness, which gives a charm to all
instruction, and an improving power even to recreation
and amusement.  How truly delightful is it to see him
in the midst of a family, who understand the value of
their privilege, and hang intently on every word he
speaks!  After dinner, on the day of my arrival, which
was Saturday, there was a prayer-meeting in the library,
when, at the request of Mr. Bickersteth, I spoke to them
on a passage of the word of God.  How quiet and sooth-
ing, how solemn and impressive, was the influence of this
occasion! and I trust the blessing of God was with us.

"The morning of the Sabbath opened upon us with
freshness and beauty.  It was the most lovely season of
the year, in a beautiful part of the country; and, amidst
the holy calmness of the day, every object seemed to
beam with pure loveliness.  My window overlooked the
village, which lay sleeping in perfect repose at the foot
of the hill, and seemed the resting-place of quiet and
contentment. . . . After breakfast, I visited the Sunday
and Infant School, which are held in two neat buildings
erected by Mr. Smith of Woodhall, who supports the
schools with much liberality.  I was much pleased with
a small Bible-class of adults, who were taught in the
church, and appeared to listen with great interest and
desire to learn.

"Mr. Bickersteth preached a solemn and impressive
sermon, on the offices and work of the Holy Spirit.  The
congregation, except the Woodhall family, seemed com-

posed wholly of villagers, and the neighbouring farmers, and their labourers. It is a rural parish, having about eight hundred inhabitants, engaged in agriculture; but they seemed a serious and attentive people, and interested in the evangelical instructions of their pastor. I preached to them in the afternoon, and delivered a familiar lecture in the evening, at the school-house in the village. It was a peaceful, happy Sabbath, and I could only look back upon it, as passing too quickly for the pleasure it gave.

" My second visit to Watton was a month later. As I stopped at the foot of the hill, my revered friend and his younger children, who were with the haymakers in the field around the church, came down to meet me; and I felt myself, amidst their greetings, as if at home. . . We passed the next morning, in a long stroll, through the grounds of Woodhall. The walk was an occasion of bringing, from the ample stores of my companion's mind, a vast amount of information and aid for me. How exalting and improving is such society ! . . . In our walk, Mr. B. had given notice for a lecture in the school-house in the evening. The place was crowded with a most attentive congregation ; and, after I had spoken to them the word of God, many came around me with expressions of their gratitude and interest in the addresses they had heard. The next morning, before I returned to London, Mr. B. had all the children assembled in the school-room, for another address to them. I felt, at parting with them, almost as if they were my own dear schools, they seemed so glad to hear the blessed truth of God from my mouth. I parted with my venerated friend, and his assistant and son, hardly daring to hope that I should see them again in this world, and lifting up my heart in prayer to God for a divine blessing to rest on them all, for time and

eternity.   In a refreshing letter which I have lately
received from him, he says ; ' Blessed be our God and
Father, for all the comforts of love, and fellowship of
Spirit in Christ.   The battles of the Lord are becoming
more hot and more general, for the Captain of our salvation is near, and means soon to win his last triumph.
May we live near to Jesus, believe all His truth, getting
more and more knowledge of it, and confess it more
boldly, and that daily.   I write hastily, but with a heart
full of love.' "

The journal of Mr. Bickersteth in this year, and his
notes to his children and other friends, while they illustrate his private character and experience, show how the
illness of the previous autumn, so critical and alarming
in its nature, had left an abiding impression on his mind
of the nearness of eternity.

" *April* 28, 1842.   Still I am spared and blessed.   The
goodness of God endureth yet daily.   O that His long-
suffering may more and more be my salvation.

" I still am enabled to go on with the Lord's work.
The book of ' Family Prayers ' is completed and published.   God prosper the three thousand copies now
issuing from the press.   I am busy with my ' Prayer
Book and Homily Sermon,' which I wish to make some
preservative against the false doctrines of Tractarianism
now abroad.   The Lord use it for that end.

" But my own soul.   O that this may never be neglected.   At my time of life, the *probability* is, that within
fifteen years I shall be in the eternal world ; apart from
the *possibility* of being there before the day closes. . . . O
that the time yet remaining of my life, whatever it be,
may be wholly occupied for God, and my talents laid out
daily for Him !   God preserve me from taking any rest

in earthly things.  Indeed every thing is shaking.  May
I receive the kingdom that cannot be moved, and redeem
the days.  May there be nothing between me and God—
but peace, union, and likeness."

*Watton Rectory, April 8.*

MY DEAR MRS. SMITH,

. . . . We much regretted not seeing you, but did not think it
right to encroach on the day you had for the country with your
children.  By and bye we shall meet in the heavenly kingdom, with
nothing to impede full communion and full joy. . . .  I like to look
at the shortness of the intervening time; at the outside, so many
years, in the probability so many, in the possibility, not a year, a
month, a day, an hour.  But take the longest time, look at it in the
retrospect, or at the eternal prospect, and what a moment it is!
Surely nothing should be precious, compared with the eternal inheritance in the Lord Himself, so soon to be enjoyed.  God give us
much grace, to have all our treasure there, or on the way there, and
to be adding to that treasure daily!

I must pass Thursday and Friday, May 5 and 6, in town, for my
Prayer Book and Homily Sermon; otherwise I do not purpose
being in London, or attending any of the May Meetings.  I find
quiet still important and needful, and have declined the many
applications for help that have come.

We did think of your child's birthday, and prayed for a blessing
on it.  Though I think we enjoy as much of God's presence in
intercessory prayer as in any part of our devotions, I find it the
one which most easily slips from its due attention.  O that we were
more like Jesus—all whose prayer is intercession!  My heart is
indeed at times drawn out in prayer for you and yours; but I know
it ought to be much more so; and in this, as in other things, sins
of omission burden me; but I trust eternity may yet show a truth
and love among Christians, which was not imagined before.  How
delightful will be the surprise of finding graces, where we had only,
from the outside appearance, discerned defects, but above all at

the unfoldings of the wisdom, grace, and love, of our Divine
Redeemer !

Most truly yours,
E. BICKERSTETH.

The following note was written about the same time, to
his sister in Liverpool, where more than one of his brother's family had been suffering from dangerous illness.

*April*, 1842.

My DEAREST K.

Your letter quite gladdened our happy circle, as we were at
breakfast this morning.   We first saw a letter in your hand-writing
from Liverpool, and then its good tidings  soon rejoiced us, and we
thanked God together, in our family worship, for the prayers He
had answered.   All praise be to His name !   I am sure you will
find, deep as the trial has been, full streams of blessing flowing
from it, and that for years to come.   God never wounds, but to
heal more entirely, and to give larger blessings than we could have
had without it.   How thankful I ought to be that the little prayer
I wrote for dearest E. was any comfort to him !   The joy of being
useful to others is a sweet reward, and we shall reap it yet more
fully in the coming kingdom of our Redeemer.

Through mercy, we are well.   Perhaps the Lord may yet spare
F. to us, but all His ways are right.   Dearest Robert's health is so
precious to us all, that we shall rejoice to hear of its being re-esta-
blished.   May we look forward to your spending three or four weeks
with us in the summer ?   I am  afraid it is a vision, but it is  too
pleasant not to be welcome ; and if a change of scene would be
useful to you all, possibly the vision may become a reality.   I do
not travel for any Society this year.

Ever affectionately yours,
E. BICKERSTETH.

"*June* 25, 1842.   The last month has been one of
many mercies.   We have had our relatives from Norwich

with us, Dr. Tyng from America, and Mr. and Mrs. Auriol, and their family. . . .

" An Abridgment of the ' Treatise on Baptism ' is passing through the press ; and I have been distributing largely the ' Prayer-Book and Homily Sermon,' and my ' Family Prayers.'

The sermon here mentioned was from the words, Matt. xiii. 52, and bore the title—" The Permanence and Progress of Divine Truth." Its double object was to enforce the duty of firm adherence to the old, fundamental truths of the Gospel, and of going on continually unto perfection, by growing in the knowledge of our Lord and Saviour. The view given, in its opening, of the character of the times, embodies the deliberate convictions of Mr. Bickersteth on many subjects of high importance to the Church of Christ, and remains, after ten years, as instructive as ever.

" The present situation of Christendom at large is very perilous. Under the general calmness, quiet and security, and under the apparently peaceful worldly prosperity of Europe, and the undisturbed surface of society in nominally Christian countries, there are the elements of judgment and destruction. There is a wide, deep, and ruinous ignorance of the blessed truths of the Gospel, full of evil and mischief. From it comes the unclean spirit of lawlessness, hating all restraint, restless, dissatisfied, given to change both in Church and State, naturally disowning God, speaking evil of dignities ; an easy prey to those who promise liberty, while they themselves are the servants of corruption. There is yet deeper evil in the unclean spirit of Infidelity, coming from Satan himself, casting off God's own word, and putting forth empty and vain substitutes for the living waters which God has provided. In perfect contrast with these evils, a revulsion from them, and an intended opposition to them, though with affecting points of union, is a most rapidly diffused contagion of error, which corrupts the simplicity of the gospel, unduly magnifies outward ordinances, judges and severely condemns even those who love Christ, if they dissent from an Episcopal church ; and will in its result, if diffused and enforced, bring on us, as its forerunner the Laudian school did, in the great rebellion, the very destruction which it expects to avert. Those who have so grievously departed from the spirit of our Church, that they openly testify, they hate the Reformation, while they honour the Roman Church ; and who shew that they think more highly of the predicted apostasy than of that heavenly gift, Reformation-truth, have also many advantages, in influential institutions, in wealth, in public journals, and periodicals, in many excellent natural endowments, with great zeal and earnestness, and readiness to make large sacrifices ; and they have used these advantages for disparaging the Reformers and their doctrines, and diffusing that which the corruption and pride of the natural heart prefer to God's truth, though full of grace and mercy. Unless the Lord mightily interpose for us, England is in imminent and peculiar peril, from that sad neglect and abuse of peculiar privileges and blessings. We are in great danger of losing the shield of Protestant truth, and sinking back into that which God accounts among the abominations of the earth, and on which his last and most dreadful judgments are denounced—judgments that must now be near at hand. The Lord grant that the danger may awaken the Church of Christ, and that our backslidings may lead on to a recovery more full of blessedness than ever, and our errors be the occasion of bringing forth a fulness of truth, and a more blessed revival than our Church has ever yet experienced !"

" *July* 29. Amidst many and great infirmities, my soul is advancing onward to its eternal home. The good Lord pardon the transgressions of each day, and each hour.

" God has given the book of " Family Prayers " a rapid circulation. The whole edition of three thousand two hundred and fifty copies have been parted with in about

three months. What a responsibility this brings with
it ! O Lord, forgive all the errors and many defects, and
accept the poor, feeble, unworthy attempts to do Thee
service, sprinkled with the blood of Jesus Christ. . . .

" The ' Christian Student' occupies me at present. It
is a laborious work, and I fear less practically useful than
others, but I seem called upon to revise it. . . .

" *August* 27. How many and how great are Thy
mercies, day by day. My children have been carried
through their journeys with many blessings. Mr., Mrs.,
and Miss Pratt have been staying with us. We visited
dear Christian friends at Dyrham Park, and have now
the Faithfulls staying with us. The Lord is full of love
in all His ways. And how is this enhanced, when I look
at my own unprofitableness ! That God should deal so
graciously with one so vile, may well be my song for ever.

" I have great cause for thanksgiving in the happy
death of M. C., one of my flock. She was only nineteen,
but through her sickness glorified the Lord. She wished
to see me before death, and as I finished my last prayer,
fell asleep in Jesus. To God be the glory.

" And I am no more zealous, no more diligent in my
ministry ! O Lord, have mercy upon me—have mercy
upon me ; quicken me for Thy mercies' sake. Make me
a faithful, laborious, self-denying minister to Watton.

" O that I may be led more to act on new principles,
earlier rising, more regular arrangement of time, more
wise instruction in visiting, more close walking with God,
more diligent waiting on Him !

" O how much more might be done for God by *me !*
I think sometimes how much more my country might do
for God. O that I did but think more of what I could
do, and set about doing it ! Lord, make me diligent

with my own proper talents. Let me not be looking
elsewhere, to think of other men's duties, but at home.
Make me, I beseech Thee, widely useful."

"*September* 24. I do hope that there has been a little
fresh impulse given to duties in the last month; but it
must be another standard yet, before my life glorifies
God as a faithful parish minister. . . .

" The Lord has been very gracious to our country in
an abundant harvest, and in putting down the distur-
bances in the manufacturing districts. Surely we have
all reason to praise His name for our many, many, national mercies.

" The general aspect of the world is but dark and
gloomy. Men live so far from God, and His Churches
are so corrupt, both Roman, Greek, and Reformed, that
we can look for nothing but judgments. Yet mercy shall
finally rejoice over judgment. O God, I ask for special
wisdom to know how to judge and act in every thing,
according to Thy mind.

" *October* 30. I returned from Brighton last night, to
partake of the communion with my beloved flock we
had seventy-five.

" I have been called to preach the fifth of November
Sermon for the Protestant Association, and have given
much time to prepare it. It is from Rev. xvi., ' the Sixth
Vial,' or 'the Divine Warning to the Church at this time,'
The Lord graciously prosper it for good. The times are
very threatening, and the present tranquillity most precarious.

" O Lord, help the preacher, at least, to mind Thy
warning, and may his words also be blessed to very
many."

A short note during the visit to General Marshall here

alluded to, shows his own restoration to health, and his employment during his absence :—

*Brighton, October* 22.

My DEAR F.

I cannot write thee much ; for when thou seest my long sermon in print, thou wilt say, Truly papa wrote enough at Brighton.

Through mercy, I and your sister are as well as troopers, and mount hills and skip over downs with all alacrity. But we have one sad drawback. Your mamma still suffers much, and this has been a suffering day. So we all need, at the Divinely-appointed time, the cross to prepare for the crown. O what a crown ! if we are but faithful to Jesus. All but this is a gaudy vanity.

With a heart full of love to you all,

Your affectionate Father,

E. BICKERSTETH.

Two notes to his kind friend, after his return, show the chief works which employed him towards the close of this year of retirement.

*Watton Rectory, November* 10.

My DEAREST GENERAL,

. . . I have had so much to do for our Master since I came home, that I see clearly it was my duty to return when I did.

God graciously carried me through the sermon, which I delivered on Saturday. I have this morning corrected the first proof, and hope next week to send you some copies for Brighton. It has already made a considerable stir. May it strengthen God's dear children to withstand the temptations of these days, and what cause I shall have to bless Him !

I am anxious about the giving up Malta in the Mediterranean Mission. It is like withdrawing our troops from Hougomont in the battle of Waterloo. Wellington said, We must all die first.

I am going to preach for the London Young Men's Church Missionary Society on Tuesday evening.

The remembrance of your kindness is still, and will always be, most grateful.   Hearty love from all here.

Most affectionately yours,<br>E. BICKERSTETH.

Watton Rectory, November 18.

. . . Through mercy I got well through the Young Men's Sermon—a large congregation and good collection ; and what is better, I believe a spirit of zeal and love kindled.   I have been attending three very interesting prophetic meetings at Mr. Villiers'. I hope we mutually helped each other.   We are going to have twelve Second-Advent Lectures at St. George's, Bloomsbury. . . .

The Lord will confound all our enemies.   Only may He give us the spirit of our dear Master—the meekness of wisdom—the gentleness of Christ—all His love—with all His boldness, zeal, and decision.

Yours affectionately,<br>E. BICKERSTETH.

The season of comparative rest had not been given in vain, and was now drawing to its close.   Public events, the wants of the church, and his own ardour, thrust him forth again into the harvest-field.   But his spirit had been ripened by the chastening ; and refreshed by months of more quiet labour, of various communion in private with Christian friends, and of sweet fellowship with his God and Saviour, he was prepared to contend earnestly for the gospel of Christ in troublous times, with the boldness of assured faith, and with growing meekness of heavenly wisdom.

# CHAPTER XXIII.

THE eventful character of the times, and Mr. Bicker-steth's own fervent spirit, soon called him to resume his post as a public labourer in the Lord's vineyard, and a watchman to the Church of Christ. His sermon on Nov. 5, 1843, was soon afterwards published, with the title " The Divine Warning," and speedily obtained a very wide circulation, attracting more than usual interest with thoughtful minds. His text was Rev. xvi. 13—15. He viewed those words, in the imagery of the Sixth Vial, as a prophetic description of recent and of passing events ; and that the spread of lawlessness, infidelity, and superstition, in Chartism, Socialism, and open or half-disguised Popery, were a striking fulfilment of them be-fore the eyes of all men. With such convictions as to the true nature of the spiritual conflict, then in progress on every side, he could not bury himself in the retire-ment of his parish and domestic circle. On the con-trary he felt bound, with recovered strength and increas-ing zeal, to use the influence which God had now given him, in bearing witness against dangerous errors ; and to contend earnestly for the faith once for all delivered to the saints, against open infidelity, ecclesiastical formalism, and the counterfeits of self-religious superstition. His reflections, at the close of the year, shew the spirit with which he entered on these difficult and arduous duties.

"*December* 24, 1842. . . . The whole world is now at peace. It looks like the calm before the storm—the pause before the judgment.

" O my God, preserve me from evil! preserve me from displeasing Thee! Keep me pure from the pollutions on every side. I see much evil in all around; and doubtless there is much in myself, which I see not. Prepare me for Thy service, and bless me in it. In contending with error, keep me from its many temptations; from magnifying the evil of the error; from want of love to those in error; from partial views of truth, and from every snare! O may the close of this year be much blessed to me, to my family, and to my parish."

The reflections written on his next birth-day, shew his deep impression of the eventful character of the times, and his earnest longing for special wisdom in the fulfilment of his own public duties.

"*March* 19. . . Never did I live in so awakening and trying a time. The Church of Scotland is shaking to its foundations, and the Church of England is so inwardly divided, that a schism seems inevitable. It looks like a great breaking-up year; and my situation has been so public, and I have in God's providence been called to take such a part in the cause of Christ generally, that I desire most deeply to feel my responsibility, and the importance of every step which I take; that I may not be ashamed of the gospel—that I may be bold in our God to testify it —that I may discern the things that differ—that I may be wise as a serpent, and harmless as a dove—that I

may not needlessly occasion division, but be of a peace-
making, and peace-loving spirit, while I hold and diffuse
His truth.   O God, my God, help me !  for Thou knowest
how weak I am ; and without Thy aid every moment I
cannot but fall.   O then, grant that, by Thy aid, I may
be made wise and strong, holy and loving, meet every
difficult, and so be a full blessing to Thy Church !   Mine
eyes are up unto Thee, in this great and critical time, for
heavenly guidance, holy boldness, fervent love, a sound
judgment, and a devoted heart !

"I cannot conceive how those who groan, as I do,
under formality and deadness of heart in outward services, can press them so much as men are now doing.
My daily grief and sorrow is, that I so little walk with
God, even in forms of worship, that my prayers are my
sin and my burthen.   I dare not seek the incessant multiplication of the form, lest I should become wholly,
dead and formal."

He was soon called to exercise those difficult graces for
which he had prayed so earnestly.   Seven years before,
in his remarks on the Progress of Popery, he had pointed
out in gentle, but forcible terms, the true character and
tendency of the Tractarian movement.   It had now proceeded so far as to threaten the total corruption or disruption of the Church of England.   The avowals in No.
XC., the open adoption of nearly all Popish doctrines,
by those who still claimed to be leaders in a Protestant
Church ; and the vague, neutral, indecisive course, pursued by too many of the bishops, created a serious question of conscience among those who loved the Church of
England for the gospel's sake, of which they held her to
be the national witness, and the appointed and honoured
guardian.   Some of the Church Societies acted on the

rule, that they were not responsible for the teaching of the clergy whom they maintained; and that such inquiries belonged solely to the bishop of the diocese where each of them might be labouring. This principle, however untenable on Scriptural grounds, would have involved little practical danger, had all the bishops been decided in their adherence to Reformation-truth, and if no serious falling away had occurred within the Church's own bosom. But when a conspiracy to unprotestantize it had been openly avowed, and was in constant operation, maintained by systematic evasions of its public code of doctrine, and when the whole cycle of Romish teaching and practices was gradually introduced, while some of the bishops maintained a timid silence, and some flattered and abetted the growing evil; grave doubts could not fail to arise, whether any Society, which abdicated the chief part of its responsibility by such a rule of action, could be fitly trusted with the free-will offerings of consistent Churchmen.

Early in 1843 this question arose in the Society for Propagating the Gospel. Some recent disclosures of evil had increased the jealousy, to which its professed rule of conduct naturally exposed it, at such a time, in the minds of those who valued the purity of the gospel far above any ecclesiastical forms. Along with Mr. Pratt, Mr. Close, and many others, both clergymen and laymen, Mr. Bickersteth was in serious doubt whether he could continue a member of the Society, without a distinct pledge that the Committee would not knowingly employ any clergyman, who held and propagated Tractarian opinions, instead of the Gospel of Christ. A correspondence ensued, of some length, which he afterwards published. The Committee made a declaration, less distinct than the

crisis required, that they would adhere to the plain sense
of the Articles and Liturgy, as their rule of examination ;
and a Circular was issued by the Archbishops and Bishops,
expressing their confidence in the Society. Mr. Bickersteth, although by no means fully satisfied, conceived that
the public pledge thus given was sufficient to warrant
him in continuing a member of the Society, while the
openings were so vast, and so many faithful and zealous
labourers were sustained by it ; and his example was
followed by most of those who had shared his own
scruples. One or two of his letters at the time will best
explain his motives, and the spirit of faithfulness to the
Gospel, and love to the cause of missions, which guided
him both in his protest and his final decision. The first
of these, to the Secretary of the Society, explains the reasons and conditions of his adherence.

*Watton Rectory, March* 31, 1843.

My dear Sir,

I have received your reply of the 30th to mine of the 16th, with
the circular containing the letters of the Archbishops and Bishops.

Nothing can be more satisfactory than the Committee's statement of their adherence to the plain and grammatical meaning of
our Articles and Liturgy ; and, strengthened as this statement has
been to me by other communications, which justify me in cherish-
ing the hope that there is a more anxious care exercised in ascer-
taining the religious views of candidates, than the Committee may
feel themselves at liberty to profess ; and not doubting that what
has taken place will confirm this anxiety, I do not feel that I am at
present under the painful necessity of withdrawing from the Society.
Its object is unspeakably dear to all Christians, being that for
which they are taught by our Lord daily to pray, so that it should
be a very plain case of departure from its great design, to make me
separate.

In continuing, however, my support to the Society, it is due to myself and to the truth to say, it is done with this understanding, that it is the real purpose of the Committee to send forth ministers, cordially attached to the doctrines of our Church in their plain and literal sense. Departure from this line of proceeding will disable me, in real consistency of conduct, from continuing to be a member.

At the same time I regret to say, I differ materially from the Society in that part of their reply, which declines making inquiry on points involved in the controversies of the present day. This seems, in its natural meaning, to contradict the other parts of the letter. It is not past, but present errors, which require vigilance on the part of the Committee. The mere existence or prevalence of views, which do oppose the plain and literal sense of the Articles, will of course make them come under the definition, a controversy of the present day. Caution against any error would thus be set aside in every case, at the only time when it is practically needed. When Arianism was unhappily a controversy in our own Church in the last century, this only made it more needful for a responsible Church Society to guard against sending out Arian Missionaries. And when there is an avowed design of unprotestantizing the Church, and an open attempt to turn the Articles from their plain and literal sense, the existence of the controversy, instead of being a valid reason for refusing to inquire on such points, appears to me to make the duty more plainly imperative than ever.

The letters of approbation, with which the Society has been favoured from our Archbishops and Bishops, are strong testimonies to the importance of the object, and its general claims on the support of Churchmen. Their expressions of confidence in the judgment and proceedings of the Committee, ought, doubtless, to have considerable weight. At the same time, I may be permitted to observe, that but few of them bear on the precise object of this correspondence; and in those which do refer to it, the approval seems to be founded on differing principles. One ground of confidence is, that the Society has never abandoned the principles of the Reformation; but another considers indifference to party distinctions as one of the excellences of the Society. At a time when

a purpose has been avowed openly, to recede further and further
from the principles of the English Reformation, these two grounds
appear to me inconsistent, and I can only fully concur with the
former.

I am led to this expression of partial dissent, only from a sense
of the supreme importance of the principles at issue ; and that no
names, however venerable, and no hopes, however reasonable or
charitable, can secure the cordial co-operation of members, conscientiously attached to the doctrines of our Church, without a consistent, practical adherence to the principles laid down in the other
part of your letter.

It is really painful to me to have principles in question, when I
should rejoice to give myself to efforts for relieving that need which
is so urgent.    Yet I cannot but hope that these differences, and this
need, may both help the great cause.    All our religious societies
greatly suffer from general ignorance, as well as from general indifference.    England as yet does nothing for missions, to what
might be done, were British hearts really alive to the magnitude and
blessedness of the work.    The conflicts through which our Societies
have to make their way, will, I trust, both purify and advance
them : *and while they adhere to the truth,* will help on their full
success.    I doubt not, I speak the feeling of revered fathers and
brethren in connection with the Society, when I say, the more open
we are in the confession of the great and peculiar truths of the
gospel of the grace of God, the more HE, our blessed Redeemer,
from whom alone all success must come, will prosper our Society ;
and the more entirely will His people yield their talents of every
kind, and their fervent prayers, to that which will then be so manifestly His own cause.    While on lesser points we ought to be forbearing, on great matters, affecting the foundation, we can have no
neutrality.

My name having been published, without my knowledge, as
having left the Society, it appeared to me due to the Society, as well
as to myself, for me to communicate publicly this official correspondence; more especially as I am able to adhere to it ; and my trust
is, that friends, over whom I have influence, may thus be prevented

from leaving it, or be disposed, if they have left it, to join it again, on the principles thus fully stated. I should have felt more confidence in this hope, if the answer of the Society had been more unequivocal. With hearty wishes for its highest prosperity, in the firm maintenance, and wide diffusion, of the blessed gospel of our Lord, I am

Yours faithfully,<br>
E. BICKERSTETH.

*Rev. A. Campbell.*

Two letters, one of them four days earlier, and the other a week later, to one of the Bishops, whose judgment had especial weight with him, explains still further his feelings in this delicate and important business.

*March* 27, 1843.

MY DEAR LORD BISHOP,

Your letter of the 25th has greatly relieved my mind on that, on which all true Christians must have a common interest, the preservation of the gospel of Christ in its purity. The answer of the Society to Mr. Percival, in December, led me and many others distinctly to the conviction, that the Committee were indifferent to the heretical perversions of the gospel, which your Lordship, as well as many other heads of our Church, had distinctly condemned; and hence to view ourselves, while members of the Society, as maintainers of those perversions, which made it impossible for us, so thinking, conscientiously to support it. Your Lordship's letter has done, what could hardly have been done so satisfactorily from any other quarter—restored real confidence in the purposes of the Committee on this subject.

I should rejoice yet more, if the Committee had taken the decided part which your Lordship has done: but I would make full allowance for the many difficulties of their situation; and on receiving the letter to which your Lordship refers, will write to the Society, and shall be indeed thankful, not to be obliged to with-

draw.   Suspension, not separation, is both Mr. Pratt's and my own
present position ; and it is the more anxious and distressing, as it
has been made public, and our conduct affects so many others.  The
Lord give us the full blessings of all the beatitudes, and the crown
of all, " the peacemakers."   I have the honour to be—very gratefully and faithfully,

Your Lordship's obliged servant,
E. BICKERSTETH.

Watton Rectory, April 6.

MY LORD,

Having been indebted to your Lordship's letter for much of my
ability to come to the purpose of adhering to the Society, I enclose
you the correspondence I have published.   O may our God give us
all, realizing faith in the unutterable importance of confessing and
maintaining His own Truth !   Soon we shall all stand in judgment
before Him, and every thing but His favour be found to be vanity ;
and that favour is deeply and closely connected with holding the
truth in love.   I doubt not your Lordship fully sympathizes in this,
and have the honour to be,

Very faithfully yours,
E. BICKERSTETH.

While this correspondence was in progress, Mr. Bickersteth was also taking an active part in a direct Protest
against Tractarianism, which was published soon after,
with the signatures of more than four thousand of the
clergy.   At a time, when the whole system of Romish
doctrine was being propagated within the bosom of the
Church, and the infection was spreading wider every day,
he felt that longer silence, on the part of the Protestant
and Evangelical Clergy, would be a grievous neglect of
the plainest duty, and that some combined testimony
was needed, to clear them from partaking in the sin of
others.   Some passages in a letter written on the subject

to a beloved friend, who preferred a different wording of
the Protest, and feared evil consequences from the number who would not sign, are characteristic of his faithfulness and affection in carrying on a difficult and responsible work.

*March* 25, 1843.

MY BELOVED BROTHER,

. . . . The matter on which we chiefly differ is here. You are
fearful that, if our numbers are only 4 or 5000, the remaining 10 or
11,000 will be claimed by the Tractarians, and the issue be perilous
to the truth. Dear brother, this is not right. This is not the new
man, but the old ; you know it as well as I do. Twelve Apostles
won the day, and the little flock prevailed over the Roman Empire.
It is truth, not numbers, that prevails; and this is simply a testimony to the truth, and it will and must grow and spread and triumph, because it is truth.

There is no fear of the effect upon those who do not sign it, and
who dislike Tractarianism, nor of the boastings of Tractarians over
us on account of it. Those who are true-hearted men, like my dear
brother, will only be stirred up to use their own artillery with
double energy ; those who are indifferent will be compelled in the
end to choose one side or other, and our Lord shews us, lukewarmness is the worst state His professing servants can be in. The
boasting will be very short. But, in the meanwhile, we are relieving
and gladdening many a faithful brother, longing for a public opportunity of testifying his adherence, before the Church, to the great
truths of the Reformation. We are getting many a confession of
Christ and his truth. We are taking a first step towards a greater
and fuller union of His faithful servants. We are learning of many
we before knew not, who are on the Lord's side. And by and by
we shall be led to a longer, fuller, and more distinct testimony to
the truth as it is in Jesus.

. . . Our brethren will allow to us that faith is the best wisdom,
and to be bold in our God, and in the confession of his truth, the

L 5

most judicious course, in days when abounding error would confound light and darkness, and bring us back again to the Apostasy.  O how guilty shall we be, if we are not now valiant for the truth ! You go along with every word of

Your very affectionate Brother,<br>E. BICKERSTETH.

In a letter, written April 10, to another friend, who had been discouraged by the opposition of his own bishop, from procuring signatures to the Protest, he wrote as follows.

It is not a thing lawful thus to forbid us to fulfil our ordination vow.  The end is imperative, the means are lawful, and a faithful testimony to the truth never can strengthen error.

But why are we so afraid of contending for the faith once de-livered to the saints ?  Has not our Saviour himself told us, I came not to send peace, but a sword ?  Has He not shewn us that the worst kind of peace is when the strong man armed keepeth his house ;  and that he must be dispossessed by One stronger than he, coming upon him ?  Why are we so afraid of numbers against us, and few for us ?  Is not the very character of our faith, victory over the world, and the very description of the Church, a little flock ?  If the first disciples, if the Reformers, had acted on such views, where would Christian truth have now been ?  We expected the measure to be much spoken against, because it is a faithful stand for real Church principles, that is, God's own truth, against heretical perversions of the gospel.  But we have counted the cost, and cannot and will not draw back, and discourage the hearts of faithful brother ministers.

. . . . Thus, my dear friend, with faith, courage, and prayer, you may more than recover all you have lost.  No human authority can *lawfully* silence our testimony to the truth.  We are the servants of the Lord, and of men *for His sake*.  Our chief authority is from Him, and we are mainly responsible to Him.  We must therefore follow His directions, so plainly and so fully given in His word, to confess His truth boldly and openly, whoever gainsays or resists, to be valiant for it, and especially at a time when it is perverted, and turned into deadly poison.

I know you concur with me, and God himself guide, strengthen, comfort, and bless you, prays,

Yours very affectionately,

E. BICKERSTETH.

Early in the Session of 1843, Lord Ashley brought forward a motion in Parliament, condemnatory of the Opium tráffic ; that foul stain on our national character, which was the immediate occasion of the war with China, and still continues the grand stumbling-block of Satan, to dishonour the name of Christ, and hinder all missionary efforts, in that immense empire. The motion was unhappily unsuccessful, and Mammon prevailed in high places over the fear of God and the love of man. Mr. Bickersteth felt himself bound, for the honour of the gospel, to depart from his usual silence on political questions, especially when the pleas of worldly men seemed to have infected some Christian minds. He protested, in a public letter, against the heinous national sin, and against the folly of those arguments, which would palliate and excuse a great public crime, by the prevalence of other iniquities. Such reasonings, he justly observed, as they tamper with the great Christian principles of the gospel, would, if generally adopted, poison the very fountains of public morality.

A few days after bearing public testimony against this great national iniquity, he wrote the following to a young friend in his own parish, with reference to her approaching confirmation :

*April* 12, 1843.

MY DEAR C.

I think I need not assure you that, amidst incessant public duties, I have not forgotten, as your own Pastor, that most interesting occasion, on which you will publicly acknowledge God as your God, Jesus as your Saviour, and the Holy Ghost as your guide, Sanctifier, and Comforter. A consistent adherence to this profession, I know, is holiness, usefulness, and happiness here, and leads to glory now inconceivable, soon to be revealed, and without end, hereafter.

Almighty God graciously pour upon you a very large and full measure of His Spirit, that as He has given you many singular advantages for glorifying His name, and benefitting your fellow-creatures, you may both feel the responsibility, and enjoy the full blessing, of thus occupying the talents entrusted to you.

The difficulty is in patiently taking up daily and self-denying duties, without finding in them that glow of feeling, which the more direct means of grace, and the powerful preaching of the gospel, in happier moments excite in us. We delight in pleasurable excitement, and are unwilling to pay the price of sharp sacrifices and patient labour, which are absolutely requisite to make us mature, steady, and consistent Christians, full of blessing to all around us, and adorning the doctrine of God our Saviour in all things.

To help you in this, my dear young friend, remember—all we receive now, precious as it is, is but the earnest of good to come. Sweet communion with God our Saviour in prayer, the full assurance of His loving-kindness, fellowship of spirit with His people, and such like rich mercies, are merely refreshments in our pilgrimage, and supports in our warfare. But oh! to look forward to the exceeding and eternal weight of glory yet to come—this animated Patriarchs and Prophets, Apostles and Martyrs, and our most precious and sympathizing Saviour himself.

My greatest fear for you is, that strength of your feelings, which is one of the best gifts the Lord has bestowed upon you, but which, without much watchfulness and prayer, may often lead you astray, when you think that you are right, and others wrong. You are necessarily yet inexperienced, and incompetent to judge on a great variety of subjects which will come before you ; and if you give way to the impulses of the moment, you may seriously mistake, and bring trouble and sorrow on yourself, and those who love you best. What you need here, is to be sensible of our deep ignorance of Divine things, to pause, to reflect, and above all, to pray much for Divine guidance, and search much the Holy Scriptures.

The Lord appoints each thing in your portion—your parents, your friends, your pastors, and all relations around you; and in honouring each relation, by consulting them, submitting to them, and seeking to be a comfort and blessing to them, according to His directions, and under the help of his Spirit, what a peaceful, heavenly, and happy course will be yours ! I yearn over you with parental affection and hope, to see you also a part of my joy and crown in the day of Christ, now, I believe, near at hand.

Your very affectionate Pastor,<br>E. Bickersteth.

The same spring had witnessed an attempt, chiefly among Dissenters, to promote a fuller exhibition of Christian union, on the part of those who held the great essentials of Divine truth. The resolutions adopted at a public meeting, with a view to this object, were forwarded to him by Mr. Sherman, and the following letter was sent in reply.

Watton Rectory, April 17.

My dear Sir,

I cannot but regard, with deep interest, the efforts which our brethren among the Dissenters are making, to promote real union in the Church of Christ, amidst their various outward distinctions ; and heartily pray that it may please the Lord of all, abundantly to prosper these efforts for the accomplishment of so blessed an end.

I will consult with my brethren, as I have opportunity, on the subject, and shall be thankful if the way should be open to us, in

any measure to concur publicly in your proceedings.  I doubt not
that matters will rapidly ripen, so as to make all real Christians
gladly unite against the increasing violence of infidelity, on the one
hand, and superstition on the other. . . . .

I feel great oneness with the spirit of the resolutions, and very
thankful that the Lord has put it into your hearts, thus to labour to
be peacemakers in the highest and best sense.  Beyond all our fears
and hopes, may He prosper the measure !

Affectionately yours,<br>
E. BICKERSTETH.

P.S.—It appears to me, that conjoint humiliation for our differences would be a more suitable close of the Fourth Resolution than
the disclaiming of compromise.  There is one ground of agreement, so peculiarly important—so truly conciliatory to all classes
who love the Lord, and in which our harmony is so full, that it
might well come in as a closing Resolution.  I mean, the practical part of Christianity, such as Christian graces, the beatitudes,
holy tempers and dispositions, relative duties, and the like.  As
far as I know the Christian men who have signed, they would all
agree on this ground of union ; and I am sure it would tend to
bring us all nearer together.

The principle, enforced in this Postscript, moulded all
Mr. Bickersteth's later efforts in the cause of Christian
union.  No one was more alive to the inefficacy of mere
professions, or mechanical expedients, in advancing so
glorious an object.  In his " Promised Glory," a few
months later, he thus alluded to the chief difficulty
attending the efforts, to which the previous letter refers.

" The nations of the earth shall yet behold with wonder the
glorious sight of myriads on myriads of ransomed sinners, all
animated by one mind, happy in one love, making a complete sacrifice of selfish partialities, pride, and vain glory; unreservedly

devoted to one Lord, joyful in one hope, and all made meet by one Spirit for the inheritance of the saints in light.

" Many excellent publications to promote Christian union have been issued in late years, and an important meeting for the same object was held June 1. 1843. May each effort of the kind be increasingly successful ! . . . . . But I fear, our Lord's rebuke, ' Ye know not what manner of Spirit ye are of,' applies yet very largely to us. While we are each magnifying the excellences of our own system, and depreciating one to which we are hostile, setting in bright colours all our fancied superiority, and in dark shades the defects in others, it is really in vain to make any call to union. More is done by forbearance, and kind constructions, and silence on the faults of others, and willingness to take the lowest seat, than by the loudest commendations, each of our own Church, or the most earnest professions of the value of union, and the most eloquent addresses to urge it on others, if there be no corresponding spirit of self-sacrifice, meekness, and love. Oh that we might all sit more at the feet of Jesus, learn of Him who was meek and lowly in heart, and seek only His exaltation. . . . . .

" It is delightful to realize the progressive growth of union, the preparation on earth for the heavenly Jerusalem. The Church of Christ is compared to the building of a temple, of which believers are the lively stones. Before the temple was built, there was a vast preparation of materials ; each stone was made ready, before it was brought. So is it in this more glorious Temple. Silently and without noise, the heavenly Architect is preparing stone after stone, exactly fitted for its place in the glorious temple. Not one is lost. Each is gathered safely, and placed surely ; and at last He shall bring forth the head stone thereof with shoutings, crying, grace, grace unto it."

The spring of the year was specially memorable for the disruption in the Church of Scotland, and the formal constitution of the Free Church. Mr. Bickersteth, without a full approbation of that movement, regarded it in

a more favourable light than many of his own brethren
in the Church of England. He was unable to agree with
those arguments, which decided the whole question by
a mere assertion of the duty of a General Assembly to
submit to the laws of the land, when once declared by
the highest authority. Such reasoning, he thought, was
a virtual denial of the visible Church, as a distinct ordinance of Christ. The union of Church and State, in his
view, was that of two co-ordinate powers, alike holding
from Christ as their supreme Head, and might be dissolved, on either side, if there were a departure from the
express or implied conditions. He believed, also, that
there were great evils and anomalies in an unrestricted
and absolute right of patronage, and inclined to the
opinion, that historical and constitutional right was on
the side of the Free Church in the first stages of the
movement. On the other hand, he thought that only
a plain departure from a scriptural law of duty, imposed
on the Church, would justify so grave a step as the dissolution of such an alliance, and that the evils of patronage would be equalled, or even surpassed, by a purely
democratic or popular election of ministers. His convictions that the path of duty was at least doubtful, concurred
with his admiration for conscientious sacrifices, to produce at the time a very deep sympathy with the pious
members of the Secession ; and though his more deliberate judgment, afterwards, was one of regret at the separation, he never ceased to honour the motives, the characters, the zeal, and the piety, of the chief actors in that
great movement. A letter of June 17, to Dr. Chalmers,
expresses his feelings at the time, and differs very slightly
from his later judgment, while it shews his watchful care
for the maintenance of Christian love.

My dear Dr. Chalmers,

I think I need not say that the proceedings in Scotland, in which you have been so deeply concerned, have excited great interest among all who have at heart the spiritual prosperity of the Church of Christ in England.   Many prayers, and much anxiety and sympathy have been called forth, though I fear you have had but little expression of this sympathy.   I am anxious to write a few lines, at any rate, to speak my own feelings. . . . .

I bless God, my dear Dr. Chalmers, for the spirit of wisdom and love which have marked your addresses, and those of Dr. Candlish, Dr. Gordon, Dr. Macfarlane, and several others.   Be assured, all expressions of faith, hope, and love, of Christian humility, self-distrust and forbearance, of the meekness and gentleness of Christ, find a ready response in the hearts of your brethren in the Established Church of England, and open our affectionate feelings towards you, as one with us.

Yet on the other hand, some of the addresses have been so marked by levity and bitterness, by hardness and pugnacious severity, that I have felt the great importance of their being discountenanced. . . . . . . . The paper entitled " Lochiel's Warning," is a specimen of what I mean ; and which it appears to me greatly to concern the honour of our Master and His cause, that the leading members of the Free Presbyterian Church should discourage.

Sufferings, real sufferings, for the truth's sake, are, I believe, before us, as the way to full victory and glory.   Earnest contention for the truth, with the meekness of wisdom, and a good conversation, are our clear duty.   But it appears to me, we look too little at the *privilege* of suffering for our Master ; and we want the kingdom, while we lose sight of the cross as the way to it—as the blessed Apostles themselves did.

But the difficulties of your situation must be very great, both from within and without.   My assured hope is, that the Lord is with you, and will strengthen you for and in every trial.   May He do so more and more.   This is the strength the world is wholly unacquainted with. . . .   Believe me, in the bonds of the gospel,

and in the love of our one and only Lord and Saviour, Jesus
Christ,

Ever affectionately yours,

E. BICKERSTETH.

P.S.  I ought to mention, that from the complexity and difficulty
of the questions at issue, many of my beloved brethren in the
English Church, whose own eye and heart are single, as far as man
can judge, for the Lord, do not concur in the steps which you
have taken; and there will be required, on the part of the Free
Presbyterian Church, much forbearance, and abstinence from censure and condemnation of those who differ from them.  Let us all
remember, ' Blessed are the meek, for they shall inherit the earth.'

In a letter, a few days later, to Dr. Hamilton of the
Scotch Church, he remarked in the same spirit of friendly
caution,—" There are rocks on every side, and I fear lest,
among any of those connected with the movement, a democratic element should overpower the evangelical.  We
need yet to learn the invincible power of the meekness
and gentleness of Christ."

The entries in his journal at this time, show that the
consciousness, daily forced upon him, of the influence he
had acquired, was attended with a deep sense of responsibility, and led him to pray earnestly for grace and wisdom from on high.

"*March* 26. . . . I am full of work with Protests, now
signing by the clergy through the country, against Tractarianism.  O Lord, help me to defend Thy truth wisely
and scripturally!  Give me courage, judgment, and love,
as well as power to maintain Thy gospel.

" But specially help me in home duties—closet—family
—parish—my immediate sphere.  Oh let me not keep
other vineyards to the neglect of my own!  Deal boun-

tifully with Thy servant, that I may live in my own circle the life of faith, hope, and love, each day.

"Great is the work before me. Oh for unction, holiness, love, strength, and zeal for Christ's sake!

"*April* 15. . . . It is a time of great divisions, even among the children of God, as well as in the world. I have been called on to write three letters to the Gospel Propagation Society, testifying against Tractarian tendencies; but hoping they may yet be checked, I adhere to the Society. It is a serious matter to cripple a Society that has done much for God, and I do not feel justified in so doing.

"Oh how greatly I need unction from above, and Divine power, to new-create my soul, and raise me out of a formal, heartless state. I contend against professed formalism! but oh, how much I am weighed down by the reality of formalism in my own course, day by day.

"Blessed Jesus, risen Saviour, let grace abound over my sin, and all glory be rendered to Thy holy name!

"*January* 28. . . . The post of each day generally brings important letters, that require much wisdom in answering, not to err on the right hand or on the left. Lord, give me that wisdom! My situation becomes increasingly responsible, as my fellow-Christians look up to me more for help and guidance. O Lord, in every thing make me a fuller blessing to Thy Church!"

In May Mr. Bickersteth, as usual, attended and spoke at several of the London meetings, and afterwards journeyed to Derbyshire, Nottinghamshire, and Liverpool, for different religious objects. During his absence, he noticed several symptoms of a decline in the interest taken in the Bible Society, and the following letter was consequently written soon after his return.

*Watton Rectory, June 7.*

MY DEAR BRANDRAM,

I write to you to bring before you my anxiety about our Bible Society. It is not in the state it ought to be. The Parent Anniversary discouraged me—that at Liverpool, at which I spoke for you, did much more. Our most devoted and spiritual Evangelical brethren stand aloof. It is bad for them, the Church, the Dissenters, the Society.

We, who love all, ought not to let matters rest so. We want more religious stamina in the Society; and the Christian Union shows us we might have it, and our Society more than recover all its lost ground, and become truly the Philadelphia of Christendom. The Socinians and the Papists may well be dropped. They cannot consistently support the circulation of our version. They really encumber; they aid us not.

I think, if an address could be prepared to all evangelical ministers, with evangelical extracts from the Reports of the Society from the beginning, it might lay hold on the consciences of faithful brethren, making an earnest appeal to them now to unite with us on principles which have been so clearly confessed by the Society. To this I would add—let all the Parent Society Meetings begin with two or three Psalms, and the Lord's Prayer from the gospels. We must make more of a profession of the truth, or we shall sink more and more. And yet, on the other hand, there are most favourable symptoms of longing for real union on Evangelical principles.

Do not, my dear brother, throw this aside hastily. I have adhered to the Society from the beginning. It may yet, I trust, be God's instrument for uniting His people, and overthrowing Infidelity, Popery and lawlessness; but I am persuaded it must take another stand of confession of Evangelical truth. I quite suffered anguish in seeing such a noble cause so deserted by men who love our Lord Jesus Christ with all their heart.

Affectionately yours,

E. BICKERSTETH.

P.S. I send you a Sermon which may interest you.

The Sermon thus alluded to was the one preached for the Foreign Aid Society, and in which the duty of Christian union was urged, but with a special reference to foreign churches only. This explains the opening remarks in the next letter.

*June* 21.

MY DEAR BRANDRAM,

I like much your sensible letter, and agree with you I have not in my Sermon " taken the bull by the horns ; " but the reason there was, that I had to take care of the Foreign Aid Society, which confines its labours to foreign churches.

I have no doubt, Dissenting ministers, holding the Head, and appointed by their congregations, are true ministers of Christ, their sacraments true sacraments, and their congregations true churches of Christ; and I hope, in publishing the Sermon I sent you in another form, to avow this. But then they must not confound the Church of England and Puseyism, and make us all Papists. Our external co-operation has hitherto exceeded our internal sympathy, and hence much of it has been hollow ; and providential events are showing our discordance and separation. Let doctrinal union take the lead, and the practical union will follow. Hence I want some more distinct exhibition of the doctrinal principles of the Bible Society, such as the extracts from the reports would give. You know that all the strength of the Society is in the true servants of Christ. Then let them confess their Master, where they see alike, and all who love their Master will join on open confession of His truth.

It is our joy, my dear brother, that the work of the Society is increasing, and that means are afforded, and blessed effects follow ; but this should increase our faith, and efforts for larger means and fuller effects.

Your *month* is so obscure, that I do not know whether you wish to convene the clergy in June, July, or January ; but I would come,

at any time in my power, for objects so blessed as promoting the
Bible Society and Christian union.

Most affectionately yours,

E. BICKERSTETH.

The notes of Mr. Bickersteth, amidst these various
engagements, to his beloved friend, General Marshall,
exhibit his earnest zeal for the cause of Christ, and his
deep sense of the eventful character of the times.

*February* 16.

MY DEAR GENERAL,

We never had, I think, in Wellington's warfare, sharper fighting
than Christians now have with error on all sides; no neutrality
will soon be allowed to any one. My correspondence is quite remarkable in this view. . . . The state of the masses of the people
is increasingly fearful; truly, the unclean spirits are all at work
obviously enough to the spiritual mind. But HE must increase,
must conquer, whom we love best of all.

I had a letter from Oxford this morning; Popery is ripening
fast. Newman has retracted every thing sharp that he has said
against Rome. The Scotch Episcopalians wanted to enlist the
Church Missionary Society against Drummond, but the Committee
is firm, and they have failed. . . . Oh let us walk closely with our
Saviour; He will come and save us from the tribulation, now, I
believe, near at hand.

Yours affectionately,

E. BICKERSTETH.

*March* 3.

MY DEAREST GENERAL MARSHALL,

It is a real pleasure to hear from you; what interesting facts
your letter contains ! . . .

It is our unspeakable comfort that the Lord Jesus presides over
all, and carries on His vast schemes of love and goodness, against,
and even by, the very machinations of those who oppose Him. Let

us rest in Him, and rejoice in Him, and get more and more of His own wise, holy, and loving spirit. When I contend with men, ardour of spirit soon inflames me, but it is a mingled fire. When I look to the love of God in Christ Jesus, tenderness and compassion, self-abasement and meekness, mingle with the spirit of zeal and devotedness. . . .

I have been so struck with the good likely to be done by Sewell's Irish College, that I have joined Lord Ashley (that noble fellow) and M'Neile, in subscribing to it. If the Tractarians fairly meet the Romanist in Ireland, (and this is the great object of the College,) they are likely both to get and to do good ; and we shew our Master's spirit, when we meet them where we can. Should you see ——, perhaps you will tell him what I have done.

Most truly yours,<br>E. BICKERSTETH.

March 23.

MY DEAR GENERAL,

. . . The " Protest " is battling through the country. Many have tried to stop it, but on it goes.

As to the College, I followed M'Neile and Lord Ashley ; and if any thing can do them good, it is fighting with Irish priests, their very object. I thought it worth a venture, and if I find myself in a snare, the Lord helping, I will get out, to their cost who would ensnare us. I never knew any thing like the movement of this day. Shall we meet in town on the 7th, when I preach a Lecture on prophecy ?

July 21.

DEAR GENERAL,

We are as full of work as the day is of hours, and enter into that expression, " hardly time to eat bread "—but thanks be to God for work to do, and health and strength to do it !

On Tuesday we have a large meeting on the lawn, if fine, to form a County Church Pastoral Aid Society. I enclose you the circular, that you may help us by prayer.   Blessed be God for all His goodness.

Ever affectionately yours,<br>E. BICKERSTETH.

A few extracts from his private journal will shew some of his engagements in the later months of the year.

" *June* 3. . . . I have been to Sapcote, Liverpool, Chesterfield, Retford, Newark, Eastwood and Nottingham. The Lord prosper what has been said and done in these places, and forgive all the iniquities of my best services.

" I am going, please God, to Cambridge on Monday, to preach and speak for the Church Pastoral Aid Society. Gracious Father, prosper Thou the effort.   Is there not a cause ? . . .

" *July* 1.   God has been very gracious in using me, at Cambridge for the Church Pastoral Aid, in London for the Accident Relief Society, and at Hertford for the Protestant Association—all glory be to His holy name.

" That one so sinful should be used by One so holy is wonderful grace.   Why am I not cast out of His service, as a worse than unprofitable servant ?   This is owing to sovereign grace.

" *July* 29.   The last month has been one of many mercies.   The Church Missionary, Bible, and Religious Tract Societies in this country have had good anniversaries ; and the Lord's Day Observance and Church Pastoral Aid, have had auxiliaries formed on the 17th and 25th. The school-children have had their annual feast ; and God seems to have prospered all.   £160, was raised within this week for the Church Pastoral Aid Society. All glory be to our most merciful Father !   May we walk very humbly.

" I have had dear Christian friends, the Auriols, staying here last month, and we have found it good to have
our Master's children with us.

" O Lord, prepare me for Thy table. . . . God make
me a real, a full, a lasting blessing to my people, to His
Church, to my country, my fellow-men everywhere, for
Christ's sake.

" *August* 16. . . . I have sent a new work to the press,
to be entitled, ' The Promised Glory of the Church of
Christ.' O that the Lord may so assist me in it, that it
may be useful to Hi s people !

" There is before me a visit to Dyrham Park, for the
Jews, and to Reading for the Church Missionary Society,
as well as other journeys.

" The state of the world is remarkable, in the shaking
of all things. Oh, that our hearts may be fixed on unseen
and eternal things, and we may walk closely with God,
in self-sacrifice, and self-denial ! "

The work on the Promised Glory of the Church of
Christ, published at the close of the year, was an enlargement of four sermons, which Mr. Bickersteth had
preached on kindred subjects, for various Societies. Its
chief topics were the Progress and Permanence of Divine
Truth, the Union of Christians, already begun, and to be
perfected hereafter, the Reward of Works at the coming
of Christ, and the Glory of the Heavenly Kingdom. The
last of these was peculiarly congenial to his fervent and
joyous spirit, and was largely unfolded in a practical
commentary on the closing portion of the Book of Revelation. The whole work contained many references to
the actual state of the Church, and the dangers it involved, and enforced the need of prayer and watchfulness among the people of Christ. Several ecclesiastical

topics of importance were treated of in Appendices at the
close.   In one of these the main doctrines of Tractarianism were briefly stated, in the form of articles, and contrasted with the truths of Scripture, and the Articles of
the Church of England.   Another was chiefly composed
of various documents, to prove the growth of direct
Mariolatry in the Romish Church.   The last was on a
subject, to which attention has been recently drawn once
more.   It contained historical proofs, from the writings
of English Episcopal Divines, including Bishops Andrews,
Cosins, Bramhall, and Parker, and Archbishops Laud and
Usher, of a friendly recognition of foreign Protestant
Churches, and of the orders of their ministers.   But the
main feature of the volume was the glowing earnestness
of Christian hope, with which the reader was led onward
through times of change and trouble, to contemplate the
sure reward of the true servants of Christ, and the
glory of His coming kingdom.

   " *September* 23. . . . The harvest I find always a time
injurious to my people.  Sad it is that the season of God's
mercies should be made the occasion of men's sins !—but
it is a little flock that is gathered from an evil world.
May God mercifully show to me, and help me to correct
without delay, anything in me that is wanting to meet
the wants of my flock.

   " There is a calm over the whole face of Christendom,
but manifestations break out, of the evil working within.
In Russia, is an Ukase against the Jews.   In Ancona, a
persecuting edict of the Inquisition.   In Spain, a fresh
revolution ; in Italy, risings of the people.   In Turkey the
Nestorians are persecuted, and a convert from Mahomet-
anism has been executed, for professing Christianity.   In
our own country, in Scotland, five hundred ministers

have left the Established Church ; in Ireland, the Repeal
agitation has spread through the land ; in Wales, a spirit
of rebellion prevails ; and in England, Tractarianism,
Socialism, and Chartism are spreading.

"*October* 28. . . . I have been blessed in several public
duties. On Monday, the 16th, I addressed the missionaries going to Africa, including Samuel Crowther, a negro,
episcopally ordained by the Bishop of London. It was an
era in the Society.

" I have before me journeys to Bristol, Bath, and
London, with public sermons for the Jews, Church Pastoral Aid, and Indigent Blind. The Lord strengthen me
for every duty, and bless me in all His work ! "

The dismissal of Mr. Crowther, and the other African
missionaries, had a double interest for Mr. Bickersteth,
from his early visit to the Sierra Leone colony, and might
be truly called a new era in the Society. At the time of
that visit, in 1815, the West African Mission was in an
unsettled and precarious state ; and in the only other
fields entered on by the Society, New Zealand and South
India, the work of love was hardly begun, and the two
Missions were infants hardly a year old. But now the
grain of mustard-seed had become a mighty tree, and the
fowls of the air had begun to lodge in its spreading
branches. About a hundred and ten clergy and nine hundred teachers were employed in the various missions, and
four thousand communicants were gathered in, by the
blessing of God on their labours. Eleven distinct and
widely distant spheres were already occupied by the Society, in West Africa, New Zealand, North, South, and
East India, and Ceylon, the Mediterranean, East Africa,
the Red River near Hudson's Bay, British Guiana, and
China. The time was now come to complete the apos-

tolic number, and add a twelfth mission, the child of
the first and earliest, to the other eleven.   The Niger
expedition, unfortunate in its direct object, was still the
means of opening fresh intercourse with the tribes of the
interior.   Soon after Mr. Crowther's ordination, and
return to Sierra Leone, the way seemed to be prepared
for a mission to Abbeokouta, his native home.   It began
in 1846, under most encouraging circumstances.  Already
it numbers more than three hundred converts ; and, after
enduring a severe persecution, and being shielded from
imminent danger of destruction, by the repulse of the
Dahomans, now promises to stretch forth its hand east-
ward, to meet the rapid extension of the East African
mission on the opposite shore.   The ordination, then, of
the first native African Missionary might well be viewed
by Mr. Bickersteth with especial interest, as a main step
towards the fulfilment of the prophecy—that " Ethiopia
shall stretch forth her hands unto God."

This autumn Mr. Bickersteth's only son, and the son of
a friend, who had been the companion of his studies at
the Rectory for nine years, both entered on their college
life.   Such a removal is an important event in the domestic history of many a Christian family ; and the following letter, written to them on this occasion, will be
read with interest by many parents.

*Watton Rectory, Oct.* 12.

MY DEAREST GEORGE AND EDWARD,

I promised to write to you before your going to College, and
though much pressed with work on every side, my dear boys, who
have been so long under my roof, and with whom I have so often
knelt in prayer together at the throne of grace, have prior claims.
You know I write in the fulness of love.

I trust that you have both now acquired habits of study, and a real love for the acquisition of useful knowledge ; and these will be very important, and should be carefully cultivated, both as leading to great means of usefulness hereafter, and.as being a present preservative from the many peculiar snares and temptations of being thrown so much on your own free choice as to the employment of your time.

You are at present but little acquainted,—you can be but little acquainted, with your chief danger, your own hearts.   I have had about forty years' more experience than you can possibly have on this point, and be assured, my dearest children, here is your chief temptation.   You know not, you cannot know, what power the lust of the flesh, the lust of the eye, and the pride of life, have to lead you astray from the paths of safety and of holy happiness.   The tremendous snares of self-confidence, self-sufficiency, vanity and self-will, beset us on every side.   The great preservative is the love of God in Christ Jesus, shed abroad in our hearts by the Holy Spirit.   What fallen creatures must we be, when nothing but our Creator's appearing in our flesh and blood, and dying for us, could reconcile us to God !   Let us then cease to place any confidence in ourselves, and place all our trust only in the Lord !

Your first, therefore, your great, your chief attention, must be fixed on your own hearts.   " Keep thy heart with all diligence, for out of it are the issues of life."   Let the care of the soul be with you " the one thing needful."   O neglect not, on any consideration, private prayer, at least morning and evening, and reading daily in secret, in regular order, and with earnest prayer, the Holy Scriptures.

Next to this, my beloved children, I would earnestly press upon you an entire separation of the Sabbath to its sacred duties.   Let it not be a day of visiting, or of receiving visits.   Let it not be a day of studies, excepting those which are strictly religious and devout. Abundance of books you both have, besides the Holy Scriptures, that may employ all the leisure hours of the Sabbath.   Attend that public ministry (after your college and university requirements) that you judge most spiritual, and suited to profit you, and do not change about, but remain under the same ministry.   If you can, secure perfect retirement and quiet, for meditation, self-examination, and devotion, during one part of the Sabbath-day.

Remember your health of body, as well as your spiritual health. Every day give a good portion of time to exercise in the open air. You will gain by it in the end, and your strength will be unbroken for future usefulness. Do not indulge in late hours, but have a well-regulated plan of rising, study, and going early to rest ; and keep to it.

Many temptations will be avoided by attention to these things begun at once ; and especially by letting it be known, from the first, that you mean to be a student and a Christian, and will not be drawn aside from a course consistent with such a profession. Oh be not ashamed of the gospel of Christ ! disregard the laughter and ridicule of the world.

The choice of friends, in so great an assembly of the young, will have a material influence on your conduct at College. The great Scripture principle is, " I am a companion of them that fear Thee." The first verse of the first Psalm makes plain to us what we should avoid. It will be a natural temptation to desire to associate with those of higher rank in life than yourselves, and to number among your friends and associates those who are superior in title or in wealth. I cannot but consider this to be attended with many evils. And, on the other hand, those in inferior circumstances may seek to gain advantages, by making themselves agreeable, and so to draw you from your duties. But a steady course of conduct, constant regularity in studies, and consistency in your principles, will secure to you the friends best worth having, and whose friendship will be a joy to you all through life. Never mingle in the society of others, without striving to speak a word for God and His truth, and to do some spiritual good to those with whom you associate.

Expensive habits ought on every account to be avoided. They are more injurious to yourselves than even to your parents. The dread of being counted mean and shabby, may become a perfect folly. Nothing really mean and shabby will ever be done by a Christian, who will aim at a liberal economy. The greatest meanness in the world, is to be ashamed of Him who died for us, to spend largely on vanities, and begrudge anything given to the cause of Christ. I should wish you to support the Cambridge Associations of the Church Missionary, the Jews, the Pastoral Aid, and the

Bible Societies. It will be one means of showing your colours, and of bringing you acquainted with those who confess our Saviour before men. Have no debts that you can possibly avoid. Your parents, be assured, according to their means, will provide for all your real wants and comforts, and pay at once the accounts at the earliest opportunity.

I trust you will seek to excel, by diligence and patient application, in the appropriate studies of the University. Your parents and friends will rejoice in any success you may attain in those studies. But let the chief motive to diligence be—it is a duty to your heavenly Father. He is present with you at all times. His favour follows all who seek to please Him in a faithful discharge of appointed work, and His favour is better than life itself.

These are the hints it has seemed to me most important to give you. My situation in life has been so public, and my writings have made me so generally known, that I cannot but feel, my dear children, that I am personally, deeply implicated in your conduct; and that the honour of our holy religion, and of the great Evangelical principles which I have been maintaining in my writings and ministry for thirty years, are affected in the eyes of many by the course you may pursue, and I can enter into the Apostle's words— "Now we live, if ye stand fast in the Lord."

You are also responsible before God, in having heard so much truth as you have heard for so many years, and having been the subject of so many prayers and hopes. Oh may you, in the great trial of your character, be stedfast and unmoveable!

You have, besides, both chosen deliberately the office of the ministry. A worldly minister of Christ is a contradiction full of evils. He is a curse to the Church, and a curse to the country, whatever his talents, or his learning, or his rank. Nothing but true conversion of heart to God, and the constant indwelling of the Holy Spirit, can make you faithful stewards of the mysteries of Christ, and a blessing to your fellow-men. Be not then, my dearest children, inconsistent with your high calling. Prepare diligently for the ministry, and be prepared of God for it, and you enter on the highest, the most glorious, the most eternally enriching, of all the offices to which the God of heaven and earth calls His people. Never have I repented giving myself to the ministry. As we are faithful in it, we are happy now, and bring multitudes to share our happiness on earth, and our glory for ever. Oh that I may have the joy of seeing you glorifying Christ, our one Saviour, and preaching His gospel fully and faithfully, to the salvation of the precious and immortal souls for whom He died!

Your most affectionate friend,<br>
E. BICKERSTETH.

A few years earlier a young person, engaged in business, who had a strong desire to enter the ministry, wrote to solicit his advice, and the following letter was written in reply. Its remarks, though brief, may not be without their interest to other students, preparing for the ministerial office.

DEAR SIR,

I was interested by your letter, which recalled to my mind some of my own difficulties in entering into the ministry, and the way in which our gracious God removed them.

I would just advise you day by day to commit all to Him. He has all hearts and means most perfectly in his control, and if He have called you by his Spirit to this work, He will make your way plain; and if He have not called you, you had infinitely better remain in any other employment, than enter, unsent of his Spirit, into the most arduous, responsible, and difficult, of all offices in which you can labour.

Your preparation may be considered as threefold: secular learning, theological knowledge, and heart experience.

As to secular learning, you require (as indeed you know) both Latin and Greek, and must take the ordinary methods of patient study of the usual school-books for this purpose: any classical teacher in your neighbourhood will direct you here. But, though I believe the Archbishop of York admits to orders without a Unisity Degree, it is, as you will find, very desirable to have the advantages of a *University education;* and I would, if I were in your place, with my present experience, labour and pray that you may gain these advantages.

As to theological knowledge, Paley's Evidences, Hartwell Horne's Introduction, Pearson on the Creed, and Burnet on the Thirty-nine Articles, with Wheatley on the Common Prayer, and Burnet's Pastoral Care, are needful to furnish you with information to pass an examination.

But there are no books (beyond the Book of books) more profitable than Milner's Church History, with Scott's Continuation, Scott's Essays, and Newton's Cardiphonia and Omicron.

As to heart experience,—the most important of all preparation, —this is only gained by diligent study of the Bible with much prayer and meditation and self-examination, visiting the poor, especially the pious, and seeking to walk very closely with God every day. This will soon shew you the exceeding vileness of our hearts and our entire dependence on the righteousness and strength of the Lord Jesus Christ, and lead you to that experimental knowledge of divine truth which alone can make you an useful minister.

But your present station may most materially fit and keep you for the future work of the ministry. God has prepared his most honoured servants in secular work for ministerial usefulness; the knowledge of the world and of business which you are here acquiring —should the Lord call you to the ministry—will be exceedingly valuable to you as a minister.

Commending you and your desire to the great Head of the Church, I am

Faithfully yours,
E. BICKERSTETH.

One or two extracts, from notes written to his son in the following term, shew the wise and loving interest his father took in his prosperity, when thus transferred from the retirement of a home education to the duties and temptations of a college life.

M 5

*October* 23, 1843.

MY DEAREST SON,

I was truly glad to receive your welcome letter, and rejoice to see that you are comfortably settled in college, and beginning your work, in a spirit of dependence on Him who is our only strength in every duty. It is my earnest hope and prayer that your trials and difficulties will be the divinely-appointed means for strengthening your faith, and confirming your whole character in that good part which our God has led you to choose. The whole experience of my life has assured me that it is the only path of real happiness here, as well as the way to true blessedness and everlasting glory in the kingdom of Christ; and, loving my dear son, as I do, with the fulness of fatherly affection, both judgment and love constrain me to make this my chief desire for you.

It must be a perfectly new scene to you, and there will necessarily be fresh temptations and occasional mistakes; but if the directions of my long letter are followed, all will work, with God's blessing, to bring you out of college, a strengthened and established Christian, with enlarged power to be an honour to the gospel of Christ, and a full blessing to your fellow-creatures.

Though unable to furnish you with those pecuniary means which the parents of some others could, I doubt not that God will always enable me to meet your real wants and comforts; and there is no money I shall more rejoice to spend than that which is requisite for your future usefulness. . . .

I need not tell you how we all think of you, love you, and pray for you. Give me your full confidence in every thing, and be assured it will be repaid with constant love, and the best advice our God enables me to give you.

Ever affectionately your own Father,

E. BICKERSTETH.

*November* 3.

MY DEAR SON,

. . . It is always pleasant both to write to, and to hear from, those we love ; and I trust this golden link of love will ever with us be stronger and stronger, even through eternity.   What a glorious hope is this !

I am sure that in giving your Sunday to God, you will have His blessing on all the rest of the week. . . . As far as regularity and order allow, hear only faithful sermons.   To have to hear error is injurious to the spirit, if not to the principles. . . .

Remember, my dear Edward, what is most desirable at college — not Bell's or any other scholarship—but a heart right in the sight of God, His favour, and fellowship with him ; so do not study to the neglect of health of body, or health of soul. . . . With hearty love from all,

Your affectionate Father.<br>E. BICKERSTETH.

*November* 18.

My dearest Son,

. . . Your whole future blessedness in life is deeply connected with present sacrifices ; only keep in health by full out-door exercise, two hours each day. . . . "We have confidence in the Lord, touching you," (such is the beautiful Scripture expression), that we shall have joy in you to the end.

Passages of Scripture that were useful to me at your age, were— " Mind not high things, but condescend to men of low estate." " Seekest thou great things for thyself? seek them not."   You need not form plans for the future.   In present application to immediate duties, the full happiness of the future is effectually sown. We are the worst devisers for ourselves—but we have a Friend who is infallibly wise, and unfailingly loving ; and He orders all, He is always with you, to guide, to govern, and to bless. . . . The spirit, dearest son, we all most want, is entire devotedness to Christ. God ever bless you and keep you, prays

Your affectionate Father,<br>E. BICKERSTETH.

The correspondence of Mr. Bickersteth, towards the close of the year, was of a most various and interesting

character. His friend, Mr. Sibthorp, had just returned
from his unhappy secession, repelled by the Mariolatry of
the Church of Rome, but still in an unsettled state of
mind ; and several letters passed between them, with Mr.
Bickersteth's usual warmth and simplicity of feeling.
Troubles had arisen at Ware, from the violent antipathy
of the parishioners to some rubrical innovations, that had
partly been occasioned by the Bishop of London's recent
charge; and he took occasion to address his Lordship, in
two respectful and friendly letters, advising strongly some
course of wise conciliation. A friend had asked his views
on the actual state of the Propagation Society, and his
reply, a copy of which was inclosed with a friendly note
to the Secretary, produced a renewed correspondence,
and elicited some facts of importance, which tended to
mitigate his previous fears as to the working of the
Society. A protest against Tractarianism was forwarded
to him by Mr. Noel, which appeared to him to err in an
opposite extreme ; and he wrote at length, to state and
confirm his objections, and his great fear lest the recoil
from one evil should betray Christians into another. His
early friend, Dr. Pye Smith, lamented, in a letter full of
sincere affection, the growing bigotry, in his opinion,
among the clergy, arising from the Tractarian movement.
The close of Mr. Bickersteth's answer is very descriptive
of his habitual feelings.

" I am sure Evangelical brethren are really desiring union with
those of other denominations, who love the Lord Jesus Christ in
sincerity. I am going, in the beginning of next week, to be present
at a large meeting, on the importance of union among faithful
brethren in contending for the truth of the Gospel, with the means
of maintaining it. I think I sent you the Sermon on the same subject, which I preached for the Foreign Aid Society, and have since

included the substance of it in a larger work I am compiling, on the ' Promised Glory of the Church of Christ.'

" But, my dear friend, we have all of us prejudices, and that on all sides ; and need meekness of wisdom, as well as earnest contention for the truth, and large charity.  Our common enemies, Infidels, lawless men, and Papists, are ready to swallow us up alive, and those who love the Lord are fighting with each other.  Let us mourn over these things, and follow the things which make for peace, and the things by which we may edify one another, and pray much for each other.  God Almighty bless you with all spiritual blessings, prays,

Yours faithfully,<br>E. BICKERSTETH.

Amidst the variety of his public work, the year closed with these reflections in his own journal.

"*November* 26.  I have been blessed in my journeys to Bath, Bristol, and London, and carried through all the duties to which I have been called.  May the Lord bless me, and use me to His glory.  I commit many mistakes; I fall short in every thing; my heart is often cold and dull towards God.  O what a mercy that I am at all upheld in His ways, and enabled to do any good to my fellow men ! . . . . .

" O Lord, how many precious interests I have to commend unto Thee ; my own soul's welfare, my wife, my children, my parish, my Church, the whole Church, my country, Jews and Gentiles !  What a circle I have to bring before Thee, in god-children, relations, Christian friends, religious Societies, and the whole cause of Christ !  God make me faithful to all my trusts, and a large blessing to my fellow-men, for His dear Son's sake !

" *December* 24.  Good and gracious is the Lord !  He has brought my scattered family together, from Cam-

bridge, and from Liverpool, in peace, and with many
blessings in their absence.   He has helped me in preaching at my old friend Mr. Pratt's Church, and enabled me
to carry through the press my address to the missionaries,
the 'Promised Glory,' and a new edition of the ' Christian Student.'   What thanks do I owe Him, if my labours
are still acceptable to His children, and useful to my
fellow-men ! . . . . .

    " Many important duties in public are before me, and
where is my strength for them ?   Only in Thee, O Lord
Jesus !   Look upon me in mercy—assist me in every
work and duty—so that I may live by faith, walk in
Thee, bear Thy light and Thy love to others ; and at
length be accepted of Thee in the day of Thy appearing."

# CHAPTER XXIV.

THE opening of 1844 found Mr. Bickersteth engaged in anxious and perplexing duties, arising out of the state of the Episcopal Church in Scotland. That body, historically derived from Archbishop Laud and the Nonjurors, had ever since retained, both in doctrine and discipline, the distinctive characters of that school of theology. Its clergy did not subscribe the Articles of the English Church ; and while they adopted the English Liturgy, another communion-service was introduced, on the model of that which Laud had endeavoured to impose throughout Scotland, but differing from it by a still plainer assertion of the corporal presence of Christ in the Eucharist. In the possession of this service the Scotch bishops and clergy were accustomed to glory, as their special badge of ecclesiastical honour. From these causes, and their more than doubtful allegiance to the reigning family, they were subject for many years to penal enactments, and great legislative discouragement. The aversion of English Churchmen, who settled in Scotland, to these features of the Scotch Episcopacy, led to the rise of congregations, in most of the larger towns, to whom clergymen, ordained in England, ministered by virtue of their English orders alone, and with a legal sanction which was then denied to the Scotch Episcopal clergy.

In course of time these circumstances were altered. After the Stuart line had become extinct, the Scotch bishops sought to obtain from the British Parliament a removal of the heaviest restrictions under which they had before laboured, and had a legal *status* given them, with regard to their own clergy ; while they solemnly re nounced any purpose of claiming authority over those Eng- lish congregations, which the law had already recognized. As a further means of obtaining the desired concession, a subscription to the English Articles was now, for the first time, required of their clergy, while the other dis- tinctive features of their communion remained as before. Still more recently, by an act in the present reign, a clerical communion, under very narrow limitations, was permitted between the two churches. The distinctions between them, in doctrine and discipline, were thus thrown by degrees into the shade ; while the revival in England of high-church principles rendered the anomaly of episcopal congregations, without the direct oversight of any bishop, more evident than ever. There arose, therefore, a strong desire in several of these congrega- tions to be united to the Scotch Episcopal Church, from which they had hitherto been entirely separate. Its bishops gladly hailed this extension of their authority. Conditions of agreement were signed, stipulating for the continued use of the English services in their integrity, and most of the separate congregations were incorporated on these terms into the Episcopal Church of Scotland.

This union, however, was still only in progress, when the Laudian spirit of the Scotch Episcopate, encouraged by the growth of Tractarian principles in England, re-

vived in full vigour, and speedily dissolved it again.   One
of its earliest signs was an act of the Episcopal Synod,
declaring the Scotch communion-office of primary authority in their church, and enjoining its exclusive employment on several public occasions, in which all the clergy,
by its own constitution, would be compelled to take a
share.   A more practical exhibition of its tendency soon
followed.   The chapel of St. Paul's, Aberdeen, had joined
the Episcopal Church in 1841, under a deed of union,
signed and ratified by Bishop Skinner ; and which stipu-
lated for the continued use, in all its services, of the
Liturgy and Catechism of the Church of England.
Within two years, in May 1843, the bishop threatened
Sir W. Dunbar, the clergyman, with penal discipline and
church censures because he ventured to claim the fulfilment of this covenant ; and required from him an unconditional submission to the distinctive canons and offices
of the Scotch Church.   The compact being thus broken
by the very party who had made it, Sir W. Dunbar and
his congregation retracted their adhesion to the Scotch
Episcopate.  The result was not a little startling.  On Aug.
10, Bishop Skinner, with a dozen or more of his clergy
sitting in synod, fulminated against Sir William a sentence of excommunication, declared all his ministerial
acts invalid, as being " performed apart from Christ's
mystical body, where the one Spirit is," and most earnestly warned all faithful people to avoid communion with
him in prayer and sacraments, lest they should be partakers with him in his sin.

A little earlier, in Edinburgh, there had been a similar
but less flagrant exercise of Episcopal authority, leading
to renewed separation.  Trinity Chapel, where an English
congregation had worshipped for many years, had lately

become united with the Episcopal Church. Mr. Drummond, the clergyman, had been accustomed to hold prayer-meetings with his flock, along with Bible classes, for their spiritual edification, and these proved obnoxious to the ruling powers. A new canon was passed, in 1838, to render all such meetings unlawful ; while at the same time the epithet, Protestant, was expunged carefully in all the other canons from the title of the Episcopal Church. The meetings were formally complained of, and Dr. Terrot required Mr. Drummond to discontinue them. Impressed with the conviction that a great Scriptural principle was at stake, he thought it his duty rather to resign his charge, than to hold it fettered by this new and unscriptural restriction, and to seek a new sphere of labour in England, where he had received his own orders. A further inquiry, however, into the Scotch Canons and Communion Service, convinced him that there were serious differences, of which he was not previously aware, between the doctrine and constitution of the two Churches. When his congregation, therefore, urged him not to forsake them, but to minister to them there on his English orders, as before the union with the Episcopal Church, and offered to build a new chapel for that purpose, no scruple prevented him from complying with their wishes, especially as his previous labours among them had been attended with a large blessing.

The controversy which had thus been kindled by a flagrant breach of contract in one case, and by restrictive and unscriptural canons on the other, was not slow in spreading to England. All the Tractarian organs were loud and fierce in condemning the two presbyters, who had been guilty, in their eyes, of a scandalous schism ; and called on the English bishops and clergy to ratify the excommunication of Bishop Skinner, and maintain the authority of the Scotch bishops.   On the other hand, Evangelical Christians, some of whom had adopted high church views on questions of order, were divided and hesitating in their judgment.   The more cautious and timorous, while they condemned the spirit and temper of the Scotch Church, blamed equally the decisive course of Sir W. Dunbar and Mr. Drummond, and would have had them abandon their flocks, and retire to England, rather than endanger the peace of the Church, and seem to contradict their promise of canonical obedience. Others, however, felt that great principles were already at stake ; the purity and liberty of the Gospel, in contrast to church tyranny and superstitious doctrine ; and that to shrink from the conflict because of present odium, would only give new strength to evils, which were daily gaining ground through a more timorous policy, and thus betray the sacred interests of Divine truth.

The question soon assumed a practical shape in the Church Missionary Society.   The Committee of its Edinburgh Auxiliary belonged chiefly to Mr. Drummond's congregation, who had been foremost in the cause of missions ; and they adhered warmly to their own esteemed pastor.   But the Society had also many friends in the Episcopal Church of Scotland.   Some of these protested against any recognition of those who had now seceded from it, as English Churchmen, and threatened, if this were done, to withdraw from it altogether.   Early in 1844 the Parent Committee, after much perplexing discussion, came to the resolution of maintaining a perfect neutrality, and of sending a Deputation to Scotland, with the instructions not to preach in any of the churches. They could not openly censure and disown those who

had separated from the Scotch Episcopacy, without seeming to countenance a service which most of them entirely
condemned, and restrictions on Christian liberty which
they all deplored ; while, if they espoused their cause,
they would revolt many of their Scotch, and also of their
English friends, endanger, perhaps, their newly-acquired
episcopal patronage, and rouse against themselves a great
amount of bitter clerical hostility.  At the same time it
was stated that individual members of the Society would
be left free to follow their own convictions, either by
preaching for the Scotch Episcopal clergy, or for those
English ministers, who had never abandoned, or had now
resumed, their original standing, and who were ministering as clergymen of the Church of England, beyond the
limits of the English dioceses.

Mr. Bickersteth was one of those who would have preferred a more decided course on the part of the Society.
He believed that the Scotch Communion Service was
directly opposed to those evangelical, Protestant principles
which the Society had ever maintained, and which were
the true secret of its strength and vitality.  He feared
that by a neutral course, on such a question, they would
be sacrificing their most attached friends, to conciliate
others of only doubtful fidelity to their cause, and would
seem to regard episcopal order as equally important with
the purity of the Gospel.  But however weighty might
be the reasons for caution, in so perplexed a controversy,
on the part of the Society, his convictions of personal
duty were plain and clear.  He felt bound to give his
full sympathy and willing aid to those brethren, who,
amidst a storm of bitter invective from the Tractarian
press, were witnessing for Protestant truth against an unscriptural communion-service, and for Christian liberty in

the pastoral office, against a yoke of ritual bondage, which, if consistently enforced, would soon be fatal to the very life of the whole church. Accordingly, when an earnest request was made to him by the Edinburgh Committee, to come and preach for the Church Missionary Society in Mr. Drummond's Church, he felt it his duty to comply. He reminded them, however, that his visit must be so arranged as to be kept quite distinct from the deputation of the Parent Society, whose pledge of neutrality, once given, he wished to be fulfilled with scrupulous fidelity.

But here new complications arose. That the step might be seen more plainly to be his own private act, he abstained at first from announcing his purpose to the Parent Committee. When, however, it came indirectly to the knowledge of the President, he earnestly desired him to make it known to them, since he feared that it might seem to the public like a breach of their engagement. The result was an earnest request that he would abandon his visit, on the ground that his long official connection with the Society, and his especial prominence with the public, among its advocates and friends, would make his act be ascribed to the whole body, and involve them in a breach of promise. Though he dissented entirely from this reasoning, in which false impressions were confounded with realities, yet, out of deference to friends whom he so dearly loved, he wrote to obtain a release, for the time, from his Edinburgh engagement. But when he found that the Sermons and Meetings had been already advertised, he could no longer withdraw, without sacrificing his own convictions of duty, and a positive promise, and even the very neutrality desired by others, to an illusive shew of neutrality, that would be in reality a heavy discouragement to faithful and beloved

brethren. He remained, therefore, immovable in his
purpose, in spite of entreaties and expostulations from
some of his dearest friends, and set out for Edinburgh,
towards the close of April, in fulfilment of his promise.
He alludes repeatedly to this journey in his private diary,
and to the deep and anxious thought it occasioned him.

"*January* 28, 1844. Truly the Lord Jesus is my only
salvation, nor can I find any rest or peace, but in Him.
But enable me to glorify Thy name, in home, relative,
and personal, and ministerial duties, day by day, hour by
hour. . . .

"I have before me anxious journeys to Edinburgh,
Aberdeen, and Cambridge, as well as an important prophetical sermon in London.

"My bodily health has been more shaken also latterly.
May all be sanctified, and help to make me a vessel meet
for the Master's use! O Lord, give the oil in my vessel
with my lamp, that I may not be ashamed before Thee
at Thy coming, but may welcome all the signs of Thy
return, and be ever waiting for Thy appearing! It is a
wonderful calm in the whole political world, and all dis-
turbances seem quieted. Lord, keep me watchful!

"*February* 24. Through mercy I am spared and blessed.
I have been to Manchester, Liverpool, and Chester, for
the Foreign Aid Society, and expect, early in March, to
go to Cambridge for the Church Missionary Society.

"I have become involved in an important subject, by
having engaged to preach for the Church Missionary
Society in April, in Mr. Drummond's pulpit at Edinburgh,
and Sir W. Dunbar's at Aberdeen. It has exposed me to
objections, both from the friends and the enemies of the
gospel; but I trust that my governing motive has been,
a desire to approve myself to my Saviour; and if I suffer

for well-doing, let me be thankful. Oh, what I want more than everything is, more spirituality, more devotion, more ready self-denial, more quiet fulfilment of immediate duties, more close walking with God ! Lord, give me these for Christ's sake."

On January the 15th he wrote to a member of the Committee :—

"I deeply grieve that our friends should think it best to continue neutral in so vital a controversy; and thus the Society should discountenance its honest friends, who have been faithful to their Lord, and encourage the enemies of the Society, who have been adverse to His truth, and to our Society also. I can conceive nothing more Antichristian, almost, than to forbid social prayer-meetings. I believe that if St. Peter had done this, not only St. Paul, but the whole body of the Apostles, would have withstood him to the face. I wish you would look at Bishop Hall's Works, and see how again and again that good bishop sanctioned it, and admits it to be sacrilege to rob the people of such prayer. Why was an English clergyman to betray his Master's cause, by yielding to such an unscriptural injunction? I believe it to be a case in which the Society might make a righteous stand for God's truth, and their own Christian liberty. If they yield here, every missionary prayer-meeting, and our own blessed Saturday-evening meeting, is left open to assault. The whole evangelical body will rally round God's truth, and the liberty wherewith Christ has made us free."

In other letters on the same day he observed ; " It is an important crisis in the Society, and many prayers will ascend, that they may be guided aright. Great ignorance exists on the subject, and we all need more faith."

On January 23, he wrote in these words, to accept the invitation :

" I should be desirous, in going so far, really to serve the cause of the Society, as well as of Christ, indeed both in one; for the

Society is dear to me, as I believe it to be the honoured instrument of spreading the truth as it is in Jesus. Thankful shall I be, if in any way I can help to heal the breach, without symbolizing with the errors of the Apostasy. The Lord himself guide and prosper me, enable me to discern His will, and ever to stand by His truth; and strengthen us in body and soul to confess Him before men, and that in His spirit, and not in ours.

" Of course it is important that my visit, and the deputation from the Parent Society, should be quite distinct, and at distinct times."

Six days later, he wrote to a friend in the London Committee.

" I desire to be quite as anxious as yourself that the Parent Society should be entirely separated from my visit to Scotland; feeling with you the vital importance, when it has fixed upon a course, that it should pursue it with godly simplicity and sincerity, and abominating from my heart all trickery. I will fully declare in public in Scotland that I come on my own responsibility, and on the invitation of the local friends, in whose pulpits I preach, without any sanction from the Parent Society. I had offered the end of next month, but, to meet your fears, have by this post put it off."

On February 23, he wrote to Mr. Drummond, who feared lest the scruples of the Committee should interfere with the fulfilment of his promise, and cause insuperable difficulties in the arrangements.

" I have no doubt of your Scriptural standing, and therefore rejoice to come, and in that respect share your cross. But the strength of our conviction on this point may well make us patient and yielding in minor matters, which do not really affect it. Do not be tempted, dear brother, by your situation, to think these lesser things of importance. Let the faith, the patience, and forbearance, of yourself and your flock, still glorify your Saviour abundantly in all."

Two days later he addressed the following letter to the Secretaries, in order to place it clearly on record, that the visit was on his private responsibility.

*Watton Rectory, Feb. 5.*

MY DEAR FRIENDS,

At the earnest invitation of the friends of the Society in Scotland, I have undertaken to visit them, and to preach in such pulpits as may be open to me, for the Society.

I understand that some of our friends in England are anxious that this journey should be openly and avowedly disconnected from any sanction, direct or indirect, of the Society; and I am myself equally anxious, after you have pledged yourselves to a course which you deem necessary, that there should be no appearance of doing indirectly, by friends of the Society, what they declined doing directly. But at the same time I feel that the Committee never intended, or could intend, to prevent individuals from doing what they feel to be right, in their private character.

Under these circumstances, however, connected as I have been with the Parent Society, it is due to the Committee, and due to myself, thus explicitly to state to you that I have undertaken the journey, and complied with the wishes of our friends, entirely on my own responsibility, and without the slightest sanction from the Secretaries of the Parent Society, or from any member of the Committee.

I believe from my heart that the English Clergymen, who had for a season joined the Scotch Episcopal Church, have done nothing that could justify harsh proceedings in any of the bishops of that church against them, or to taint their character, as consistent and orderly clergymen of the Church of England. I believe, also, that it is a special duty to sympathize with those in trial, when standing firm for the liberty and truth of the Gospel. I dare not, therefore, as a Christian Minister, stand aloof from beloved and devoted brethren in these circumstances.

I know the difficulties of the Committee, and would be far from condemning their minutes. I cannot, however, but earnestly pray that a gracious Saviour may ever guide you to those decisions, which are most for His glory, in the faithful maintenance of those pure truths of the Gospel, which are the whole foundation of the Church Missionary Society,—which God has so largely blessed in time past, and I trust will yet more largely bless in time to come. Let us also stand fast in the liberty wherewith Christ has made us free, reverencing authorities, but obeying God rather than man.    I am only anxious, for my own part, to fulfil my duty in godly simplicity, to Him whose I am, and whom I serve.

In Him affectionately yours,

E. BICKERSTETH.

Anxious to meet the wishes of the Parent Committee in the fullest manner, he wrote to Edinburgh on February 10, requesting that his visit might be fixed two or three months later, so as to disconnect it entirely, in point of time, from the deputation early in April.    But when he learnt, by their reply, that his coming at the close of April had been advertised, with the Sermons and Meetings, he felt bound to adhere to his promise.

The great caution, however, of the London Committee, and the efforts which had been used to dissuade him from the journey, produced a natural jealousy in many of the friends to the cause in Edinburgh; who thought that real neutrality was sacrificed for a mere shadow, and that it would have the moral influence of a positive condemnation. In fact, where great religious principles are involved, absolute neutrality, even when honestly sought, is practically impossible.    The moral influence must preponderate in one scale or the other ; and all indecision in the cause of truth will commonly give a real advantage to the progress of error.    Mr. Bickersteth was most desirous to prevent the growth of a feeling, which circumstances rendered almost inevitable, and wrote the following letters on the same day, February 21, to Mr. Drummond, and to a member of the Parent Committee.

MY DEAREST DRUMMOND,

. . . Your letter of the 16th places all in a different position from what I knew when I last wrote. I have promised to you, and you have promised to the public. Unless, therefore, you have made subsequent arrangements in consequence of my letter, I see it right to adhere to my original promise.

I am very anxious, however, that you and our dear brethren in Scotland should not think the worse of the Committee in London for the part which they have seen it right to act. Let us admire their delicate sense of honour, to adhere scrupulously to their neutrality, as they viewed it. Let us enter into their difficulties, from so large a proportion of their most devoted friends viewing the matter differently from myself. Let us consider their just having come out of a painful collision. Let us remember that a corporate and representative body has necessarily to consider, not only what is right, but also what is the best way of doing what is right, so as to commend it to the judgment of their supporters. Let us remember, also, the consideration due to faithful brethren in the Scotch Episcopal Church. And then consider how, to this hour, I am identified with the acts of the Society.

In these views I cannot judge harshly of the Parent Committee. They will have the whole battle to fight, and it becomes them to be very cautious in their movements.

I am also peculiarly anxious about your beloved flock. The zeal, the decision, the faith and the love, which has made them stand firmly by you, is admirable. But oh, let it be joined with patient forbearance, meekness of wisdom, long-suffering, and charity! Let patience have its perfect work among you. For your position is peculiarly perilous, and warmth, zeal, and indiscretion, might soon mar your excellent standing. Adhering to a noble institution, like the Church Missionary Society, will be a great stay to your whole flock. I do trust, our Evangelical Societies may help us, in the coming war, to bind all who love Christ more and more firmly together.   Tell them, with my hearty Christian love, I entreat them to think well of the Parent Committee.   There is a real desire in the whole body to do what they think to be right in the sight of God.   We must not let the common enemy divide the little flock; but if any are weak, while others are strong, the strong must bear with the weak. . . . . . God graciously guide us all.   May the season of Lent lead us to what is becoming to us all—humiliation before our God.

Ever affectionately yours,<br>
E. BICKERSTETH.

DEAREST ——,

I send you the enclosed copy of a letter I have written to Mr. Drummond, as I wish to act with perfect confidence and openness.

It appears to me that the Committee have now taken every step which they could, and more than was required, to disconnect the journey I take from the Deputation of the Parent Society.   May they be equally anxious to disconnect themselves from the contamination of the tendency to Popery in the Scotch Episcopal Church—a duty, to which faithfulness to our Redeemer calls them. The fact is palpable.   Their Canons and their Communion Service are published and gloried in.

O beware how you put a stumbling-block in the way of faithful, but reviled and suffering servants of Christ !   I am sure that this is the farthest thing from the heart of my beloved brethren in the Committee.   May our common God and Saviour give us all wisdom, in every part of this intricate business, to do that which will promote His truth, and glorify His name.

Ever affectionately yours,<br>
E. BICKERSTETH.

The following note was written to a valued friend, who, under a false impression of the circumstances, as he owned a few months later, had written to dissuade him from the journey, and taxed him with a desire to fight his own battles at the expense of the Society, and involve it in a breach of promise.

DEAR ——,

If you had known the whole case, you would not have written as you have done.

In the Committee of Jan. 18, it was distinctly stated that the minutes then passed did not affect the members of the Society, individually.

I have promised to the Edinburgh Committee to preach for their Auxiliary; and in consequence of this, they have promised, in an advertisement of February 10, to their subscribers. I cannot break my promise.

The Society has no right, the public has no right, to identify me, nor will I be identified, with any Society, but as they hold the truth as it is in Jesus, which ought to be dearer to us than all other considerations.

Thank you for your love in writing, but when I feel conscience-clear, and conscience-bound to a course, I hope God will keep me stedfast.

Ever affectionately yours,<br>E. BICKERSTETH.

The journey which was thus undertaken, amidst reproach and difficulty, in the full conviction that it was required by faithfulness to the cause of the gospel, was attended through its whole course, with many tokens of the Divine blessing. Mr. Bickersteth was welcomed by the English congregations, at Edinburgh, Aberdeen, and Glasgow, with deep, and almost enthusiastic love; and there was perhaps none of his previous journeys, in which so large a measure of his Master's spirit seemed to be given him. His whole conduct agreed with his expressed desire, before he set out, to heal breaches, if it were possible, without unfaithfulness to the cause of the gospel. In this spirit he sought an interview, when in Edinburgh, with Bishop Terrot, that he might offer a kind and friendly explanation of the motives which had led to his visit. He hoped that, if agreement in their maxims of judgment was unattainable, this conscientious difference might at least be freed from any appearance of personal disrespect on the one side, and from all bitterness of feeling on the other. This object of the visit was fully attained. The last sermon which he preached before he left Edinburgh, was published, on his return home, with the title "The Christian Blessing." Its text was the customary benediction, 2 Cor. xiii. 14, and its character was a powerful enforcement of Christian love.

A letter addressed to the Secretaries of the Society, on May 9, after his return, explains the course and the result of the journey.

My dear Friends,

Having completed my visit to Scotland, it appears to me desirable, with reference to the future course of the Society, to give you particulars of my journey, and the information which it furnished.

I thank God that His providence made the way clear ; for I should otherwise have been deprived of the privilege and comfort of brotherly sympathy with tried brethren, in their faithful adherence to the Standards and Formularies of our Church, and of strengthening the attachment of their congregations to our Church Missions.

I preached for the Rev. Sir W. Dunbar, in St. Paul's Church, at Aberdeen, on April 21st, to a large and highly-respectable congregation. I had on the following day the pleasure of personal intercourse with many of them, and was refreshed by their Christian spirit.

On Wednesday, the 24th, I preached for the Society in the Rev. C. P. Miles's Church, St. Jude's, Glasgow. He is a faithful

Minister in connection with the Scotch Episcopal Church, but has the same liberty in conducting his ministry according to our Church services, that we have in England.   I was glad to find that the Bishop of Glasgow has patronized the formation of a Glasgow Auxiliary to the Church Missionary Society.

On Sunday, April 28, and Monday the 29th, I preached for the Society in Mr. Drummond's new Church of St. Thomas, Edinburgh, to large congregations.   The interest felt by his flock for the Society will be seen in the amount, £112, collected after the sermons.   I have never been more delighted with the manifest spirit of devotion and Christian feeling, in any congregation during my ministry.   Truly the presence of our God was with us.

I felt it respectful to call on Bishop Terrot, and had a lengthened conference with him : he received me with courtesy and kindness. I also saw, in the course of my journey, several clergymen of the Scotch Episcopal Church, and made such inquiries as were in my power, respecting the position of that Church, and of the English Churches in Scotland. . . .

I rejoice to know and testify that there are, in the ninety ministers serving in the Scotch Church, men of much piety and faithfulness.   They naturally sympathize with the efforts of the Church Missionary Society, and count it a privilege, as it really is, to be partakers in its blessed work of Christian love.   Through the Episcopal Association recently formed in Edinburgh, and the Glasgow Auxiliary, under the kind patronage of its bishop, I am thankful that they have an opportunity of doing so, in harmony with their views of Church order, which I desire to respect ; while I trust that their liberty, as English clergymen, will be guaranteed by the failure of the efforts to displace Sir W. Dunbar and Mr. Drummond.   I see no reason why, in congregations thus connected with the Scotch Episcopacy, where the English Liturgy only is used, clergymen in our deputations should not be at full liberty to preach for the Society.

Still less do I see reason, why they should not have that liberty, to preach in the pulpits of faithful and orderly English clergymen, like Sir W. Dunbar and Mr. Drummond.   I have been a witness of the piety, zeal, and love of their flocks to Christ and His truth, and of the evangelical and devotional spirit of these faithful ministers of our Church, and of their conformity of worship with us in their congregations.

Only in this way, it seems to me, can the Committee be relieved from undue interference with questions, which, as a Society, we are not competent to solve ; or from dissipating a bright flame of Missionary zeal, which has been kindled in Scotland, and which, I trust, may yet spread, and be a large blessing, not only to the heathen, but to all the churches which thus shine as lights, holding forth the word of life.

God Almighty graciously guide all your deliberations, and make your work an increasing blessing to yourselves, to our Church, and to the benighted heathen world, prays,

Yours very affectionately,

E. BICKERSTETH.

In a note written May 1, from Liverpool, to his son at College, he thus expresses his own feelings, in the review of his Scotch visit.

I left Edinburgh on Monday, the 29th, after a journey more full of spiritual mercies and blessings than any that I ever undertook. Thanks be to God, and thanks be to you, my love, for your prayers, which were abundantly answered. . . . . The Lord, when we are trusting in Him, and doing His work, will always abundantly meet our real wants. O what a good Father our common and best Father is ! All my love to you, which is not small, is from His first love ; and there are unsearchable heights, and lengths, and depths, and breadths, in that unfathomable ocean of goodness. . . .

I should like to send you a long account of my journey. It was brim-full of God's goodness, at Aberdeen, at Glasgow, and at Edinburgh ; and the love of the Christians at each place was most precious. None love like real Christians, and you know the sweetness of this love.

A few days later, May 11, he alluded in another note
to the same subject, and his own feelings under the praise
or censure he might receive.

My views were greatly strengthened and confirmed when in
Scotland. Those who love our Saviour are with Sir W. Dunbar
and Mr. Drummond; and their congregations are the salt of the
earth where they are settled.

You were quite right about the Secession Churches. I wish to
do nothing irregular, having plenty to do as a consistent clergyman
in my own Church.

My account of my journey would occupy a long time. I have
just sent it to the Church Missionary Society. The matter is now
getting into all the London papers, and I shall be plentifully hated
and abused, and plentifully loved and praised. But the only thing
of real importance is,—Will the blessed Saviour approve and
accept? I have a good hope that He will, and then it is of little
consequence having to pass either through good or through evil
report. God bless you, my dear son, prays,

Your affectionate father,

E. BICKERSTETH.

The decision of Mr. Bickersteth in maintaining a righteous cause, amidst the invectives of adversaries, and the
misconceptions or timorousness of beloved friends, had a
speedy recompence. His communications, on his return,
to his own diocesan, who had been applied to by some of
the Scotch Bishops, and through him to the Archbishop
of Canterbury, had the effect they would naturally produce on candid minds; who were not disposed to sacrifice scriptural truth and liturgical consistency, law, and
precedent, to interdicts framed in miniature on the
Romish model. The following note, which he received
in June from a member of the London Committee, who

had strongly dissuaded him from the visit, shows the new aspect in which the subject now appeared.

My dear Bickersteth,

I received your note with great joy. Surely the overruling hand of the Lord is manifest in the whole affair.

You now stand clear of all annoyance, and you have cleared the way for any other clergyman to go down to Edinburgh and Aberdeen; and we have vindicated our honesty of intention. But at the same time it is clear that we cannot again interpose a word against any one, however closely connected with us, who may choose to preach our sermons in the proscribed pulpits.

Whether under these circumstances it will be necessary to interdict our deputation from preaching, is a matter of very little moment, and may be well deferred till the time arrives for decision. I have read your sermon, (preached at Edinburgh) with great interest and thankfulness.

While this change of feeling was still only in progress, he thus expressed his own principles of action, in a note to one of his Scotch friends.

I am indisposed to mix further controversy with the spiritual triumphs which our God has so clearly given us, and which will be more and more manifest, if we leave it with Him. I can say this the more freely, as it is simply personal suffering for ourselves. . . . The ignorant account me rash, in acting contrary to the wishes of the Society, and your standing as a church is not fully cleared. This is the evil: I am willing to bear it, and I dare say you will see it to be right. We make a present sacrifice for the good of missions, as we have often before; and while leaders in the Society here are softening, all the rest will come right in time. It is the patience of Christ, leaving it to the Lord to clear up all, that gives us the full victory.

The whole course of events, during the seven years which have passed since this journey of Mr. Bickersteth, has proved how clear and just a view he took of the real nature of the conflict. It is hardly too much to say, that if all, even of the evangelical clergy, had been equally prompt to discern the inroads of Romish doctrines, and to resist the assumptions of abused and unscriptural authority, the canker of superstition could never have spread so widely, and the country and the Church might perhaps have been spared the insult and the danger which now threatens them, from the growing pretensions and direct aggression of the Church of Rome.

The other engagements of Mr. Bickersteth at this time, and his views of passing events, are seen in these extracts from his journal.

"*March* 19, 1844. I this day complete fifty-eight years of age—a life full of singular mercies and blessings, and greatly wanting in corresponding returns of love to my God. The last year has been strongly marked, in the separation of the Free Church from the Established Church of Scotland; in the increased conflict with Popery; and many shakings in the Church of England, as well as in the movements affecting the Jewish nation.

" In the mean while, we have each to be watching, praying, and waiting. Through God's mercy I published this year the ' Promised Glory of the Church of Christ ; ' and the ' Christian Student,' the ' Treatise on Baptism,' ' Scripture Help, ' and ' Practical Guide,' are going through fresh editions. May all these works be more and more used for good, and become a blessing to others. For myself, I am more and more compelled to see that I can hope for nothing but through free and abounding mercy. I am compelled to exclaim, when I look at the state of my soul, and the deadness of my affections, and my wanderings in religious services, ' Can these dry

bones live ? ' O Lord, quicken me and raise me to newness of life."

"*April* 6. . . . I trust there is a little stir for good
among my dear people at Watton. Fresh communicants
are joining the Lord's table. Oh ! with what joy should
I see a decided work of grace among them. It would be
more to me than all the wealth and glory the world
could give.

" O Lord Jesus, leave us not ; come near and help us.
Give testimony to the word of Thy grace, and may we
all be quickened by Thy Spirit ?

" I had three important sermons in London last week ;
the Prophetical at Bloomsbury, and for public charities
in St. Olave's, and in St. Dunstan's. Thanks be to God
for strength for His service."

"*May* 25. Since last communion, I have been carried
through many weighty and important duties, thank God !
with comfort, and I hope with usefulness. . . .

" I have in London pleaded also for various Societies,
the Jews', the Indigent Blind, the Widow's Friend, the
Religious Tract, and the Foreign Aid Societies. To God
be glory for any good or blessing. May He pardon all
the many sins of my poor services, prevent evil from
them, and accept of what I have done, for Jesus' sake.

" I am compelled more and more to renounce all confidence in my own doings, and cling only to Jesus. If I
look at my defects as a father, a husband, a minister, a
friend, a master, in my home, my parish, in my church,
in my country, towards all men, in my devotions, in
public, in private—all, all, is stained and defiled, and I
can have no peace, no hope, but as I wash every robe
in the blood of the Lamb, and look to the sprinkling of
that blood on all I do and have done.

" O go with me now to Thy house and table, and let not my soul be formal, dead, dry, and barren ! Give me realizing communion with Thee, my God, and with Thy people, in prayer and at Thy table ; and let Thy blessed unction be largely granted in my ministry, and through the worship and services of this day. Oh, how empty are all, unless Thy presence be in the midst of them !

" The confirmation, in my parish-church for the first time, is on Friday, June 7. The Bishop of Lincoln stays at my house : my two youngest children are to be confirmed."

"*June* 29. I have been more stationary in the last month, though I have preached for the Foreign Aid Society at Clapham and Sydenham, and for a new church in Christ's Chapel, John's Wood. . . .

" The times continue shaking and difficult, and vital godliness has little favour from the authorities in State at least. A false liberalism, in a conservative government, favours both Socinians and Papists, and who can tell the sad issue ?

" But the main thing I have to regard is my own faithfulness to Jesus. O that I may not be wanting there ! O Lord, uphold, preserve, and keep me, and guard me from temptations on every side ! "

"*June* 30. I desire most gratefully to record the loving-kindness of the Lord, that I could admit my two youngest children this day to the Lord's table ; and so had the privilege of seeing my whole family, my wife and six children, with, I trust, penitent, believing, and loving hearts, commemorating our Saviour's death. What am I, that the Lord should thus be gracious to me and mine ! To Him be all the glory ; and may He largely vouchsafe His grace to all, that we may continually seek

His praise, and spend ourselves, and be spent, in doing
His will.   Oh! how utterly unworthy I am of all the
mercies which the Lord has shewn me, in this and
innumerable other things.   Glory, glory, glory, only
unto Him!

" I have been to Wanstead for the Church Missionary
Society.

" *July* 27. . . . Through mercy we have had good
meetings of the Church Pastoral Aid, here at Watton, of
the Church Missionary at Hatfield, and the Lord's Day
Observance and Bible Society at Hertford.   O Lord, accept each feeble attempt to serve Thee.   I attended and
spoke at a large meeting in London against the Dissenters' Chapel or Socinian Endowment Bill, but it has, alas!
been carried through Parliament, and is now the law of
the land.   The Lord pardon our guilty country.   The
Lord pardon my own personal sins.   O Jesus, wash me in
Thy blood.   May I wash my robes, even all my graces,
gifts, and doings, and make them white in the blood of
the Lamb!"

The absence of his son at college, earlier in the year,
was one of the first separations in the domestic circle,
and led to some characteristic letters of affectionate
advice and encouragement, of which the following is one
specimen.

*January* 16.

MY BELOVED EDWARD. . . .

. . . Though you are from home, you are really present with us
in spirit.   We bring you before our God in prayer, and before each
other in our conversation, and we joy in the thought that you are
now in the very scene, where all our wishes for your future usefulness
may be best promoted.   I rejoice in the thought that you are in a
circle of friends, who think with us in those all-important things,

in which our real happiness is bound up. May your delight be only in the excellent of the earth!

God is beginning to teach us, by our present separation, that we belong to a larger family ; that we must not have our hearts selfishly bound up in each other only ; that we must comprehend all members of the heavenly family, and seek ever to enlarge that happy number. O what a glory this opens out to us, that unites all the sweetness and enjoyment of family love, with all the innumerable hosts of God's children in all ages, and makes us one with them all! What a joy to think that, in the ministry, we have the fullest opportunity, and the richest advantages, for enlarging that company! How may it compensate for all the dryness of mathematical studies, to be assured that it will enable you more accurately and justly to plead and reason with the wisest of the world, that there is a wisdom beyond what they have before perceived, and a " way of life above to the wise," to be infinitely preferred to all the ways of the world! Go on, then, my dear son, steadily in all your studies ; and with all, walk closely with God, keep fast by Him, and He will use you abundantly to His glory here, and to the good of others, and secure for you, in pursuing them, the highest happiness on earth, and hereafter, the prize of our high calling.

Your ever affectionate father,

E. BICKERSTETH.

The same jealousy that spiritual objects should be kept foremost, amidst the excitement of college studies and literary emulation, marked all his letters. At the time of a scholarship examination he wrote to him—" Cast all care on your best Father and best Friend, who is always near, always loves us, and receives our attempts to serve Him with constant acceptance and favour. With Him is the best, pure, and the full reward. . . . O let us walk close with Him, and seek only to please Him, or we shall be driven about with every wind. I had rather you had the three prizes of faith, hope, and love, than all

the prizes that all the universities of the whole world
could confer, and I do trust the Lord of all will not fail
in giving them.   Covet earnestly the best gifts."

The following letters in the course of the summer, explain his impressions with regard to the state of the
Church, and the general aspect of the cause of Christ.
The longing for brotherly union among pious Christians,
amidst the perilous delusions of the age, was gathering
strength in his mind.   The first of them was written to
the Rev. D. Brown of the Free Church of Scotland, in
reference to a sermon, bearing on the subject, which he
had published.

*June* 24.

MY DEAR SIR,

I took the opportunity of going to town, to call on H., and left
with him the Sermon, bringing before him this sentiment, that we
should bend all our strength to the forwarding of those great
things in which Christians agree, the growth and extension of
spiritual and evangelical religion, for the conversion and salvation
of perishing souls all around us, and through the earth.   I shall be
thankful if he takes up the subject, and brings it before Christians.
But oh, when I look at the state of the Church every where, my
heart sinks within me !   I fear that nothing but uniting afflictions
and judgments will at length give full efficacy to our testimony to
the truth as it is in Jesus.   It is out of the last tribulation that
the great multitude comes, Rev. vii. 9—14.   Yet none of our
efforts shall be wholly thrown away : they shall be productive beyond our largest hopes ; sowing in tears, we shall reap in joy.   I
wish our Churches in England were more in the penitent, prayerful
state, of the Free Churches of Scotland.   In our one Head,

Affectionately yours,

E. BICKERSTETH.

*Watton Rectory, June 25.*

MY DEAREST D'AUBIGNÉ,

I thank you for your welcome note of May 28, and your interesting little volume of " Rome and the Reformation." . . .

We were delighted with Monod, and rejoiced to welcome him as a Christian brother. I have a great hope that the real children of God are more and more coming together, and as we do, we shall be greater blessings, first to each other, and then to our fellow-men. Popery and lawlessness, with Infidelity, are our great foes. May we have wisdom and grace, earnestly to contend for the common faith, once delivered to the saints. I hope that Puseyism has received some effectual checks; but it has done, and is still doing, much injury to mere professors.

We deeply sympathized with you in your personal trials; but who is largely used of the Lord without such trials? They are part of the cost of being a real blessing to others.

I was much pleased with your address on the one body of Christ. Many are looking out eagerly for your fourth volume of the Church History of the Reformation. May you be largely assisted from on high in the work! I have been prefixing remarks to translations of Gaussen's Discourses on Rome and Jerusalem, and publishing them for the benefit of the Foreign Aid Society. I hope they will do much good in England. . . May we so labour for our blessed Master, Jesus, that we may rest in fulness of joy at His right hand. In our one Lord,

　　　　　　　Ever affectionately yours,

　　　　　　　　　　　E. BICKERSTETH.

*Watton Rectory, June 25.*

MY DEAR SIR CULLING,

Right glad shall we be to see you in England on your return, and obtain some of the benefits of your long absence from home. I thank you for your interesting letter. I am most anxious about the religious state of the continent; but geography has its interest as connected with the higher elements of truth.

I cannot but hope that one good effect will arise, amidst numer-ous evils, from the Dissenters' Chapel Bill. It will bring the true children of God of all denominations, who hold the Head, more to real unity. They will see how few they are, how weak they are in themselves, and how wicked it is for them to fight for minor things, instead of pressing the great things.

Not that we must relinquish truth. I firmly believe that it is a national duty to establish and maintain true religion; and that writers like Vinet, Wardlaw, and others, are unscriptural in their opposition to this. You, I fear, agree with them; but there are so many deeper truths on which we are agreed, that I will not separate from my brethren in the Lord on this ground. I believe that the true religion shines clearly in the word of God, and that all who reject it or oppose it, do so sinfully—but to their own Master they stand or fall; and God forbid that I should judge my fellow-servants, or say what is the measure of light necessary for their salvation.

I trust that these things are beginning to be more seen. The contrasted dangers of Popery, lawlessness, and infidelity, are oblig-ing us to take the whole armour of God. And the more truth we get from God's word, the more links of union we have with each other; while all error is dividing and separating.

I mourn over the state of our country; and blessed as England may be with reference to other countries, there is an indifference to our privileges, a worldliness, and high-mindedness, and a disregard of the things of Christ, that are most humbling. Oh what might not England be, had our rulers a zeal for God's truth and His glory. . . .

Very truly yours,

E. BICKERSTETH.

On October 10, 1844, the Rev. Josiah Pratt was called to his eternal rest, and Mr. Bickersteth was invited by the family to preach one of the funeral sermons for his aged and venerated friend. Almost thirty years before,

Mr. Pratt had been the means of introducing him into
that sacred ministry, and that sphere of missionary labour,
in which he had since been crowned with so large a blessing. They had worked together, for nine years, as Secretaries of the Church Missionary Society, and had been
united nearly as long in the pastoral charge at Wheler
Chapel. The attachment thus formed, and which was
founded on their common love to the great truths of the
Gospel, was cemented by their general concurrence and
harmony of judgment, in the practical questions that
successively arose in the Church of Christ. They were
alike strongly attached to the doctrine, the principles,
and the essential constitution of the Church of England,
and were alike of a catholic spirit, in their love and
willing fellowship of heart towards Christians of other
bodies, who loved the Lord Jesus in sincerity. Their
mutual feelings at first resembled those of a beloved son
and an honoured father ; and passed insensibly, with Mr.
Bickersteth's growing years and experience, and widening
influence, into those which endear an elder to a younger
brother. There was perhaps no one to whose judgment
Mr. Bickersteth looked with more instinctive deference.
In a letter to the Bishop of Calcutta, in July of this year,
he had observed—" Dearest Mr. Pratt is still spared to
us, though getting feeble. I and Mrs. Bickersteth spent
three or four days with him in the beginning of May. O
the beautiful Christian simplicity, humility, and love of
our revered father, and his beloved wife ! " On the other
hand, Mr. Pratt's letter, on Mr. Bickersteth's illness of
1841, shows that only the wisdom of a deeply-experienced
Christian withheld him from expressions of most affectionate admiration towards his beloved friend. There
was in both of them, the union of deep spirituality with

great practical energy, and a single aim to glorify their
Saviour. Their occasional divergence of judgment, which
was very rare, only rendered their mutual esteem more
striking and beautiful. Mr. Pratt paid his last visit to
Watton in the summer of 1843, and their intercourse at
that time was marked by an almost playful confidence of
deep and long-tried friendship. He had never adopted
those views of prophecy, which gave so distinctly their
tone to Mr. Bickersteth's later writings and ministrations ;
and the adoption of them naturally seemed to him some
drawback on the usually sound judgment, and practical
excellences, of his beloved host and friend. In a time
prolific in excitement, he felt called upon to be a spiritual
conservative ; and could not help expressing, now and
then, his affectionate jealousy, lest one who was so justly
honoured in the Church of Christ, should either indulge
himself, or encourage in others an appetite for novelties, and thus indirectly obscure the prominence, which
needed to be given, in his view, more than ever, to Jesus
Christ, and Him crucified. These cautions, as they were
given, were received and returned in the spirit of love,
by one who felt their real value, but who was perhaps
more alive than his friend to the danger on the opposite
side ; and who knew that, with regard to Christian doctrine, as well as Christian practice, there is no surer mark
of decay than to think that we have attained, or are already perfect. Some allusion having once been made by
Mr. Bickersteth to the signs of the times, as confirming his
own convictions of the near approach of Christ's second
coming,—Mr. Pratt turned to him, and said very signifi-
cantly ; " I stand just where I did ! " Mr. Bickersteth
answered at once, with his joyous tone and beaming
smile—" I hope that I am getting on a little." The playful

repartee was full of meaning. If stability is one characteristic of living faith, progress is another. It is needful
for the Christian, not only to be rooted firmly against
the winds of false doctrine, but to grow continually in
the knowledge of Christ and His word.

The text chosen for the funeral sermon was Josh. i. 1, 2.
After describing the character of him who was taken
away, like Moses, in an important crisis of the Church's
history, Mr. Bickersteth made the words an occasion for
unfolding the duties to which the survivors were called
by such a loss, in the progress of the Church to its better
and heavenly inheritance. " I was struck," he said,
" when I visited our departed friend, and saw him for
the last time, on September 23, with the earnestness with
which, in a voice almost inarticulate, he spoke of his own
feelings, of the duty of preaching Christ more earnestly,
and labouring far more zealously than he had ever done,
for Him. O, could he now return from the heavenly
mansions, how would he return with every feeling deepened, with every exhortation full of power, to call British
Christians to use their many advantages for the Lord !
Every thing calls us to tread firmly, and with enlarged
hearts, in those steps, which our revered friend has marked
out for us ; following confessors of the truth in every age.
To save a soul from death—to bring a soul to Christ and
glory—oh this is worth living for, and labouring for, and
dying for ! It is the highest happiness to ourselves. It
diffuses the highest happiness on earth. It makes us the
largest blessings to our fellow-men. It is preparing for
us the highest crown of glory in the world to come. The
issue of it is glory unspeakable, joy unutterable ! "

The same month deprived the writer of the privilege
he had enjoyed for more than eight years, of daily inter-

course with Mr. Bickersteth under his own roof, by removal to another sphere of duty. It was a privilege for
which he cannot be too grateful to the Father of mercies.
Every year seemed only to render his society more precious, and a purer and deeper fragrance of holy love
breathed around him, as his spirit ripened continually for
its translation to the bosom of the Saviour. There was,
in his daily affection, a tone at once of such mature,
experienced thoughtfulness, and of such frank, open-
hearted confidence, that it was like the love of a father,
and an elder brother, both united in one. His private
journal alludes to the change of duties, consequent on
this removal, and to other domestic incidents, and exhibits the reflections with which the year came to its
close.

"*August* 30. The Lord has blessed me, wherever I
have been, in His happy work and service. I have to be
thankful for mercies of this kind in Buckinghamshire and
at Barnet. O Lord, purify my heart, and raise my mind
to Thyself.

" I have before me lengthened journeys from September 13 till October 8, to Exeter, Bristol, London, Norwich,
and their neighbourhoods, for the Jews' Society, while
Mr. Birks will preach a course of parting sermons at
Watton. He leaves me for his new living at Kelshall in
the middle of October.

" *October* 26. God has graciously carried me through
long journeys and important duties for Him, and in
pleading His cause. Last Sunday, I was called to preach
Mr. Pratt's funeral sermon at St. Stephen's, and at Wheler
Chapel in the evening. . . . . On Thursday I preached
at Rugby, for the Church Missionary Society. Blessed
be God, who calls me from time to time to special acts of
service, and strengthens me for His work ! . . .

" I have now the whole duty of the parish upon me, which I prefer to having a fellow-labourer, if the Lord strengthen me for it, while my son is at college. I hope that my heart will thus be more drawn to my work in the parish.

" My heart needs quickening, and drawing near to the Lord. It is clear that changes are about to take place, materially affecting the Church of Christ ; and oh, how needful is it to walk closely with God, in a faithful discharge of known, plain, and immediate duties ! O Lord, make me a blessing to my parish, that I may not labour here in vain for Christ's sake.

" *November* 24. Very gracious have been the Lord's dealings with me in the past month. I have been strengthened for my duties in the parish, and have found, I trust, increasing comfort in my work. I have commonly ten public services in the week ; four on the Sunday ;—the Bible class at ten—morning and afternoon service—and evening lecture ; a school lecture on Monday, Bilton's Cottage on Tuesday, Wempstead and the school-room on Wednesday, Bishop's Cottage on Friday, and the Prayer-Meeting on Saturday. O that, in each of them, there might be tokens that the Lord is giving testimony to the word of His grace !

" I have this week been to London for the prophetical meetings, and have found them very profitable and edifying. O that I may be grateful, and improve all the means and blessings which the Lord so graciously provides !

" Yet I find these London journeys very distracting, as it regards home duties, and I must now be as little as may be away from my parish, since I cannot be so without loss to my flock. O for closer communion with God in all His work !

" *December* 31. This has been a year of very many spiritual mercies and blessings to me and to my family. How good has the Lord been to me in scenes of public usefulness, in my journeys to Scotland, to Devonshire, and to Clifton, and in my publications. All glory be to His name !

" O that there may be a closer walk with Him ! My heart breathes after His image and likeness. My soul longs to be sealed with the Father's name in my forehead. The likeness of Jesus is indeed a prize above all value. O Lord, give me this ! Then only shall I be satisfied, when I awake up after Thy likeness !

" I desire also especially to record my gratitude to God, that I have been strengthened in body for my duties, without a curate. It gives me a more direct interest in my flock, and enables me to continue charities which otherwise I must have restrained."

# CHAPTER XXV.

## THE ENDOWMENT OF MAYNOOTH—COMMENCEMENT OF THE EVANGELICAL ALLIANCE.

### A. D. 1845.

TOWARDS the close of 1844 Mr. Bickersteth's friend and late parishioner, General Marshall, whose hospitality he had repeatedly enjoyed at Brighton and at Clifton, was seized with a dangerous illness, which in the course of half a year carried him to the grave. On April 2, Mr. B. preached his funeral sermon, from Rev. xiv. 13.

The following notes, occasioned by this illness, shew his habitual sympathy with Christian friends in their times of sorrow.

Walton Rectory, Sept. 9, 1844.

MY DEAREST GENERAL,

How we grieve over your illness! but it is of the Lord—the God of light and of love; and we shall not cease to pray that all may be sanctified. . . . .

Oh how every thing tells us—This is not your rest! And blessed be God, how all His word tells us—"I will give you rest!" "Come unto me." Look at the freedom—*give ;* look at the certainty—*I will ;* look at the personal application—*you.* And, dear friends, the Lord himself shower the blessing richly upon you! You have comforted many, many hearts with your love. May the Lord now comfort you with *His* love.

Ever gratefully and affectionately yours,<br>E. BICKERSTETH.

*Norwich, October 6.*

I must write, on hearing the sad tidings of your being worse. We cannot but suffer with you, for we are members of one body. I have three sermons to preach to-day; but my heart flies again and again to Clifton, and then upwards to our heavenly Father, to be graciously present with you; if it be His will, to remove the disease; and especially to grant that, while the outward man decays, the inward man may be renewed day by day. O what a sweet hope is added! " Our light affliction, which is but for a moment, worketh out for us a far more exceeding and eternal weight of glory," while we are looking at unseen and eternal things. Christ, Christ only, is our sole foundation. He will be with us through the valley. He will receive us, when it is passed through. He will present us faultless to the Father. His blood, His righteousness, His Spirit, His image—these are the glorious dress which He gives. Let us day by day put on Christ; so shall we be found clothed with the garments of salvation.

These are our common hopes, my beloved friends, which infinitely out-balance all the sufferings of this life. O may Jesus be very precious to you now! And dear, dear Mrs. M., the Lord greatly strengthen her for all that He calls her to, and be her constant refuge and support. " The name of the Lord is a strong tower; the righteous runneth into it, and is safe." He gave us all to each other; and if He separates us, it is but to restore us, more perfect than ever. I have rejoiced in seeing His work advancing in your souls, each time I have been with you; but O how advanced will it be, when we wake up after His likeness, and meet in the heavenly kingdom, pure as He is pure, and see Him as He is!

The Lord bless you and keeep you! The Lord make his face to shine upon you, and be gracious unto you! The Lord lift up His countenance upon you, and give you peace, prays,

Your very affectionate Pastor and Friend,

E. BICKERSTETH.

*Watton Rectory, November* 8.

Thanks be to God for all His love to you. The two last letters have been quite refreshing.

I am very busy now in my parish, and God is giving me comfort. Two are dying—a child about ten who has just told me, " I am so ill, I do not know what to do." I told him, " but Jesus knows what to do for you, and He will do it." He replied, " Oh yes, He is all my trust, He is my shield and my strength." I went from him to old Farrer, who is dying, and he said, " Jesus is my rock and my salvation." The old and the young disciples have one voice for our precious Saviour. His name be glorified for ever! God bless you both, my dear friends, and perfect that which concerneth you, prays,

Your ever affectionate,

E. BICKERSTETH.

*Watton Rectory, December* 20.

My conscience has just been saying to me—do not forget your beloved friends in Harley Place, in a letter, as well as in prayer ; and I seize pen and paper, to silence that all-important and precious monitor, so good a friend if we yield to his monitions, and so sad a foe if we neglect them.

O my dearest friend, what a precious Saviour is our blessed Jesus. Amidst the shaking of every thing here, we seem driven by every thing to cling closer and closer to Him. You have had an afflicting disease, to draw you near to Him ; and we have changes, and agitating fires,* and such fearful movements as we see in Exeter diocese and elsewhere, to send us to Jesus. But He is carrying on His own work in the midst of all. . . .

The Church Extension Fund is a noble plan. What a magnificent seed-time God is giving to His Church, in the midst of all

---

* An incendiary fire had taken place, a few days before, in Watton parish, in which many ricks of corn were destroyed, and the dwelling-house narrowly escaped the flames.

these confusions, and what a glorious harvest is before His faithful people !

Our hearts are always with you both. We know you love the Lord Jesus, and this eternal bond unites us for ever.

*February* 24.

MY BELOVED GENERAL MARSHALL,

Our hearts are with you, and often lifted up to God, in all your trials and sufferings. They are perfecting the vessel of mercy, to be a vessel of glory ; to purify all the dross away, and make you quite meet for the Master's use. I had hoped that the Lord would yet have raised you up for more service here on earth ; but should this not be so, should He want you now to swell the choir in the heavenly kingdom, His holy will be done ! O what thanks we owe to Him, that He revealed to us Christ, and His free and full salvation, and led us to trust in Him only, to glory in Him only, and to be open and decided in testifying of Him !

I was preaching yesterday on the words—" They washed their robes, and made them white in the blood of the Lamb." It is different from the other—" He washed us from our sins in His own blood." But we need also the same blood, that our robes, every grace and service, faith, hope, love, prayer, alms, kindness to others, &c., may also be perfectly cleansed ; and then there is joined with it, " great tribulation." O how sweetly will you sing that song, when you see our blessed Jesus, and cast yourself at His feet, and He welcomes you into His kingdom !

You have been a great help and comfort to me, my dear friend, both in my ministry and in my family ; and how glad shall I be, if I can speak a word of comfort to you. God Almighty bless you both.

Most affectionately yours,<br>E. BICKERSTETH.

The following was written to Mrs. Marshall on the first tiding of her husband's removal.

*March* 27.

My beloved Friend,

Our hearts sank, as we read your deeply-affecting note. The will of the Lord be done!

Any thing I can do for His blessed character, and for your comfort, is entirely at your command, as to the funeral or the sermon. . . . . We must think how we can make so great a loss to us a real blessing to the Church below, as it is a joy to the Church above. Though we must give all the glory, from first to last, to the Lord, so upright, and faithful, and open, and bold a confessor of the truth as it is in Jesus, is an example that must be held out in these days of trimming and time-serving. The Lord enable me, and direct me, so that many may be quickened by his course.

And now, my dear friend, be not cast down. Do not sorrow as those who have no hope! The time is very, very short, even for you who are much younger, as well as for us who are elder; but our Master will use us a little longer ; and we shall have more of a pilgrim, devoted spirit, I trust, while that time is continued; and then—oh what a meeting, what a glory for ever! Comfort yourselves with this hope. He is with Christ, which is far better, ever happy in the presence of Him, whom we all love the most—loving even each other for Jesus' sake ; and soon we shall join the blessed company.

Most affectionately yours,

E. BICKERSTETH.

The return of his birth-day led to the following reflections, in his journal, on his own duties, and the state of the Church at large.

" I this day complete fifty-nine years of my life. Glory be to God for fifty-nine years full of mercies. Shame and humiliation to me, for fifty-nine years full of defects, infirmities and sins.

" I find my work continually increasing, and am obliged

to decline many things that daily come before me. But it is a day in which much may be done for the Lord. May my time be more and more redeemed for Him ! I have completed 'The Signs of the Times in the East, a Warning to the West,' and a new edition of the ' Promised Glory ' is now in the press.

" The state of the country occasions anxious thoughts. The present Government seems set on bringing in measures falsely called liberal, really infidel, for giving political power to the Jews, and support to the teachers of Popery. The dispensation of grace to the Gentiles seems fast closing, and the Jewish restoration at hand. At least the signs of the times are such as may well increase our watchfulness.

" But oh that I may not, in public duties, lose sight of that which infinitely concerns me, seeking the glory of God in every thing, and to approve myself in His sight in all my thoughts, and words, and works.

" Easter Day being earlier than usual, my birth-day falls in Passion-Week. May the sacred season be very quickening to every resolution to love and serve the Lord.

" O Lord, direct my soul in all its plans and purposes, that in the important subjects which come before me, I may ever be guided to that course, which will be according to Thy word, and at the last approved of by Thee ! "

" *March* 22. I desire to go to the Lord's table in a humble and contrite spirit, with a believing and devoted heart, and in full purpose of soul to walk more consistently hereafter, as a Christian minister. Many things are needed for this.

" In private—a far deeper meditation daily on God's word—a much more close walking with God through the day—a greatly enlarged pouring out of the heart to God in prayer, (many things that ought to be brought before God in prayer are hardly ever mentioned)—a habit of self-denial and self-sacrifice.

" For my family—a more diligent seeking of the improvement and profit of all—a more constant remembrance of each in private prayer.

" For my friends, especially my relatives—to think of them more in intercessory prayer.

" For my parish—the searching out of sheep that wander altogether—the more diligent noting of their actual state—greatly enlarged visiting of them in their own houses—the habit of speaking to them about their souls.

" For my god-children—to remember them more before the throne of grace.

" For my church and country. To do what I can to maintain truth, and bear witness against error, and to save the souls of others, as well as to shew mercy to the poor and afflicted.

" For Christendom—gladly to help efforts for the salvation of Papists, the revival of Protestant Churches, and to prepare all for the day of Christ.

" For Jews, Mahomedans, and Heathen—oh how much is yet to be done !

" O Lord, help me to walk in every good word and work according to the wonderful preparation which Thou hast made in Thy providence, that Thy name may be glorified in me and by me.

" *April* 18. ' The Signs of the Times,' my eighteenth volume is now published. O that the Lord may use it to His glory, and the promotion of His truth, and mercifully grant that I may ever practice, myself, what I strive to teach to others.

" At this time the Parliament in the Commons are
debating on the increased grant to Maynooth.  The Lord
himself frustrate this iniquitous attempt to support the
training up of the teachers of Papal idolatry."

The Maynooth Bill, to which allusion is here made,
awoke in Mr. Bickersteth a mingled feeling of grief and
indignation.  Accustomed to look on Popery as a fearful
apostasy, clearly predicted in the word of God, believing
it as plainly idolatrous in principle and practice as heathenism itself, and to be so pronounced by the very Church
which the State continued to recognize, he felt the measure
to be an enormous national sin, and a direct provocation
to the God of truth and holiness, by whose favour alone
Britain had been so highly exalted among the nations.
His grief was especially stirred, that any of those whom
he loved or esteemed in private, for their personal piety,
should take part in a measure which he viewed with a just
and deep abhorrence.  The following letters, two of them
written to an opponent, and one to a supporter of the Bill
in Parliament, explain his principles and feelings ; and
present events are throwing new light on the justice of
the views, which he, along with many others, then maintained.

*March* 10.

My dear ——,

You would probably perceive by the papers that I have felt it
right to testify publicly against the grant to Maynooth.  The more I
consider the subject, the more fearful a measure it seems to me
really to be. . . . . But I know the peculiar temptations of benevo-
lent minds, like yours, and Wilberforce's, and Buxton's ; that you
instinctively shrink from the severity of doing what seems harsh,
though it may be real mercy to Romanists as well as Protestants.

We have no support here from foreign countries.  They have

preceded us in these infidel measures. England has stood alone in principle, and therefore alone in blessedness and glory—not sending forth from the same fountain sweet water and bitter. Our only support is the sure word of God, which clearly describes Rome, and threatens judgment to all who partake of her sins.

If government is too blind to discern between truth and error, at any rate there would be some consistency in supporting neither : but there is both infidelity and folly in supporting both. Protestants are awaking to it, and will be indignant, and grieved to the heart, at such a dishonour put upon God and His truth.

True it is, the political difficulties of Ireland are great, and this through our sins; and the grant to Maynooth among those very sins. But if God have given us power over Ireland, as unquestionably He has, what an affront to Him to use that power in paying to train up teachers of idolatry ! Shall we do the like in India with Mahomedans and Hindoos, and pay teachers of the Koran and priests of Juggernaut ? Power is a trust, to be used for God, and not against Him.

I see, as clearly as can be, the harlot mounting the beast, before she is drunk with the blood of the saints; and as a patriot, as a Christian, and as a minister of our Reformed Church, I would lift up a voice, humble and feeble though it be, against it.

*April* 12.

My dear ——,

I venture to write to you again, after reading Peel's, Gladstone's, and Roebuck's speeches. Peel's is worldly conservatism, Gladstone's is superstitious Romanism, Roebuck's infidel liberalism—the three unclean spirits of this day (Rev. xvi. 13), all perfectly opposed to the word of God, which abides for ever.

Gladstone denies that Protestantism is anything more than a negative term, as knowing and feeling nothing of its life-giving doctrines, common to all the Reformers; and so defames that which God accounts in his word (Rev. x.) an unspeakable blessing.

He insists that we should look upon it in the way in which the Irish Papists must regard it—that is, we must give up our truth to adopt their error. His speech is more revolting than even Sir R. Peel's. He professes to look for principles, and has not one scriptural principle to stand upon.

Roebuck thinks it requires omniscience to know what truth is. Was there ever such a Pilate-like state of mind?

The real strength of the case seems to me very simple. God says, " Thou shalt not bow down to an image." The Papists bow down to images. The Queen is made by the legislature to say, " This is superstitious and idolatrous." The same authority now proposes to educate persons, who shall teach what the Queen then declared to be superstitious and idolatrous, at the expense of the country. It is monstrous infatuation, apart even from the testimony of Scripture against this corruption of Christianity.

It is more than ever the turn of England's future history. We are Christians, but we are patriots. We love our country and our families. Now is the special opportunity to be faithful to God our Saviour, and to our fellow-men, and to save ourselves and those that hear us. . . .

I write in the fulness of my heart, hoping that God may strengthen you to stand up for His truth where it is so little regarded.

Most truly yours,

E. BICKERSTETH.

*April* 11.

MY DEAR ——,

Your letter gave me pleasure, as opening the grounds on which conscientious minds may concur in such a grant. Thankful should I be, if I could show you as clearly, as I think I see myself, the insufficiency of those grounds for such a course.

Government is a real trust from Almighty God, for the good of the governed. They are appointed of Him for this end, the punishment of evil doers, and the praise of them that do well. (Rom. xiii. 1 Pet. ii. 13—15.) The principle which is to guide their conduct is clearly laid down. (Ps. ci.) The administration is to be paternal.

Now it will not do for a child, who wishes for that which is evil,

to receive from his father support in doing evil. The father, however much the son may wish it, must not help in giving him tutors,
either to teach him to *steal*, or *to bow down to an image.* His
duty is of an opposite kind. True, the son may help in earning
the income that maintains the family ; but while the father has his
authority from God, he must use it according to the will of God.

All revenue is really the Lord's—the earth and the fulness
thereof; and governors, as well as the governed, are accountable
to Him for every part. . . . I quite agree with you that mere penal
enactments will only do mischief, when tried as they were, alone.
The children of God, not the government, have been roused in the
last twenty years to Christian exertion, in setting the truth plainly
and affectionately before the people of Ireland in their own tongue ;
and God has blessed their efforts, notwithstanding all the counter-
acting influence of government-favour to Papists, and withdrawal of
favour from Protestants. But the efforts to quiet Ireland have
utterly failed, as the present measure abundantly shows. It will
have the dreadful issue of implicating Britain in the idolatry of
Rome, and of teaching Romanists that there is no danger in their
religion. God preserve you from sanctioning that apostasy which
you abhor.

Most truly yours,
E. BICKERSTETH.

About two months later, the entry is found in his journals—" The Lords have just passed the second reading of
the Maynooth Endowment Bill by a large majority—the
most painful public measure that the Legislature of this
country have passed within my recollection. My heart
sinks to the dust for my beloved country. The Lord
give us true repentance !" A little earlier he had written
in a private letter, " O what an amount of false principle
this bill has disclosed ! I fear it will be carried ; but
the worst thing is the disclosure of inward faithlessness
to Christ and His truth."

Amidst the deep anxiety of Mr. Bickersteth, occasioned
by the dangers of his country, and of the Church of Christ,
and the ceaseless pressure of his correspondence and
other public duties, he was still surrounded by an atmosphere of peace and love in his own quiet home. The
constant flow of affection, from a husband and a father
so justly beloved, and returned by those who felt the
greatness of their privilege; the frequent resort to him,
for advice or comfort, of so many Christian friends; the
full tide of daily correspondence, embracing subjects of
the most various interest, and the harmony of an united
family, had rendered Watton Rectory one of the most
sunny spots on the face of the earth  The influence
which he had exercised at home, began to be now diffused over a wider domestic circle.  His son was already
in the second year of his course at the University; and
this summer witnessed the first marriage among his children.  The frequent visits, also, of his many nephews
and nieces, who were dispersing from their homes, to
prepare for new duties, and occupy posts of influence, or
to become the heads of new families, and who all looked
up to their uncle Edward with peculiar affection and
reverence, gave to his domestic life, from this time, an
almost patriarchal character. His journal of this summer,
while it alludes to the changes in his family, records his
own personal and deepening experience of the Divine
goodness.

" *May* 11—*Whitsunday.*  I have been spending a busy
week in London at the great May Anniversaries.*  The
Lord pardon every thing said and done, not according to
His word ; and accept my poor, feeble attempts to speak
for Him and His truth, amidst all the mingling of my

* He preached this year for the Church Pastoral Aid Society.

own grievous infirmities and sins. Jesus is all my confidence, hope, and glory, now and for ever."

" *June* 28. This last month has been one of very special mercy and loving-kindness from our God.

" I have seen my eldest daughter married to my beloved friend, Mr. Birks, and they have had a journey, full of mercies, to the north.

" My weakest daughter, F., has had a much better state of health, and all my other children are well. My son has again got the Chancellor's medal for the best prize poem.

" And what I count a special mercy, I have had some sweet seasons of melting of heart before God, and refreshing views of His grace and loving-kindness.

" There have been many deaths in my parish, and several of them have been attended with real comfort, in the sweet hope that they fell asleep in Jesus. May the season be blessed to my people !

" O that the Lord may graciously open doors for the union of His people, who love Him, and for their separation from the world that lies in wickedness !

" I think I find the advantage of having the parish entirely upon me, in giving me a deeper interest in it, as the primary work, and chief object of my daily labours. O Lord, give me more wisdom, faithfulness, earnestness, and love, in dealing with all classes for their eternal welfare !

" *July* 26. This month has been again full of mercies, as is each day of my life. Oh, how great a debtor I am to Divine grace ! . . .

" We have had very good meetings for the Church Pastoral Aid and Bible Societies. Thanks be to God for permitting us to labour in these works of love. I have also been to Cheshunt and Hatfield for the Church Missionary Society.

" I have begun some letters on Christian Union, to be inserted in the Record. The Lord guide and prosper me.

" But I fear that my soul is not in so lively a state this month, as the one before. What a poor, fluctuating creature I am ! Lord, revive Thy work, and never leave me to myself."

" *August* 30. The letters on ' Union ' are published, and will, I trust, have a wide circulation.

" I am going with my whole family to Sandgate, God willing, on Tuesday, for a month, to exchange duties and houses with my friend Mr. Green. May it be much blessed to both our families, and both our flocks !

" I visited the Southboro' Church Missionary Association, preaching for the Society ; and attended the Barnet Jews' Meeting.

" God is graciously sending us a good harvest, after a season of much anxiety. May His goodness to our nation lead us to repentance ! "

The letters, to which allusion is here made, were one public expression, amongst many, of that longing for closer union among the children of God, which had been awakened at this time in the hearts of Christians, and which led, in this and the following year, to the formation of the Evangelical Alliance. The object itself was eminently dear to Mr. Bickersteth's heart. His intimate connection with the Alliance, both in its origin and its progress, and the large place which it occupied in his private thoughts and public labours, render a brief account of it indispensable in his biography.

There were two main causes which led to this movement, and seemed to justify and require some effort of the kind, to heal the breaches of the visible Church, and bring Christians into nearer union with each other.

The first of these was the growing conviction, in the minds of sincere Christians, belonging to different bodies, that their real union of heart and judgment was far greater than the outward appearance. It was, however, almost entirely hidden from the eyes of the world, by the variety and frequent bitterness of ecclesiastical controversies. The evil thus arising was great and notorious, and had a most pernicious effect in weakening the hands of Christians, and hindering the spread of the gospel. It seemed, then, a duty to meet this public evil by some public remedy. There was also another powerful motive for such efforts, in the progress of Popery. The recent passing of the Maynooth Bill, in spite of strenuous opposition from such multitudes of British Christians, had rendered this danger more apparent than ever; and proved, in a striking manner, how the divisions of the Church of Christ had weakened its moral influence, and were imperilling the cause of truth in our own country, and in every part of the world.

Several steps had been taken previously, which tended to this fuller union. Among these may be mentioned Mr. Stewart's annual invitation, for many years, to united prayer for the outpouring of the Holy Spirit; an Address of Mr. James, in 1842, to the Congregational Union; the appointment of a Committee by the Scotch Church in the same year, for brotherly intercourse with other bodies,* —the public meeting in London, June 1843, in furtherance of the same object, an address from brethren in Switzerland, and another from Dr. Patten of New York, who urged the duty of a general conference in London, with a view to mitigate the dissentions, and if possible, to repair the breaches, of the Churches of Christ. But

* A volume of Essays, by eminent ministers, on Christian Union, was printed and circulated by Mr. Henderson of Glasgow.

the more immediate occasion of the Alliance was the
united opposition of British Protestants to the Maynooth
Bill, in the spring of this year.  The intercourse of those,
who were brought together by their common efforts to
avert that national sin, led to a growing desire for union
with each other, and with all Evangelical Protestants;
while the need of it, from the aspect of the times, seemed
more urgent than ever.

It was thought inexpedient that the invitation should
be given by the Anti-Maynooth Committee, which had
been formed for a distinct and political object.  Several
members of the Scotch Free Church had already taken
steps for the promotion of Christian union ; and by the
consent of their English brethren, the task was devolved
on them, of inviting to a preliminary conference the
leading members of various evangelical bodies of Christians throughout the empire.  The invitation was issued
August 5, and Liverpool was fixed upon as the most convenient place for their meeting.

The letters on " Union," which Mr. Bickersteth wrote
and published in the course of July and August, arose
from the depth of his own personal convictions ; but they
concurred remarkably with these other steps of Divine
Providence.  The Spirit of God was working simultane-
ously in many hearts.  It was while these letters were
publishing, that he received the invitation of the Scotch
brethren, many of whom he knew and esteemed, to take
part in the proposed conference, which was to be held on
the first of October, and had the very same object in
view.  From such a request, coming at such a time, it
seemed unnatural and inconsistent to turn away.  Mr.
Bickersteth was well aware, however, that the practical
success of the conference would be likely to depend, under

God, on the presence of adequate representatives from
the various evangelical bodies, and more especially from
the Church of England. He endeavoured, therefore, during
his visit to Sandgate, to procure promises of attendance,
or of sympathy, from those of most influence among his
brother clergymen. The general tenor of their answers
was discouraging. His spirit was weighed down with fear
and heaviness, and he was led, with increased earnestness, to commit the whole matter in persevering prayer
to God. All approved highly of the object; but some
were suspicious of the parties by whom the circular was
sent forth, others deemed co-operation impossible, and
thought the attempt likely to cause increased division;
while those who sympathized more hopefully with the
movement, were afraid to commit themselves to it, till
they could reckon on the support of some large number
of their brethren. When one refusal followed another, it
became a serious question with him, whether the possible
sacrifice of influence, in his own immediate sphere, might
not outweigh the benefit which the cause of union would
gain from his presence at the meeting, since the same circumstance diminished also the hopes of a very successful
issue. The simple faith, which led him to say thirty years
before;—" There shall be a Church Missionary Association at Norwich, if I have to stand alone on the Castle
Hill,"—guided him now in a similar perplexity. He
knew that the object was immensely important, the duty
of promoting it by all lawful means, clear and imperative;
and he saw nothing but a risk of incurring odium, or a
vague fear of possible dangers, to place in the other scale,
against an apparent call of Providence, and the obligation
of consistency, in his practice, with his published sentiments. The line of conduct which he pursued, and the

feelings which guided him, appear in his journal and letters, and in his own publications connected with the Alliance. He went to the Conference in October with fear and trembling, under a simple conviction of duty in the sight of God, and with considerable sacrifice of personal feeling. His fears were disappointed, and his hopes surpassed, by the character of the meeting. The Spirit of God seemed to be specially present with His people, amidst their many infirmities, to bless them in their feeble efforts to obey the command of Christ, and cultivate the love of the brethren; and he returned to his home, praising the Lord for His goodness, with renewed zeal to labour in the furtherance of love and union.

On September 9, he replied thus to the Scotch circular of invitation.

DEAR SIR,

It will give me real pleasure, God permitting, to meet my brethren of different denominations, holding the Head, at Liverpool, for the furtherance of Christian union and brotherly love, and in withstanding, at this critical time, the common enemies of our blessed Lord. May He himself graciously direct us to those measures which shall be for His glory.

I feel strongly that mutual humiliation before God is needed from us all. O may the spirit our Lord has pronounced to be blessed, in his Sermon on the Mount, be granted to us! We shall agree in devotional and practical things, I trust, to a large extent; and there is a wide field of doctrine also, in which we are one—if we can keep subordinate things in their due place.

It appears to me, it would much strengthen our standing before the true Church of Christ, if we included expressly Socinianism, as well as Popery, as one fatal error with which we have to contend. They were both nationally discouraged at the Revolution; they are both now nationally favoured, and need therefore the express protest of real Christians.        Yours, affectionately,

E. BICKERSTETH.

In another letter, a few days later, he observed :—

It is clear the true children of God will soon have to stand alone against all the mighty hosts of this world. Politicians and Statesmen, men of learning, talent, and genius, earthly-minded men, the superstitious as well as the Infidel, the Papist and the anarchist, will all combine against those, who, cost what it may, denounce their errors as fatal and ruinous ; and who will hold forth the word of life at every sacrifice of ease, peace, advantage, and honour.

There are two grand impediments to real union.  On our part, the spirit of the Canons * is a dead weight, confining, cramping, and keeping us from recognizing Dissenting bodies as true Churches of Christ ; and on their part, the anti-church spirit is like a fiery poison in the veins.  Both these evils, I think, will be greatly diminished by the mutual forbearance of brotherly meetings, with the determined purpose—' whereto we have already attained, let us walk by the same rule, let us mind the same thing '—and not pressing any thing on which we differ.  If we can get into common actings of brotherly love, for the spiritual benefit of Papists, and the strengthening of Protestants, in Ireland first, and then in France, Germany and elsewhere, either by already-formed Societies, or a fresh Society, we shall by well-doing put our adversaries to silence.  It would be a glorious object, worthy of our meeting, to bring on the Philadelphian state of the Church, which I believe has yet to appear.

He wrote, a few days before the journey :—

We can never take any step onward in the cause of Christ, without obstacles as mighty as the Red Sea before us, and the Egyptians behind us. . . . May the Lord himself give us the wisdom that is

---

* In Mr. Bickersteth's deliberate judgment, the letter of the Canons was not morally binding on the conscience of any clergyman, since no assent to them is required.  Their obligation, in his opinion, was like that of obsolete and injudicious laws in the state ; and implied merely the duty of submission to their penalty, or compliance with their injunctions, when enforced, as a small price for a great ecclesiastical benefit.

profitable to direct. I go in weakness, fear, and trembling, and yet with a full conviction that it is our dear Master's work; and with readiness, I trust, to suffer reproach for His sake.

The meetings lasted three days, Oct. 1—3, and two hundred and sixteen Christians, of seventeen denominations, were present. They commenced with prayer and devotional services, and continued with free discussion on the great object itself, of Christian union, and the various difficulties which stood in its way. Mr. Bickersteth had the privilege of being the first called upon to supplicate the gracious presence of God, and His blessing on a work of love. He also occupied the chair on the morning of the second day, at the third sitting of the conference; and on the third day, after the conversations were ended, moved the first of the resolutions, both in the morning and evening. It was in accordance with the spirit which he so earnestly desired to cultivate, as the surest pledge of real union, a common humiliation for sin in the presence of God. In his parting address he made these remarks on the aspect of the times, and the duty of faithful Christians.

We shall have to buckle on our armour for a more arduous conflict, only not with each other, but with a common foe. We shall feel that we are in one great army, under one Head, the Lord Jesus Christ, fighting against the Devil, and Antichrist in all its forms. From my own knowledge of the state of Popery, and of Christendom, and from some study of the Divine word, I think that we must prepare for a very serious and awful conflict with that great apostasy, which has so long deluded the Church of God. My great hope and joy is, that all who love the Lord Jesus Christ in sincerity, will then be more and more as one army united together, and that they will have such joy and such triumph in the midst of their conflicts, such comfort of love in Christ Jesus, that trials and afflic-

tions themselves will be full of blessedness, enabling them to glorify
God in the fire.

I am anxious we should all convey the spirit we have felt in
these meetings to our respective neighbourhoods, though I feel that
there has been a spirit manifested, which cannot be conveyed by a
mere recital. I trust our hearts are so fully knit, that, as the
mouth speaks out of the fulness of the heart, when this conference
breaks up, it will spread blessings all over the land. The Resolution is as follows :

> "That this Meeting desires to express its humiliation before God
> and His Church, for all the divisions of the Christian Church,
> and especially for every thing which we ourselves may have
> spoken, in theological and ecclesiastical discussions, contrary to
> 'speaking the truth in love ; ' and would earnestly and affection-
> ately recommend to each other in our own conduct, and parti-
> cularly in our use of the press, carefully to abstain from, and to
> put away, all bitterness, wrath, anger, clamour and evil-speaking,
> with all malice ; and in things whereon we may yet differ from
> each other, to be kind, tender-hearted, forbearing one another in
> love, forgiving one another, even as God, for Christ's sake, hath
> forgiven us ; in everything seeking to be followers of God, as dear
> children, and to walk in love, as Christ also hath loved us."

When I remember that the first of the beatitudes is, "Blessed
are the poor in Spirit," and that they ascend in a climax, till we
read, "Blessed are the peace-makers," I cannot but trust that this
meeting will ultimately inherit all the blessings there pronounced.
May God enable us to go forth in the spirit of the beatitudes to
our respective homes, and circulate those impressions of humility
and love, which have been made on all our hearts.

After one or two touching and beautiful confessions,
made by those who spoke next, of their previous offences
against Christian love, Mr. Bickersteth was obliged to
leave the meeting ; and all who were present rose, as he

left, in token of their deep respect. On the following day he wrote from Watton to a private friend.

I am just returned from the most touching, truly Christian, and most profitable three days' meeting, I ever passed in my whole life. They will ever be memorable to me, for the oneness which our God gave, first in heart, and then to a large extent in judgment, to the leading ministers of more than a dozen evangelical denominations, from England, Scotland, Ireland, and Wales. More than two hundred were present, of ministers and laymen. Many weighty resolutions were passed, as the basis of union, and then of future action. They were much discussed, but not one dissentient voice disturbed the passing of those resolutions. The last, while I was there, was one of humiliation before God for our divisions, confessions of our sinfulness, and purpose to abstain from angry, irritating things hereafter.

I went, at great personal sacrifice, not merely of time, &c., but what cuts infinitely deeper, without my brethren who so generally think with me; but I doubt not, I shall thank God, in the day of judgment, for His grace in disposing me to go. . . . The first meeting for two or three hours was simply spent in prayer, reading the Scriptures, and singing. This brought us into a heavenly and devout state of feeling, and then two meetings were given to mutual conference. Sub-committees arranged business, and subjects to be brought forward; a solid basis of union was fixed, and then plans of future action, the whole being preliminary to a larger meeting, if God will, in the summer of 1846, in London.

The Lord prosper it yet more abundantly to His glory and the good of His church! The God of peace and love was with us throughout. Help us not only by your prayers, but also by your pen.

In a letter to Sir Culling Eardley, of the following week, after some expression of his feelings with regard to the practical evils of the Anti-State Church movement, he continued :

It is always a privilege to submit ourselves one to another in the fear of God, and he who is first in this is really highest with the Lord. I feel the vast importance of our meetings at Liverpool, and if we have grace from the Lord, rightly to improve the opening which He has given us, no tongue can tell the sweet joys of light, union, and love, before the children of God. But oh, how much there is yet to bear and forbear! I am writing daily to influential brethren. . . . In the light of prophecy, I fully hope that the Philadelphian state of the Church is coming on. God give us the blessing of the peace-maker, though it be, as I believe, followed with the higher blessing of suffering for Christ's sake. Matt. v. 9—12. Phil. i. 29. Rev. iii. 7—13. May you have a rich reward in devoting yourself to this blessed cause! It will fill Lady C. with joy, and bring a rich reward on your dear children.

Very affectionately yours,<br>E. BICKERSTETH.

He wrote on the same day to his beloved friend, Mr. Stewart, who soon after joined the Alliance.

Never, in all my many meetings, did I attend such truly blessed ones as these. Cast down as I was, with not having my brethren with me, and standing so much alone, yet there was such a manifestation of Divine grace through the meetings, in frank declarations of sentiment, in forbearing one another in love, in manifested unity in great things, in the spirit of devotion in every prayer, and the spirit of praise and joy, as we came to unanimity in the basis of union and work before us, as filled our hearts with gratitude to God and love to each other. . . .

I would now earnestly, through you, entreat all my dear brethren, whom I love in the Lord, and at many of whose feet I have sat with such profit, not to impede or oppose a work which God seems graciously to have owned: or to be any stumbling-block to those, who, like themselves, loving truth and peace, are seeking to be peace-makers among brethren. I would write separately to others, but am overwhelmed with work.

The cheering dawn, however, which delighted the hearts of many in these first meetings, was speedily overcast with clouds, and the hindrances and difficulties in the way of union began to appear. The following note, towards the close of the month, alludes to discussions which had taken place in a synod of the Free Church, and to other difficulties which were rising in various quarters.

*Watton Rectory, October 25.*

My dear Dr. Candlish,

I see that you in the north have difficulties with some of your brethren, as we in the south have with brethren of another cast of mind. But it is sad when we fight against all Popery, but the Popery of the inner man in our own bosom ; and when all opinions are heresy but those at which we have personally arrived, and the strife becomes—Who is the infallible interpreter ?

But I would write on a more difficult subject—membership of our alliance : all who join us now will influence and govern us hereafter. If we leave it quite open to all who acknowledge our basis, we are in great danger of unsuitable men pressing in. I am disposed to think that limiting it to *communicants* of Protestant churches, who concur in the basis—though it might diminish, perhaps, our numbers, would purify and strengthen the body. I should like to have your mind on it, before any recommendation in our Committee.

Very many of my brethren are with me in heart, who do not join. Their difficulty is this : While the Dissenters, as a body, maintain their present attitude of hostility to what they call the State Church, if I unite, I shall be compromising interests I ought to defend.

The goodness of God in the Liverpool meetings was so great, as may encourage us to hope that He will yet use us in furthering the union of His people. God bless and strengthen you in your many weighty duties, prays

Yours affectionately,

E. Bickersteth.

The following alludes, in part, to the same discussion, and to an article in one of the Scotch papers, containing, with some praise of the Alliance, a strong invective against the Church of England.

*Watton Rectory, Oct.* 31.

My dear Mr. H.,

Your letter has given me great pleasure. Thanks be to God for leading you to this view of the subject. G.'s speech is singularly clever, and yet absurd. " You must agree with me in every point, as the first step, and absolutely essential."

We are really feeling our way towards fuller union. The true view of our effort is, an immediate purpose to co-operate for definite ends, on the strength of that partial union which really exists, and a hope that, by strengthening and cultivating the actual union, and a careful abstinence from needless causes of irritation, it will please God, in his providence, to open the way for a deep and full union. We must not mar the first and easier stage, by confounding it with another for which we are not ripe ; neither, if the movement is to be real, must we in our hopes abandon the other, which ought to be attained.

I was sorry to see the article. It is not true. The Evangelical Clergy are not an insignificant fraction of the Church ; and even the errors in other pulpits are much oftener defect than positive falsehood. The preaching has commonly a higher standard than the preacher, and with the Lessons and Liturgy, a nearly full system of truth is before the eyes of the people. This cannot make up for the want of heart and power ; but still it is a libel to describe it as, in the vast majority of cases, the constant inculcation of deadly error. The spirit of Christ, which rejoices in truth, wherever it finds it, is wanting in such statements.

Affectionately yours,

E. BICKERSTETH.

The general feeling of Mr. Bickersteth on the difficult,

though blessed work, in which he was now engaged, appear in his private journal.

" *October* 25.  The events of the last two months have been very important.  I spent the month of September at Sandgate, preached at Dover, and went to Fredville (Mr. Plumptre's residence).  God greatly prospered several charity-sermons, and I hope good was done.

" On Wednesday, Thursday, and Friday, October 1—3, I attended a series of meetings at Liverpool for promoting Christian union.  There were representatives from twenty denominations, and God was very graciously present with us ; so that, amidst the thousands of meetings I have attended for the last forty years, I never was at any so full of unction and blessing.  We came to very harmonious conclusions, and I hope, laid a basis for more extended efforts to promote the same blessed cause.

" But this is likely to meet with violent opposition from all quarters, and at present, I fear, but little support even from faithful ministers, who love the Lord.  It is so new and untried.  I desire to move with prayer, wisdom, and faith.  Lord ! give me all needful grace !  Specially quicken me in Thy way, for Thy name's sake. ·

" A new edition of my ' Divine Warning' is passing through the press.

" *November* 28.  The importance of the Liverpool meetings is, I think, beginning more and more to appear.  The Alliance thus formed, is rapidly increasing and spreading, amidst much coldness and opposition from many, who, I hoped, would have favoured it.  It has brought a great increase of correspondence and labour upon me, and frequent journeys to London.

" I have had the joy of seeing one of the most unlikely numbered among my communicants.  Truly the Lord is manifesting His grace in my parish more, since He has led my heart to seek the union of His Church. To Him be the glory.

" My ' Family Expositions,' taken down by one of my daughters, have been sent to the press. May they be blessed of God. We had important prophetical meetings last week. Thus work abounds more and more; but thanks be to God, that He gives me health and strength for it all. O may He be with me now at His table!"

The perplexities, which arose at this time, were from three different sources. Severe reflections on the Church of England were made, soon after the Conference at Liverpool, by one or two of those who had been present, both in meetings connected with the Free Church, and in those of the Anti-State Church Society; while these, and similar causes of offence were collected in the pages of the ' Christian Observer,' and were made the ground for a charge of treachery and deceit on the part of those who gave, and those who accepted, the invitation to Liverpool. Mr. Bickersteth endeavoured, amidst all these perplexities, to keep steadily in view the great object,—the removal of offences in the spirit of meekness, and the promotion of real unity and forbearing love. The following are extracts from three notes, written about the same time with this view.

*Watton Rectory.*

My dear ——,

Knowing from my experience at Liverpool your Christian principle, and your brotherly heart, I venture to direct your attention to an article in the Christian Observer of this month, on our Evangelical Alliance. I exceedingly disapprove of the article, and grieve over it as a one-sided view, and have written to the Editor freely; but I think it may be useful to shew you the real difficulties of our standing, who are of the Established Church, and how those difficulties are aggravated. . . . . I do not complain of your address as any departure from the stipulations of the meeting, but I should have numbered it, in your case, among things lawful, but not expedient, considering especially the exceedingly tender state of our infant Alliance, the immense blessing it may yet be, and the position of those brethren in the Established Church, who have cordially joined it, in the hope of attaining its great ends.

O may our God give us grace to meet all difficulty and opposition in the mind of Christ, not being overcome of evil, but overcoming evil with good, and remembering the perfect example of our blessed Redeemer, 1 Peter ii. 19—24. Excuse the freedom of my letter, and believe me,          Affectionately yours,

E. BICKERSTETH.

*Watton Rectory, Dec.* 14.

MY DEAR ——,

The brotherly spirit which you manifested at Liverpool, and which drew my heart to you, leads me to write to you direct, respecting the expressions in your address at Edinburgh.

There was nothing contrary to our agreement, and I fully admit the lawfulness, in that view, of your statements. But amidst the mighty difficulties we have in every way in bringing the children of God into oneness, there appears to me an undesirableness, at union-meetings, in speaking against bodies that hold the Head ; as placing our fellow-Christians under increased difficulties in working out the great object.

There are, blessed be God, several thousands, I might almost say to my own knowledge, of ministers of Christ who love and preach Him, in the parishes scattered over England ; and amidst all the defects we mourn over in our Church, we prize its institutions. Say, this is our infirmity ;—but we know enough, my dearest friend, of Rom. xiv, to bear with each other, even in infirmities.

My perfect confidence in you as a Christian brother makes me write freely.          Very affectionately yours,

E. BICKERSTETH.

My dear Dr. Candlish,

I write now respecting an article of this month in the Christian Observer, on our Evangelical Alliance; to meet which in the mind of Christ, overcoming evil with good, will require peculiar grace in our Scotch brethren. I believe the designs charged against you are as alien from your minds as possible, and I grieve at the sending forth of such suspicions. O may our God give you grace to act in the sweet spirit of the Gospel! (1 Peter iii. 8, 9). I believe, if we do so, these sharp accusations will give us our happiest victories. I should hope you or Dr. Chalmers, or Dr. Buchanan, will set the key-note of love again in answering this. I have myself written privately to express my grief.

I have had a very important adhesion from 130 ministers and laity of Geneva, stating more distinctly their doctrinal views. All seem afraid of going *much* further than we have done in a doctrinal statement, and anxious to impress the importance of the real spiritual life existing in the heart, and flowing from the articles we have confessed . . . . May the Lord guide us and bless us.

Affectionately yours,<br>E. BICKERSTETH.

The letter of the foreign brethren, alluded to above, and Mr. Bickersteth's reply, exhibit another, and perhaps a still more interesting view, of the practical working of the Alliance.

*Geneva, Nov. 19.*

Reverend and dear Brother,

We have the pleasure of communicating to you the accompanying address, and beg you to set it before the General Committee for the Promotion of Christian Union.

We have seen that the London Committee were authorized to inform the foreign brethren that you are a member of that Committee, and also that you were one of the presidents at Liverpool. These motives, added to the respect we feel for your Christian

character, have determined us to resort to your intervention.   Permit me to add two or three words in our private capacity.

The brethren whose signatures we have sent, concur in what has
been done in Liverpool, and in all with which they are hitherto
acquainted ; but it is clear that they cannot pledge themselves to
concur in what may hereafter be done without their knowledge.

We believe that all those who have signed, are earnestly and
prayerfully desirous that this Christian Union should be completed,
without any obstacle being thrown in the way.   But if the Committee in London make any considerable addition to the number of
the dogmas contained in their confession—if they enter into details
of doctrine on difficult points, it is possible that some, who now
adhere, might not be able to go along with such additions.

Articles are necessary ; but it is not in articles that we must seek
for Christian union, but in the word of God believed in the heart
in the work of the Spirit, in the blood of the Lamb, in communion
with the same Head.   Christian union can only be realized by much
faith and life on the one hand, and by much prudence and modera-
tion on the other.

Accept, dear brother, the assurance of our respect and Christian
affection.

C. BARDE, Pasteur.
MERLE D'AUBIGNE.

This letter was accompanied by another, signed largely
by the Christians of Geneva, explaining at length their
views of the basis proposed for the Alliance, and to which
the following was the reply.

*Watton Rectory, Dec.* 15.

BELOVED BRETHREN IN CHRIST,

Your letter was received by me with deep interest and brotherly
affection.   It very much accorded with the principles and feelings
which our gracious God has given me, respecting His glorious
gospel ; and having communicated it to leading members of our
Alliance, there is a considerable response in their minds.   You may

be assured, there is not the least probability that any thing will be made articles of the union, at all opposed to those sentiments.

At the same time it would be unwise to make limitations, which might exclude real brethren in the Lord. Our object was to make the opening so wide, that as many as possible of those who love the Lord Jesus Christ in sincerity, might be brought into our Alliance, and yet so distinct, that it might not be latitudinarian, and include those who hold vital errors. The brief statement which I enclose, will give you a clearer and fuller view of our aim than has yet appeared. I prepared it at the request of the London Committee, and they approved it. If it commends itself to your minds, perhaps you will be kind enough to get it translated into French, and circulated, to diffuse information among your brethren.

We deeply feel how much we need the special guidance of the Spirit of our God in every step of the way. We feel also, how ignorant we still are of the brethren on the Continent, who would cordially join with us in this blessed work. Our only hope is in the Lord, and we wait on Him continually in prayer. The impediments are great, every where, to real, cordial, full, Christian union. But the mighty Spirit of our God, who has already converted to the Lord the thousands and tens of thousands of His people in every land, has accomplished, in that conversion, the great elements of the union we desire to make visible to the world, by a manifested oneness of confession, and by a real brotherly feeling, notwithstanding all diversity in subordinate things. Thus will our Saviour be glorified, and the Papist and the Infidel be left without the excuse, so often urged, of the variations of Protestant Churches.

You may render us great help, by furnishing lists of brethren on the Continent, with whom we might correspond on this great object; and especially such leading brethren, as it would be desirable to have at the London summer conference.

May I add—British Christians have much sympathized with our suffering brethren of the Canton de Vaud, and grieve over the harsh and unchristian spirit in the government, which has dealt so severely with faithful ministers of Christ. It is one object of our Alliance, to shew brotherly love to brethren, suffering for the truth in any part of the world; and I hope that, when our plans are matured, ways for doing this effectually may be opened.

You may be pleased to hear that this cause is daily gathering strength in the country. Ministers of Christ in all denominations are giving in their names. We have good hope that our God will increase us, and bless us, and make us a blessing. . . The Lord bless you and keep you, and make his face to shine upon you. You have much refreshed our hearts by your brotherly letter, and strengthened the principles on which we are united. Pray also for us, that we may be guarded from every thing that would mar this work, and guided to all that may strengthen, confirm, and enlarge it.

Your affectionate brother in Christ,

E. BICKERSTETH.

This eventful year closed with the following reflections in his journal.

" *December* 24. Goodness and mercy follow me and mine. All glory be to the Lord.

" The Evangelical Alliance spreads, and calls forth the opposition, alas! of good men. Lord, grant that their opposition may so purify this work, that at length they may be brought to join us! There is to be, God willing, a meeting on January 8 in London, and others on the 15th and following days at Liverpool, which I hope to attend. O for heavenly wisdom, patience, forbearance, and love! Surely I need especially to abound in prayer.

" God has been very gracious in providing an opening for my child F. to pass the winter at Torquay, in Sir C. Eardley's family, and for help being found to provide me a fellow-labourer. All glory be to His great name for his many mercies.

" I have suffered much in the last fortnight. Thanks be to God for sufferings, which humble me, and draw me near to Him.

" I entreat Thee, make me a larger blessing to my people ! Oh that there may be in my parish that Christian union, which I desire to spread and diffuse ! But I had need walk softly, when I see how hard it is to walk in union with my own flock and people. Of all my duties the most humbling is my public worship, so dead and formal. O Lord, at length give me some life there !

" *December* 31. Through mercy I am brought to the close of another year. How excellent is Thy loving-kindness, O my God !

" Certainly the most important work, in which I have been concerned this year, is the Evangelical Alliance. The difficulties seem to thicken, so that unless God marvellously appear, and give us special wisdom, I fear it will yet fail. So many of the excellent of the earth hold back from it, after full consideration, as necessarily to keep us very humble, and very dependent before God. He can crush us in a moment. He can also in a moment raise us out of the dust.

" O my God, I especially pray for my parish. I thank Thee from the heart, that in the past year several truly hopeful additions have been made to the communicants, and I have reason to think Thy Spirit has been at work in their hearts. Carry on Thine own work.

" We hope to begin the year to-morrow with a special prayer-meeting for a blessing, as we have just closed this year with a service in the Church.

" O Lord, I commit all unto Thee ! Without Thee I am nothing, and can do nothing, and all that has been done comes to nought ! With Thee every thing prospers. Never leave me ! O never forsake me ! "

# CHAPTER XXVI.

WITH the new year, Mr. Bickersteth continued his labours in the cause of Christian union, which was now more than ever dear to his heart. Even those who doubted the expediency, and feared the results of the proposed Alliance, could hardly fail to recognise, in his recent efforts, the simple integrity and earnest zeal of an upright and loving spirit. He was not exempt, in some quarters, from bitter censures and malignant aspersions; but most of those who loved him before, even if they now differed from him in judgment, loved him the more deeply for the Christian charity, and ardent desire for the glory of Christ in the closer union of His people, which evidently promoted his labours. He was, on his side, very jealous that no diversity of opinion, on a question of expediency, should create fresh suspicions, or weaken mutual confidence, among dear Christian brethren. His zeal was for the great object itself, the love of the brethren; and while his judgment thoroughly approved of the Alliance, he was far from being disposed to idolize it. His views of prophecy made him hopeful of great and real good, but kept him from being sanguine, like some of its zealous friends, of immense results, and of a speedy success that would dazzle the eyes of the world. In all his public speeches and private counsels, he chiefly dwelt on the need of mutual confession, of abasement and humility, if the work was to be prospered by the Divine blessing. An extract from the close of his address on January 8, at a public meeting in London, shews the real nature of his hopes and feelings :—

"Union with all who love the Saviour is not a matter of choice ; it is a commanded duty. To join the Alliance is optional, and very many real Christians will stand aloof. But we must not, therefore, love them the less. O how much of the power of the movement depends on our adhering to this spirit, especially those who take a leading part in it ! God forbid that, by unholy tempers we should increase disunion, instead of healing it.

"Let us not think too highly of this effort—let us not expect too much from it. It is not the mechanism of a society that will heal our divisions, but God's truth that we may bring out, and the aid of the Spirit that we may obtain by prayer. Let us abase ourselves—let us abase our society, as altogether feeble and insufficient in itself, and magnify our great object as all-important. This will be the secret of our strength, and God may then use us far beyond our expectations."

On the 17th of January he wrote from Liverpool, where he had attended a further conference, and introduced some practical resolutions for the furtherance of humility and forbearance :—

MY BELOVED CHILDREN,

God's loving-kindness continues abundantly. Our Liverpool conference of four days went on very well throughout, and in parts was intensely Christian and edifying.  The Manchester meeting last night was prodigious, five thousand people at least in the magnificent Trades' Hall, and a truly Christian spirit.  How good the Lord has been in every part of the progress of this work !  Nothing on the Lord's part could more effectually have furthered our blessed object. . . . At times, things seemed threatening, and this brought out the best feelings of all : difficulties were prayed away.  Let us all praise the Lord for ever.

Your own father,<br>E. BICKERSTETH.

On his return he wrote in his journal ;—

" *January* 24.  I have been to Liverpool and Manchester, and was carried graciously through weighty duties for my Saviour.  I think and hope that the Alliance will, by its Christian spirit, manifest clearly to God's children that it is of God.  In the week before this, we had six important meetings ; and I trust that real good was done, in laying a more humble and wide foundation for our future proceedings ; but it will require time to win my brethren to join in it.  At present comparatively few of those, who love the Lord, have united with it in my own church.  Lord, draw them.

" O Lord, only let my heart be right with Thee—only let me be accepted of Thee !  This one thing I desire— Thy favour, Thy approval.  Truly life is a vapour ; the favour of man is vanity. . . .

" All my temporal as well as spiritual concerns I leave with the Lord.  May He provide for all, and enable me to be a far larger blessing in doing good, than I have ever yet been.  O Lord, thanks be unto Thee for any and every instance of Thy goodness, in using me for the good of others.  Yet more largely use me in this way, for the glory of Thy great name, and especially in my own parish, and among my own flock ! "

On Jan. 29, he wrote to a clergyman, who had referred to some proceedings of the Anti-State Church
movement, as a difficulty which prevented his own
adhesion to the Alliance, and after some remarks on that
subject, concluded with this statement of his views :—

How are we to overcome evil? There is tremendous evil in this
war of brethren, Protestant brethren, biting and devouring one
another. It is the scoff of the Infidel and the Papist. I believe
that we shall best overcome it, by men of the beatitudes presenting
another spirit, that shall commend itself to the minds and consciences of all men, overcoming evil with good. It is not necessary
that all who have a heart-union should visibly unite, but it is needful that enough should do it, to produce the effect of a brotherly
recognition.

It is with the Lord whether it prosper or not. I feel that hitherto
the design is hopeful, though full of difficulties. I endeavour to
commit it all to the Lord; my conscience being clear that His
truth and His love are my main motives in what I have done. Be
also fully assured of my entire conviction of your brotherly spirit
and faithfulness to Christ.

Very affectionately yours,

E. Bickersteth.

Watton Rectory, Feb. 2.

MY DEAREST MR. BEVAN,

Peace and every blessing be with you and yours. I have read your
letter with deepest interest, and fully enter into your difficulties.

I think that we, whom God has honoured to be leaders, must
expect to be the special objects of Satan's enmity, and to be specially tried in this very character, that we may be proved, and
approved, and further used. God has singled you out to stand in
the fore-front of the battle, and no wonder Satan should specially
aim his darts at your ease and comfort in it. Let us gain our
lesser victories, and it will be a token of the greater triumph.

I hope also that —— will have learned by past experience on the one hand, and that the spirit and atmosphere of our meetings may have a sweetly subduing power on the other, and then all his energy may have a right direction. Surely we have seen this already.

I know how hard it is, when we see inconsistency, to believe there can yet be grace; but look at David, living months in sin, and Peter cursing and swearing, at well as into our own hearts, and till the Lord come, we can despair ot no living being.

Your very affectionate friend,

E. BICKERSTETH.

*Watton Rectory, February 2.*

My dear Mr. Garbett,

Your beautiful Christian letter, so full of thought, and unction of spirit, has much interested me. No doubt the difficulties of manifested union with those whom we know to be brethren in Christ by their fruits of faith, hope, and love, while they differ in many things which we think important and precious, are very great.

But some things are clear. Fulness of confession of truth does not exclude disunion. There is a much greater disunion between me, and Dr. Pusey, or a mere worldly clergyman, than between me and Mr. James, or a spiritually-minded Dissenter. Yet I quite agree, the more truth we *cordially* receive, the greater is our fulness of union.

But the state of the heart is the main thing; and we have had much on our thoughts to press a Christian state of mind in our differences, such as is brought out in Rom. xiv.; 1 Cor. xiii.; Phil. ii.; Eph. iv., and in many other passages. A little light in the understanding, if we walk faithfully by it, and real love in the heart, will do much for the union.

All human language is vague and indefinite, and can never exclude false professors. God's own word is the highest and clearest light which our world possesses; and our own Articles and Homilies are very plain and explicit, yet what differences they are made to cover!

It is wonderful to see the strange alliances against this movement.

. . . It appears to me as if each had cherished an idol, which is in danger of being broken. The warm combatants, too, of the powerful minds, are not prepared to come in; but other dear brethren are with us, and I do believe, what is of all things most important, the God of peace and love is with us. He has helped us in our difficulties, cheered us in our trials, and strengthened us to stand. . . .

Ever most affectionately yours,

E. BICKERSTETH.

It pleased God within a few days to fulfil the anticipation expressed in his previous letter, of special trials to be expected by those who were leaders in a work of love. On Feb. 11, while on his way to a Committee of the Evangelical Alliance in London, Mr. Bickersteth was thrown out of his carriage by meeting a cart loaded with bricks to build a Roman Catholic chapel, at Old Hall Green ;* fell under the wheel of another that was passing in the opposite direction, and which passed over the lower part of his body, crushing him very severely. For two or three weeks his life was in imminent danger ; and one of the smaller bones in his leg was doubly fractured. Some extracts from a journal kept during his illness, will give a more vivid impression of the trial, and of the special grace and consolation with which he was accompanied :—

" *February* 8, Sunday. Our dear father preached twice on the words—" Grow in grace and in the knowledge of our Lord and Saviour." His mind was so full of the blessedness of the knowledge of Christ, that we said, in coming home, he never seemed so near heaven before.

---

* It is due to the gentlemen of that establishment, to notice the courteous visit of inquiry, which two of them were sent to make after Mr. Bickersteth's health, on hearing of the accident, and the circumstance which occasioned it.

" *February* 11, Wednesday.   Papa left home at seven
for a Committee-meeting of the Alliance.   After prayers,
E. was called out to speak with a poor woman.   She
said to her, ' Your father has got hurt—thrown out of
the chaise—the back of his head is cut, but not much ;
and I heard him say, his feet are the worst.'

" Mr. Dalgleish had received the account before us, and
while his carriage was got ready, came to relieve us, by
telling us he was going to bring him back immediately.
We had a prayer together.   After an hour and half the
carriage drove up quickly.   It was with difficulty they
lifted him out, and three men supported him up stairs,
but he fainted, and nearly threw them down. They lifted
him into bed, and Mr. D. gave him a strong cordial, and
waited anxiously to see its effect, for, though he did not
tell us, breathing was suspended, and he feared that all
was over.

" After a few minutes he breathed, and said, ' Sarah.'
Mamma hastened to him.   ' Praise God that I am preserved ! '—and then to us, ' The Lord is very good, dear
children.'

" Active means were used to restore warmth, but the
pain was racking, and for some time every breath was a
groan.   Calling one of us to him he said—' Good and upright is the Lord.   You see I thought I was to serve the
Lord in London, now I am to serve Him here in suffering.'   He then said, smiling, ' The Lord is very good,
dear H.   I was just thinking myself very important ; that
they could not do without me in London, and now I am
to be taught another lesson.   You have all to praise God.'
While he was trying to sleep, and groaning with pain, he
whispered to us, ' Praise the Lord.'   He added soon after
—' There is much to praise for, much to profit by, and

much to be submissive under.   I am all sores and bruises
—I can lie nowhere in peace : that is a picture of the
state of the soul.   From the crown of the head to the
sole of the foot there is no soundness ; but wounds, and
bruises, and putrifying sores.'   When we repeated to him
Psalm xlvi. he added. ' The Lord is my salvation and my
healing.'

" Constant fomentation, and incessant calls of friends
and parishioners, filled up the day ; the fulness of sympathy has been most refreshing.   In the midst of his pain
he remembered his little godchild's birthday, (Miss L.
Smith), and dictated the following note.

> My dear Lucy,
> I have not forgotten that this is your birth-day, though I am
> sorry to say I have met with an accident in being thrown out of my
> gig, which confines me to my bed, so that one of my children writes
> for me.
> I shall not forget to pray that God will give you His Holy Spirit,
> and help you to love Jesus very much, and to try and please Him in
> being very obedient to your dear parents.
> Your affectionate god-papa,<br>E. BICKERSTETH.

" Our dear father was in great danger all that night.
(Mr. D. said afterwards that he feared every hour he
should have to break the tidings, that mortification had
begun, and the case was hopeless.)   He seemed aware of
it, for in the whispered prayer on his lips we caught the
words—' The Lord's will be done, if I recover, or if I go
hence.'   When suffering much from the bruises in the
night, he said—' He was wounded for our transgressions,
he was bruised for our iniquities.'   The extreme pain

allowed him only an hour's sleep, after taking an ano-
dyne. . . . .

" As soon as we heard of the accident, we sent a letter
to the Committee, to account for his absence, and all
the members present united in prayer for him.  Sir Culling came down the following night, and could scarcely
speak to us for grief when he came in.

"The whole of Thursday tho pain scarcely abated.
Our dear father speaks only of mercy.  ' All is well ; the
Lord is full of grace.'  When told of the repeated and
hourly inquiries, he said, ' The sympathy of my family
and my friends has been more overwhelming than the
accident.'  ' I have not a grain of the medicine too much,'
was his remark when he saw us distressed by his sufferings.  He had formed many engagements for work, and
we had to write to five different quarters to say that he
could not fulfil them.

" *Saturday.*  Still not out of danger.  Mr. D. fears the
formation of an abscess, which might prove fatal.  At
night E. came from Cambridge, and left on Monday with
a lightened heart, thankful to have spent a little time in
that chamber which is indeed, as our dear father calls it,
' A chamber of light and love, and peace and praise.' "

On Monday he seemed slowly recovering, and dictated
the following letter to the London Committee of the
Alliance.

*From my sick-room, Watton Rectory.*

MY DEAR BRETHREN IN THE LORD,

I cannot but be grateful to our merciful Father, and to you, that
as soon as you heard of my dangerous accident, in that brotherly
and sympathizing spirit which has hitherto distinguished all our
meetings, you united at once in prayer for my recovery.  This
comfort of love, this fellowship of spirit, will be our great support

in the trials and difficulties of our most blessed work. I have had opportunities, in the seclusion of a sick room, of reviewing the way in which we have been led, and the objections made to our efforts, as well as the difficulties which impede those who are most friendly to us, and I am only the more confirmed that we are walking in the way, in which the Lord would have us walk ; and if He give us grace to proceed in patience, forbearance, wisdom, and love, we shall have a blessing beyond our largest hopes. It is so peculiar a privilege and honour, to have been early and prominently engaged in this work of love, and it is likely, if prospered of God, to be recompensed with such full spiritual blessings, that those who are thus circumstanced, as all the history of the Church teaches us, must expect to pass through peculiar trials, and some even be laid aside for a time ; that the Lord may shew more distinctly, it is not their work, but His, and we may all rejoice the more to give undivided glory to His great name.

The delicacies and difficulties experienced, not only between the different sections, but within almost every section of the Christian Church, in this matter, are just what we ought to have expected, had we comprehensive knowledge of each other's situation. They call for continual forbearance in love on all sides. The more we can be forgiving and forbearing towards one another, the more we can bear one another's burdens, the more we can exhibit the meekness and gentleness of Christ, in our dealings with each other's infirmities and ignorances, the more speedy, the more happy, and the more peaceful will be the triumph of love. While the more we clothe ourselves with mailed, impenetrable armour, in a fancied, perfect, and minute system of theology—though it be really Scriptural, and seek to maintain it only by controversy, in the prominent urging of our respective peculiarities, the more difficult we shall find it to arrive at the fulness of Scripture truth, as well as to come together in love in the far greater things in which we are agreed. Not that I would call on any one to suppress what he believes to be truth; but if the spirits of the prophets are subject to the prophets, it is clear that we need not, at all seasons, and never except in that spirit of faith and love, meekness and fear, which our Divine Pattern justifies and demands from blind and erring creatures, urge what we believe to be a part of God's truth, revealed to our own minds, in which we differ from those we believe to be our brethren. The law of love, also, is to receive as a brother, him that is weak in the faith, but not to doubtful disputations. . . .

Thankful indeed shall I be, if my trials and helplessness, and lengthened hours on the bed of languishing, should, among the innumerable family and local blessings already given, be also honoured of God to the furtherance of Christian union and love, among all who love the Lord Jesus in sincerity. If the Lord should raise me up, as I trust He will do after some weeks, may He enable me to give myself more wisely, more lovingly, and more heartily, with you, to the attaining that manifested oneness of the people of God, which has never yet been fully realized, except in the truly primitive Church of Christ.

The God of love and peace be with you, and guide all your deliberations to His glory, and the furtherance of this manifested unity.

Your affectionate brother in the Lord,

E. BICKERSTETH.

" *February* 16.   Twenty-five answers to letters of sympathy and love were sent off to-day.   His pain drives away sleep, except from anodynes, but his great refreshment is a verse of scripture.   I read John xiii. at his request, and he added a beautiful prayer ; first for himself, that if it were God's will to restore him, he might be a fuller blessing to all in his works, publications, &c. ; then for dear Mamma and ourselves, that we might obtain fuller spiritual blessings through this trial, and that God would enrich us with more faith, love, hope, and experience ; thanking Him above all that He had made us one in Christ, near to Him, and thus nearer to each other, of one mind, and the same spirit ; then, he earnestly sought God's blessing on sympathizing relatives and friends, and especially for the parish, and for the Evangelical Alliance.

" While he prays for others, God gives others a heart to pray for him.  To-night a hundred of the parishioners, of their own accord, met in the school-room to pray for him,—a cheering earnest of his recovery."

" *February* 19.—*Thursday.*  Through mercy the alarming symptoms are removed, and our dear father scarcely suffers.  The privileged night-watchers have a chapter, prayer, and sometimes a hymn with him, in the morning. I never saw any thing like his deep humility.  He did not sleep so well last night, but told us he had quite as much as his best Friend saw good for him.  We expressed a wish he had slept better; he added, ' The only safe wish is, that the will of God may be done.'  Every morning brings a multitude of letters of sympathy.  Those of some of his Dissenting friends in the Alliance are full of affection, and he often blesses God for having taken a step, which has unsealed so many springs of love to him. This post brought one from Mr. Stewart full of comfort."

On Friday morning, amidst the restlessness which followed a sleepless night, he dictated the following letter.

My dear Mrs. Smith,

O what thanks to God I owe, more than I can utter or express, for all His mercies to a poor sinful creature, graciously vouchsafed in this most blessed trial.  His goodness has overflowed on every side, and you must allow me to speak good of His name, and to testify of some of His loving-kindness.

When I look at the way in which my poor dear people, in their trials, are often left, who am I, that God has made me to differ ?  A precious wife, whose watchful care and love has been my joy and relief for more than thirty-three years, has been strengthened to be my constant nurse.  My three dear daughters have by turns, day

and night, anticipated and supplied every want, and been spiritual
as well as temporal comforts.   Our skilful friend, Mr. D., has
always provided the best remedies; and sufferings and weariness
have literally been swallowed up in the tide of loving-kindness,
flowing in from all quarters.   It may show something of this, that
one hundred and twelve letters, in reply to expressions of sympathy,
have gone forth from the Rectory, only in the last five days.

But all this, in itself, might be empty and vain, and serve only
to the exaltation of the flesh.   Blessed be God, He is making my
trial fruitful in good to others, and first to my own dear flock.   He
has enabled my beloved son-in-law to improve the occasion for their
best good.   They have of themselves had repeated prayer-meetings,
which are described to me as peculiarly earnest and affecting.   Joyfully would I suffer far more, for a revival of religion among them.

But yet further, that most blessed object, which it was the design
of my journey to further, is, through the mercy of God, far more
promoted by my suffering through it, than if I had been permitted
to give my presence and counsel.   It has called forth most touching manifestations of sympathy and love from faithful ministers of
other denominations.   O what fields of unopened blessedness the
Lord has in store for His people!   Without the least thought of
mine, prayers were offered for me in more than a hundred churches
and chapels in London.   Is not this, my dear friend, true Christian
union?   Oh, when the restraints are removed from all the Josephs
of the brotherhood throughout the land, what gushes of endearment
and affection will be realized!   Is it not a singular mercy that,
before the Lord returns in glory, He should give His people such
fresh fountains of love?   O taste and see that the Lord is good!
It is my hearty prayer to Him, that you may have a rich experience
of the same goodness.   You also are encompassed by the loving-
kindness of the Lord in a special degree, and oh, may He give you
the joy of seeing this loving-kindness full of spiritual profit, in the
wide sphere which He has called you to fill.

Especially it is my prayer, that your earnest longings for the
spiritual health of your dear children may be so gratified that your
songs may have to burst forth continually, in gratitude to God.

O let us live not to ourselves, not even to our families, but to Jesus ; and we shall then live best to ourselves, and for our families, for ever.

My kind remembrances to Mr. Smith.   Much have I thought of him also during these trying seasons, so peculiarly trying to him. . . . But the Lord reigneth, that is enough for us all.   Still pray for me, for without Jesus I am nothing.

Most truly yours,<br>E. BICKERSTETH.

On Monday the 23d, when he seemed still advancing to recovery, he dictated the following paper to his children.

" *Gracious indications of the Divine goodness and loving-kindness, connected with the accident of Feb.* 11, 1846.

" My mind had been oppressed with the great amount of public duty, to which for many weeks and months the Lord had been calling me.   The difficulties of that blessed Society, the Evangelical Alliance, had been multiplying ; though the happy effects of it were becoming more and more apparent to those who had formed it.

" It seems the Lord's plan, that those who are called to peculiar service for our heavenly Master, must pass through humiliation and trial ; and especially, where the work is consolation, union, and love, that they themselves must be sufferers.   It appears to me that, to accomplish the great ends of personal sanctification, meekness for the Master's service, capability of being useful to others, and particularly of being a blessing to my family, to my parish, to my evangelical brethren in the Church, and especially to the cause of manifested oneness of the people of God, it was important that some providential trial of a marked character should occur, if the Lord should favour me

with one great object of my desires, to be a large blessing
to my fellow-men.   This providence was just of that character.   It was so marked and public, that it was brought
into the public journals ; it was known immediately to
the London Committee of the Alliance, whence it has
spread rapidly through the country.   It is just the Providence which goes so far to accomplish, through the
Lord's grace helping, (which may He grant for His Son's
sake,) all the benefits which my circumstances required.
I have a bruised body that confines me to my couch ; but
there has been no concussion of the brain to impede my
mental faculties.   It is also a singular mercy that this
occurred so near home, so that I was brought here within
a few hours, to· receive those rich blessings which the
Lord by this affliction has been pouring upon me.   By
His mercy I have enjoyed the constant care of a skilful
medical adviser, of my beloved and most tender and affectionate wife, and of three dear daughters who have felt it
their privilege to watch over me with unwearied love.

" The blessing to my people will not, I trust, be small ;
they have gathered together in increasing numbers to
remember their minister before the throne of grace, and
to intercede for the continued light of the Gospel in this
place.   The Lord make any sufferings of mine turn to
their good, and it will be joy indeed.

" The streams of love from relations and friends have
come in with a gush of kindness quite overwhelming, when
I consider my personal weakness and unprofitableness.

" Especially endearing and refreshing have been those
from members of the Alliance of other denominations ;
showing me from what streams of loving-kindness we are
turning away, in turning from our Dissenting brethren.
. . . . How good the Lord has been, to give such precious

tokens of brotherly-kindness, and such spiritual blessings, at so small a personal sacrifice ! He did not give me into the hand of Satan, to do as that adversary would, but just to do that which He saw would bring the richest blessings. My hope is, that as St. Paul's imprisonment, which apparently might have damped the zeal of friends, and so have impeded the Gospel, through the grace of God made them more confident and bold to speak for Christ, so my trial, incurred in going to the work of the Alliance, may perhaps make my brethren more willing to come to its support."

The three next days were a time of increasing danger, and growing anxiety, from the return of inflammation, and the severe shock to the whole system. The private journal continues as follows.

" *Thursday, February* 26. At three A.M. he said to Mrs. B.— ' I think it right, dear, to tell you, that though I got through the accident, I do not think I shall get over this.' She had hitherto kept up, but now her heart quite sunk within her. When Mr. D. came up, he confirmed all her fears, and soon after set off to London for Sir B. Brodie. The inflammation increased frightfully, and spread rapidly upward. Since Tuesday morning he has eaten almost nothing. He was calm and peaceful, but very solemn, and called me to read Psalm lxii. Seeing my distress, he directed me to the words, ' only,' and ' at all times.' He dictated the following letter to the village prayer-meeting."

*From my sick room.*

MY DEAR PRAYING PEOPLE,

I bless God who has given you grace, thus to unite in prayer for me. Such an affliction as this calls for great searchings of heart,

both in you and me.  Blessed be God, I feel fully assured that the
great truths I have preached to you have been those truths of the
word of God, which will judge us in the day of Christ.  But I
mourn before God innumerable defects, omissions, and negligences ;
the blood of Jesus is my only hope.  I pray God, my dear people,
that you may also be led to much self-examination and prayer, as
to how you have received the truth.  O be sure, nothing but the
word of God will do to build your hopes upon, and nothing but a
sound conversion of heart will answer at the last.  Make sure
work, I entreat you, in the one thing needful, the salvation of your
never-dying souls.  Whether the Lord will raise me up or not, I
know not ; but the great Shepherd ever liveth, and to Him I commit you day by day.  From the sick-bed of

Your affectionate pastor,

E. BICKERSTETH.

" He then bade E. write to Mrs. Smith, and tell her it
had been a great comfort to him to think that, if the
Lord were pleased to take him, Mr. Smith would certainly
provide a faithful pastor for his people.  In the afternoon,
after another severe attack, he fell back fainting.  We
all gathered round him, and he said—' If I were not sure
that the Lord is good, I should be so grieved to be trou-
bling you all thus.'  Mamma said—' God will be with
you and support you.'  ' Oh ! for myself I am quite
sure it is all good, for Thou, Lord, in very faithfulness
hast afflicted me.  It is you, love, of whom I spoke ;
but if it be God's will that I should sink under this,
He will support you.'  Again, he said to H.—' It is
the Gospel that supports me now.  Jesus is my only
hope.'

" B. and T. drove over by half-past four, but he was so
weak they did not see him at first.  When T. came in,
papa said, ' I have been thinking of that sweet text—

"I die, but God shall be with you."' 'Yes,' he answered, 'but there is another sweet text—" I shall not die, but live, and declare the works of the Lord."' 'Yes, he replied with a calm but feeble voice—' That is very true;' plainly meaning that he felt the will of the Lord to be the best, whether for life or death. He said again to Mamma—'If anything happen to me, God will be your support.' And soon after, to B.—' I have had no shaking of my peace; but if the Lord permitted, Satan could buffet me.' He asked them for Psalm li., and after a few minutes, added—' The Lord is my salvation; I will trust, and not be afraid.'

" The people are very anxious; the door is besieged with inquirers. A voluntary prayer-meeting of two hundred parishioners seemed a pledge of an answer in mercy, and encouraged us to hope."

" *March* 3. A most affectionate letter from Lord Ashley, and another from Mr. Stewart, mentioning the earnest prayers of many brethren at Liverpool. These and many others of the same kind, fill his heart with love and gratitude, which overflow in words of praise and letters of thanksgiving. When one of us said— ' This has been a week of trial,' he replied, ' It has been a week of full, rich mercies.' He dictated the following to Mrs. Smith.—

Glory be to God! What a flow of mercies have I been enjoying for the last three weeks. My expositions, just before my accident, were on the Apostle's desire to depart, and willingness to stay; and how good the Lord has been, in giving me something of the same blessed state of mind! And now there seems every prospect of the same issue, my being raised up for the service of His people. Thanks to you for all your kindness! If the giving a single cup of cold water does not fail of a reward, a cup of cream, every morning and evening, will, I am sure, be remembered by Him we love and serve.

How far beyond our thoughts, how deep, how comprehensive, is the wisdom and loving-kindness of our God! I had thought of great scenes of usefulness, in active exertions for my blessed Master. He says, " No, I will lay you aside, and teach you better, that you may be fitted for my service." My friends had thought, " Our minister gives too much time to the Church at large, he should give himself wholly to his parish." The Lord seems to say, " I will take him wholly from you for a time, that you may gladly see him surrender some of his time to the work of Christ at large, and yourselves and the whole parish obtain a richer blessing in his enlarged usefulness." I only desire to know, suffer, and do, the will of my heavenly Master, and be the joyful and spiritual father of many spiritual children, who shall be my joy and crown of rejoicing in the day of Christ. . . .

With kindest regards to Mr. Smith, believe me,

Most truly yours,

E. BICKERSTETH.

" His mind is again busy with schemes of usefulness. His ' Divine Warning' was now just completed ; and he was much interested with distributing it in quarters where he thought its stirring message was needed. He is busy, too, in looking over the ' Expositions on John and Jude,' and pencilling alterations for the press. He has begun also to read a little the fourth volume of Merle D'Aubigné's History, and Dr. McNeile's ' Church and the Churches.' "

" *March* 7. This day he dictated the following letter :

MY DEAR PRAYING PEOPLE,

Through the mercy of God, in answer to the prayers of many, I am going on most favourably. On Thursday last week, I almost thought the Lord was calling me home; but now I hope yet again to preach the glorious gospel to you. I shall now be your minister in a double sense, not only appointed by the providence of God, through my beloved patron, whose aim in fulfilling his trust has always been the best welfare of the parish, but also the minister of your own asking from the Lord. May it be the token of a re-vival of grace among us, and of more rich and abundant blessings in my ministry. . . .

I am anxious to bring before you, for your prayers, my choice of a fellow-labourer. Earnestly pray that the Lord may guide me to choose one, who will be a true yoke-fellow to me, and a constant blessing to yourselves. The prayer-meetings lead me to the sweet hope, that my dear people will hereafter be more perfectly joined together in one spirit; and so exhibit at home, what has been so much laid on my heart, the oneness of all who love Christ truly. I really hope God is about to give a large growth to this blessing in His church. Your minister has taken a very open part in pro-moting it. O that his dear flock may help him by their prayers, and by their example in forwarding this blessed work!

Nothing more expresses my feelings at this time than Psalm ciii. It just describes how good the Lord is, and has been to me. The principles I have preached to you, I have found every day powerful to sustain and comfort me in the time of trial. I can well recom-mend them to you, and say, " O taste and see that the Lord is good; blessed is the man that trusteth in Him." Let me however specially commend to you Rom. xii, as that which peculiarly adorns these principles. The source of them is, the Lord Jesus, our only and complete Saviour. My heart clung to such passages as these : " Look unto me, and be ye saved." " Behold the Lamb of God, that taketh away the sin of the world." May Jesus be all in all to every one of you, prays

Your affectionate pastor,

E. Bickersteth.

" *March* 19. Our dearest father's birth-day—a day to be long remembered. It was like a jubilee of thanks-giving for his restoration. He had a little family ser-

vice of praise with us, and in hearty prayer he commended each and all of us to God ; praying that, as in
God's providence his illness had been made so public,
and such fulness of sympathy and affection had been
received from all quarters, we might not pervert these
gifts of love, to nourish pride and self-conceit, but receive all the spiritual benefits designed by the trial.

" *April 25, Saturday.* Our father's first lecture on
the close of Matt. xiv. The room and the passage leading to it were crowded."

On May 3, after eleven weeks' silence, he preached
once more, and his subject was the practical benefit of
trials, from Acts xiv. 22, 23. The impression made on
those about him was thus described in a letter written
just after leaving his sick room :—

He has been so lively, so earnest, so confiding, so genuine, and
his conscience so tender ! First, he saw nothing but love even in
trial. All was right ; no pain, no weariness too much. Then he
seemed quite afraid lest, in the abundance of mercy he should forget
that it was meant as a humbling chastisement. I cannot but think
his light will shine more brightly than it had ever done before.
Mamma almost trembled to see him so ripe for glory. I felt rather
that an especial work is before him. The union of the Church is
to be brought out by a mutual recognition of the badge of union,
loving holiness ; and the man appointed to be a leader in this task,
must bear the badge most prominently. It was no intellectual training that he wanted, but soul-quickening trials. It was no work on
baptism, no exposition of prophecy, he was about to write. These
he has accomplished without any special exercises to prepare him ;
but when the loving work of union is to be promoted, even this
fruitful bough must be purged, that it may bring forth more fruit.
Oh that we were more like him ! Our religion seemed so superficial
by his bedside ; he little knew what an undertone of reproof there
was in his whole conduct, while so full of love.

The marks of deep sympathy from all parts of the Church, elicited by his illness, were most touching and beautiful. Out of a multitude of letters, three may be given : one from the Committee of the Church Missionary Society ; another from one of the most honoured servants of Christ, among his Dissenting brethren in the Alliance ; and another from his beloved and honoured friend, Dr. McNeile. The last of these, beside its interest in itself, led to a reply no less interesting.

*March* 11, 1846.

MY VERY DEAR FRIEND AND BROTHER,

I have received with deep emotion the affectionate letter which you have sent to *me*. I yesterday read it to the Committee, and it is in their name, as well as my own, that I write to assure you of our sincerest Christian sympathy with you and your family, under the dispensation with which our heavenly Father has visited you. We humbly thank Him for the abundant mercy which He has remembered in the midst of judgment ; and we fervently pray that He may continue and confirm this mercy to your family, and to the Church of Christ, by your restoration to health and strength ; so that you may yet be enabled, by future labours, to animate, to direct, and to strengthen, as in former years, your brethren in the Lord.

One especial mercy we recognize, in that the Lord has made you, by this very event, the object of abundant prayer throughout His Church at home and abroad ; and these prayers will avail much, to procure enlarged blessings upon your own soul, and upon the many great works with which your labours have been associated. Amongst these works we rejoice to regard this Society as standing in the first place. The joy which you describe, with which you contemplate the work of the Society under your present circumstances, is a cheering testimony to its Divine character ; and if such be the blessedness of being associated with it below, what will be the joy in the presence of our blessed Lord and Master above—when our labours are ended—when multitudes from all parts of the heathen world rejoice with us before the throne, and before the Lamb !

May these refreshing views still comfort your heart in your present confinement, and may they animate and quicken us to renewed exertions. Continue, my beloved brother, your prayers for us, that the power of Christ may rest upon us, and that He may be glorified, even by the weakness and infirmities of our labours.

Ever in the best Christian bonds, very affectionately yours,

HENRY VENN.

*Edgbaston, March* 3.

MY BELOVED AND VENERATED BROTHER IN CHRIST JESUS OUR LORD,

.... I cannot refrain any longer from conveying to you the assurance of my tender and prayerful interest in your present situation, and future recovery. With what deep concern I heard of your accident, as *we* call it, He is witness, who alone knows how much I love you, and how much I glorify Christ in you ; and with what gratitude I praised Him for the preservation of your invaluable life, which seemed in such imminent peril, my congregation can testify. Never was public prayer presented by them more fervently for the restoration of any one, except in the case of their own pastor, when his life seemed trembling in the balance. Thanks to the God of all power and grace, dearly-beloved servant of our common Lord, that in your case has been exemplified the truth of David's words in their true import : " Precious in the sight of the Lord is the death of His saints," which evidently means, that God does not readily allow His servants to die, but watches over them as a rare thing, which He values and protects. So has it been in your case ; and so, I trust, it will be. With our Divine Lord, the source of all life, all power, all wisdom and grace, at the head of His church, and the helm of the world, I dare not say of any human instrument —" We cannot do without him," but as far as I can with propriety say this, I say it, dear sir, of you, in reference to our glorious cause of Christian union. Oh what an affliction is it to me, that we shall not see you in Birmingham! With this however we may be content, now that you are likely to be spared to us for future service, and spared with all the new treasures acquired in the purifying process of affliction. Yes, honoured and beloved brother, we shall love you more, and see more in you to love than ever, even as we shall love Christ more, not only for giving you, but now for sparing you to us. The Lord Jesus be with your spirit. Believe me to be, what you have owned me in public,

Your Brother in Christ,<br>J. A. JAMES.

Liverpool, March 6.

MY DEAREST BICKERSTETH,

Occupied as I am, I must not attempt to express to you, either my deep anxiety, on hearing that your dear brother was gone to see you, or my relief on hearing his report when he returned. You have been in our thoughts of love, and our prayers, I trust, of faith, ever since it has pleased the Lord to intimate to you, and through you to us, that He is independent of human instruments.

It is a blessed thing to be willing to labour for Him. I sincerely believe it is even more blessed to be willing to be laid aside. He doeth all things well. The most advanced in His service and likeness require more advancement still; and if through a stroke, that lays us low, He convey the sweet voice which says—" Come up higher," oh how exquisitely well done it will appear in the light that shall make all things manifest! For the last few months I have felt deeply the pain of publicly differing with you in any thing. Since your hurt, this pain has been increased. But indeed, dearest Bickersteth, it is inevitable, since the more I meditate and pray over our present circumstances, the more I am convinced that your ardent and loving spirit will meet with a distressing disappointment in the issue of the Alliance. That even this, should my worst fears be realized, will be overruled as a great blessing to your own soul, I cannot doubt; since there is nothing but good to the glory of the Lord, and the happiness of His Church, in your intentions.

Q 5

Well, our love to one another requires, perhaps, this test of its sincerity, that it can live, and breathe, and pray, with undiminished warmth, through the uncongenial season of a dark and cloudy day. The mists will soon be dispersed, and we shall see eye to eye, when the Lord shall bring again Zion. May the Comforter, in the mean time, strew your couch with the soft sweet flowers of patience, gathered under the cross, and greet your ears with strains of joy, which are not very far off !

Dear love to your family, and thanks to your sweet child for her notes to me. I shall long for another.

Yours in Him,

HUGH McNEILE.

To this beautiful letter, which alone was a sign of the real difficulties besetting that work to which his own heart was so powerfully drawn, Mr. Bickersteth dictated the following characteristic reply :

*Watton Rectory, March 9.*

MY BELOVED McNEILE,

Glory be to God, all is going on well in my poor body, and I hope, in my soul. My whole soul was touched by your most brotherly, tender, and consoling letter, and never in my life has my heart been knit closer to you.

It may indeed be asked, How can those, who have equally sought the Lord, come to such opposite conclusions in so important a point ? But we are both partially blind, and partially sinful ; and so the Lord in part only shews us His truth in the matter. Yet, I doubt not, from Rom. xiv, even in our differences we are equally accepted of Him.

We cannot be wholly disappointed in this work of love; we have already tasted so largely the comfort of love, the fellowship of spirit, the consolation in Christ, as constrain us amidst all difficulties to go on,—against hope, to believe in hope, casting ourselves hour by hour upon the Lord, who can bring us, through all, to the largeness of blessing we seek.

But I am anxious, dearest brother, that the difference should be for the greater good of our own Church. I believe no Church on earth possesses more objective truth than our own beloved Church. We are far too ready to boast of this, but I believe it to be our duty to maintain these truths in wisdom, firmness, and love. We must not yield to the temptation, to which our divine Master was exposed, of casting Himself down from the pinnacle. Here we are one. But then, dear brother, we must on the other hand accept the punishment of our sins as a Church. The hard severities against Puritans and Papists, till the grand rebellion was provoked, gave occasion to that insurrection on all sides against the laws of Christ, of patient suffering, and victory by faith and love, and overcoming evil with good, in which so many godly men, of deeper piety than ourselves, were led astray.

Instead of learning wisdom by experience, our forefathers passed the Act of Uniformity, and added to our guilt by the persecution of the nonconformists, and were themselves punished by two evil kings, till God brought about the Revolution. Still we learned not wisdom by experience, we repented not of our sins, and our Church sank into dead formality. God then gave a glorious revival in the time of the Wesleys and Whitfield ; but instead of being welcomed, it was mocked and scorned, till there was no room in our Church for the faithful men who began this work. We are reaping the bitter fruit of three centuries of sins. It is not enough to say, our Church has most truth to present in its constitution to the people of England. The Lord may well say ; ' Look at your sins in the appointment of bishops, and the exercise of patronage generally. See tens of thousands in your parishes, and under the appointed ministry, starving for want of the bread of life. I have called other faithful men to the ministry, to help to supply this need. I have given to them also precious gifts of my own Spirit, important truth to testify souls to their ministry, and a large proportion of my Church in England is now to be found amongst them. I have indeed divided the land for the Church of England, but I have given them also a legal sanction for their worship in every parish of that land.' Thus, my dearest brother, the Church of England is not the whole Church of Christ in England.

It probably was so once ; and but for our sins, particularly the way
in which the Act of 1662 was passed, and our own Church sins, it
might to a great extent have been so now.   Now you aim to bring
our whole country to this state of unity.   But my view is, that
though we should aim at this in the way of truth, forbearance, and
love, we must also humble ourselves before God for our exceeding
Church sinfulness, which has prevented our dissenting brethren from
recovering the light of truth which we really enjoy, and has (for with
them also there are many sins) engaged their zeal even directly
against what we believe to be the truth of God.

Our disunion is our weakness.   Now what I wish from you, dear
brother, is, that you should be God's voice, calling the Church of
England to true repentance for three centuries of sins ; that you
should charge home on the present generation all these sins ; that
you should obtain, by prayers from God, and by manifestation of the
truth, from men, frank confession, deep humiliation, and tender forbearance towards others, because of our own exceeding sinfulness.

I would further suggest that our repentance for our sins, as a
Church, should be proved, by leading us to humble ourselves before
God, in joyfully acknowledging their call of God, their ministry,
their gifts, and their success, and thanking Him that, notwithstanding our unfaithfulness, He has carried on His precious work, of
gathering His elect from our land, even by those who are, as we
believe, in many things defective labourers ; if indeed we may say
so of so many, who, like Baxter and Owen, Watts and Doddridge,
Benson, Hall, Fuller, and Watson, have by their writings profited
the whole Church of Christ.   We ought to cultivate intercourse and
kindness with them, as Archbishop Sancroft so sweetly recommended.
All this may be done most effectually, even by those who do not
join the Alliance, and now is the time for you, dear brother, to
do it.

Having done this, I further want you to be the spring of a union
of all the Evangelical brethren in our Church, in an avowed and
decided opposition to Tractarianism, to secularity, and all Infidel
perversions of the gospel.   Let the true ministers of Christ in the
Church combine.   Let them have an organ like the Christian Penny

Magazine, among the Dissenters, and of which, by arrangement
with faithful ministers, half-a-million a month might be circulated
for the diffusion of sound, interesting, Protestant and Church truth;
and in the spirit of love and forbearance to all who love the Lord
Jesus in sincerity. Thus should we be working together, in different
sections of the Church of Christ, to one common end.

I, equally with you, view John xvii. 23, as only to be accomplished at the return of the Lord; but it is the ideal at which we
are to be aiming; as " Thy kingdom come," is the ideal at which
we aim in missions.

Farewell, my dearest brother; the Lord forbid you should use
your powerful mind and your deep piety, against Christian union.
The Lord use you very greatly, for His glory, and the good of His
Church.

Your affectionate brother,<br>E. BICKERSTETH.

The following were his remarks in his journal on the
trial through which he had now passed, and his merciful
recovery.

" *April* 12.—*Easter Day.* Very remarkable have been
the dispensations of Providence with me in the last two
months. . . . For some time I was in great danger, and
for two months I have been confined to my room, and
kept from all public duty.

" Now what was the special design of my God in this
affliction? How may I most profit by it? Besides those
rich mercies which I have received, doubtless there was
a message of instruction to my soul. See what thy life
is—a vapour. Live as on the borders of eternity! Be
bold and decided for God and His truth, while thou hast
time. Count the cost of aiding such a work as the Alliance, and the sufferings to which it may expose thee!

Be specially careful that this be not a lost, but a sanctified affliction.

"I have been especially awakened by seeing how
God's most eminent servants, after deliverance from affliction, fell into sin—Noah, David, Hezekiah, and others.
O Lord, I shall do the same, if Thou leave me to myself.
Leave me not, I beseech Thee ; sanctify all, uphold me
to the end, nor for one moment forsake me    In the time
of need and trial let help be given.

"A further trial has arisen, from the illness of my
dear child F. at Torquay, of a nature so serious, that she
cannot be removed home, and two of her sisters are obliged
now to be with her.    We know not what may be the
Lord's will concerning her ; and the separation, distance,
and suspense, have been distressing to us all.    The will
of the Lord is wise, and kind, and good ; we need the
whole.    May this also be sanctified ! "

The notes of Mr. Bickersteth to his absent children,
from his sick chamber, breathe all the fragrance of sanctified affliction.    The first of those which follow was dictated while he was still unequal to the effort of writing.

*February* 17.

MY BELOVED CHILDREN,

At first I grieved you should have to partake in our distress ; but
when I considered that it is only in this way we arrive at the fuller
joy, and how blessed the oneness of our family has been, I am sure
that this, like every thing else in our trials, is full of choice goodness and loving-kindness.    Our sympathies are now transferring to
Torquay.    The Lord fill each with heavenly consolation and peace.
Dear F., is in the same kind hands, which have blessed, and will
bless even to the end.    The rich fruits of this affliction are springing up on all sides.    .    .    As to myself, I have now no pain, but

ten thousand comforts and blessings, which humble me in the dust, while they fill me with joy and gratitude to the Giver of all. All is well, all will be well, now and for ever.

Your own Papa,<br>E. BICKERSTETH.

April 6.

MY BELOVED CHILDREN,

Truly affecting to us were your letters this afternoon. Our beloved child's sufferings go to our hearts, and we can only bow in submission to our heavenly Father's wisdom and love, who assuredly orders all this trial for our child's good, as well as our own. We know we deserve severer chastisement, and we know that this chastisement is full of loving-kindness. Be of good courage, then, my children; wait on the Lord still, in faith and patience, and we shall yet see His tender mercies. It is our greatest trial that we cannot be personally present with our beloved child, and minister to her; but all this is also ordered, and we feel grateful that she has such help, and is in the dwelling of such tender sympathizing friends.

Tell my dearest child that her work is now, simply looking to Jesus, as the Israelites, bitten by fiery serpents, looked to the brazen serpent on the pole. So looking, so trusting in the dying Saviour, no malice of Satan, no mental darkness, no want of preparation, can hinder her sure and complete salvation. Should we not meet at Watton, which yet we would pray and hope for, happy as our home has been, it is nothing to that far happier home, in which we shall shortly meet and dwell for ever. Let our affections be more set on things above, and all these severe trials will be rich in spiritual fruit.

I thank God for the wisdom given to my children. . . . I doubt not, He will yet give grace for every exigency; only let us speak good of His name, and glorify Him.

We grieve that Sir C. and Lady E. are involved so painfully in our afflictions, but the Lord grant in it, even to them, richer and fuller blessings, and mercies, as I doubt not that He will, and may

it be so ordered, if it be His will, that they may not suffer further
for all their love.

Your ever affectionate father,

E. BICKERSTETH.

*April* 14.

MY BELOVED F.

So, my dearest child, it pleases the Lord to shew His love to you,
by severe sufferings and trials of darkness, and keeping you at a
distance from your dear home, and precious parents, and beloved
family; and you have to spell out, by faith, His tender goodness,
and His loving-kindness, in these dark signs.

This, my sweet child, is the privilege and glory of faith, to see
love in these things ; and when they come, to lift up our heads,
assured that they are tokens of faithful and covenant love.

An eternity of glory is worth a momentary affliction ; nay, the
sufferings of the present time are not worthy to be compared with
the glory that shall be revealed in us.    But we are always fancying
this is our home, when it is only the passage thither ; and that here
is the time of rest, when it is only the time of preparation for the
true rest.

Especially be careful here, not to mistake darkness for sin, and
the effect of disease for anything wrong in the sight of the Lord.
This would be, to think your food and medicine, sent in love from
God, were the poison of Satan.    Oh no, my child, it is because the
Lord loves you, and would have you quite meet for his presence,
that He sends these trials, according to His own precious word.
1 Pet. i. 3—9.

This is perhaps as much as you can bear, and I will write the
rest to your sisters.

Your most affectionate father,

E. BICKERSTETH.

A letter to his son at college, during his recovery, contains his sentiments on a work which was then attracting

much attention, and has continued, probably, to exert a powerful influence on many minds.

*March* 21.

MY BELOVED EDWARD,

I have just got from my bed to the sofa, and through the rich mercy of God, go on favourably every day. His mercies have been great indeed, and specially sweet, as given in answer to so many prayers. . . .

I have been reading Arnold's Life with considerable interest, but I feel that there are very weighty objections, to hinder its solid usefulness.

His ignorance in Theology is really great, with all his claims to study and knowledge; and this has begot a rashness and presumption of judgment, full of self-conceit and imagined superiority, and seeking to put down those who differ from him, whether Puseyites or Evangelicals, by harsh words, such as priestcraft, fanatics, men of narrow minds, bibliolaters, and the like. The acquirements of sixty years, instead of his limited studies, would never justify such railings; and so he was left to fall into infidelity about Daniel, and into many rash speculations about Church and State.

But, on the other hand, there is a frankness and thorough honesty; there is a real devotion, there is genuine piety, there is a kind, affectionate spirit; and so, not being an evil man and a seducer, he did not wax worse and worse, but better and better, and his last days were his best days. His great glory is his bringing Christian principles into schools, and training up the young as immortal beings. God honoured him as His servant for this.

May you, my dearest son, be guarded against what is evil in this work, proving all things by the word, and "holding fast that which is good."

Your affectionate father,

E. BICKERSTETH.

The return of his beloved child, after a time of suspense and danger, and the close of his own illness, are
thus noticed in his journal of May 30.

"The Lord's mercies have been very great to us. My
dear child has been brought home in safety, though she
suffered greatly on the journey. And now I hope again
to go to the Lord's table, after being absent nearly four
months, and with my people to remember the Lord's
sacrifice of Himself for our sins.

"O let me not, O my God, be slothful in business, but
fervent in spirit, serving the Lord. Let me not be slothful in prayer, but pray without ceasing.

"The love of Christian friends has been very great.
O Lord, make me a blessing to them, I entreat Thee!

"My 'Family Expositions on John and Jude' have just
left the press. The Lord prosper even this feeble effort
for good. In none of my works do I take pains enough
to make them permanently useful. Eccles. xii. 9—11.

"O Lord, assist me for all the weighty duties that now
again come upon me!"

At the beginning of the month, when his recovery
was almost complete, he wrote to the Secretaries of the
Alliance, expressing his thanks for the sympathy of his
beloved brethren, and his hopes for the cause which now
engaged his heart, amidst its many difficulties.

*Watton Rectory, May 5.*

My dear Friends,

I have gratefully to acknowledge your kind sympathy in my
restored health, and especially your prayers for my future usefulness.
I believe it to be the highest and greatest of the beatitudes to be
among the peace-makers; and I rejoice in the thought of again
being employed, with beloved brethren in Christ of all denominations,

holding the Head, our one Saviour Christ, in promoting that blessed object. But we have all seen that, like our blessed Master, in whose glorious titles the Prince of Peace seems the last and highest, (Is. ix. 6.), in being peace-makers we shall have to be sufferers, and that even beloved brethren will be afraid of our proceedings, and oppose us. Yet, if God give us grace to persevere in prayer, and real love to the brethren and to all men, I feel assured, notwithstanding all the many predictions to the contrary, from those who do not join us, our Heavenly Father will greatly own our efforts to heal the divisions of the Church of Christ, and to restore the first brotherly love of Christians. What a glorious consummation of our best desires will this be!

Gratefully and affectionately yours,

E. BICKERSTETH,

Mr. Bickersteth came forth from the retirement of his sick chamber, not only with increased zeal in the cause of Christian union, to which he felt that the providence of God had specially called him, but with those spiritual perceptions deepened, which made him keenly alive to the dangers of the Church, and to the need of incessant watchfulness against the besetting evils of the day. These feelings are apparent in the following letters. The first relates to the spiritual condition of the Irish Church, and the other to a proposed change in the Newfoundland School Society, which took effect at the time, but has been reversed after an experience of its practical evils.

*Watton Rectory, May 5.*

My DEAR ——,

Since I sent you my short note, I have received your affecting letter about the Evangelical body in Ireland. I fear there is too much truth in it, as a *general* representation of our present state, and it is the very thing which renders the trials that are manifestly before us, so needful. We have sunk into the spirit of the world; and so our faith, and boldness, and zeal, have all languished, and Popery and Puseyism, and infidelity and lawlessness, rise up on all sides to punish us. Oh that men could be brought more to prayerful study of the Scriptures, to retired duties, to lean only on the Lord, and not on an arm of flesh! . . .

The temporary triumph of ungodliness seems close at hand. It is, in my view of the Scriptures, rapidly joined with the Lord's return, and the rapture of the saints. Let us make it, then, our constant and great aim, at every cost and sacrifice, to be approved of Christ, and accepted in His sight at His appearing. The Alliance is, I feel assured, a work entirely accordant with His mind; and in confessing it, and adhering to it in a right spirit, I fully believe we are approving ourselves in His sight.

Affectionately yours,

E. BICKERSTETH.

*Watton Rectory, June 5.*

MY DEAREST ——,

I had not heard of the proposed extension of the Newfoundland School Society, with the concession of a *licence* being requisite for the schoolmasters.

I am sure that these are not times in which such a licence can be safely conceded to the Colonial Bishops by the Society. Neither the general feeling of the evangelical contributors to the Society, nor the understood principles of some of the Colonial Bishops, make such a change safe or prudent, for the enlarged usefulness of the Society.

Why should we revive in our Colonies the 77th Canon, which the common sense of England has sunk into disuse in our country? It is the revival of an injurious, self-destructive, and impracticable system, which looks at externals, instead of looking to the power of Divine truth, in the living experience of a Christian life and Christian teaching.

Surely there is much greater safety to the subscribers, that we shall have faithful men of God under it, in the character of a known Committee at home, of men of piety, dependent for the continuance of the work on the confidence and love of true Christians. I have rejoiced to support the Society on its present principles. I should feel trammelled by the proposed alteration.

Affectionately yours,<br>E. BICKERSTETH.

After the experiment of the change, here deprecated, had been tried for a few years, it was found necessary for the Society to revert to its original constitution ; and it has more recently, while both its principles and its object are retained, been merged in the Colonial Church and School Society.

Mr. Bickersteth had not long been raised up himself from the bed of sickness, when he was called upon to perform the last service of Christian love for a dear and beloved brother. He alludes to it thus in his journal :

" *July* 25. It has pleased God on Tuesday, July 14, to take my beloved brother-in-law, Mayor, to himself, in the full triumph of faith, at Acton, near Namptwich. I have seldom heard of a more truly peaceful, holy and happy death. He wished me to preach his funeral sermons, and, please God, I am to do so on August the 2d. May they be accompanied by the power of God to the salvation of precious souls. He has left my dear sister a widow, and ten children. He might as much have been expected, in February last, to preach my funeral sermon, as I to have preached his. Charlotte Elizabeth also has been taken to her rest.

" Please God, I go to Liverpool, Coppenhall, Acton, and Bristol, next week and the following. The Lord give me rich blessings in all the work to which He calls me, and carry me through all to His glory, and the good of many.

" Oh how I need Thy quickening grace; else everything is dead and formal, no thirstings after God, no sense of His presence, no spiritual desires in prayer, no lifting up of the mind, nothing but cold, dull, drowsy, heavy form. O Lord, deliver me from this. Give me unction and reality, and life,—a real communion with Thee, a stirring up of myself to lay hold on Thee, and may the Lord's Supper be specially blessed, to help me to walk in newness of life."

" *Acton, August* 2. I preached my two sermons to large congregations ; that in the afternoon was the largest they had ever seen in Acton church, (1200 or 1300 people,) and they were most attentive. I got many fresh facts, and the sermons are to be printed."

He wrote to one of his younger children on this journey, who was with her cousins at Liverpool—

What wonders love does ! how it makes every house a palace, and every heart where it fully dwells, a little type of heaven. The Lord give it to us abundantly more and more ! . . . The Lord bless you, my love, with every temporal and spiritual blessing, and grant that each year may see you increasing in knowledge and grace, in usefulness and happiness. You have been a great source of comfort to your parents, and I trust in the Lord's love that you may yet have much happiness in each other, while spared by Him in this world of change and temptation—this scene of our constant and busy preparation for eternity, and the very seed-plot of our future harvest. . . . It is beautiful to see how much grace can do to make a female the largest blessing to all around her—her feelings, like the flow of a deep river, with an unruffled surface, quietly carrying forward a full tide of blessings.

In the same month he thus expressed his habitual feelings, with reference to some suggestions on Church Reform.

I am not disposed to lessen much the incomes of the Bishops, when I see the nobleness of charity in which the Bishop of London, the Archbishop, the Bishop of Chester, and others, have spent theirs. Their multiplication, however, seems very desirable. I would not deter from attempts to do good, by my own natural incapacity; but I feel little fitted for the rough work of reforming others, and shrink from it, except as it comes before me in the way of positive duty. After all, the great spring is something quite different. The whole Church might be thus re-formed, and be a dead form. Extempore prayer would be no remedy; the Divine Spirit is the great and all-essential Reformer.

The month of August was occupied with that work on which his heart was set with earnest desire,—the actual formation of the Evangelical Alliance. Nearly a thousand Christian brethren, from England, Scotland, and Ireland, from France, Germany, Switzerland, and the United States, beside some from the British Colonies, were gathered together in London; and their meetings for united prayer and friendly conference lasted fifteen days, from August 19 till September 2. It was naturally a time of deep interest and of intense excitement; and though several difficult questions were raised in the protracted discussions, especially on the subject of slavery, which alone threatened to be an insuperable difficulty, the general character of the proceedings, and the issue of the whole conference, were causes of deep thanksgiving to all those who desired the prosperity of a work of love. The services of united praise and prayer were particularly interesting and solemn. Mr. Bickersteth presided at the first of these, and took an important part in the whole of the business. It was remarked of him, and of two or three others among the more aged leaders, that whenever the Christian tone of the discussion was in danger of being lost, amidst the necessary details of business, or the partial clashing of opinions, their rising was the signal of its instant recovery, and their voice a watchword of holiness, peace, and love. The resolutions, which he had introduced at the second Liverpool Conference, and with which his name is honourably connected in the lips of many, as " Mr. Bickersteth's Resolutions," formed one of the latest parts of the public business, and may perhaps be viewed as the practical quintessence of the whole movement.

He wrote towards the close of the meetings to his family at home—" God has been graciously with us in the most difficult part of our meetings, which have been more trying than last year, but I think may have even a fuller blessing. Sir Culling has conducted our business with his usual judgment, sweetness, and influence. To God be all the praise. The devotional and loving spirit triumphed over all difficulties. Such days I hardly expect to pass again on earth, of intense interest and incessant exertion."

The following are his remarks in his private journal.

" *August* 29. I have been engaged for the last three weeks in almost incessant labours, in the formation of the Alliance, and I trust that God is bringing it to a safe and happy conclusion ; though there are many difficulties in the way, which call forth our Christian principles.

" Much progress has been made, but probably another week will have to be spent in prayerful deliberation. My soul, bless the Lord, for being permitted to take part in a work so calculated to bless the whole Church of Christ.

" The scenes have been so exciting, prolonged, intensely interesting and exhausting—that private devotional exercises have been much interfered with. The Lord pardon my many sins and infirmities, use and accept my poor services, and grant that I may be now refreshed and strengthened at His holy table, so that my soul may suffer no loss, but every grace be quickened and enlivened."

" *September 26.* In the last week, Monday was occupied with the Herts Lord's-day Observance Society; Tuesday, with Committees of the Alliance in London, and journey to Norwich; Wednesday, Norwich Bible Meeting; Thursday, two Norwich Jews' Meetings; Friday, Norwich Evangelical Alliance, and Norwich Jews' Sermons; Saturday, journey home and Committee Meeting on the way. To-morrow, God helping, the Communion, and Jews' Sermon at Tewin; Monday, Hertford Jews' Meeting; Tuesday, Aylesbury Jews' Sermon and Meeting. Thus from day to day the Lord provides work for me. . . ."

" *October 24.* I have been much occupied the last month in preparing ' A Brief Practical View of the Evangelical Alliance.' I grieve that several of the bishops have spoken against it, and none have appeared for it. Unless the Lord graciously appear for us, we shall fail of our hopes, at least in that extent which we desire.

" The way in which those who have taken a part in it have been called to pass through the furnace, is instructive. One after another has suffered. The American brethren, one part shipwrecked in the Great Britain, another in fearful peril in the Great Western. One has lost a wife, another been disabled by sickness, another

cast out of his curacy.    May we count the cost, and take
up the cross !

"But O my God, where is my heart ? where is the
inner temple, cleansed for Thee, and sanctified for Thy
use ?    O come Thyself, and cleanse the thoughts of my
heart, expel every thing that would keep Thee out, and
banish every idol from my soul ! "

"*November* 29. I have been very greatly occupied from
home last month, though not absent on Sunday.    One
week at Manchester, in the organization of the Alliance ;
another at Cambridge for the Female Refuge ; another
at the Prophetical Meeting, and preparing an Appeal for
a special fund for Ireland, the last week on the Alliance
Committee in London.    Glory be to God alone.

"Gracious Father, let not work for Thee lead my soul
from Thee.    Thine I am, Thee I rejoice to serve, it is my
privilege.    Give me not less work, but O give me with it
all a constant looking to Jesus ! "

Thus, in the course of the present year, in the sufferings and perils with which it began, and the labours with
which it continued and came to its close, the words of
our Lord were eminently fulfilled in his beloved servant.
"Every branch in me, which beareth fruit, He purgeth
it, that it may bring forth more fruit."    And the fruit
which he brought forth, in all his thoughts, prayers, and
labours, was the choicest, sweetest, and ripest, "the fruit
of righteousness," which " is sown in peace, of them that
make peace."

# CHAPTER XXVII.

THE opposition to the Maynooth Bill, among the great body of British Christians, who loved and prized the Gospel, had from the first a double tendency. That spurious charity which thought peace attainable by setting aside the most vital distinctions of religious truth and falsehood, had triumphed only by the divisions of Protestant Christians. The desire was thus increased for a purer union, not based on religious indifference, or the sacrifice of conscience even in lesser things, but on the real and substantial agreement of Evangelical Protestants in all the vital doctrines of the Gospel ; and this gave birth to the Evangelical Alliance. The false benevolence, which pretended to heal the miseries of Ireland by an ampler supply of Popery at the expense of the State, called equally for vigorous efforts of real Christian love, in a more earnest diffusion of the Gospel, the only true remedy for Ireland's distress and moral degradation. This conviction gave rise to another work, in which Mr. Bickersteth also took a very prominent part,—" The

R 2

Special Appeal for Ireland,"—issuing soon afterwards in
" THE SOCIETY FOR IRISH CHURCH MISSIONS."

While the Maynooth Bill was still in progress, he was
deeply impressed with the importance of both these objects,—the closer union of true Christians, and direct
labours in spreading truth among the Roman Catholics
of Ireland. In May 1845 he wrote as follows.

" I feel that nothing more weighty ought to be on our minds, than
that so vast a religious movement should have a right direction.
We want a great Protestant Institute. We are at present placed in
quite a false position. Really loving Ireland, and because we love
it, resisting this aggression, we are brought before men of the world
as resisting conciliation, full of bitterness, and opposed to the men
of liberality and kindness. We must not let Satan get this advantage over us, by perverting the real truth. This Institute should
be, to receive information on the institutions now in existence for
the relief of the temporal necessities, and promoting the spiritual
improvement of Ireland, to circulate that information through the
country, and to convey help to such societies, each subscriber to
appropriate his subscription to such of these objects as he most
approves. The word of God, in the vernacular languages, to be
circulated with those funds which may be left at the free disposal of
the Committee. . . . . . . . I have written in haste, and amidst dis-
traction ; but the ideas have been much on my mind, as needful to
give strength to our resistance of the Maynooth Grant, and to place
us in our right position, by legitimate actings for Ireland, that will
shew real love."

Circumstances delayed, for a little time, the fulfilment
of a duty, which was already felt, by Mr. Bickersteth and
many others, to be alike seasonable and important. But
the providence of God began to conspire signally with
these instincts of Christian benevolence. The same judg-

ment, which blasted the hopes of worldly politicians, who had sought to conciliate by the sacrifice of truth and righteousness, opened a way for efforts to benefit Ireland, of a purer and higher kind. The measure had scarcely passed for providing an ampler supply of spiritual poison, when the staple food of the island was turned to rottenness, and famine set in with unparalleled severity. The distress kept increasing throughout the year 1846, and the recurrence of the evil, in a second harvest, seemed to fill the cup of Irish misery. All the resources of government, and of private benevolence, were exhausted by the claims of millions, reduced to utter starvation. But some gleams of hope appeared amidst the very greatness of the calamity. The famine loosened the chains of priestly bondage. The sympathies of British Christians were rendered deeper and more intense, by the awful spectacles of misery spread before them. The alms of Protestants, which were dispensed largely, without distinction of creed, and indeed mainly to Roman Catholics, since Popery and poverty went hand and hand in Ireland, broke down a vast amount of religious prejudice, and thus conspired with heavy affliction to prepare the minds of thousands for the seed of divine truth. While Englishmen, in general, felt the plain duty of relieving temporal distress, there were a smaller number of earnest Christians, who saw, in this visitation of God, a still louder call to care for perishing souls, and to raise them from the darkness of sin and superstition into the glorious liberty of the gospel of Christ. The religious societies of Ireland were all crippled by the famine, at the very time when the spiritual necessities of the country were most urgent. The cry of need was heard plainly from across the channel, " Come over and help us ! " The servants of Christ assuredly gathered, that the Lord was calling them to new efforts in that land of trouble and sorrow, and a Committee was formed, towards the close of 1846, to provide " a Special Fund for the spiritual exigencies of Ireland."

The first mover, perhaps, in this work, and certainly one of the most active and liberal contributors, was the late Enosh Durant, whose mind had been deeply affected by the claims of Irish Roman Catholics for spiritual instruction. Mr. Bickersteth and Mr. Dallas were very early associated with him, and while the latter was employed in direct efforts to ascertain the true state of Ireland, and prepare the soil for the preaching of the gospel, Mr. Bickersteth entered zealously into the task of awaking the zeal, and securing the aid of British Christians. The following notices of the subject occur successively in his journal.

" *November* 29, 1846. I feel that a great opening is now made for doing good to Ireland. O Lord, prosper the effort I have made in the Appeal I have now been writing. I lodge this prayer with Thee, O Redeemer, who delighteth to use the weakest.

" *December* 25. Glory be to God for the measure of success given to the ' Irish Appeal,' above £1000 having been already raised. O how merciful the Lord is, in any measure to use one so unworthy, for advancing His own purposes of truth and love.

" O take my soul unto Thy special care, O my God! Amidst incessant occupations, it is seriously injured by want of more communion with Thee. Lord, give me more of the spirit of prayer. I loathe and abhor myself, and humble myself in Thy sight. O that the closing Sabbath and week-days of another year, may, by Thy mighty grace, have a quickening power, reviving every good thing, and quickening every grace of faith, hope, and love !

" *January* 30, 1847. The Lord has most graciously prospered the Appeal for Ireland. More than £4000 have been contributed, and several of the Bishops have aided it. It has also been greatly opposed by the Infidel and Papal party, and by Lord Brougham in the House of Lords. May it indeed be owned of God, in doing a great work.

" *March* 7. 1847. The Lord has specially blessed the Appeal Fund, which has reached about £6000. Glory be to His name ! "

In the Appeal itself, Mr. Bickersteth stated clearly the broad Scriptural principle, on which the effort was based, and which proved it to be specially seasonable in the hour of distress.

" A calamity, fearful in extent, and occasioning wide and severe suffering, has befallen our sister country, Ireland. Famine, with its many sad and distressing attendants, has come upon vast multitudes. Their sufferings cannot fail to awaken our deepest sympathy, and to call forth our cheerful contributions. Something has been done by private benevolence, but more may, and we trust, will yet be done, in channels that are open to individuals, and by unexceptionable societies. We have also to thank God that a provident government, though it can never reach all the details of such a calamity, has done much to alleviate this national affliction.

" But such afflictions come from the hand of God, they are His chastisement for our sins. They are His voice—' Hear ye the rod, and who hath appointed it.' He tells us, in the day of adversity, to consider. They issue from his mercy and love, to recal us to Himself, from whom we have grievously departed.

" The primary, the very chief remedy for all temporal destitution, is a real return to that God who smites us. If the appointed weeks

of harvest bring no harvest, the reason is especially stated. ' Your
iniquities have withholden these things from you,' There is no principle more sure than the divine promise—' Seek ye first the kingdom of God and His righteousness, and all these things shall be
added unto you.' In making this Appeal, therefore, to set before
the Irish the word of God, we may be assured that we are taking
the right and principal means for remedying the evil under which
Ireland is now suffering."

Such an effort, however, was too thoroughly in accordance with the mind of Christ, not to ensure the opposition of the world. It brought the principles of Christian faith into direct collision with those maxims of false
peace and hollow expediency, which had brought on the
terrible judgment. An outcry was speedily raised, that
it was a scheme to take advantage of Irish starvation, by
bribing the peasantry to renounce their faith. O'Connell
was forward, as usual, in the work of poisoning the minds
of his countrymen, and denounced all the benevolence of
England, which was pouring into the island, as a conspiracy worthy of the fiends of hell. Lord Brougham, in
the House of Lords, condemned the Special Fund, and
Mr. Bickersteth as its promoter, in language of almost
equal violence. But what was still more deplorable, an
Irish clergyman of some eminence was found willing to
repeat in one of the London papers, the wretched and
calumnious misrepresentations, and thus to hold up the
best and wisest friends of Ireland to the condemnation
of the irreligious public. Mr. Bickersteth, in a further
Address of February 19, disposed in a few words of the
groundless calumny, and of the antichristian maxim
on which it was based, which would shut the mouth from
imparting a knowledge of the gospel, because of the pressure of unusual distress. " The Fund," he remarked, " is

entirely unconnected with any plan for temporal relief whatever. The contributors will be found to have given, in other ways, for the temporal relief of all classes, without reference to their creed, whether Romanist or Protestant, but wholly apart from, and independent of this ' Special Fund.' When Christians have thus shewn their sympathy for the physical wants of the people in Ireland, the Committee feel justified in calling their attention, if not to a more urgent, to a higher and more enduring charity, the care of the soul. On the principle that the time of affliction is specially the time, when it is a pastor's duty to impart religious instruction, and that every infirmary should be provided with its chaplain, they could not hesitate as to the propriety and importance of raising this fund. . . . . . . Believing that there is none other name under heaven, whereby we must be saved, but the name of the Lord Jesus, they would thankfully avail themselves of a season, when the heart is softened by affliction, to spread before our afflicted brethren in Ireland that one name, as set forth in the word of God."

A few days later, having received from his Irish brother a reply to a kind letter of private expostulation, he wrote again as follows :

*February* 1, 1847.

My dear ——

My love to you obliges me to write again, though entirely at issue with your letter in its conclusions, but at one in its kindness.

You can never surely mean that when God's hand is over us in judgment, is just the time when we are not to obey His commands, and make known the love of Christ from His own word to dying sinners. This would be indeed to read things backward. The objections to V.'s plan are quite as groundless as to the Special Fund.

Surely the Apostle was not guilty of bribery, when he says, " Do good to all 'men, and specially to them which are of the household of faith ; " nor our Lord, when He made the feeding of the five thousand the direct occasion for teaching them the great truths of the Gospel.

Nor was that paper a right channel for censure of the children of God. I wrote a very friendly reply to you, which I sent to it, as soon as I saw yours. This they refused to insert. It may show you that it is not an honourable vehicle for your letters. . . . . The Lord forgive us all our mistakes, make us a blessing to our fellow-men, and bring us to rejoice together in His heavenly kingdom, prays

Yours affectionately,

E. BICKERSTETH.

It pleased God, however, amidst all opposition, to prosper this work of Christian love. For several months Mr. Bickersteth alludes in his journal to its continued success. On April 3, he wrote :

" The Irish Appeal has raised nearly £7000, and has been the means already of sending forth many fresh labourers, as well as of upholding the excellent religious Societies of Ireland. O Lord, prosper it more and more ! I do count it Thy especial love, to be in any way used and owned of Thee, in doing Thy blessed work of faith and love."

And again, in the following months.

" *April* 24. Through mercy a ' Second Appeal ' has been prepared by me, and is now circulating. The Lord prosper it for the good of Ireland, and dispose his children to aid in it.

" *June* 26. The ' Irish Appeal ' has raised £8021. Glory be to God alone ! "

The funds thus raised were employed, during the same

year, in aiding the " Irish," the " Church Education," and
" Additional Curates' " Societies, the " Irish Scripture
Readers'," the " Hibernian Female Schools," the " Cork
Pastoral Aid " Societies, the " Achill and Dingle Missions," and the " Irish Islands Society ; " while a small
portion was devoted, towards the close of the year, to a
direct mission to the Roman Catholics of Galway, which
has since borne very abundant fruit to the glory of the
grace of God.

Along with his efforts for the good of Ireland, Mr.
Bickersteth continued to labour, with unabated zeal, for
the furtherance of Christian union. His loving spirit
knew how to turn passing causes of offence into blessed
occasions for the triumph of forbearance, candour, and
charity. One of the brethren from America, who was
present at the August conferences, had written home,
a little before they took place, in a moment of excitement, reflecting severely on the religious state of England, and especially on the Established Church. The
letter was printed, and found its way back across the
Atlantic ; and its strongest passages were produced, in
an Irish journal, as a convincing proof of the futility of
the Alliance, and the insincerity of its professions. Mr.
Bickersteth, at the request of other friends of union,
wrote a private letter of kind and affectionate remonstrance. One or two extracts will shew his feelings with
regard to the actual state of the Church of England, and
his habitual candour towards those who differed from him,
whether within or without the pale of the establishment.

" For above thirty years I have been a minister of this Church,
and I may say, without condemning other denominations which
hold the Head, it is the Church of my deepest conscientious con-

victions and affections, as being truly Scriptural, evangelical, and catholic towards other Churches.

" For fifteen years after I was in the ministry, I travelled in connection with the Church Missionary Society, over every part of our country; and since that time, from my connection with different religious Societies, I am well acquainted with its situation. I deny not many humbling and fearful inconsistencies. Throughout the Protestant Churches much of the spirit of the Reformation has decayed, and hence the door has been opened to many evils. I deny not our participation in this decay. . . .

" There are fifteen or sixteen thousand clergymen in our Church. The chief proportion are in country parishes,—the great stay, support, and comfort, of the retired villages of our country, from their conscientiousness, intelligence, and benevolence, and this in many cases where there is not the fulness that might be wished, of enlightened, deep, and experimental religion.

" There are, it must be admitted, to the grief of every true Christian, unconverted, worldly, and formal ministers, and perhaps at the same time exclusive and extreme in their notions of Church authority. But faithful rulers and ministers in our Church have again and again testified against these evils. A fervent and zealous spirit may also greatly mistake as to the proportion of evil-doers. Elijah thought that he only was left a true worshipper of God, when there were seven thousand such in Israel. I mourn that there should be any such in a Church, where the most eminent holiness and devotedness are required by her principles and ordination-services. But the tares will grow with the wheat; and while it is our duty to testify against that which is evil, let us remember also the solemn admonition, ' Judge not, that ye be not judged.' We may exaggerate the extent of the evil, and are incompetent judges of others.

" As to Tractarianism, the general voice of the bishops and clergy has been against it, and the middle and lower classes of Churchmen strengthen faithful brethren in firmly withstanding it. Its character has been manifested by some open secessions to the apostacy of Rome, and this shipwreck of faith has not been in vain. Others, yet with us, in my view overvalue their own notions, as to the visible Church, its sacraments and ministry, and episcopacy; but are there no contrasted errors in other denominations? And where there are these errors, there is often much conscientiousness, seriousness, real devotedness, enlarged bounty, and self-denial,— though mingled with statements erroneous in themselves, and leading to still more dangerous errors.

" Blessed be God, there is also a great revival in the last thirty years, a growth of earnest attention to religion, as the one thing of supreme moment. These errors have quickened many to deeper studies, and a more bold and open confession of evangelic truth. It remains yet to be seen whether the Church of England may not, in the great mercy of God, be a means of preserving this kingdom from national apostasy, and preparing the way of the Lord on earth. Sure I am, a very large body of ministers are labouring in retirement, with patient zeal, for the salvation of their flocks. There are thousands of such ministers, who count the salvation of souls their highest preferment, and the reproach of the cross their greatest honour. They, with faithful brethren of other denominations, are the true salt of Britain.

" As to the higher authorities, they have large incomes, and these may be abused, but often their charities fully correspond. The Archbishop of Canterbury and the Bishop of London, for instance, give immense sums for charitable objects. . . . Our Church authorities have also taken many decided steps, to bring in and carry through Parliament, laws to diminish and put away various evils. . .

" God forbid that I should justify sin or error, either in my Church or out of it. I would rather cry and sigh for every abomination. Any mixture of truth in the sharpest statements, or the most unfounded principles, may well occasion grief and humiliation, in one who loves the institutions of the Church, while he is aware that the administration of them is defective.

" My hope is, that this frank communication, in the full spirit of brotherly love, will meet with a kind reception, and that now I have pointed out what I think was wrong, none will grieve more at it than yourself, if convinced it was so ; and a foundation will be laid for deeper and fuller union than we could otherwise have attained.

" What merciful deliverances God gave on your return ! He is
the Hearer and Answerer of prayer.   Glory be to His name ! "

The reply was such as Mr. Bickersteth had hoped to
receive—frank, affectionate, and ingenuous; and was
prefaced with a brief tribute of hearty esteem and
love.  " I thank God, and glorify God in you, my honoured brother, that whatever I have done, it has been
overruled as the occasion of displaying your Christian
urbanity, your heavenly temper, your brotherly faithfulness, your wisdom, your benignity." The whole explanation was worthy, in its tone, of the affectionate remonstrance by which it was elicited. The result was a striking
proof of the real tendency of the Alliance, as a powerful
influence on the side of forbearing love ; and showed how
far more blessed it is to seek the cure of offences in the
spirit of meekness, than to blazon them abroad, as ex-
cuses for alienation, distrust, and bitterness, among the
servants of Christ.

The correspondence of Mr. Bickersteth was, at this
time, of a most extensive and interesting character. Very
frequently he would receive more than twenty letters by
a single post, and many of them on topics, either of great
delicacy, or of public importance, in connection with the
general interests of the gospel.   Some of his more prominent engagements in the course of the present year are
briefly recorded in his journal.

" *January* 30.  I was called on the 13th, at the Islington meeting, to speak on the way in which St. Paul encountered error in his ministry.  It was a very profitable
meeting, and many spoke very seasonally.  I go next
month, if it please God, to preach on the 14th, at Clapham, for the Church Missionary Society, and on the 21st,

for the Jews at Brighton. May the presence of the Lord be with me !

" My brother's family has been specially afflicted in the last six weeks. The Lord relieve, comfort, and sanctify. As to my own soul, I hope there has in some things been more unction and communion with God. O that there might be a full tide and flow of blessings, much spiritual grace and fruit to the glory of God, and the good of my fellow-men ! When shall it be ? I am much pressed with work, but God has graciously given me a most valuable curate for my flock.

" *March* 7. The Lord has disposed Government to appoint a national fast-day. May it be greatly blessed ! I was carried through my duties at Clapham and Brighton ; and on the 28th we had a large collection of £30 for the Irish at Watton. On March 4, I preached for the London City Mission at Woolwich, and the next day a lecture at St. George's, on Prophecy. The Lord be blessed for strength in these duties !

" *March* 19. I this day began my 62nd year : so long has my God spared me and preserved me in this world of sin and sorrow. The last birth-day was spent in my sick room, while slowly recovering ; this birth-day I am surrounded with many peculiar blessings. . . First, the birth, this morning, of my first grand-child, born the same day as my father and myself. It was a time of special answer to prayer. Glory be to God.

" Secondly, God is graciously prospering my little tract on the Fast, and 80,000 have been printed. May it be owned of the Lord, to help in bringing the nation to repentance !

" The blessings given to my dear children make our home one of special happiness and blessedness. These

are some of my mercies. What is my return? Very unworthy, very inconsistent. If there be some outward
zeal, O how little real communion, fervent prayer, and
self-sacrifice, in seeking only the glory of Jesus! Lord,
help me, even at sixty-one, to begin to walk in newness
of life.

"*March* 24. This is the National Fast-day, for the
famine in Ireland. I have preached two sermons on Isa.
xxvi. 9. There have been unusually crowded congregations, morning, afternoon, and evening; and I trust the
Divine blessing will rest largely on the labours of the
day. O how much I have to be thankful for! It appears
that 120,000 of the Tract have been published. Glory be
to God! May it please Thee to give some blessing to the
sermons also.

"How very different may be my heavenly Father's
judgment, from that of partial admirers; and though
enemies say hard things of me, which are false, friends
speak, as they judge, far too highly of my doings. Nothing is of the slightest value, but Thy approbation, O
Jesus; nothing a real injury, but Thy displeasure. O
Jesus, pardon, accept, and bless me!

". . . The Lord guide me, in accepting and in de-
clining invitations to journey for, and to help Religious
Societies. Many I am obliged to decline, and often I am
in great perplexity what to do, the applications for this
help are so numerous. My correspondence also is so
much increased, that I have sometimes twenty or twenty-
five letters and packets by the post. O let not work lead
from, but lead to Thee, my God, and be for Thee, and
give me strength for it, and then the more the better.

"*April* 24. Last Tuesday and Wednesday I was at
Birmingham for the Jews' Society. . . . For many weeks

I have important engagements : the Prophetical meetings and Religious Societies next week, several Societies the two first weeks in May, the Evangelical Alliance in Edinburgh at the beginning of June, and then journeys to Inverness and Aberdeen. O Lord, give me heavenly wisdom for all Thy work, and a large blessing on the furtherance of Thy truth ; and, along with this, give me to grow in grace, and in the knowledge of Christ Jesus my Lord.

" *May* 22. . . Thanks be to my God for help in duties in London. I spoke for the Foreigners' Evangelical Society, the Wesleyan Missionary, the Church Missionary, the Irish, the London City Mission, the Jews, the Home and Colonial, the Religious Tract, the Church of England's Young Men's, Societies. I then went to Nottingham for the Church Missionary Society, and on Tuesday returned to town, and spoke at the Church Pastoral Aid, the Protestant, and the Reformation Societies. Thanks be to the Lord for health and ability to plead His cause. May He make what has been said a blessing, and pardon all that was sinful in His sight.

" I went to Kelshall, last Sunday, for the baptism of my first grandchild. The Lord pour his grace upon her !

" The conflict is manifestly increasing. O Lord Jesus, give me this one thing—let me be faithful to Thee, cost what it may ! Hold up my goings in Thy paths.

" How uncertain is all before us ! What an important journey that to Scotland ! How shall I need heavenly love and wisdom from above ! Lord, make me faithful !

" *June* 11. *Edinburgh* (Alliance Meetings.)

" Every moment is full of work for our blessed Saviour. Oh it is sweet to work, and to promote the love of the brethren ! The meetings have been very blessed, beneficial, and striking hitherto. God is with us of a truth.

"*June* 14. *Glasgow.* God graciously carries me through my work, and blesses me in it. I preached twice in Edinburgh yesterday, and have come here for the meetings of the Alliance. Oh how much there is, each hour, for which to praise God !

"*June* 16. *Aberdeen.* I go fifty miles further to Banff to-morrow, please God ; then to Huntley, back to Aberdeen, and on to Perth, Edinburgh, Newcastle, and London, and then to happy home, where, if it please God, the Watcher over all, I hope to arrive this day week, after a journey of 1500 miles, hitherto full of mercies and blessings.

" How sweet to commit all that is dear to us to the Lord ! His truth, His kingdom, the union of His children, the spread of His gospel, the communion of saints, and the greatest things we have to do with ; and then wife, children, relatives, friends, parish, church, and all our immediate relationships. God give us singleness of eye and heart for Him !

"*June* 26. I have been safely carried through my long journey. I preached for the Irish Scripture Readers at Edinburgh, for the Colonial Church Society, and the Evangelical Alliance, and three times for the Church Missionary Society. I was strengthened to speak often at public meetings, and brought home in peace. All glory to the Lord my Saviour.

" As a clergyman of the Church of England, I am apparently called, with a few brethren, to walk in a solitary path, and find my brethren on all sides shrinking from that course which seems to me the plain path of duty. I can fully free them from blame ; and yet, seeing as I do, I cannot act otherwise.   Yet it will most likely bring upon me trials and sorrows.

"My soul thirsts for more grace; more of God's presence; more preparedness for the Lord's coming; more self-denying labours.   O Lord, time is short, the work to be done is immense; make me faithful to Jesus, faithful to souls, faithful to my parish."

"*July* 23.   The chief public work has been in reference to county Societies, the Herts Reformation, the Hatfield Church Missionary, and the Herts Gospel Propagation Society.   Glory to God for help in these!

"I trust that there is a blessing on the labours of my dear fellow-labourer, Mr. Ogle, in the parish, and that more communicants are added to the Lord.   The elections make it a time of great national moment, as well as the ingathering of the harvest that now covers the earth."

"*August* 28,   Months roll rapidly away, each bearing its solemn account for the judgment.   O were it not for the promises, of the grace of the gospel, I should have no hope!

"We have had Church Pastoral Aid and Church Missionary Meetings, and I am at present trying to get a day of National Thanksgiving.   The Lord in mercy prosper a feeble instrument.

"My time has been much occupied preparing a lecture on Popery in the Colonies.   Lord, help me to speak in much faithfulness on a subject so important to the welfare of my fellow-men in distant lands.

"My dear child F—— continues most distressingly ill. It ought to be a very serious inquiry with us before God, wherefore He thus contends with us.   I know that I am not walking closely enough with God.   O Lord, give me repentance and newness of life!   I would humble myself before Thee: quicken me for Thy name's sake."

" *September* 26.  Still mercies are prolonged.  There
appears the prospect of a day of National Thanksgiving,
as indeed there ought to be.  I am preparing a Tract for
its due improvement, and another on the due observance
of the Lord's Day.  The Lord own and prosper them.

" In the last month we heard of the heavy trial of our
dear friends the Auriols, in the loss of their only son in
the lake of Geneva.  They have been wonderfully supported in the fiery trial, and enabled to glorify the Lord,
as doing all things well.  May we glorify Him also under
F——'s affliction.  Lord, we commit all to Thee.

" My faith is very weak, hope very feeble, and love
very cold.  Lord, pardon all my follies, inconsistencies,
and everything in me short of thy mind and will.  O
fulfil Thy new covenant promises, and write Thy laws in
my heart, for Christ's sake ! "

The affecting trial of his beloved friends led to the
following letter of Christian sympathy,

MY BELOVED AURIOL,

Our hearts have been greatly crushed by your letter.  We got it
just after family prayers, and your most touching account thrilled
through all our feelings, so that I could hardly read it.  It is the
Lord !  This silenced us, and we knelt down together again in
prayer, that you might be supported, sanctified, and strengthened,
and that it might be sanctified to us all.  Ever since, the painful
stroke has been like a weight upon us.  O may it indeed come
with purifying power to every one of us !  Our own dear child has
been under aggravated suffering the last two days ; but your fearful loss is most upon our minds.  And yet what alleviations and
consolations !  No father's, no mother's love, can do for E. what a
few moments did—bring him into the presence of Jesus, and make
him happy in his love for ever.  All was foreseen and foreordained,
in deep love and infinite wisdom, that he might be removed from

conflict, temptation, and trial, to rest, and holy love, and full joy ; and that you, dearest friends, might have fresh experience of the all-sufficient grace of Jesus in the greatest of earthly trials parents can have, the sudden removal of an only child. And I doubt not that God may be greatly glorified before all, and especially among His people, in the grace given you, to testify His faithfulness, wisdom, and love, in such a stroke as this ! And I doubt not further, many spiritual children you would never otherwise have had, many comforted children of God you would never otherwise have been able to comfort, a heavenly-mindedness you would never otherwise have attained, will be given to you through this trial, and will increase the perfected joy and glory, with which you shall both rejoin your son in the speedily coming day of the Lord. That all glorious day cannot be far off ; and then lost E. and harassed F. and afflicted relatives, all remember no more the present sufferings ; or rather, in the sweet words of that precious promise—" I will turn their mourning into joy ; and will comfort them, and will make them rejoice from their sorrow." They shall have joys they could not have had without their sorrow.

O my dearest friend, we know these things are ours ! we know the truths we preach are realities, not fictions ! Our only sorrow is, that they do not impress us enough, and so we fail to impress others ; but such dispensations deepen every inward conviction, and give strength and power to our utterance of God's own truths for our people's salvation.

The Lord bring you back again, then, with even a fuller blessing for His church than when you went out. The Lord anoint you with a fresh unction from above, " to preach good tidings to the poor, and to bind up the broken-hearted, and to comfort all that mourn." And your dearest wife and sister, the Lord be gracious to them, and bless with especial help to glorify Him in this trial, that all may see His grace is all-sufficient, to sustain those who confide in Him, in the very darkest day of earthly sorrow. I need not say how my dearest wife and our children sympathize with you in all this trial—it is like losing one of ourselves ; for he had endeared himself so to us all, we felt him to be like one of our own family.

And so he is now, in the highest of all senses, removed to our safe and happy home, to welcome us there.

> Yours most affectionately,
> E. Bickersteth.

About the same time a letter of Lord Ashley, (now the Earl of Shaftesbury) in reference to the great perils of the social condition of the country, led to the following characteristic communication.

*August* 11, 1847.

My dear Lord Ashley,

Thanks be to God for your deeply interesting and truly Christian letter. I bless Him who has given you this deep insight into the actual state of our country. It is just that to which the study of the prophetic word has long led me, though the visible signs of it have not before been so apparent.

We have, then, just to rise to the mind of Christ and His apostles, as patriots in the Jewish State, labouring intensely, though they knew the people would fill up their sins and bring down Divine judgments, for the highest good of the State ; and who were eminently and remarkably blessed of God, first in bringing out of that state the purest and most efficient Church of Christ that has ever appeared on earth, and then by that Church, in sending the Gospel through the known world, and founding the whole of present Christendom. This is our mighty mission, to prepare the way for that happier state, near at hand, when the whole earth shall be filled with the glory of the Lord ; though all our hopes have the humbling and sanctifying sorrow, that our country as a country, with Christian kingdoms in general, nationally rejecting the gospel, must previously undergo national judgments.

God is so wonderful in all His grace, that it is possible He may give a temporary ministry in the State for good, before our trials ; as He gave a cabinet of grace for a short season in the reign of Edward VI., before the martyrdoms of Mary. But our brightest views must be drawn from the scene beyond all this, which Scrip-

ture opens out to us ;—The Lord of heaven and earth, notwithstanding all our infirmities, approving and accepting our confession
of His truth, blessing it to the awakening of many, and the salvation of multitudes, through our beloved Societies, that would otherwise have perished ; and so the seed sown of a harvest, joyful beyond all our imaginings, in the day of Christ. And, as it regards
our country itself, prolonging the day of grace, the long-suffering
of God, in the meanwhile, bringing salvation to multitudes, and
lengthening out our tranquillity.

Those who are so prominent as your Lordship in what is good,
will of course be special objects of the wrath and malice of those,
whom your faithful conduct especially condemns. It was so with
Wilberforce. The revilings of that good man, which I heard above
thirty years ago, are still remembered by me. So Sir T. F. Buxton
called on me once in London, much depressed with the obloquy
which he encountered.  When I told him of those who sympathized
with him, he seemed greatly comforted, and said he met with little
of that sympathy in the circles in which he moved. Yet see what
these men effected ! Wilberforce opened the door to the Gospel,
through the East and the West Indies. Buxton has made the
Christian instruction of those, who once were slaves, to be now
coveted through the Islands, and even in Africa the Gospel is pervading that dark continent.

Of our Lord it is said—" He shall not fail nor be discouraged,
till He have set judgment in the earth, and the isles shall wait for
His law." This is firmer than heaven and earth. His approval in
this work, carried on by us, is our present joy, and will be our everlasting reward.

The excess of lawlessness is needed to show liberalism its false
position,—and extremes beget their remedies. Yet immense mischief may be done in the mean while ; and our best comfort is—the
Lord reigneth, and orders every thing to the glory of His name, the
triumph of His truth and love, the good of His people ; and finally,
to the everlasting happiness of this lower world, in the full glory of
His own Church.

In that day, my dear Lord, what fulness of joy will be yours, and what praise will you give to Him for the course which He has put it into your heart to pursue ! May He uphold you to the end, and continually give you wisdom and judgment, grace and strength, for all the trying and difficult exigencies through which He is leading you.

Most affectionately yours,

E. BICKERSTETH.

The tone of deep, calm faith, mingled with strong and pure affection, in this letter, will explain the words of his Lordship, in replying to another of the same kind, about two years earlier, at a time when he was exposed to very bitter reproaches. " Your letters are always to me a balm of Gilead, grapes of Eschol, which show that there is a better land than that in which we now are."

" *October* 33. The Lord graciously strengthens me for his work. About 45,000 of the Thanksgiving Tracts have been circulated. On Monday last I delivered my lecture on Popery in the Colonies, at Islington, speaking more than two hours. It is now printing. I have since been to Huntingdon for the Malta Protestant College. Thanks be to God, if He uses and accepts me in anything for His service. The Thanksgiving was on Sunday, October 17. I regret that it was not a week-day.

" The one thing I need and desire is to be approved of Thee, O Lord. Revive Thy work, and quicken all my graces ! On the morrow I hope several of my young people will come to the holy communion. May there be a gracious outpouring of His good Spirit upon us all !"

The Lecture, to which the journal here alludes, was one of the most laborious, and perhaps of the most seasonable and striking, of Mr. Bickersteth's small occasional publications. He briefly unfolded the extent of the British colonies, and the solemn trust thereby committed to our nation; the character of Popery, and its direct opposition to the gospel of Christ; the zeal of Romanists in its diffusion; the support of it, by the British Government, in most of our colonies; the conflict in every sphere of Missionary labour, first as deduced from Papal, and then from Protestant testimony; and lastly, the practical measures which it becomes Christians to adopt, in order to withstand the apostacy of Rome. His remarks, on this first point, are still highly seasonable.

"It becomes important to discern with what forces Popery shall be overthrown. There are many unhallowed weapons which a Christian can never use. Lawlessness, Infidelity, Unitarianism, and Rationalism, are opposed to Popery, as well as to Evangelical Protestantism. We cannot combine with such hostile forces. Let them unite against us, if they think it will promote their cause to do so; they have done it in times past, and are very likely to do it again. God will divide and destroy all His enemies; we cannot, may not, will not, unite with any of them. The only effective weapon is the sword of the Spirit, which is the word of God.

"What is further wanted now, is to combine and greatly enlarge all the scattered efforts made by Protestants for resisting Popish aggressions, and for extending and diffusing Protestant truth. . . We must out-preach, out-pray, out-work, and out-give the Papist, if we would gain the victory. We do not wish to see England under spiritual bondage, like Austria, Spain, Portugal, or Italy. Should Popery again triumph in Britain, by God's grace we will not lay up for ourselves the agonizing reflection, that we were careless, supine, and indifferent, while its hosts were thundering at our gates, or traitors within were admitting them into our strong places. We will do what we can to hand down, unimpaired and strengthened, to our children, that Protestant constitution which we received from our forefathers, and which has been such a mighty means of national greatness and blessedness to Britain. The spirit of delusion is mighty and energetic to overcome worlds, but the

Spirit of truth is mightier still.  " He that is in us is stronger than he that is in the world."

" Let it be seen that none magnify Jesus so much as faithful Protestants ; that none dwell so much on His grace, all-sufficiency and love; none more continually exhibit Him as "made of God unto us, wisdom, righteousness, sanctification, and redemption;" none more rejoice in the blessed hope of His return, His kingdom, and His glory. Thus lifting up Christ, we present the great magnet of souls, and God will prosper all our labours."

The year came to its close amidst premonitory signs of the tempest which quickly followed ; and Mr. Bickersteth continued his course of unwearied labour in the cause of Christ, while ripening apace for his heavenly rest.

" *November* 27.  Goodness and mercy daily follow me. I went the Sunday before last to Bath, for the Church Pastoral Aid Society, and am going next Thursday to preach in London, for the Young Men's Society.  I am also preparing a Manual of Prayers for the Young.  On October 31, 102 communicants were at the Lord's table.

" I hope that, through Mr. Ogle's zealous labours, much good is doing in my parish, though I have much to be humbled for.  Two have been excluded from the communion, and two have died this week, one of them suddenly.  O Lord, lay not the blood of souls to my charge ! I cast my many and great sins on the Lord, and entreat that, in the sense of His forgiving love, I may live more to His glory.

" *December* 24.  Public events are full of agitation. Government are introducing a bill to bring Jews into Parliament, and a violent controversy is rending the Church of England on Dr. Hampden's appointment.  Our consolation is—The Lord reigneth !

"My Tract on the Lord's Day, and the Lecture on Popery, are now printed and in circulation.

"But what most condemns my soul is within. Whatever I may be before men, I am indeed a poor wretched sinner before God. Such a twofold character is in my soul; sometimes a burning flame of pure zeal, thirsting for God, and longing to live wholly to Him, and then a spirit feeding on ashes. O Lord, expel Satan, and come and dwell wholly in my soul!

"*December* 31. I come to the close of this year—a year of many trials in our country, and of many mercies. Judgments seem now impending over us; distress in Ireland, with many murders; cholera approaching; and our country endangered, by not being prepared to meet powerful enemies; and with this, the government support of the admission of Jews into Parliament.

"My own soul is barren, even at a time when the Lord has been graciously using me in the ministry, and blessing me in my parish with an increased number of communicants. My dear son is preparing for the ministry, and hopes to be ordained February 6. Glory be to God for the grace, I trust, given to him."

The year 1848 was one of storms. It opened with the French Revolution in February, and continued with a series of convulsions, that shook or overthrew nearly every state on the Continent of Europe. Mr. Bickersteth looked with peculiar interest on these great and solemn changes, which seemed to him the beginning of the last vial of judgment, and a fresh warning to the nations, to prepare for the coming of that kingdom which can never be moved. The time of public alarm was also marked, in his domestic circle, by special mercies, and

S 2

his journal records his feelings of humility and thanksgiving.

" *January* 29.   Wonderful is the Lord's love to a most unworthy servant, very negligent of His work, very unfaithful to His trust.   And yet He spares and blesses me ; that I may be ashamed and confounded, and deeply humbled in His sight.

" I have been preparing a ' Manual of Prayers for the Young,' and hope that the Lord may graciously bless it for much good.   God graciously grant it !

" The signs of the times, in the country, are very fearful.   The Parliamentary measures for the next month, if carried, would go far to unprotestantize and unchristianize our country.   The Lord stop them, if it be His will."

The measures here condemned were the Bill for the admission of Jews into Parliament, and that for diplomatic relations with the court of Rome.   To both of these he was earnestly opposed, from deliberate conviction, as destructive of that national testimony to Christ and His truth, which he accounted the chief honour and privilege of Britain, and the true secret of our national greatness.   His views on the former are stated, at some length, in an Appendix to his ' Guide to the Prophecies ; ' while his lecture, a few months before, on ' Popery in the Colonies,' was a warning against the misguided policy, which prompted the other measure, as if to link our nation with the mystic Babylon on the very eve of her judgment.

On February 6, Mr. Bickersteth's son was admitted to Deacon's orders by the Bishop of Norwich, and the following Sunday was a time of peculiar interest to himself, his family, and parish.   He preached in the morning on 2 Tim. ii. 1.   " Thou, therefore, my son, be strong in the

grace that is in Christ Jesus ; " a sermon, says one who
was present, " with such an opening out of the fulness of
Christ, that it might well be comfort to the sorrowing,
and strength to the feeble." In the afternoon he had the
pleasure of hearing his beloved son preach his first sermon, to a crowded congregation, on 1 Cor. i. 30. It was
a time well suited to awaken a thankful review of God's
mercies through forty years. It was nearly at the same
age that he himself had begun to desire the ministerial
office ; and after patient waiting, his desires had been fulfilled, and he had been led in that course of ministerial
labours, which was crowned with so large and rich a
blessing. The next entries in his journal allude to the
Revolution in France, and his own impressions of past
unfruitfulness.

" *February* 26. On Thursday the 24th, at Norwich, I
married my dear and only son, Edward, to Rosa Bignold.*
I have great joy in hoping that the marriage will be full
of blessing. The day this was taking place, Paris was
the scene of another Revolution, that seems a step onward
to the terrible convulsions of the last tribulation. I also
preached at Norwich a Jewish lecture.

" O that the Lord may quicken me by His own ordinance. Changes, travelling, bustles, and distractions, are
great impediments to the steady following out of earnest
devotional exercises.

" A fresh revolution seems to be now opening a new
and eventful era in European history—perhaps the beginning of the seventh vial. The Lord prepare His people
for all His purposes.

" *March* 19, *Rugby.* Having been called here to preach
for the Church Pastoral Aid Society, I spend my sixty-

* The daughter of Samuel Bignold, Esq. late Mayor of Norwich.

second birthday at Rugby. The last year has been specially full of mercies, particularly in my dear son's entrance
into the ministry, his happy marriage, and settlement at
Banningham in Norfolk. The Lord bless him, and make
him a blessing.

" God has been very merciful to me, but my returns to
Him are very poor and ungracious. It is so difficult to
live by faith in the Son of God, who loved me, and gave
Himself for me ; and when I cease to do this, all is dead.
Prayers are formal ; self-indulgence creeps in at a thou-
sand crevices, and the work of the ministry is neglected.

" But it becomes more and more evident, that the day
of the Lord is approaching, and that all His ministers
should be energetic and zealous, and sound an alarm in
His holy mountain, for the day of the Lord cometh. I
have entered on another year of my life ;—Oh that it
may be more fruitful than any past year in labours of
faith and love ! I have been much struck with St. Paul's
description, of approving himself as a minister of God, ' in
much patience, afflictions, necessities, distresses, stripes,
imprisonments, tumults, labours, watchings, and fastings ;
by pureness, by knowledge, by long-suffering, by kindness,
by the Holy Ghost, by love unfeigned, by the word of
truth, by the power of God, by the armour of righteousness on the right hand, and on the left.'

" What poor, little, puny ministers we are ; at least, I
am. Blessed Saviour, Oh, at length, touch my heart more
with the fire of Thy love, and enable me more to follow
Paul, as he followed Thee. Seventy years is the ordinary term of life. If spared such a lengthened period,
there would be eight years more of seed-time for eternity.
Lord, help me to redeem the time ! to be very watchful,
very dependent, very prayerful, very zealous for Thee !

Washed afresh in the blood of Jesus, may I, with an enlarged heart, run in the way of Thy commandments."

A few days before, he wrote to his son, on his return to settle at Banningham. " Our hearts and thoughts are much with you. Now, my children, form your plans early. You can easily modify them, but have regular plans for steady work, each hour, for the Lord. Time for solitary communion with Him, time for social prayer, time for family prayer, time for exercise out of doors, time for study, time for the poor and for all parishioners, and time for conversation on all. In short, time so laid out, as in the review will give you most joy, and enable you to do most for Him, to whom you owe, as we do, everything. The Lord make your ministry full of blessing.

" Order and discipline, are very good, as means to an end, but not to be pressed, so as to destroy the end itself, the salvation of our hearers. Shew a loving spirit in every thing to Dissenters who love the Lord, and a forbearing spirit to others, and all will work well in the end. Your difficulties will be more, as you are successful ; but grace will always be given."

" *April* 1, 1848. I am losing my valuable Curate, Mr. Ogle. The Lord graciously supply the want.

" The revolutionary movement seems spreading over the kingdoms of Europe ; Berlin, Vienna, Rome, Naples, Turin, Sicily, Hanover, Bavaria, have been undergoing great changes. The Lord, through all these, open doors for the spread of His gospel !

" In the mean while may my soul be watchful and prayerful ; may I keep my garments unspotted, and be preserved from all spiritual defilement in these trying times. I do desire of the Lord, in the name of Jesus, these great blessings ; that I may be preserved from these

evils—dishonouring Him, injuring others in body, goods,
or soul—defiling my inner man by any allowed sin : that
I may obtain, from His mercy and grace, these three great
blessings—to glorify His great name, to be a blessing in
every thing to others, to grow continually in inward purity
and holiness.

" O Lord, let this ordinance strengthen these desires,
and do Thou give to me these blessings !

" *April* 22.—*Easter.* A great deal of public business,
through the post, comes daily upon me, but from a want
of vigorous self-denial and industry, little that is widely
useful comes forth. I am now left alone for my parish
duties, and hope that I may earnestly and faithfully fulfil
the sacred trust, for which I am accountable to Thee, O
my Lord and Saviour Jesus Christ.

" I am struck with seeing, in all the great French histories, and in the present revolutionary proceedings, how
exactly France realizes the words—' They repented not
of their evil deeds,'—' they repented not, to give Him
glory.'

" The Lord grant me true repentance for all my present
sins, and help me to lie very low in the dust before Him.
Truly, O Lord, if Thou be extreme to mark what I have
done amiss, I cannot for one moment abide it. In every
character, in every relation of life, I plead guilty. I have
nothing to mention, but only as it is washed in the blood
of Jesus—that cleansing, purifying blood ; nor hope for
any thing better, but in the power of Thy quickening
Spirit and strengthening grace.

" *May* 27. In the last month I have been one week
at the London Anniversaries, which have been much
blessed this year ; another week at Sheffield, with visits
to Manchester and Nottingham, and part of a third week

in London at the prophetical lectures, besides the parochial work, which now lies wholly upon me.

" It is pleasant to work for the Lord ; only let personal
religion, heart, family, home and parish work, be preserved from neglect and injury. I am looking for another
fellow-labourer : the Lord guide every step, to His glory,
and the good of my parish. I hope that we may resume
our clerical meetings on an improved plan.

" I am very anxious about the young men of my
parish, who seem growing up in a headstrong, self-
willed spirit. The Lord help me wisely to seek their
improvement.

" My ' Manual of Prayers,' and ' Child's Book of Prayers,' are now published. The Lord prosper them.

" *June* 9. The Lord's mercies are innumerable to me,
to my wife, to my children, married and unmarried, and
my sick one, to my servants and my parish. Oh how
great is His goodness !

" I have had to prepare two addresses for the Evangelical Alliance ; one for the missionaries of all Societies,
and the other to those who have not yet joined us. I
have also been requested to prepare an Address on the
approaching Jubilee of the Church Missionary Society,
November 1st. The Lord help me in these important
duties.

" I have been thinking how good the Lord is in my
trials. While some, both in and out of my parish, prize
me too highly, some are ready to find fault. The trial is
the needful ballast to the mercy. While I am so largely
blessed in the spiritual state of all my children, the constant and severe illness of one is the needful ballast to
this mercy. Let me then be ever truly grateful for my
trial, and bear even those things which trouble the spirit,

but yet, so far as they come from the Lord, are only mercies and blessings.

" *July* 1. O how great are our mercies! What desolations and judgments the Lord is sending on the nations! In Paris there has been in the last week an insurrection, which was not subdued without the loss of several thousand lives. Who are we, that we should be spared such dreadful evils! Not because of our righteousness, but from the Lord's great mercies.

" Lord, help me to remember Thee at Thy table, and obtain there new strength against corruption, and new power to fulfil all my duties, to Thy glory and the good of others."

In a letter of June 29 he wrote to his son—" They stick up in the streets that 35,000 Frenchmen have been killed or wounded in the late terrible scenes. It is clear that there has been a fearful slaughter! O for the Lord's coming, and happy kingdom! Our own country is shaken with the heavings of this terrible earthquake."

" *July* 29. The last week has been specially full of mercies. My dear brother John from Acton, my son from Banningham, my son-in-law, his wife and child, have been staying with us. At our Pastoral Aid Meeting we had a larger attendance than before, and more abundant contributions. This evening three Africans, George Nicol, Thomas Maxwell, and Thomas Macauley came from London, to visit the old African visitor of the Church Missionary Society. All glory be to God.

" I visited Sir Culling Eardley at Belvidere, and found it a profitable and refreshing season, preaching on board the Thames Church Ship at Erith."

The visit of the three African youths, from the Institution at Islington, was full of interest to Mr. Bicker-

steth, and awoke his grateful recollection of the Divine
goodness.   Thirty-three years had passed since his own
voyage to Africa, when he admitted the first-fruits of
the Society's labours to the table of the Lord—six boys
from one of the native schools, whom he had himself examined and prepared for that sacred service.   The little
one was now become a thousand.   More than 13,000
communicants had been gathered into the fold of Christ,
in various parts of the heathen world; and in Africa
itself the cords were lengthening daily, native Africans
were preparing to spread the Gospel among their sable
countrymen, and Abbeokouta, an off-shoot from Sierra
Leone, had assumed its place among the twelve leading
fields of labour, now occupied by the Society.   It was an
interesting sight to see Mr. Bickersteth in his own school-
room, introduce his three visitors to his own people, and
then cede his own place to them, that they might speak
of the gracious Providence by which they had been res-
cued from slavery and heathenism, and were prepared to
go forth shortly as messengers of grace to their own
brethren.   They came to Watton for the purpose of
receiving the communion at his hands, and the contrast with that earlier communion, on the shore of
Africa, might well awaken the feeling, What hath God
wrought !

"*August* 26.   How good the Lord is, day by day !
The Bible and Church Missionary Meetings at Hertford
were full of interesting details, and our collection at
Watton just double that of last year.   I have been writing
tracts for the Jubilee, and shall be very thankful if the
Lord bless them to the furtherance of His cause.   I have
also been appointed to preach one of the Jubilee Sermons
in London, and felt it a duty to comply; and God has

disposed the beloved Archbishop Sumner to agree to preach the other.

" But in the midst of blessings, signs of judgment abound.  The potato-crop has again failed, and the weather has been such as to injure the general harvest, while the cholera seems impending on our shores.  While Government is passing a Bill for Diplomatic Relations with Rome, God himself seems destroying the Pope's temporal power.  O that the Lord may deliver our rulers from the infatuation of being reconciled to Antichrist.  At such times how important is the office to which I am called, rightly to improve the present season, as to our national duty in more extended missions to the heathen !

" I hope that I have been favoured with more earnest communion with God in some seasons of private devotion; but there is great room for quite another standing of communion and devotedness.  O that the Lord may give it me !  May I shrink from every defilement of the inner man, and may the light in my soul be purer, brighter, and more blessed to others !

" Please God, in the next month I go to my son at Banningham, and to Cromer, Yarmouth, and Norwich, for the Church Missionary Society, and then to Liverpool for the Colonial Church Society."

Several notes to his children were written on this journey.

*Banningham, September* 15.

MY BELOVED F.

The sick one has the strongest claim, from her very weakness, on the absent father ; and so I begin my letters with one to you. And if it be so in earthly parental love, which is only a drop from the ocean, it must be infinitely more so in heavenly parental love, the very ocean from which all other love originally comes. . . .

My child is called to glorify God in a more difficult path than her father has to walk in; by quiet, patient, confiding, and loving acquiescence in the Lord's will, amidst daily suffering; and I rejoice to see how the Holy Spirit is mightily aiding her to learn the lesson, which will help her joy for ever. I have to wait on Him and to walk with Him, in active work, and there is great danger of losing the fellowship, even in the midst of the Master's own work. But He is all-sufficient for us both, and will never leave us, till He has accomplished His own good pleasure in us and by us. Let us ever joy in God, through our Lord Jesus Christ. My hearty love to your sisters. Remember me to the servants, and to our friends about you. . . .

Your ever affectionate father,

E. BICKERSTETH.

*Banningham, September* 18.

We had a very happy Sunday yesterday. The four parents and their two children met, and we had the Lord's Supper in Banningham Church, with about twenty-five communicants. I preached in the afternoon for the Church Missionary Society, and in the evening at Felmingham, for the Jews, and go with Edward, please God, to Cromer to-night, and to Yarmouth to-morrow. The most delightful thing to me was to hear my dear son preach a very faithful sermon on Luke xii. 32, and to be cheered by the hope that the Lord will be gracious to him, as He has been to his father, in blessing him to promote His holy and happy kingdom.

I am engaged continually in the work of our blessed Master here; and I trust my dear children do not cease to pray for me, as we do for them.

*Caistor, September* 22.

MY BELOVED SICK ONE,

A father's heart yearns after his afflicted child, going through lengthened trial; but a better, wiser, more loving, heavenly Father, directs it all. A Saviour sits by as a refiner and purifier, watching over all. It will not last one moment more than He sees good, for

the best good of my child, her sisters and brothers, her kind
nurse and servants, and the parish, and a far wider circle; and
then, too, for a far higher object—His own glory, in buffetting
Satan by a weak earthen vessel, and the perpetual expulsion of that
malignant foe, from a temple which the Lord will consecrate to
Himself for ever.

O how much is suffering better than sin, and victory over
temptation better than not being tried (Rom. i. 2; Rev. ii. 10,)
and the haven after a storm, than to have had no experience of the
power, wisdom, and loving-kindness of the Lord, in carrying us
safely over every stormy wave. . . .

Your ever affectionate father,

E. BICKERSTETH.

" *October* 28.   Glory be to God for all his mercy, in
carrying me through trying duties, and prospering me
hitherto in His work.   Next week is important in various
respects.   On Monday I observe the Jubilee by preaching
and a meeting at Watton.   On Tuesday I go up, please
God, to London, and preach my Jubilee Sermon at St.
Ann's.   On Wednesday the Archbishop preaches; Thursday is the Jubilee meeting; and Friday evening, the Young
Men's Church Missionary Meeting, when I am to be in
the chair.   O Lord God, my Strength and my Redeemer,
assist me and Thy servants in these weighty duties and
engagements, and grant that they may be full of blessing
to many souls !

" On the 14th, please God, I am to go to York, where
the Archbishop of York is to be in the chair.   May all
these efforts very widely awaken the Missionary feeling
through the country.   And, O Lord, kindle in my heart
true zeal for Thee, and true love to Thy cause !

" *November* 25.   Through God's great goodness I have
been carried through my duties.   Through His loving-

kindness the Jubilee has been accompanied by many blessings in all parts of the country. Glory be to His holy name. I hope also that good is doing in my own parish, through the labours of my children. O for more of the spirit of grace and supplication ! Lord, grant Thy grace for this end."

The season of the Church Missionary Jubilee was an era in Mr. Bickersteth's life, as well as in the history of the Society. He had been a member of it for more than forty years ; and for three and thirty years, which was two-thirds of its whole existence, had been one of its most active and zealous friends. Fifteen years he had laboured as one of its official secretaries ; and the eighteen years since his resignation, had been marked by annual journeys to plead its cause in almost every part of the kingdom. He had joined it while he was still a clerk in the Post-Office, and when he was comparatively unknown ; he had founded one of its auxiliaries when he was a layman at Norwich ; his first work, as an ordained minister, had been to visit its African stations ; he had admitted there to the Lord's table the first-fruits of its heathen converts ; he had toiled in its cause, when it was still exposed to obloquy and reproach, and neglected or discountenanced by those who should have naturally been its patrons ; and now, in its old age, amidst the convulsions and overthrow of earthly thrones and kingdoms, he joined his brethren in celebrating the mercies of the Lord in its growth and prosperity, and was called to share with the Primate of All England the honourable and blessed office of recounting those mercies, and publicly enforcing its claims on British Christians. His Tract, entitled, " A Pastoral Address to British Christians on the proposed Jubilee," was very widely circulated before the time

arrived. On Wednesday evening, October 31, a crowded
congregation assembled in St. Ann's, Blackfriars, the
church where Scott, Simeon, Cecil, Biddulph, Venn, Ro-
binson, Richmond, Buchanan, had successively pleaded
its cause in early years, to hear him, as its oldest surviving Secretary, proclaim with the silver trumpet of the
Gospel its blessed year of Jubilee. His text on this occasion was Rev. xiv. 6, and the Sermon is printed at length
in the Jubilee Volume of the Society. His intimate connexion with the whole progress of its work will justify
the insertion of one extract, in which he reviews the
course of its labours.

" Feeble, like all the great works of God, the Society, in its
first appearance, seemed little likely to effect much on the earth.
But God raised up the men, both at home and abroad, and fitted
them for His own work. Its first preacher, the venerable commen-
tator, Thomas Scott ; its most efficient secretary for twenty-two
years, my beloved and departed friend, Josiah Pratt, whose heart
would indeed have been filled with joy in reviewing with us these
fifty years of mercies ; the departed Venn, who modelled the rules
under which we have acted ; these, with others dear to us all, and
our lay brethren, Grant, Wilberforce, and Admiral Gambier, laid the
foundations. But Melville Horne, who went as chaplain to
Sierra Leone, by his celebrated letters, in 1794, eminently prepared
the way for British Missions. The Society sent forth its first two
missionaries in its sixth year. They gradually increased, but for
seventeen years it had none of the converted heathen that its
missionaries could welcome to the Lord's table. Unhealthy
climates cut off many of its labourers, and its first English missionaries were only sent out in 1816. But the Lord sustained the
faith of its conductors and contributors, and enabled them to persevere. In 1816, on my visit to West Africa, I had the opportunity of placing Johnson at Regent's Town, and Düring at
Gloucester, who were so owned of God. I had also the privilege

of finding some in a prepared state for the communion; and on Easter Day, 1816, I admitted the first six communicants to the Lord's table, at Bashia, on the Rio Pongas. It has now twelve missions, in West Africa, Abbeokouta, the Mediterranean, East Africa, Western India, North India, South India, Ceylon, China, New Zealand, the West Indies, and North-west America. In these its missionaries preach the gospel in twenty different tongues, and congregations worship in our liturgy in seventeen languages. It has 102 stations, 138 ordained clergymen, of whom fourteen are natives, and 1342 lay teachers. From places whence we have returns, not including one of our principal missions, New Zealand, we have 561 schools, and 23,965 scholars. Glory be to our God. There are also now 13,010 communicants in our different missions· If the Apostle could say, within sixty years from the birth of Christ, "Their sound went into all the earth, and their words unto the ends of the world," now that the utmost regions of our earth have been unveiled, we may adopt in a yet larger sense the same heart-cheering language. "Glory be to God on high, on earth peace, good will towards men!" Thousands in different classes, of different colours, and different tongues, but who all believe in the same Saviour, have received and know and obey His word, and worship Him in our beautiful prayers in spirit and in truth, sing His praises, commemorate His dying love at His table, and tell others of His grace, and hope for His glory. The sending of the gospel has also everywhere been the revival of the gospel at home. In the apathy and darkness of the Protestant Churches, we might have lost our Christianity, had we not the reviving home re-action of our Foreign Missions, realizing the Divine promise—" Give, and it shall be given to you." " He that watereth shall be watered also himself." . . Oh! let us praise our God, as we ought, heartily, fully, and consistently. This is the right improvement of past success; this is the sure precursor of triumphs to come! Let us realize the predicted position of the Church of God in the last days—" Ye shall have a song, as in the night when a holy solemnity is kept, and gladness of heart, as when one goeth with a pipe, to come into the mountain of the

Lord, to the Mighty One of Israel." This is the true, fearless, and blessed position, amidst all earthly shakings, of the children of the living God, who have received a kingdom that cannot be moved.

His address at the public meeting, October 2nd, began in the same spirit of earnest praise.

" Glory be to God, our heavenly Father, for the scenes He has permitted us to witness during the last few days! Glory be to God, that we have been permitted to see, in this great metropolis, such gatherings of His servants in the truly Christian cause of missions to the heathen. Amidst the shaking of the whole earth, amidst the revolutions which are overturning kingdoms, and dynasties and thrones, the Christian Church in this land is graciously permitted to hold this happy jubilee! We cannot thank God sufficiently for what He has done for us. Never was it more needful that the Church should continue stedfast in the faith, and exhibit to the world a glorious light in the midst of the darkness, holding forth the word of life. The falsehood and failure of all worldly schemes, makes our duty to glorify God, by diffusing His means of blessing the world, more manifest. Men may now see that no real good can be conferred on mankind, but by His Gospel, and the regenerating and sanctifying influence of His Spirit. The great object we ought to keep in view, is to make our Church a really missionary Church; and then, through the Church of Christ, the nation must and will become a really missionary nation. . . . Britain will never be destroyed while Britain is zealous for God. This is our surest bulwark, the protection of the Lord."

In two notes, a few days after, he alludes to the joy of this happy season.

*November 6.*

My beloved E. and R.,

. . . . You will be glad to hear that all went on prosperously to the end. The dinner at Mr. Venn's, the evening sermon on 1 Thess.

iv. 16, and the conversation afterwards on Thursday evening, were deeply interesting. On the Friday morning such a meeting and breakfast, and addresses at the Institution, I never witnessed, for love and deep instruction and joy. An important Irish Committee Meeting, and then the Young Men's Meeting in the evening, crowned the whole of this memorable week of jubilee. From my conversation with ——, I hope we may establish a Mission in the Holy Land. It was very pleasant to me that you had a part, not only in seeing it, but in helping it by your hymns. God bless my dear children.

Your affectionate Father,<br>E. BICKERSTETH.

November 7.

MY DEAR MRS. SMITH,

. . . I never spent such a remarkable four days as the jubilee days in London. It was really heaven upon earth. The dismission of the missionaries on Tuesday, the Archbishop's Sermon, and the five or six hundred communicants on Wednesday, the immense public meeting on Thursday, the meeting of the old missionaries and missionary students, on Friday morning, and the crowded meeting of young men in Freemasons' Hall on Friday evening, were specially interesting. Had you been able to have been present, I feel assured, Mr. Smith would have had increased joy in all the support which God has enabled him to give to a cause so emphatically His own. . . . I spent an hour, along with two or three friends, with the Archbishop after his sermon, and thanked God for the remarkable spirit of meekness and of wisdom, which God has given him. I feel assured that he is raised up, in a most critical period, to be a blessing to our church and to the world. A Pastor's prayers and best wishes for all.

Very truly yours,<br>E. BICKERSTETH.

Amidst the joys of this happy festival, another chord was touched of deep and feeling interest. Between the

time when the jubilee services were announced, and their
actual celebration, the Rev. H. W. Fox, the youngest
secretary of the Society, after a brief course of eminent
devotedness, was called to his eternal rest. He had
written one of the Jubilee Tracts, to invite Christians to
this gathering, and a hymn to assist their worship, but
was himself summoned away to the nobler assembly of
"the spirits of the just made perfect." Mr. Bickersteth
in his Jubilee Sermon, made a touching allusion to this
event. He introduced himself as the oldest surviving
Secretary of the Society, and spoke of the sacrifices which
his younger brother had made, of his wife, his child, his
health, and life itself, in the missionary cause, with the
hopeful words, "From his ashes will rise those, who will
yet bless the untold millions of the heathen." In his
speech he alluded to the double privilege of being a
member of the Society for forty years, and of seeing all
his children its members also. The next speaker took up
the allusion, with reference to the changes before another
Jubilee ; but in this case only sixteen months fulfilled
the too prophetic warning, and gave force to the practical lesson. "The speakers of to-day will all be gone.
Some of the children just mentioned may be here, but
the voice of the beloved father will have been silenced.
And what is the conclusion ? That we all remember,
Time is short. We must be like the drops of the rainbow,
—each falling, but each reflecting the Lord's light in the
brief moment of our rapid fall, so that the whole combined may form a bow between earth and heaven, a
standing testimony to the covenant of God."

# CHAPTER XXVIII.

## IRISH CHURCH MISSIONS—LATEST JOURNEYS.

### A. D. 1849.

THE influence of Mr. Bickersteth, in his last years, was so widely felt, and the works of benevolence in which he took an active part were so various, that a full account of all the subjects which occupied him from day to day, would almost require a large volume of Church history. Beyond the immediate circle of his family and parish, he was the mainspring of religious activity in his own county, where most of the Societies had been set on foot, and some of them were chiefly maintained, by his efforts. He devoted himself to the work of missions, among the Irish, on the Continent, to the Jews, and to the heathen world. He also laboured zealously, both in his numerous writings, and by his public addresses, to resist the inroads of Popery, to maintain the national testimony to Christ, and to promote peace and love among Evangelical Protestants ; while, as a preacher and writer on the subject of prophecy, he fulfilled the office, in a time of startling and convulsive changes, of a heedful watchman to the Church of Christ. The unobtrusive simplicity of his zeal, and the variety of his exertions, makes it difficult to convey a just impression of their collective amount, and of the real eminence of blessing and usefulness which he

had attained.  His course was like that of a river, which
sends a thousand little streams into the adjoining valleys,
and loses in apparent volume, only by enlarging the
range of its fertilizing influence.  It is impossible, within
a few pages, to give a full view of all those fields of
Christian activity in which he laboured.  The notices in
his monthly journal, during the last year of his life, will
give occasion for a few remarks on those which were
most characteristic and important.

The first entry after the Jubilee alludes to his domestic
mercies, and to several events of public interest, in which
he was actively occupied, on his return from those happy
and quickening services.

"  *December* 25, 1848.   Goodness and mercy, O how
great they are to one so unworthy !   God has placed me
in a position of wide influence, but I by no means use it
as I ought, for his glory in the good of others.   But His
blessings abound.   He has given me another grandchild,
the first-born of my son.   He is using me in making our
Special Fund a means of Church Missions to the Roman
Catholics of Ireland.

" The triumphs of the Jubilee are accompanied by one
humbling lesson to us all.   Mr. Baptist Noel has left our
Church, . . . which, with all its defects, I believe to have
been God's gracious and chief means of blessing our
country, and making it a blessing to the world.   The
Lord avert the evil, and bring great good out of it.

" I have been preaching, this Advent, on the Church
of Christ, in the position of waiting for the Lord's coming.
I have engaged to speak on Wednesday at the Sabbath
Prize Essay Meeting, and to go to Brighton on the 6th,
for the Jubilee.  The Lord strengthen me for these duties!

" This winter my children have established a working

school for the young women, and adult evening schools
for the young men, which I hope will meet the wants of
two inaccessible classes."

The event just referred to naturally caused Mr. Bickersteth deep regret, and involved him in a large correspondence. With a deep and heartfelt sorrow for many
practical defects and abuses in the Church of England,
growing years had rather strengthened, than weakened,
his conscientious and deliberate attachment to it, as the
noblest witness to Divine truth on the face of the earth ;
and as affording, in spite of the laxity of its discipline,
abundant helps, wherever there was a faithful and zealous
ministry, for the quiet, practical growth of true godliness.
His strong desire for union with true Christians of other
bodies was no result of diminished love to his own Church,
but of a fuller and deeper sense of the supreme importance of those great common truths, which they all believed, and of which the secret glory dawned more and
more upon him, as he drew near to the borders of eternity.
His own view of his friend's work was summed up in a
sentence written soon after.  " Most of the arguments
would apply to the Divine ordinance of marriage.  There
are so many unhappy marriages, and so many bad hus-
bands and wives ; therefore marriage is so very mis-
chievous." But his chief regret arose from the fear, not
that Churchmen would be led to copy Mr. Noel's example, but that they would be repelled from that cause
of Christian union, which had become increasingly dear
to his own heart.

The distribution of prizes to Working Men, for Essays
on the Sabbath, at which Mr. Bickersteth was present,
cheered his mind as a hopeful sign, amidst so many causes
of fear and alarm. He had written one of the Tracts,

which were contributed by several distinguished men on
this important subject, with the title " The Spiritual Observance of the Lord's Day," and had taken a lively interest in the general movement.    A branch of the Lord's
Day Society had been set up in his own county by his
exertions.    The Sabbath had long been to him " a delight,
holy to the Lord, and honourable ;" and from forty years'
experience of the greatness of the blessing, he was earnest in his desires for its fuller private and national observance.

" *January* 27, 1849.    Mercies encompass me largely.
The meeting for delivering the prizes was a very useful
one, and I have to bless God for the Brighton Jubilee.    A
first grandson has been added to my family.    Glory be
to the Lord.    May he continue His grace to all my children from generation to generation.

" The whole work of the parish is now upon me.    The
more regular duties are these :

" Sunday :  Bible  class—morning  and  afternoon  service—and evening lecture.

" Monday : Cottage lecture—catechizing the children
—and  Parish Friends' meeting, in the different classes,
weekly.

" Wednesday : Wempstead Lecture in the afternoon—
Watton Lecture in the evening.

" Thursday—Adult Evening School.

" Friday—Cottage Lecture.    Adult Evening School.

" Saturday—Prayer Meeting at the Rectory.

" O may the Lord pour out His Spirit on these means,
for without Him none can prosper.    I feel sadly how
easy it is to go through a round of religious duties, without any heart-communion with God.    Vain thoughts,
pride, and  neglect of self-denying duties, still beset me.

O how low shall I stand at the last! Only the wonders
of redeeming grace and love can at all help me in the
day of Christ.

" Lord, let this first communion of the year be blessed,
as a help to my own soul, as well as to my people.  Amen."

The love of children had always been one feature of
Mr. Bickersteth's character, and his three grand-children
naturally came in for a large share of his affection.  A
note to his son at this time expresses the habitual feelings of his heart.

*Watton, Jan. 19.*

My beloved E. and R.

It is very pleasant to hear of you both, and of our little grand-
child.  I am so rich now with three grand-children, I may well be
very thankful.  My brother John tells me he has twelve ; so
altogether, the Bickersteth tribes are growing.  O that they may
all belong to the sealed tribes, that shall stand with the Lord on
Mount Zion.

The difficulty of leaving a parish, now of 930, without a curate,
obliged me to give up visiting you ; but how I rejoiced to hear that
our beloved friend, Captain Trotter, is coming to the baptism.  It
is truly kind and Christian.  Our poor F. continues our cross and
our blessing.  We seldom keep very near to God, but when we
have a burden for Him to bear ; only too often we are unconscious
of our worst burden, that should ever bring us near to Him.

Our hearts will be much with you on your birth-day.  Believe
me, my dear children,

Your ever affectionate father,

E. Bickersteth.

His parish engagements now occupied much of Mr.
Bickersteth's time.  From October 1844, to April 1846,
while his son was at College, he had dispensed with the

aid of a Curate ; until his severe accident, by disabling
him from active work, led him to seek for help again.
Mr. Ogle, who had previously had a charge at Wellington,
was led to offer his services, partly from a wish to benefit
by intercourse with one so highly esteemed in the Lord's
work ; and continued to labour zealously, and with marks
of the Divine blessing, till he was called away, in April
1848, to another sphere  Though no signal revival of
religion, at any one time, had taken place during Mr.
Bickersteth's stay at Watton, there had been a gradual
progress.  The number of communicants, which was about
twenty-five when he first came, had increased to an average attendance of eighty or ninety persons, and sometimes above a hundred met around the Lord's table, as at
the communion before the missionary Jubilee.  The word
of God, though the results were far short of what their
pastor earnestly desired, had not been spoken among them
in vain, and many a peaceful and holy death-bed had
borne witness to the blessed power of the gospel of Christ.

The Bible Class, which stands first among the Sabbath
engagements, was a little company of from twelve to
twenty old or middle-aged men, who met in the chancel
at ten o'clock, to read a chapter, and hear Mr. Bickersteth
give a simple explanation.  At eleven the morning service began, and when he was without a Curate, Mr. Hudson, a clergyman residing near, and who attended the
Church, assisted him by reading the morning prayers, so
as to enable him to keep up the bible class, along with
three other services.  He preached from notes, and usually
continued the subject of the morning in the afternoon.
His style was earnest, homely, and above all, affectionate.
His really spiritual hearers prized his sermons for their
ripened fulness of divine truth ; while the attention, even

of the careless, was often secured by their heartiness of
tone, and the plainness of his illustrations. There was
seldom or never the logical continuity of a sustained
argument, or the lofty style of a fervid and poetical imagination, but clear divisions, fulness of thought, simplicity
of statement, and warm-hearted earnestness of love. The
evening lecture was held in the school-room. In this he
frequently took a course in the Epistles, Psalms, or Gospels,
and at one time went in succession through the Articles
and Services of the Church. His expositions were perhaps more striking than his sermons, especially those
in family worship. Few have ever had more power to
seize the force and scope of a scriptural passage, or to
bring out its lessons, with such loving and simple energy
as to reach the understandings, and touch the hearts,
even of the least cultivated hearers.

The " Cottage Lecture," one of which, at this time,
was held on Monday, and the other on Friday, at the
opposite ends of the village, were simple gatherings of
from twelve to twenty of the poor, chiefly the women,
about three in the afternoon, when a hymn was sung,
a prayer offered, and a chapter or shorter portion read
and briefly explained. At four, on Monday, it was also
his custom to visit the schools, and examine the elder
boys and girls, on the heads of the sermons preached the
day before, impressing on them a few of the plainest and
most important lessons. The hamlet of Wempstead was
about two miles from the village, and usually his Curate
gave a lecture there every Lord's day, and every Wednesday, in the evening ; but when the whole charge rested
on himself, a lecture on Wednesday afternoon replaced
these two services.

On the morning of the Lord's day, before the bible

class, he often went down to open the Sunday school ; and
the following explanation of the second collect in Advent,
given on one of these occasions, is a specimen of the simple style of his addresses to the children of his parish.

"*Blessed Lord.*" What a sweet title to give to God!—*Blessed* or
happy—happy God—yes, God is a Being, full of joy and bliss ; he
is " God over all, blessed for ever." Dear children, do not forget
this, God is happy, those who love God are happy—God continually
is devising ways to make His people happy. One of these ways
is mentioned in the collect. What has God caused to be written
for our learning? " All holy Scriptures." Why do you call the
Bible *Scripture?* what does *Scripture* mean? " Writing." The
Bible, you know, when God first gave it, was written down; there
were no printing-presses, all had to be written. How was it
written? " Holy men of God spake as they were moved by the
Holy Ghost." What other name is given to the Scriptures?
" The Bible." What does *Bible* mean? " Book." Yes, this is
*the book,* the only book in the world of which it can be said,
God wrote it. What was it written for? " For our learning."
Learning to spell, or to read does it mean? " No." What
then? " Learning the way of salvation—learning to know God."
Repeat the rest of the collect. " Grant that we may in such wise
hear them, read, mark, &c." *Hear them*—when this prayer was
first made, very few people could read ; in St. Paul's, London,
there were six Bibles, and crowds gathered together to hear them
read—it was a very precious thing to hear. Then " read them." Oh
happy children, happy boys, happy girls—you can read, you have
been taught to read, and you have this precious word in your own
hands. " Mark them." Some people have a plan, when they read
their Bibles, of taking a pencil, and marking under such passages as
they have found a comfort, that when they come to them again
they may know.—Does the collect mean this? " No." Perhaps,
children, you have lately been in some new road where you had
never gone before—how diligently you marked the way, you noticed
this tree, and that house, and if two roads met, you marked the

right one, that you might not forget it ; now just so carefully, diligently, mark in your mind, what you read in the Holy Scriptures.

" *Learn.*" Just as David who said, " Thy word have I hid in
my heart, that I might not sin against Thee." Keep fast hold of
God's word, grasp it tightly. " And inwardly digest ; "—well, this
is a strange thing indeed. What, does it really mean we are to
eat the Bible, as you eat your breakfast ? No ; I do not think it
means this. You know, children, that you all had your breakfast
before you came to school, but now, whatever it was, it is (I hope),
all digested—turning, i. e., into your flesh and blood. Now, when
we read the Bible, we must *digest* it with our souls, make it a part
of our spiritual life and strength.

" *That by patience.*" Read it patiently, day after day. Some
there are who begin to read, but soon get tired ; read it daily, and
with prayer. "*And comfort.*" Oh, there is such sweet comfort in the
Bible ! It tells you, God will pardon all your sins through Christ
Jesus—that Jesus died to save you—that God loves you, that He is
your friend. " *We may embrace and hold fast the blessed hope of
everlasting life.*" Oh what a thing is this—poor children, and
dependant as you are on your parents, there is open to you the
blessed, happy hope of everlasting life, of joy and bliss eternal, of
being with God, of joining the glorious hosts of angels and arch-
angels, sharing in their songs of glory on their golden harps. Oh
embrace this hope, hold it fast ! You know, when a mother has
been parted from her little one, and meets it again, how glad she
is, how she puts her arm round the child and hugs it to her heart—
so, dear children, hold this blessed hope, take it home to your heart ;
let it gladden your mind. Who gives this hope ? " Thou hast
given us." Yes, God gives it. Through whom ? " Our Saviour
Jesus Christ." What a beautiful close to this precious little prayer !
It began, " Blessed Lord,"—it ends, " our Saviour Jesus ; "—as
if to say, that God, to make us happy as Himself, spared His own
Son to die for us, and to be our Saviour.

This winter two fresh plans of village usefulness had
been set on foot. Every Monday evening was devoted to

social meetings at the Rectory, for distinct classes of parishioners. One week the meeting was of personal friends, when Mr. Bickersteth gave a short lecture on the Articles and on Church History, followed by a general conversation; the next was for the school teachers, and farmers' wives; the third, for the daughters of the small tradesmen, and the fourth for the district visitors. On Thursday and Friday an evening school for adults and elder boys was held in a building adjoining the Rectory conducted mainly by Mr. Bickersteth's family, and sometimes forty or fifty were present. The Prayer Meeting on Saturday had been begun, when he first came, after the pattern of the one at the Missionary House, which he also originated on his return from Africa; and closed the spiritual privileges of the week, while it prepared for the fuller instruction of the coming Sabbath.

"*February* 24. This day last year, Louis Philippe fled from France, while the Republic was proclaimed. Still England is spared, though tried and corrected. O may my country be yet more spared, and yet more helped and used to bless the world!

" But what is the state of my own soul? what is the state of the closet? for that is the thermometer of the Christian life. Alas! not as I would, and hence my spiritual strength is weak. O Lord, draw my heart, and we will run after Thee! No man cometh to Jesus, unless Thou draw him. I need continually this divine drawing. The position which God has called me to occupy is very influential, and hence the responsibility is very great, and the duty of living to the Lord with all diligence and earnestness, very weighty. This can only be done by constant fellowship with God in Christ, and receiving daily out of His fulness. Lord, help me thus to live!

" O what a responsible trust, that of immortal souls !
Three are now dying in my parish, whom I have been
visiting some time, and with hope of good.

*March* 19.  Through the goodness of my God I have
now attained sixty-three years of age.  O how gracious
my God has been to me a sinner, sparing me, upholding
me, and blessing me to this day.  May He still uphold
and bless me with His own Spirit.

" I most want fellowship with the Father, and with
His Son Jesus Christ ; more singleness of eye to His
glory, more purity of heart in His sight.  Lord, give me
these blessings.

" My family mercies have been very great.  I have had
with me, at this birth-day, my six children, and my son-
in-law, with his two children.  What a blessed circle God
has given me. . . .

" My parochial mercies are great, in the piety and
bounty of the Woodhall family, in the increase of communicants, and in the good doing by my children ; but
many things are very humbling and trying at present.
The Lord bring good out of evil.

" My general blessings, in wider scenes of usefulness,
by my publications, and by the Societies in which I have
been privileged to work, have been very great.  O how
good is the Lord !  O how sinful and weak I am !  May
His name be magnified for ever and ever !

" *April* 6. *Good-Friday.*  Very weighty duties are now
before me.  Not only are the usual anniversary meetings
in prospect, but I have a special mission to Dublin, leaving home on the 16th, to meet the Irish Brethren, and
consult on plans for more effectually promoting Church
Missions to the Roman Catholics.  Having no Curate, I
have also the weighty charge of my own parish.  The

Lord graciously help me to fulfil every work, to which He calls me, to His glory !

" The wonder is, that one so utterly sinful should in any way be used for the good of others, and not dealt with as a cumberer and removed. O Lord, still spare me; create in me a clean heart, and renew a right spirit within me !   Carry me safely, if it be Thy blessed will, through my long journeys ; assist me, in these momentous duties, with heavenly wisdom and sound judgment, and bring all to a happy issue, to Thy glory, in the salvation of many precious souls."

This journey to Ireland was one of deep interest, and, to the spiritual eye, full of brighter hope to that unhappy land, than could be drawn from all the laborious plans and conflicting expedients of worldly senators and states-men; expedients sometimes perverse, and always abortive.

The greater part of the Special Fund, raised in the year 1847, had been spent in aiding various existing societies. A smaller portion was applied to the same purpose in the following year, and a small surplus remained at the dis-posal of the Committee.   Meanwhile several circumstances conspired to shew the need of a more direct missionary effort for the Irish Roman Catholics.   Dr. Kalley, at the request of the Committee, paid a visit to Ireland in August and September, and stated, as the result of care-ful inquiry, that there was a great readiness in many places, to listen to Divine truth.   In November, Mr. Gordon addressed an earnest letter to Mr. Bickersteth, enforcing the duty of direct and vigorous efforts to make the Gospel known to the Irish Romanists, and woke a response in many hearts.   During the same year, Mr. Durant, at his own expense, had already set on foot an experiment in one of the darkest districts in the West of Ireland, and

in the course of a single year it began to be crowned with
unlooked-for-success.   Hence the Committee in 1848,
amidst the distractions of a year of revolution, and of
attempted rebellion in Ireland, besides continuing their
aid to other Societies as before, devoted about £800 to
direct missions in the county of Galway, and to assistant
ministers, expressly for the Roman Catholics, in two other
dioceses.  The success in Galway was so conspicuous, that
the Bishop of Tuam, after strict and searching inquiry,
departed from his usual rule, and ordained one of the
chief agents in the work as a minister of the Church of
Ireland. Encouraged by these tokens of the Divine blessing, and the pressure of the famine having now ceased,
the Committee, after grave and prayerful consultation,
determined, at the close of 1848, to reconstitute themselves as a distinct Society for missions to the Irish
Roman Catholics.   In January 1849 they issued a further Report, with an Appeal to British Christians for
their aid.   They said, truly, that "the importance
of the work could not easily be overrated, as it regards
the safety, prosperity and peace of the  British Empire, and even the temporal interests of England, now
burdened with Irish poor. . . . . They are our fellow-
countrymen ; they are our neighbours, and next to the
neglected masses in England, they have the first claim
on our missionary exertions." A general arrangement
was made with the Irish Society, that, except in Galway,
which was already occupied, the new Society should
chiefly devote itself to the English-speaking Roman Catholics, leaving a wide sphere for the valuable labours of
the elder institution.  But as many questions of detail
arose, and it was very desirable to learn the feelings of
the Irish clergy, and their willingness to help on the

great work, it was resolved that Mr. Bickersteth and Mr. Dallas should visit Ireland in April, and confer with their brethren, who would then be gathered in their annual meetings.

The visit thus undertaken was one of deep interest. The chief subject proposed at the clerical meetings, usually held at that time, was this—" What are the most prudent and efficacious means, consistently with the discipline of our Church, of bringing the truths of the Gospel to bear upon the minds of the Roman Catholics of Ireland ! " It was fully discussed, with much thought and prayer, and the result was a judgment almost unanimous among the large number who were present, that it was their duty to consider their Roman Catholic parishioners as direct objects for missionary instruction, and to co-operate with all their power in every practicable means for imparting to them the Gospel of Christ. " The mission of the honorary Secretaries of the Special Fund," an Irish journal wrote at the time, " has been attended with the most cheering results. We gladly and thankfully hail their coming among us, and trust that the hopeful symptoms they have witnessed will not only cheer them in their work of faith and labour of love, but that the bold, steady activity and zeal, which shall be carried out in the several parishes to which the brethren have returned, will open a new era, and diffuse new life through the spiritually-desolate regions of our beloved native land." After hearing the statements of the deputation, two hundred clergymen signed an address, expressive of their hope and gratitude, closing with these words :

" In conclusion, we beg them to accept our warmest and most cordial thanks, for the interest they have on the present, and on all former occasions, manifested for

the welfare of Ireland, and the untiring energy with
which they had laboured to advance its good, and request them to offer to the members of the London Committee their acknowledgments for the kind feeling which
prompted and matured their plans, which will issue, we
trust, under the Divine blessing, in the temporal and
spiritual prosperity of our country."

The service, thus undertaken, was not in vain. A new
impulse was given to the spread of the Gospel in Ireland ;
and before the close of the year, abundant proof had been
given, that amidst the ignorant and deluded peasantry of
that land, as well as in heathen countries, it is still the
power of God to the salvation of sinners, and the true
remedy for superstition, demoralization, and social wretchedness. A leading clergyman in Dublin wrote of Mr.
Bickersteth's visit—" An impression of the loveliness of
his character was left on all who approached him. My
children, though unused to strangers, were fascinated to
familiarity by his gentleness ; and his uniform habit of
seeing every thing in God, and investing every thing with
an atmosphere of religion, affected even the youngest
amongst them ; and the little books he gave them, and in
which he wrote their names, were laid up among their
most valued treasures. . . . The acceptance of the plan
for the Church Home Mission by the clergy, and the
smoothing down or the removing of any feelings on the
part of individuals, unfriendly to its reception, or suspicious of its tendency, is mainly to be ascribed, under
God, to the spirit of love, meekness, and wisdom, that
animated every word uttered by him."

Mr. Bickersteth, on his return, thus noticed the general result of the journey.

" *April* 28. Through the abounding mercy of God, I

have been carried safely, and I hope usefully, through my visit to Ireland. Glory be to God, the faithful brethren in the Irish Church heartily concurred in our plans of Church Missions to the Roman Catholics, and I was privileged to bring back the intelligence to our Committee on the 26th in London.

" My beloved sister, Mary Anne, the wife of Mr. Cooper, died on Wednesday, April 18. I saw her the day before, when she told me she was very, very happy ; resting on Christ the Rock of ages ; and that I had much helped her, all her life, in serving Him. Glory be to God for this blessed testimony !

" O that I may go to the Lord's table, in a deeply penitent and contrite spirit. My only solid ground is—' This man receiveth sinners.' In this feeling I would go. O Lord Jesus, quicken my dull affections by Thy omnipotent grace ; raise within me spiritual, holy, and heavenly feelings, and make me wholly Thine."

The parting interview with his beloved sister was held under deeply interesting circumstances. He saw her on his way to Ireland, and his engagements made it impossible to stay with her, though plainly near her end. On his return, the happy spirit had departed to be with Christ, and he was just in time to be present on the day when her earthly remains were committed to the grave. His letters to her, in early years, had been the chief means of awakening and confirming her religious impressions ; and the affection which bound them together grew stronger and stronger, till death put its seal upon it, and, within ten months of each other, removed them both to the presence of their Saviour.

" *May* 26. How good the Lord is to me a sinner ! This is my daily surprise. This week, on Tuesday the

22nd, we had a large gathering in London, to form the
Society for Irish Church Missions to the Roman Catholics ; or, rather, to hold its first public meeting. It was
a very blessed occasion. The large room in Hanover
Square was filled, and much sympathy called forth. I
have since been to Hadlow, preaching for the Society,
and forming an Association. We have had many difficulties, and shall doubtless have many more : but, O
Lord, do Thou give wisdom, boldness, and fidelity !

" I most of all need close walking with God in every
thing. My inner man is feeble indeed. O that this
Whitsunday may be blessed to the revival of pure religion
in my own soul, in my family, and in my parish ! "

Mr. Bickersteth moved the first resolution at this public
meeting, to the purport that it was the bounden duty
of every member of the Church of England, to protest
against the false doctrines and idolatrous practices of the
Church of Rome, and to aid in rescuing the Irish popu-
lation from the degrading effects of Romish superstition.
His address, as usual, was simple, faithful, and impressive. " Our mission," he said, " like our common Christianity, is aggressive, but aggression in real love to those
whom it assails. We wish not their destruction, but their
salvation, and would use no methods but speaking the
truth in love !—no bribery, no Roman anathemas, no Inquisition. The only remedy we desire to apply is God's
own remedy—the proclamation of the Gospel of Christ in
love to their souls. . . It is a false charity for Protestants
to be indifferent to the conversion of the Roman Catholics. It is a selfish cruelty, and places them in a false and
indefensible position. It is infidelity to Christ and His
Gospel to remain silent with His truth in our possession,
while so many millions are perishing for want of that

truth. The Irish Roman Catholics must be considered as our neighbours, our brothers, and sisters. Their misery springs from Popery. Popery enslaves the intellect and brings men under an intolerable yoke of bondage. Ignorance is made the mother of devotion, or learning prostituted to oppress the soul. There is need of the royalty of true faith, in a Divine testimony of the liberty wherewith Christ makes free. . . , Great trials, however, are to be expected, and many reproaches; but let us be strong and courageous, and we are assured by God—' Then thou shalt make thy way prosper, and shalt have good success.' The urgency of the work has brought me out of direct parochial duties to seek to promote it. We must all make sacrifices to advance it; and oh how thankful shall we be, if we thus bless our Roman Catholic brethren, bless Ireland, strengthen our Church, promote the welfare of our country, and honour that Divine Saviour who is our only Lord and Redeemer. Let the work be carried on in the spirit of prayer, and in the spirit of love, and God will confer His blessing on the Society. Without prayer the hearts of Protestants will not open to aid us, nor the hearts of Roman Catholics to hear us; and deep intense love to their souls is the quickening and powerful motive for doing them real and lasting good."

Among the Anniversary Meetings of this year, in which Mr. Bickersteth took a part, were the Dublin Bible Society, and the City Mission and Bible Society in London. His brief notes for his speeches at the two former, are a specimen of his usual preparation for those public addresses, though these were sometimes written on a fuller scale.

"*Dublin, April* 19, 1849.—Bible Society.

" Have rejoiced to be a member of the British and Foreign Bible Society for forty years.

" 34 millions of copies.

" Bibles, from the great demand, so reduced as to be accessible to all.

" Gradual progress : the first ten years 1,026,650.

" In the last 33 years, 33 millions.

" In 1804, Bibles in print in 49 languages, now in 140.

" Probably then hardly accessible in their vulgar tongue to‾200 millions, now to 600 millions.   Openings on the continent.

" Italy, Diodati's Bible printing.   Austria, the liberty of the press.

" Why do we rejoice ?   Because we have found light and peace in the Bible ; a plain path to walk in.

" Are we to be charged with Bibliolatry ?   So was David charge-able.  Ps. i. 2; cxix. 97.  So St. Paul.  Col. iii. 16 ; 2 Tim. iii. 15.  So our Lord, Matt. v. 18; John v. 39.

" May it ever be the glory of Evangelical Christians, that they prize the word of God.

" London City Mission, April 28, 1849.   The vast exigency requires the efforts of all Christians.   Increasing conviction that the London City Mission is the enemy of no true Church, nor of any true minister of Christ.   The nearness of the evil to us.   Special delight in its taking up labours among foreigners.   The blessed openings now before us in England.

" The change making in our destitute and neglected classes.   If they remain, that they may remain to be a blessing.   If they go abroad, no longer as convicts, to poison colonies, and spread moral infection ; but as Christian emigrants, to spread the gospel.   So, again, that foreigners may no longer stay here, to learn our vices, but to hear the gospel.

" Rome—the Inquisition—the New Testament.

" The London City Mission has spread the gospel in new modes. Thank God, the principle is gained.   Thank God for the Scripture Readers' Society, and that our Bishops now plead for lay-agency.

"It is pregnant with blessings for the salvation of London. Push, then, the London City Mission. Vastly more is yet to be done. The most important of all charities—charity to the soul is the soul of charity. The peculiar temptations and sufferings of the Missionaries. The messengers of the Churches are the glory of Christ.

"Descend to the lowest, and so rise to the highest honour. Mrs. Fry, and others; not that they sought it, but God gave it. 'He that humbleth himself,' &c. Christ exalted in the labours and success of each Missionary. Irish Society—have just been to Ireland. The Protestant Irish Societies all increasing—spirit of the Irish Clergy."

The meeting of the Bible Society in London this year, had circumstances of peculiar interest. Several speakers, as well as the chairman, had uttered sentiments expressive of their regret, that a Society, designed to circulate the word of God, could not honour God and His word more openly, by commencing with prayer. Mr. Bickersteth, who for many years had shared this feeling, was one of those who gave it expression. Just as he was leaving the room, the excellent Secretary, Mr. Brandram, a rigid conservative of the existing practice, stated his unaltered objection to any change, and that it could not be introduced without the assent of the Society. Mr. Bickersteth returned to his seat, and wrote quickly a resolution, which he at once proposed to the meeting, that the Committee be invited to reconsider the practice of the Society, with a view to the regulation, that its meetings in future be opened by reading the Scriptures, and a short prayer. The motion was at once seconded, and carried by a large majority, at least three-fourths of the whole assembly. The result was a series of deliberations, which issued in the rule that a portion of God's word should be read at the opening of each public meeting.  The chief importance of the incident was the light which it threw upon the altered tone, since the discussion first arose in 1830, among the great body of the friends of the Society ; and the deeper feeling, which now prevailed, of the need that religious efforts should be openly, as well as secretly consecrated, by the word of God and prayer, in order to secure the fullest measure of the divine blessing.  Allusion is made to this subject in the next entry of the journal.

"*June* 29.  Another month's mercies and sins :  the two streams, alas ! flow together.  O when will the stream of sin  be for  ever  dried up, and the flood of mercy everywhere prevail over the earth !  The Lord hasten that day.

" At the beginning of the month I went to Winchester for the Jews' Society ; a journey of many mercies.

" My chief trial at this time is conflicting with beloved brethren, for prayer, or rather, reading a devotional portion of the Scriptures, before the Bible Society's Annual Meeting.  It was debated on the 11th, and it is to be again on the 25th, and I have been called to a prominent part, from what passed at the Annual Meeting ; when they concurred in the proposal which I made.

" Would that my own soul lived more in prayer ; then I should be more victorious over my temptations and corruptions, and more successful in all my works of love."

Early in June Mr. Bickersteth enjoyed a privilege, highly congenial to his affectionate heart, in welcoming under his roof Mr. Fast, and Mr. Elgqvist, two young Swedish Missionaries, the first-fruits of their country in that holy work, who were passing through England on their way to China, and who sought an introduction to one, so long connected with the cause of missions, and so widely known and honoured through the foreign Churches of Christ. Their short visit, including the Sabbath, was a time of great refreshment and joy to these young soldiers of the cross, who were just entering upon their arduous work, and to the aged servant of the Lord, whose time of departure was now really at hand. It was at their parting that one of them referred to the delight of their visit, as a breeze of the eternal summer passing over them ; and the memory of their brief intercourse is rendered the more touching, since not a year had elapsed, after Mr. Bickersteth's own removal, before Mr. Fast fell a victim to the violence of pirates, and was translated, in the first glow of his faithful zeal, from the work of missions to his heavenly rest.

" *July* 28. By God's mercy we gained, not indeed all I wished, but the reading of a portion of Scripture, before the Annual Meeting of the Bible Society.

" I have since been for a deeply interesting meeting, to Weston-super-mare, where I preached before, and addressed, between seventy and eighty clergymen, to strengthen and encourage us in our labours, in conjunction with Haldane Stewart. Our Sermons and Addresses are to be published. May the Lord's blessing follow.

" One of the most pious of my parishioners was called to his heavenly rest this week. His whole course adorned the Gospel of our Lord Jesus Christ.

" I had an attack of cholera, now largely spreading in our country, but mercifully it was slight. O may all these warnings of what a vapour life is, lead me to holy diligence in improving time for God's glory ; specially, O specially, in the only truly powerful way, earnest prayer !

" The various Annual County Meetings are before us, Bible, Church Missionary, Church Pastoral Aid, Protes-

tant Associations, Tract Society.   The Lord prosper our
poor efforts.

" It has been a great comfort to me, this last month,
to have had my dear son with me, helping me in the
ministry, and faithfully preaching the Gospel of the grace
of God.   Glory be to God ! "

His friend, Archdeacon Law, has thus recorded his
impressions of Mr. Bickersteth's Weston-super-Mare visit,
to which he himself frequently referred, in the few
months that he survived it, with the deepest pleasure.

" He was at the time personally unknown to most of
us ; but the respect and love, which his writings and character had excited, caused great expectation of instruction
and edification from his lips.   But though our expectations were high, I can truly say, they fell far short of
what was realized.   He arrived at this Rectory in company with his dear friend Mr. Haldane Stewart, on the
evening of Monday, July 9.   When the time for our evening service arrived, he begged to have the hymn, ' Great
the joy when Christians meet,' and he then opened out to
us, as appropriate to the occasion, the concluding verses
of Rom. xv. ; and truly did he come to us ' in the fulness
of the blessing of the Gospel of Christ,' and, as he testified when parting, greatly did he participate in the blessing that he communicated to us.

" Our two next days were occupied in examination of
scripture, and public services.   I say nothing of his address and his sermon, because they are in print ; but I
cannot forbear to say, he was the animation, the spirit,
and the power, of all our discussions.   He was full of life
and vigour, which never seemed to flag for a moment, so
that he spoke on every point. I will not attempt to repeat
his striking observations, which went to many a heart,

and I believe, still abide and live there in sanctifying freshness. The passage on which he entered most fully was 2 Tim. iv. 5, &c. How little did we then think that the sixth verse was so predictive of his own removal! The impression on all our minds was quite different. We fondly thought that his energy and strength gave promise of labour for years to come, and when he expressed his affectionate hope that the visit might be renewed, tho idea occurred to none of us, that we were never to see his face again on earth. Some engagement in London caused his departure from us, before the discussion of the second day was ended; and I can never forget the feeling which pervaded the meeting, when he arose to say, ' Farewell.' It was the signal for every one to arise, and every eye followed him with expressions of grateful admiration and love. Some time elapsed before attention could be brought back to our subject, and perhaps we did not fully realize the exceeding value of his presence among us, until, at every succeeding point, we missed the perspicuity and the unction which he had thrown into each discussion. His visit to us was not in vain. His Lord was with him, and a rich blessing from on high attended almost every word. He appeared among us as one whose conversation was in heaven, and who experienced the joy and peace that are in believing. His looks of love, his words of love, are still present to many minds, and while we glorified God in him, many were filled with desire, humbly, and at a distance, to follow him as he followed Christ."

" *August* 15, 1849. I have to glorify God for refreshing meetings, at which my dear brother, Dr. M'Neile, has been assisting this week. On Monday the Church Missionary, on Tuesday the Reformation Society, and this Wednesday the Church Pastoral Aid Society. For the

Herts Reformation Society, £45. was collected, and for
the Church Pastoral Aid Society, £201.   All glory be to
God.

" The most delightful thing, however, was the really
practical and holy character, for personal edification, of
my friend's addresses and intercourse.   May the savour
of it remain for many days.   An address to my poor people this evening, on Exod. xxviii, was full of spiritual
unction and blessing."

The visit of Dr. M'Neile, the first and the last which he
ever paid to his beloved friend at Watton, was a season of
high social and Christian enjoyment.   The whole family
circle, and one or two intimate friends, were gathered at
the Rectory, and a feast of Christian thought, feeling, and
friendship, was enjoyed, of which the memory will not
soon pass away.   All the great subjects of interest, affecting the kingdom of Christ, with which the thoughts
of both were daily and hourly occupied, were brought
out in all the freedom of unrestricted communion ; and
memories of the past, and hopes for the future, and grave
reflections on the actual state and dangers of the Church,
were mingled now with all the variety of playful anec-
dote, and now with calm and serious conversation on the
deep things of God.   Variously gifted by their common
Lord, and alike highly honoured in His service, each
seemed to give a free scope to his feelings of quiet joy in
the other's presence and society, while the sickness of a
beloved daughter shed a mellowing and tender influence
of deeper sympathy with patient suffering, amidst the
else unclouded sunshine of domestic and Christian joy.
It was like the culminating point of God's abundant
mercies, bestowed on the home and family of his beloved
servant.   The meeting on the lawn for the Church Pas-

toral Aid Society was felt to be one of intense interest, and Mr. Bickersteth's words were like a presentiment— " This is the climax of our meetings, but what shall we do after this for next year?" The recollection of this meeting has now an added tinge of sorrow. The next time that Dr. M'Neile visited Watton, it was in the promptness of his Christian sympathy, at a sudden call from the house of mourning, to preach a funeral sermon for his beloved friend, whose body had been already committed to the grave.

" *August* 25. I have been this week to Erith, Belvidere, to attend a meeting there of the London City Mission.

" We are greatly tried now by Sir H. J. Fust's decision. in reference to necessary regeneration in baptism, (the Lord avert the evil !) and by the cholera, which is spreading over the country. May He lead us to repentance !

" But the greatest evil is to live at a distance from God, with but few thoughts of His presence and His love. I hope my heart has been helped, by giving more time to thought on, preparation for, and real prayer. Glory be to God. But I am yet very far from what it would be to my infinite interest, and that of many others, to be. The Lord bless this communion for this end.

" *Sept.* 28. This day is appointed by the Bishop, in this part of the diocese, for humiliation and prayer on account of the cholera. O give us a heart to see Thee, O God, and to turn to Thee in weeping, and fasting, and prayer. We have all great reason so to do !

" I have before me a long journey to Glasgow, Edinburgh, Doncaster, Liverpool, and London, for the Evangelical Alliance, the Irish Church Missions, the Church Missionary, the Jews,' the Church of England Young

Men's, and other Societies. The Lord use me for good, and to His glory, and bring me back, if it be His will, to be a double blessing. But the real ground of all good must be, that all is straight between Him and my soul; —my sins pardoned, my soul justified, and I myself delighting in Him. O Lord, let these things be clear in my soul! Let thine own Spirit effectually teach, lead, and sanctify me!

"*October* 27. Through God's mercy I have been brought prosperously through my long journey for the Societies to Scotland, &c., above a thousand miles in seventeen days, and speaking, perhaps, to twenty thousand souls. What a responsibility! and if the Lord use it to His glory, what a blessing! May He pardon all the sins, and accept in Jesus all the services of the journey!"

The following notes to his children were written at the time of this northern journey.

*Kelshall, Sept. 5.*

My beloved F. has seldom a letter from her father, as he is mostly with her. I look on you as a vessel of mercy, not only preparing by your trials for the Master's house above, but as already bearing supplies for others. You are the missionary to our family, and God is by you drawing out for us views of His truth, not only profitable for you, but unspeakably profitable to ourselves. We are taught the wise, and deep, and unfathomable love of our God, in that which seems all severity; we are taught the power of His grace in sustaining a weak creature; we are taught that perfected family bliss is larger and fuller than earth can afford; we are taught that nothing but God himself is the rest, portion, and full joy of the soul; and you are the missionary, by whom God brings home these precious lessons. Glorify God, then, my child, not by being a foreign missionary to the heathen, nor a city missionary to London, but a Watton Rectory missionary, to the rector and all his family day by day; and they will try to realize,—" He that watereth shall himself also be watered." And then, when we reach our heavenly home, we shall see how wonderfully, beyond all our thoughts, God was blessing us, and making all to work for our good.

Your affectionate Father,<br>E. BICKERSTETH.

Edinburgh, Oct. 15.

DEAREST E. R. AND H.,

. . . I had a most pleasing account of the Bishop of Norwich's last thoughts upon 2 Cor. v. &c.; particularly the last verse.— Glory be to God. I always loved him for his eminent devotedness to what he thought right.

The best way of answering your desire for information about the Alliance, is to send you the enclosed. . . . Glory be to God! such blessed accounts of our Irish Church missions! There was an immensely overflowing evening congregation last night at Mr. Drummond's, while I preached on Dan. xii. 3. In the morning on 1 John i. 3. God has heard the prayers of my family for rich blessings on this journey. Continue to pray.

Your ever affectionate Father,<br>E. BICKERSTETH.

Liverpool, Oct. 19.

MY DEAR SICK ONE,

With a great deal of work, I must yet give you a token of Sunday remembrance. What a comfort is the promise, " I will never leave you." Your other best friends have their leaving times; God never leaves. He is your shade at your right hand, from the burning sun of temptation. He is your fountain, perhaps invisible, like Hagar's, Gen. xxi. 19; but God can open the eyes, and enable us to draw living water. Dear child, cleave to Him. He loves you with intense love.

God is prospering my journey. I have already travelled above eight hundred miles, protected by His love.

Your affectionate Father,

E. BICKERSTETH.

This last visit of Mr. Bickersteth to Scotland, only a few months before his death, like the one to Ireland in the spring, and to Weston-super-mare in the summer, was attended with a peculiar blessing. It seemed to be felt by all his beloved friends, that a double portion of the Spirit of God rested on His servant. The affectionate testimony of Mr. Drummond, whom he had often cheered before, amidst trials and difficulties, by wise advice and loving sympathy, and who looked up to him as a son to a father, expresses the thoughts which were passing through many minds.

" His visits were indeed precious and soul-refreshing ; they were such as to make us feel as though we were entertaining an angel unawares. The announcement of one spread cheerfulness and happy expectation, and the joy in the prospect was more than equalled in its fulfilment. Faith was confirmed : the mere earthly admixtures, that mingled with contending for the truth, were rebuked, and love and forbearance were enlarged. His was the spirit that rejoiced as little in iniquity, as it rejoiced much in the truth. The impressions made by his sermons and public addresses were uniformly deep and extensive ; the influence of his private intercourse was pervading and sustained. The garden of the Lord seemed to give forth its special sweetness, when this spiritual labourer appeared, laden with the precious fruits of the gospel, peace and love.

" The last visit he paid us, in October 1849, is ever to be held in sweet remembrance. Blessed as all the former

had been, this was twice blessed. In his public duties
there was a power and unction, beyond what we had
ever witnessed, even in him. The last sermon which he
preached in Edinburgh, and which has since been published, was on that glorious passage.—'They that be wise
shall shine as the brightness of the firmament, and they
that turn many to righteousness, as the stars for ever and
ever.' He seemed already half in heaven. A powerful
impression was manifestly made on all who heard him.
A solemn stillness pervaded the congregation, every word
fell with weight and energy, and the heavenly spirit of
the preacher was never more deeply felt ; his crown of
glory seemed almost to be encircling his brow.

" And corresponding to this was the delight and profit
of his private intercourse. He rem ᵕ ᵕd five days under
my roof, and I was much exhausted at the time from
long illness. How shall I describe his sympathy ? He
had ever a word of encouragement ; he made me begin
to hope, even against hope. His prayers were my best
medicine. He strengthened me by his counsel, he refreshed
me when I was weary ; his fellowship was ever ' comfort
of love,' and I can truly say, that, with much bodily
and mental trial at the time, those few days were among
the happiest I ever spent on earth, they seemed to partake
so much of heaven."

One little incident, at the time of this last visit, shews
the deep interest which had been awakened. When he
set out with a friend to the chapel, before preaching his
last sermon, they were alarmed by the crowds who were
coming away, and feared that some disaster had occurred.
On their arrival, they found the large building completely
crowded, and that the multitudes whom they met were
those who had tried unsuccessfully to gain admittance.

In a note of November 3, Mr. Drummond wrote to him, on recovering from a severe attack of illness; " Your visit, dearest friend, was just my preparation for this season. It was an angel's visit. O how we all prized it! How we mourned over your departure! How we blessed God for the savour that was left! How we rejoiced with unutterable joy at the prospect of that glorious day, when such sweet and blessed communion shall be perfect and everlasting."

The visit to Glasgow, chiefly for the Evangelical Alliance, was hardly less marked by spiritual blessing. Mr. Bickersteth thus describes it, in a letter, soon after his return home, to one of the American brethren, whom he had met before at the August Conference.

*Watton Rectory, Oct.* 1849.

DEAR SIR,

I promised my friend Sir C. Eardley to comply with your request, in sending a few lines to your Christian Union respecting our Evangelical Alliance.

We have just had, in the second week of October, very blessed meetings at Glasgow of the Annual Conference; and I feel assured that we were generally and practically convinced that God was with us, and that this is His own cause, and that it is a real privilege to have a part in carrying it forward.

I need not enter into the proceedings, as you will see them at length in " Evangelical Christendom." I had to address the meeting on " Fellowship with Christ, leading Christians to fellowship with each other,"—a subject in itself enough to warm our hearts, and draw us nearer together. Mr. Noel, Dr. Cunningham, Dr. Leifchild, Mr. M'Leod, Dr. Smyth and others, made useful and practical addresses; but Dr. Wardlaw's, on " Separation from the world, prompting to brotherly union," was a most convincing, holy, and peculiarly profitable manifestation, with Christian wisdom, of the great principles of the Alliance.

We acted practically, in adopting the petition of which I enclose a copy, and raising subscriptions to send a deputation to the continent, for promoting the release of Achilli from the dungeons of the Inquisition; being convinced that his great offence was his zeal in distributing the word of God in Rome.

At present we are a little flock from each denomination, who thus unite together, but the hearts of God's children are manifestly with us. The numbers gathered together, morning and evening, meeting after meeting, on Wednesday, Thursday, and Friday, were very gratifying. At the one on Thursday evening, when the Provost was in the chair, it is supposed that four thousand were present, and many were unable to get in. I have seen nothing in the Alliance to weaken my hope that it has been raised up of God to promote the Philadelphian spirit in the churches of Christ. No doubt its enemies may find in us all, plenty of weakness, imperfection, and even inconsistency. But we will glory in our Divine Saviour, and His spirit of love, and His precepts and prayer for unity. It rejoices us to see that we have hearty friends of the good work in America. Give my Christian love to the faithful brethren there, whom I know in the flesh; a very small part of that glorious company in America I hope to rejoice with for ever in the presence of Christ in perfected unity; but still, though so small, dear to me in a more especial manner, as having had communion with them, face to face on earth. O may we spend ourselves, and be spent, in labours to bring others to share with us the fulness of joy, still to come in the presence of God and the Lamb!

In Him, faithfully yours,

E. BICKERSTETH.

The address referred to above, will be found in " Evangelical Christendom," January, 1850. It closed with a beautiful thought, soon after realized in his own experience.

" Fellowship with the fulness of Christ most of all helps us to fellowship with others. The gushing fountain-springs of mighty rivers come not originally from the basin where they are first visible. They have a secret connection, unseen but constant, with a hidden, unfailing, exhaustless reservoir, in unknown distance and depth. By continual supplies, thence received, the fountain overflows ; and the streams flow on, and come into fellowship with other streams, having a similar reservoir ; and at last they all unite in the mighty ocean. So let us all draw from the hidden, unsearchable fulness of Christ, the exhaustless reservoir, hid from the eye of flesh, but known to the eye of faith ; and we shall come in due time, after refreshing many a thirsty land in our way thither, into the full ocean of joy prepared for the whole Church of Christ."

The ministrations of Mr. Bickersteth, and his private intercourse in these closing months, had the same ripe and holy character, which marked his northern visit and journey. On Sept. 30, before the sacrament, his subject was those words of St. John, " Truly our fellowship is with the Father, and with his Son Jesus Christ ; " " sermons," says one of his hearers, " which almost translated the hearer to heaven by the vividness he imparted to the soul-gladdening themes. He dwelt on God's fellowship with us, the High and Holy One, condescending to all our wants, sympathizing with all our sorrows, numbering the very hairs of our head ; on the fulness of intimacy the term implies ; and then our fellowship with Him, through the Holy Spirit working in us, raising up our earthly minds, and creating in us those tastes and affections, which alone can prepare us for complete fellowship with Him for ever." On October 28, soon after his re-

turn, he preached on Melchizedec ; and after speaking of
him as a type of Christ, in his origin, his union of offices,
&c., he closed with " a glowing description of the feast,
which this Royal Priest, the King of righteousness and
of peace, will make to His warriors, after the toils of
their long conflict are over, and when the crown of victory shall be theirs for evermore."

The journal of these closing months of the year thus
continues :

" *Oct.* 27. The Church of Christ has been greatly
stirred up by attempts to desecrate the Sabbath in London by Post-office employment.  I hope, through God's
mercy, it may yet be the means of having a rest through
the land from Post-office work on the Lord's day."

Mr. Bickersteth attended several meetings in London
at this time, in connexion with the important question,
thus re-opened.  It is remarkable that, after beginning
life in the Post-office, one of his latest and most earnest
efforts should have been to relieve those employed in the
same work, from the compulsory desecration of the Lord's
day.  It is earnestly to be hoped that the fresh difficulties which have arisen, from the vacillating course adopted
by Government, may not hinder the accomplishment of
this great object.  It continued dear to his heart, even to
his dying hour.

" *Nov.* 24.  I have just been passing a very busy week
in London at our prophetical meetings, which were this
year more interesting than usual.  We had also a very
important meeting yesterday, in Exeter Hall, for the Irish
Church Missions.  I trust that much interest was awakened for that blessed object.  I met also a large body of
the clergy on the Gorham cause.  The Lord deliver His
church from enemies to evangelical truth.

"Incessant moving has been unfavourable to health, both in body and soul; and yet I am pressed much for the aid I can render to good causes. O Lord, let grace abound, to pardon sin, and to strengthen for duty."

"*Dec.* 23. We are coming near the close of another year. This month has been one of great excitement in our Church, from the progress of the ecclesiastical cause on Baptismal Regeneration, before the Judicial Committee of the Privy Council. It has taken a long time, and is yet undecided. The Lord grant that His truth may not be oppressed and hindered. I have published several letters on the subject.

"O that it were with me personally, as it ought to be, in all close walking with God; and personal faith, hope, and love! There is a wonderful mixture of right and wrong in all I think and feel, and say and do. Sometimes I seem to be serving God vigorously, and at other times I am cold and earthly, dead and fruitless. May I walk after the Spirit more and more."

During the whole progress of the Gorham cause, to which the Journal here alludes, Mr. Bickersteth took a deep and anxious interest in a question, which seemed to him of vital importance to the spiritual welfare of the Church of England. His feelings and judgment found expression, towards the close of the year, in five letters on the subject, which were his latest separate publication. The first of these was on the express renunciation, by the Reformers, of the Romish doctrine of absolute, unconditional efficacy in the two sacraments, or the *opus operatum*. The second adduced briefly some leading testimonies to their own sentiments. The third, on the evangelical character of the Baptismal Services, dwelt on the fact, that similar expressions are used, in Scripture

itself, for covenant privileges or federal relations, and for
inward grace and vital godliness; and applied the principle, as a sufficient key to the Service for Infant Baptism. The fourth unfolded the vast and momentous
importance of the new birth, or inward and vital regeneration of heart; and the last replied to some objections
of a friend. The words of the preface, which are dated
on the following New-year's day, are, except the brief
obituary to be presently noticed, his latest printed testimony to the Church of Christ, and enforce a truth em-
bodied in his own experience, and the mainspring of all
its beauty and blessedness.

"One great temptation of the enemy of souls in this
day, I believe to be, substituting the form of godliness
for the power; the name to live for the real life; the
outward and visible for the spiritual and invisible church
of Christ; baptism by the minister for baptism by the
Spirit; the receiving of the Lord's Supper for living faith
in Christ; traditions of man for the word of God; the
outward sacraments for the blessings signified by them;
—and then to cry out, 'The temple of the Lord, the
temple of the Lord, the temple of the Lord are these.'
Christ, and His Spirit, and His word, are thus displaced,
that the ministry of man may be magnified, and immortal souls are left exposed to serious delusion. Let
the ministry have no undue exaltation. Let us not as-
sume what belongs to our Master. We are only instruments in His hand, used by Him as it pleases Him. We
cannot, by baptism, at our will communicate the new
birth of the Spirit. John i. 13. Salvation, from first to
last, belongeth unto the Lord. Let us diligently use the
means, in dependance on Him. Let Him have all the
glory. He gives promises to the children of believers.

He gives faith and repentance in His own time, and at His own will. Let us rejoice it is in His hands, and not in ours. Love to our heavenly Master, and love to all men for whom He died, require a decided testimony against this danger."

At the opening of Advent, in a letter to his son, he thus alluded to the cause which he had so specially at heart—the Missions in Ireland.

*Watton, Nov. 26.*

MY BELOVED EDWARD,

I should like to write a long letter, but I am greatly pressed with work. I thought of taking parables for this Advent (1) the Tares, Matt. xiii; (2) the Servants waiting for their Lord, Luke xii. 36; (3) the Ten Virgins, Matt. xxv; (4) the Talents, Matt. xxv. If your mind turns the same way, it will be pleasant for father and son to be telling out the same truths, at this remarkable crisis.

Our prophetical meetings were very good; but the crowning meeting of the week was our Irish Church Mission on Friday. The large room in Exeter Hall was quite filled, and the speeches were good, and the interest kept up to the end. We shall receive, I hope, between three and four hundred pounds from the meeting, and I hope that it will be the beginning of larger funds from the country. God is greatly blessing the missions; and if it be His will, we shall commence a new day for Ireland. Glory to Him only!

Let us be faithful to Christ, dear son, and He will welcome us in the day of His appearing; and our wives and our children too. Remember not to idolize your babe, but to think of her as more the Lord's than yours, and to be trained, not in softness, but in good discipline for Him.

Your affectionate father,<br>E. BICKERSTETH.

The meeting of Nov. 23, the last London public meeting in which Mr. Bickersteth took a part, was one of

almost romantic interest—a fit and worthy close of those
abundant labours, in which he had been occupied for
more than thirty-five years in the cause of Christ.  Mr.
Dallas and Mr. Wilkinson, who had just returned from
Ireland, recounted at length the mercies of God which
they had witnessed, and the cheering triumphs of the
gospel in districts which had long been seated in spiritual
darkness.  More than four hundred recent converts had
just been confirmed by the Bishop of Tuam, and had continued faithful in the midst of trying persecutions; the
bitter but natural fruit of those principles, which the
British Government were training five hundred priests,
in Maynooth, to disseminate throughout the land.  After
these reports of eye-witnesses, Mr. Bickersteth, who had
been the main-spring of the cause in England, as Mr.
Dallas in Ireland, was called upon to move the first resolution, expressive of deep thankfulness to Almighty
God.  His remarks were in his usual spirit of glowing
praise and fervent love.

" Let God our Saviour have the glory ; it is His work !
a work of the Holy Spirit, bringing men out of darkness
into the light of the gospel of Jesus Christ. . . . It rests
now with British Protestants to enter in at the breach
that has been made.  This is the only real love we can
show to our Roman Catholic brethren.  I hate love with
dissimulation ; we must abhor that which is evil, and
cleave to that which is good.  I denounce all grants to
Maynooth as miserable bribery and transparent selfishness.  It is an attempt to bribe Popery with a sop ; but
Papists have too much sense, earnestness, and zeal, to be
bribed in that way.  They will rightly feel only encouraged to seek for more ; but let us tell them that their
souls are endangered while under Popery ; then their

consciences are awakened. Nothing but God's truth will
enable us to achieve the victory. We plant our standard
here, that Popery is an apostasy from true Christianity.
The noble Christian revenge we will take on the Romanists shall be this—while they would take away from
the Irish Church its revenues and honours, we will enrich them, if we can, with the best of all blessings, the
knowledge of Christ for their own eternal salvation.
The heavenly voice to those in Babylon is, 'Come out of
her, my people !' We desire to have a full harvest in
such a time, of ransomed Roman Catholics, recovered
from that fearful apostasy. I can appeal to themselves,
if they will give us credit for believing the Protestant
faith to be the true faith, that ours is the only honest,
the only loving, the only really Christian course."

This was the last time that Mr. Bickersteth addressed
a public meeting in London. The providence of God,
within less than two years, has set a double seal upon
the truth of his parting testimony. The attempts to
bribe Popery, which he denounced so earnestly, have
failed more conspicuously than ever ; and the recent
aggressions of the Church of Rome have so far opened
the eyes of the country to their folly, that a revived effort
is just begun, with cheering hopes of success, to repeal
the Maynooth Bill, and roll away the reproach which it
has brought upon our national legislation, of a blinded
ignorance of the first laws of human nature, as well as of a
hateful indifference to the honour and truth of God. On
the other hand, those direct and honest efforts, in which
he took so forward a part, to take revenge on the Romanists by imparting to them that gospel, which rejoiced his
own heart, have borne still more abundant fruit since his
death. They are extorting the notice and the praise of

neutral or adverse journals, and awakening loud lamentations among the priesthood, that their creed and their church, in Ireland, are in danger of an entire extinction ; while Roman Catholic journals admit that the success of these Protestant labours exceeds their worst fears before actual inquiry. So signally has God, in His providence, condemned a crooked expedient of worldly policy, and put His seal upon a direct and earnest effort of real Christian love to the souls of men.

Three days before this parting testimony, in public to the duty of Protestant Christians, to resist Popery by the sword of the Spirit, and spread the gospel among their fellow-countrymen in Ireland, Mr. Bickersteth gave a similar expression to his feelings on the subject of mutual love and brotherly union, in a letter to M. Bland, of Fontainebleau, who was about to edit a journal in harmony with the principles of the Evangelical Alliance. This double testimony, with a journey to Birmingham in January, for the Foreign Churches, closed his long course of public labours for the cause of Christ.

*To the Editor of the Bulletin du Monde Chretien.*

*Watton Rectory, November* 20, 1849.

MY DEAR SIR,

It gave me great pleasure to hear, through my friend Sir C. Eardley, of your projected publication, to promote the love of the brethren of our one Head and Elder Brother, Christ Jesus, throughout Christendom. Under the solemn warning of our blessed Master—" Because iniquity shall abound, the love of many shall wax cold "—it becomes us to be especially watchful against the predicted evil, and in every possible way to foster brotherly love.

God has honoured the Evangelical Alliance, formed amongst us in 1846, for this end. It brought us acquainted with many beloved

Christians, from France, Germany, the United States, and other parts of the world, whom to know was to love. And amidst all the shakings of the nations since this, brotherly love has continued, with real consolation and true blessedness.

My hope is that your proposed work will bring us more acquainted with Evangelical Brethren, especially in France, and with all they are doing to maintain and extend the gospel of our Lord Jesus Christ. The union of brethren of various nations is as important and as blessed, as the union of brethren of various denominations in the same country. We belong to one kingdom, the kingdom of righteousness, peace, and joy in the Holy Ghost. Whatever our respective systems of Government, in Church and State, we have all one great Sovereign, Head over all things to His Church, who alone raises others to power; and wherever we are, we rejoice to submit to the powers that be, as ordained by Him, and His ministers for good; our loyalty to Christ helping, not hindering, our submission to every ordinance of man for the Lord's sake.

But that which draws us near to each other, really and effectually, is the sense of our common ruin in Adam, and by our personal transgressions; the most wonderful love of God in giving His only Son to die for us; the common faith we have in this rich grace of our God; the quickening of our dead souls by His Spirit; the fellowship we have with the Father, and His Son Jesus Christ; the glowing love His Spirit has kindled in our hearts, first to Himself, then to the household of faith, and then to all men; the work now to be done, to glorify His name; and then, the bright hope of the coming glory, when we shall be gathered together from all lands into His blissful presence, and ever be with the Lord.

While looking at these great things, we seem almost to lose sight of all the lesser differences, of country, and form of government, and denominations of Christianity; and we cry from the heart, "Grace be with all those who love our Lord Jesus Christ in sincerity."

And this must make us sympathize with our brethren, in their joys and in their sorrows, in their successes and in their disappointments. What we wish for our brethren is, that they may be greatly honoured of God, in spreading that heavenly joy and peace and love, which are to be found, as we know by happy experience, in Christ Jesus alone ; blessing man here with true rest of soul, and righteousness of life before God and man, and blessing us for ever in that eternal kingdom to which we are hastening.

The state of the whole Christian world, whether we look at the Greek and Eastern Churches, at the Roman or the Protestant, has become so apostate from these Scriptural principles and this holy practice, that never was the union of the true children of God more needed, to manifest the true light and love of the gospel.

And thanks be to God, never were there fuller opportunities given, and greater doors opened, for the widest diffusion of the gospel of the grace of God. All other remedies have failed to supply men's thirst for righteousness and love. The gospel, the gospel only, is God's effective remedy. As our brother Merle d'Aubigné has said in one of his valuable discourses, the word of God only, the grace of Christ only, the work of the Spirit only—these are the mighty instruments which God has given, to regenerate the human race, and prepare us for the coming, the kingdom, and the glory of our Redeemer.

Being greatly pressed with many duties, I have written the first thoughts that have arisen in my mind, on hearing of your publication ; and if they will be, in your judgment, of any value in promoting mutual love, you are quite at liberty to use them. In our one Lord, affectionately yours,

E. BICKERSTETH.

# CHAPTER XXIX.

A. D. 1850.

THE public labours of Mr. Bickersteth had now nearly
reached their close. Incessant work, and the mental
activity of more than forty years, without exhausting, in
other respects, his strong constitution, had worn out the
organ of thought, and brought on a fatal disease, which
baffled the efforts of medical skill. Though others of his
friends had discovered the traces of growing bodily infirmity, his habitual cheerfulness had so disguised its ad-
vances when he was in the bosom of his family, that the
blow came suddenly upon them. In the very midst of
his abundant labours he was removed to his rest.

The second week of January was full of varied interest.
Along with three of his family, he went up to London,
that he might take part in the annual meeting of clergy,
at the Rev. D. Wilson's, the next door to his former residence. He had assigned to him for his subject, 'the
Dangers of Rationalism, and the proper means of resisting
them.' It was observed by several that he did not speak
with his usual power and freedom, which was probably
due to the unsuspected approaches of his fatal disease.
He preached his last sermon in London the same evening,
in the Church of his old friend Mr. Charlesworth, St.

Mildred's, Bread Street, for the Church Missionary Society. The next day he accompanied some of the party to Greenwich Observatory. The weather was most inclement, the ground being entirely cased in a sheet of ice, and he seemed more than usually sensible to its influence ; and referred, several times afterwards, to Mrs. Airy's hospitable refreshment with expressions of peculiar pleasure. The same evening the whole party returned to Watton, for one of those happy domestic gatherings, in which he had so often diffused light, love, and cheerfulness around him. On Friday afternoon, Spencer Thornton, who had also been at the Islington meeting, called at the Rectory. The writer was present at their short conversation in Mr. Bickersteth's study, and little dreamed how soon he would be the sole survivor of the three who were met together. It was delightful to see the mutual affection and honour of these servants of Christ ; tempered, on one side, by deep respect as to a father in Israel ; and mingled, on the other, with delight in the grace given to a son in the ministry, more gifted, perhaps, than himself, in the one special work of pastoral visitation. When the party was increased by the rest of the family coming in, Mr. Thornton took Mr. Bickersteth's little granddaughter on his knee, to tell her the names of his own seven children. The very next morning, while he was passing through the streets of London on his way to his home, he dropped down suddenly, and expired in a few minutes.

This mournful event, the tidings of which came on Monday morning, made a deep impression on Mr. Bickersteth. His son arrived from Banningham that day ; but a shade of more solemn thought had passed over the happy new-year's gathering, as if to prepare the family for their own approaching sorrow. He preached on the subject, on the next Lord's day in the morning, from those words of our Lord, " What I do thou knowest not now, but thou shalt know hereafter." " How far more likely, ten days ago," he said, " that he should be preaching a funeral sermon for my death, than that I should now be preaching his." His own funeral sermons were preached only seven weeks from that day. Several incidents occurred during this family meeting, which seemed afterwards as if there were the presentiment in his mind of his approaching change ; as when, after caressing his little granddaughter, he said more than once—" I think she is old enough now to remember Watton."

On Monday, January 21, the writer parted from him for the last time, and under peculiar circumstances. He had engaged to speak for the Foreign Aid Society, a cause always dear to him, at Birmingham, on Tuesday evening. The day had since been changed to Monday, but he had omitted to note the alteration in his paper of engagements, and, what was still more unusual, it had escaped his memory. When he was consulted about the train by which he should go on Tuesday, the change was pointed out to him. He seemed to recollect it with some effort, and proceeded at once, with his constant and careful fidelity to engagements, to make speedy preparation for setting out, so as to arrive early that same evening. We felt that he would be more harassed by the sense of having broken his promise, than even by the hurried journey, and only prevailed on him to take a more convenient train, so as to reach Birmingham after the meeting had been some time begun. His arrival was hailed with joy by the friends who had been anxiously awaiting him, and had almost ceased to expect him. His speech was earnest and effective ; but the excitement of this journey was probably the last strain under which his nervous system, long pressed to the uttermost, finally gave way.

On his return he employed himself busily in preparing the brief obituary of his dear friend, Mr. Thornton, which appeared in the Christian Observer the day after his own death. Almost his last act, before his illness began, was to request that it might be forwarded to the Editor, for further correction and revision.

On Saturday the 26th, before the communion, he made the last entry in his private journal. The words which close it are very expressive of that growing humility which marks the children of God, as they draw nearer to the presence of the Infinite Holiness.

"*Jan.* 26, 1850. It has pleased God very suddenly to take to Himself my beloved friend and brother, Spencer Thornton, in the midst of apparent health, while walking in the streets of London. What a lesson to be ever mindful of our latter end.

" I have been to Birmingham for the Foreign Aid Society ; the Lord watching over, strengthening, and prospering. O that He should ever condescend to use one so sinful and unworthy. The fifty-first Psalm is the Scriptural prayer that most suits me. Lord, give me more and more self-loathing ! "

The following day, January 27, he preached his last sermons, from the remarkable text—" Come, ye blessed of my Father, inherit the kingdom prepared for you before the foundation of the world." He seemed peculiarly drawn out by the glorious subject, and spoke energetically of all earthly joy, when compared with God's favour, as only " like a farthing rushlight, compared with the brightness of the noon-day sun." After the two sermons

were ended, he took, as usual, the evening Lecture in the
school-room, a service in which he always seemed to have
great enjoyment. His last Sabbath of public labour
was closed by singing with his family the beautiful hymn
—" Jerusalem, my happy home," which had long been
one of his especial favourites. Already his spirit longed
to join the society of heaven.

On the previous Friday (his son's birth-day) he wrote
to him the following note of parental affection, of which
the last paragraph has now a touching significance.

*January* 25.

My beloved Son,

We cannot let your birth-day pass, without a word to show that
we remember it and you, with all grateful affections. Your visit
was most pleasant to us all, and we bless God for the blessedness
He has bestowed upon you; first, in his quickening grace, and in
calling you to be faithful in the ministry, and then in your very
precious wife and child. He loves you much, and us also, in thus
blessing you; and who can tell what he means to do for you, and
by you? Be of good cheer. In our family reading we had the
passage—" If God be for us, who can be against us?" This is
for you, my E. and R. The most sunny part of our letters this
morning was your description of your child's recollections and
greetings. Dear little one, if I may judge by my own children,
she will love you more and more, as she grows older.

We are much as usual, except your beloved mother, It was well
I went on to Birmingham. They had not given me up, and my
arrival was warmly greeted.

I have written an account of Spencer Thornton for the next Observer. Blessed be God for sparing our own beloved son to us.

Your ever affectionate Father,

E. Bickersteth.

On Tuesday, for the first time, Mrs. Bickersteth and his daughters were seriously alarmed by his lassitude, which they had ascribed simply to influenza, and sent for Mr. Dalgleish, his medical adviser, to whose skilful and zealous care they had been so much indebted at the time of his accident. He saw the danger at once, and told them that the drowsiness and languor were premonitory signs of a second paralytic stroke; and forbade every kind of mental exertion, and even the usual exposition in family worship.

For two or three days active remedies were used, but he could only with great difficulty be persuaded to give up his various engagements, including a Bloomsbury Lecture, which he had just begun, on the Goodness of God in His dealings with Israel, and a journey to Torquay, with sermons and meetings for more than one Society. On Friday he made a very characteristic remark, with reference to an accident in the village, in which a boy had narrowly escaped death in a chalk-pit. "My mind," he said, "has been a good deal exercised about him in the night. I was thinking of the way in which they drew him out, as a parable; in digging him out, they hurt him with their pickaxes. This should be a lesson to us, to deal very gently with the souls we would draw to Christ. ' If any man be overtaken in a fault, ye that are spiritual, restore such an one in the spirit of meekness.' "

On Saturday, in the intervals between the remedies, he read "Curzon on the Eastern Monasteries," which had been kindly lent him as a relaxation, at a time when his usual studies were prohibited. His usual cheerfulness continued. "The daggers of the leeches," he said to his wife and children, "were as sharp as those which

threatened Mr. Curzon, but it was well they sought his
health and not his destruction." In the evening he was
persuaded not to take part in the usual prayer-meeting,
but to receive Mr. Waterman, an American clergyman,
who was expected to arrive soon after it had begun. The
first distinct signs of a failing memory occurred on his
arrival. He seemed surprized when he found that the
meeting was over, called together those who remained,
kneeled down, and offered a prayer for a blessing on
the morrow's services, and then asked for the hymn,
numbered " Second 125 " in his own hymn-book, written
by the lamented Henry Kirke White.

> Oft in sorrow, oft in woe,
> Onward, Christian, onward go ;
> Fight the fight, maintain the strife
> Strengthened by the bread of life.
>
> Let your drooping hearts be glad,
> March, in heavenly armour clad ;
> In your very weakness strong,
> Fight, nor think the battle long,
>
> Let not sorrow dim your eye,
> Soon shall every tear be dry ;
> Onward still in battle move,
> More than conquerors shall ye prove.

It was the last hymn which he ever sung on earth.

That evening he seemed to have some strong impression that his time was short, and with his usual practical
thoughtfulness, explained to Mrs. Bickersteth about his
private papers. In the night he complained of distracting pain in his head, and said to her the next morning—
" Heaven is near." He went down by himself into his
study. On entering it, a few minutes later, she found
him stretched on his chair in a state of unconscious and

alarming stupor. Prompt measures for restoring consciousness were used at once. Throughout the day powerful remedies were applied, but with very partial effect.
His clear, happy faith shone out, amidst his weakness,
as unclouded as ever. " What a comfort it is," he said
to them, "not to have to seek salvation now; I can enjoy
a salvation found! I know whom I have believed. The
Gospel is a reality. I find it to be so now." And again,
after an interval—" Salvation sought is with fear and
trembling; salvation found is always ready." When a
cup of tea was offered him, he said—" I will take the cup
of salvation, and call upon the name of the Lord." Soon
after, he added—" That is a noble testimony of St. Paul,
' I know in whom I have believed, and am persuaded he
is able to keep that which I have committed to him until
the day of Christ.' " Then, turning to his wife—" We
ought to bear testimony to the truth of His promises."
She asked what message she should send to Kelshall—
" Say, I am very happy in God's love." Yet a playful
cheerfulness mingled with his deep, solid joy, and his
bodily sufferings. When some severe remedies were applied, he said—" These are fiery serpents. I wonder the
Papists have never used them for instruments of torture,
to extort confessions." Then, soon after—" I have so
many mercies, I ought to be full of praise. How easy
love makes every thing, when we know the love of God!
This is a sweet direction. ' In every thing give thanks,
for this is the will of God in Christ Jesus concerning you.'
There is more divinity in that verse than in all the
Fathers. It is a bit of gold that enriches; they talk
of the gold of California, but the gold of *that* land is
good."

Something led him to allude to the forests of America,

and the early settlers, when he added with much energy, referring to their expulsion from England—" There can be no peace without liberty of conscience. 'They made a solitude, and called it peace.'" Then to his daughter, who was nursing him—" You have a very angelic office, my child, ministering to an heir of salvation."

During the night, the text Isa. xxvi. 3, being read to him, he repeated the words—" ' Because he trusteth in Thee.' That is—the Lord delights to honour confidence in Him. What a God He is to trust in ! "

On Monday, February 4, he seemed much better. His brother had come from Liverpool, on receiving a telegraphic message. On his arrival, he walked down stairs, and had an hour's conversation on the Gorham cause and other matters, and spent much of the afternoon in reading, when his brother had returned. But the excitement was followed in the evening by a relapse into torpor and debility. After a restless night, he called his youngest daughter to him, and said—" I will give you a text— ' The Lord is my keeper, my shade upon my right hand.' He keeps us from all the most subtle temptations of the enemy : what a Deliverer He is ! " The following night he called his daughter, who was then watching with him, and said,—" I want to give you a Father's blessing : ' The Lord bless thee, lift up the light of His countenance upon thee, and shine upon thee, give thee peace, and make thee happy, now and for ever.'" Again he asked— " What have you been reading ? The Bible. That is best. What different aspects it has under different experiences ! Passages read in a sick room come with more power than ever they did before. What part did you read ?" " ' Because Thou hast been my help, therefore under the shadow of Thy wings will I put my trust.' "

" That is past experience, leading to future joy and future faith. 'The shadow of Thy wings!' beautiful expression! under the mercy-seat! under the parent-hen! So near to Him! Yes, nestling in all His warmth and love." Afterwards, when a cup of tea was brought to him—" I will give you a cup of living water for your cup of tea. I have been thinking of it for a long time; it is this: ' But, beloved, building yourselves up in your most holy faith, keep yourselves in the love of God, looking for the mercy of our Lord Jesus Christ unto eternal life.' There may be pleasant rooms here to dwell in (mentioning one and another;) but the best room of all to keep in, is the love of God. What a prospect we have from it! looking for the mercy of our Lord Jesus Christ, unto eternal life! What boundless mansions of glory are these!"

This day his son arrived from Banningham, and one of his daughters returned from Kelshall, where she had been spending a few days. To the latter he said; " The heights of glory are what will humble us; there is no humiliation like that." On his son asking how he felt, he said; " Pretty well: the visions of glory have been quite indescribable. ' Eye hath not seen, nor ear heard, neither hath it entered the heart of man to conceive, the good things God hath prepared for them that *love* Him.' All the images of revelation fall far short of the reality." " Do you want any thing, dearest father?" said one of them. " No, dear, only a more thankful heart." " The medicine makes you weak." " But grace makes me strong. They that wait on the Lord shall renew their strength."

Mention was made by his nurse of a Christian who had wished for death. He continued—" Like St. Paul, longing to depart, and be with Christ, which is far better. Why is it better? No pain, no fears, no sorrow, no sepa-

ration, no absence—with Christ.   Here, even in our best
times, we have pains and partings ; there, no more."

On Friday his mind, sometimes incoherent, seemed to
roam amidst its literary stores.   " I am in a whirl of
genius, perplexed with M. and transcendentalism."   He
then spoke of his poor people, and schemes of instruction
and amusement for them.   When he rallied, his son said
to him ;  " The Lord says, I will make all their bed in
their sickness."   He replied ;  " That is the case with me.
I have three dear daughters, and a dear son, and kind
servants—and what (looking to her) should I do without
my wife now ? "

In the afternoon, when Isa. xxxii. 2, was read to him,
he remarked ;  " That is all we want—protection—shade
—refuge !

On Saturday, February 9, he lay in a stupor most of
the day.   His son came over to Kelshall, where we were
detained by his sister's indisposition, to bring the latest
tidings.   On his return, leaning over him, he said, " I
have been to Kelshall."   With a great effort he answered ;
" I doubt not you found goodness and mercy following
them."   " They are praying for you."   " Yes, thanks be
to God for loving and obedient children."   Soon after,
when every word was an effort, his tongue being swollen
with the medicine ;  " I have no confidence in any goodness or merit of my own.   I place my whole trust in the
Lord Jesus Christ.   I believe I have faithfully preached
His gospel ; " and then, taking the hand of his sick child,
" Renounce every confidence, but in the death of the
Lord Jesus."   Then, in a whisper, " O death, where is
thy sting ! O grave, where is thy victory !   Thanks be to
God who giveth us the victory, through our Lord Jesus
Christ.   For I am persuaded that neither life nor death,

nor principalities nor powers, nor any other creature, shall be able to separate me from the love of God, which is in Christ Jesus our Lord." Then to one of his daughters, apparently with the impression that his end was very near,—" Tell Mamma, ' he that believeth in Jesus shall not die eternally ; ' this is my last message to her. She is worthy of a last message." Soon after, alluding to his sister Cooper's death, " I shall soon follow her ; who would wish to linger in this dying world ? "

In the night he whispered, as one of them was raising him ; " I pray God this may be sanctified to me and to my family : it will be, with God's grace, it won't without." To his suffering child : " Wearisome days and nights are appointed us, my F——, but all will be well." On Tuesday, he was excited and feverish, and his thoughts turned much on his funeral. He seemed to wish the Hymn 73, which was read to him, to be sung then, and repeated the lines,

> Mercy's full power I then shall prove ;
> Loved with an everlasting love.

Wednesday and Thursday were days of langour, and of comparative, though not entire, unconsciousness. In the evening he said to his son, looking earnestly on him, " He is not dead, but sleepeth ;—Edward, take that," meaning for a funeral sermon. He had before suggested the passage, " Those that sleep in Jesus, will God bring with Him." Then to another he said,—" The Lord bless thee, my child, and make thee a blessing. If we honour our Saviour, and His truth, He will honour us ; if we rally round His truth, He will give us strength to support it."

On Thursday night the drowsiness deepened into total stupor, and all thought that his end was very near. We were sent for from Kelshall. As his son wrote soon after, " It was a lovely spring-like morning, the lark was singing its first spring welcome, the soft sunshine poured through the open window into that room, where we all, as we thought, were watching our father's dying hours ; but the loveliness of creation, when the pang of parting was over, seemed not to jar, but blend with the peace of the dying Christian. All hope of recovery had died in our hearts, and his children from a distance were sum-moned to watch his departing spirit, when, by the tender loving-kindness of our God, he was yet restored for a few more days, to animate, and cheer, and bless."

The revival took place about noon, within an hour before our arrival. It was indeed a joy to find a bright eye and restored consciousness, when it was feared that the spirit might have fled, before the mournful privilege had been given, even of witnessing its departure. He held out his hand, saying, with a serious smile—" Well, dear T——, I am a mass of infirmity, but Christ is the strength of my heart, and my portion for ever." When his daughter arrived soon after, he gave her an affectionate greeting. " I am so glad to see you, my child. You see me a poor wreck, but Jesus is on board, and all will be well." Then to F——, "You have long been a sufferer, my child ; now I have had to suffer for a little while, but it will soon be over now."

On drinking some cold water, which was his greatest refreshment, he said—" I want to connect it with spiri-tual blessings. ' He that drinketh of this water shall thirst again ; but he that drinketh of the water I shall give him shall never thirst ; but it shall be in him a well of water, springing up unto everlasting life.' Its coldness, its abundance, its refreshment, are types prefiguring just

what the soul wants. . . . . Nothing seems to me so to
resemble the pure, refreshing waters of salvation." Then,
to his eldest child—" My B——, I don't want to be weary
of God's dealings with me. I want to glorify Jesus in
them, and to find Him more precious."

On Saturday he seemed much recovered, but his eye
was almost unnaturally bright, for the torpor of the brain
was followed by excessive action, but calm peace sat upon
his suffering features. He said to his medical attendant
—" You have had a troublesome office, Mr. D., but it is
nearly over now." " No, sir, you have had the trouble and
the suffering." " Nothing compared with my deservings.
I find all my principles confirmed by my last hours. I
have believed in the Lord Jesus Christ, and He supports
me now. I commend Him to you, my dear sir, as an
only and complete Saviour. You have done all you could
for my poor body, it is right that I should commend
Christ to you."

He sent this day for myself and my beloved wife, and
said to us, calmly and deliberately—" I have been so
public a character, and God has called me to so prominent a part, that it will be needful that some memoir of
me should be written. I have great comfort, my children, in entrusting it to you." Then, turning to myself,
—" You will take care that every thing is put in its right
place, not exalting the creature, but humbling the sinner,
and exalting the Saviour." Then, after a pause—" I am
afraid where so many arrangements have to be made,
some things will be forgotten ; but we serve a loving and
gracious and compassionate Master." I feared that he
was exhausting his feeble strength, and begged him to
rest. " Quiet rest," he answered calmly, " is in the sense
of duty performed."

He said, soon after, to another of his children—" I am anxious lest my sufferings should be a stumbling-block to my children and servants.   When you see an aged Christian, who has tried to serve God, suffering in this way, it may be a difficulty to you ; and I wish to testify to you, that the sufferings of this present time are not worthy to be compared to the glory which shall be revealed. Besides, have I not ten thousand alleviations ? and among the greatest is to have pious children attending my dying pillow."

His son, as he helped to move him, having spoken of his suffering, he said—" Though I walk in the midst of trouble, Thou wilt revive me.   Oh that resurrection-glory ; what will it be when these vile bodies are fashioned like unto His glorious body !   This hope supports me through all."   " I fear I am trying you, dear father." " You never tried me, my Edward, but you have always supported and helped me ; you never tried me."   After an interval—" You preach the Premillennial Advent.   I know you do, because you believe it.   I have never regretted the Lord's giving me to grasp that blessed truth."

To his youngest daughter, he said—" You never saw a death-bed before ; did you ? "   " No, dearest father, but we hope the Lord may yet raise you up again."   " That is not in the least probable, nor do I in the least desire it. I desire to depart and be with Christ, which is far better. What should I be raised up for, except for my family ? and God will be with them.   If I were raised, it would be to a body of much weakness and suffering ; if I am taken, it is to glory : the sufferings of this present time are not worthy to be compared with the glory that shall be."

This day, Saturday the 16th, he called one of us to him, and dictated this message to his people for the next

day : " The prayers of this congregation are desired for
the Rector of the parish, not that his life may be spared,
but that he may throughout his affliction glorify God, by
fresh exercises of faith, patience, and resignation ; and
that, when the Lord's work is accomplished, he may depart hence, and be with the Lord ; to which he has always
looked forward as the highest consummation of a faithful
minister of Christ."

Early on Sunday morning his brother and sister came
again from Liverpool.  It was a day, throughout, of full
consciousness, though mingled with slight incoherency,
but the medical aspect of the case was not improved.
He thought much about his people and the school-children, and wished them to have copies of " The Sinner's
Friend."  " O that I could get a warning and invitation,"
he said " to the careless souls of Watton !  ' Ho, every one
that thirsteth, come ye to the waters.'  I think, Edward,
that would be a nice invitation."  To myself he said—" I
have finished my work, I long for my rest.  Tell my children they must not detain me by their prayers."  And
again, when several were present—" I hope the faith of
my dear children will not be weakened, but confirmed, by
their father's last hours."  Soon after, he said to his son
—" I have been talking with my dear brother, whether
this will be my dying illness.  He tells me, he does not
say there is no hope.  Now what he calls no hope, I
call the most hopeful of all things, to go to be with my
Saviour.  He said, it would be so for me, but I must che-
rish the hope of life for my family and parish, and the
Church of God.  Well, the comfort is, it does not depend
on our wishes ; it is God's will that orders all."

To his sister, Mrs. R. Bickersteth, he said—" I am so
delighted to see you."  Then, speaking of Dr. M'Neile,

who had sent a message by them—"Dear M'Neile, I shall always be grateful to him for the spiritual good he has done in my family. I know no one who so unites talent with earnestness and singleness of heart as he does, and I pray God there may be a large blessing on his ministry."

While one of them was employed in waiting on him, he said to her—"This is a self-abasing dispensation." "Yes, dear father, but a Christ-exalting one." "I hope so. With all our knowledge and all our acquirements, we cannot rise above the whirl of trial and temptation." "But He has said, ' I will never leave thee, nor forsake thee :' you will not be left in the temptation." " ' I have prayed for thee, that thy faith fail not.' "—he answered, —"that intercession of Jesus is absolutely necessary."

On Monday, February 18, he called one of his children and said, "My child, I want to dictate something to you on the mercies of God in my last illness." When entreated to leave it, as there was danger of injury by any excitement, he replied. " No, the desire for God's glory will enable me to do it. I think such a paper might be blessed to my family when I am gone. . . . There is the mercy of my dear brother Robert being here, of our all being together, a united family, and of knowing that all things work together for our good."

After alluding to his brother's great kindness, in leaving his important practice, to see him at such a distance, and give him all the help of his skill and experience, he continued. " Another singular mercy is, that all my family have been enabled to gather round my bed, and the greatest of all, that they have one heart and mind with me in the things of Christ. Glory be to God for all. God has so blessed my little store, that I have no anxiety for their temporal wants : it might have been far otherwise. Goodness and mercy have followed me all the days of my life, and my cup runneth over with His love. I record it as my dying experience of God's faithfulness, that though weighed down with a suffering body, I have found it true, —'As thy day is, so thy strength shall be,' and, 'They that seek the Lord shall want no manner of thing that is good.'" She begged him to leave off, saying, that she hoped he would have other opportunities of finishing it. He looked at her earnestly, and said, "I do not deceive myself, a dying man has not many opportunities. I desire to glorify God, and to be a blessing to my flock and children. 'He died for all, that they who live, should not live unto themselves, but unto Him who died for them.' I trust my children may be better Christians for the experience of the past week. God grant it." To another, who came in, and begged him to leave it for the present, he said,—" Let us do what we can, while we can."

To his eldest daughter he spoke with tender affection. " My B——, you have been a comfort to me ever since you were born. God return to thee a thousandfold all thy filial love, and make thy children the same blessing to thee, or a greater ; and return into thy bosom full measure, pressed down, and running over. I have nothing but glowing love to you and yours." Again, "I do not know how to be so long without a kiss of my little ones, when I know they are not far off ; they will forget their grandpapa." " No, dear father, little F—— often prays for her grandpapa." " God bless her, and give her more grace than her grandpapa, and less suffering. Yet perhaps this is hardly a legitimate prayer for a child : suffering is so needful for growth in grace."

Before his brother and sister returned to Liverpool, the latter had a parting interview. " The great thing in love," he said, " is to seek each other's spiritual benefit. Remember that, dear Katherine, for yourself and for your children. Seek to glorify Christ yourself, and seek that your children may glorify Him." "Your prayers, for them, dear brother, are a great comfort to me." He answered, with peculiar solemnity, " No prayer is lost ; they are lasting and living things. It is a wonderful thought, that no prayer is lost. They ever live ; they are, as it were, indented around the throne of God ; and when God looks around, He sees the prayers of His people, covered with the sweet incense of the Saviour's intercession."

When he was awake and conscious, extreme quiet was always enjoined, and Mrs. B., with a painful self-denial, kept out of sight, lest the effort to make her hear should exhaust his strength, and destroy the very faint hope which still remained, of possible recovery. He repeatedly asked for her, and begged her to sit by him. She said she feared it would tire him. " It tires me, dearest, not to have you." He afterwards called for a slate, and tried to write messages upon it, as his voice was too weak for her to hear it. Then to his children, " I am afraid my children should think what I say is oracular. It is nothing at all, except so far as it is according to the word of God, and I am anxious you should bear this in mind." The day before, he said to his son and myself ; " I hope you will make arrangements to stay at Watton for a few weeks. I hope the time of my illness will be a great blessing to my dear poor people ; and how delightful it would be to have my two dear sons the fountain-springs of these blessings."

When the 63rd Psalm had been read to him, he asked for Psalm cxxx. When it was finished, he said : "*Beautiful* it is : that is your father's only ground of confidence."

X 5

" How truly this is called the body of our humiliation. Well, it is sown in corruption, it shall be raised in incorruption ; it is sown a natural body, it shall be raised a spiritual body. Precious in the sight of the Lord, is the death of his saints."

The following night, when the daughter who watched with him expressed her fear that he was uncomfortable, he answered, " No, I am very comfortable, I have had a pleasant dream ; I thought I was in the green pastures with all the flock of Christ, wandering beside the still waters, and resting in those cool, green pastures : was not that pleasant ? " "And did you see Jesus there ? " " Yes, that was the delight of it, you know, to be with Him, and while He was there, every want was supplied. ' The Lord is my shepherd, I shall not want.' He supplies the wants of the whole world, by the atonement he has made with His flesh and blood. That is a wonderful thought. ' My flesh is meat indeed, and my blood is drink indeed.' While we have that, we cannot want." In the course of the same night, " Such multitudes of thoughts come into my mind, passages of my past life. I have had a busy life ; and ' in the multitude of my thoughts within me, Thy comforts refresh my soul.' "

The post of that morning brought a letter from Merle d'Aubigné, who, of course unconscious of his illness, sought his advice on a subject of great delicacy, and ended with saying ;—" I commit this to your wisdom, your judgment, and your fraternal kindness." I told him simply that Merle d'Aubigné sent his affectionate Christian remembrance. " Tell him, from me," he answered, after a short pause, to collect his thoughts, " my heart is with him, and the dear foreign brethren, and I hope the Lord will bless them greatly in their efforts to spread His truth among the foreign churches." It was at the same time, I think, that he added, "I think you should write to Dr. Steane, and say to him, I found so much benefit, in my former illness, from the prayers of my brethren in the Alliance, that I should be sorry to lose it now." Indeed there was no fear of this neglect. Perhaps there was no one, of whom it was more widely true, that prayer was made without ceasing of the church unto God for him ; and these petitions were largely answered in the peace and blessedness of his dying hours.

On this morning alone his extreme weakness appeared to cause a passing cloud of depression. He said to his son, " I have been accustomed, all my life, to take a cheerful view of things, but I find it difficult to do so now. I am ready to say, " All these things are against me.' " The text was suggested, " If God be for us, who can be against us." " Yes, that is the right answer." He afterwards repeated the words, "When I walk through the valley of the shadow of death, Thou wilt be with me ; " and when he heard his nurse say, while moving him, " He is a great sufferer," he replied in a whisper, " If we suffer with Him, we shall also reign with Him."

On Thursday, as his son was waiting on him, he spoke of his wife and their little one, the only absent members of the family circle. " I want you to take a message to her from my dying pillow. Tell her she has never given me one moment's uneasiness as a daughter, but met and gratified every wish ; and I bless God for His grace given to her, and I pray God to multiply His grace to her and you and yours." Then, with deep emphasis, " R—— cannot tell how much I love her. I have found the greatest comfort through my life with your mother ; now I love to leave her to you and T——." Then, alluding

to Mr. Thornton's sudden removal, he expressed a hope
that this, and his own experience, might be " as lamps
in the dark valley of the shadow of death." After some
other directions, he said to his eldest daughter, " I am
afraid I have been putting confidence in other things;
thinking too much about arrangements for your dear
mother, and not looking simply to the Lord Jesus; and
that is the reason, perhaps, that I am left to some gloom.
I wish T—— to make it clear in my Memoir, that I
have no other ground of confidence but in the Lord Jesus
Christ : Christ first, Christ last, Christ all in all."

" All that patience and love can do, I have, both from
children and nurses." Soon after, he said to me, as I
was standing by him—and they were the last words I
heard from his lips—" I have been thinking much of that
precious promise—' Let not your heart be troubled : ye
believe in God, believe also in me.' Believing in Jesus
is the greatest comfort. We must try to be better ministers. The good of the people is the great thing : all
beside is a passing dream."

No murmur ever escaped his lips, though his sufferings,
from various causes, were great and distressing. Each
of those who helped to wait on him had some word of
counsel or of comfort. To one he said, " There are only
two classes ; mind you choose the right way." To another, an old and faithful servant, " You must forgive my
faults : I have served a kind and faithful Master." None
could come near him, without being struck by the calm
and holy earnestness of love, in the broken utterances
that fell from his lips, even when his mind was wandering, or his tongue, accustomed to the law of kindness,
almost refused its wonted office.

On the evening of this day (Friday, the 22nd) he sank

into a heavy sleep, which lasted nearly three days and nights without intermission. But on Monday, about midnight, while one of his children was holding his hand, his eyes lightened up again. "Dearest father," she said, "is Jesus with you?" His lips tried in vain to move. "If He is, press my hand." He did so, looking earnestly upon her. "Have you no fears?" He again tried to speak, but his voice failing him, pressed her hand again. She asked a third question, but the gleam of consciousness had disappeared. When all had hastily gathered to his room, and stood around him, the conscious light again returned, and his eye rested on each, but chiefly on his wife, with a look of calm and quiet love. When his nurse, towards morning, gave him his usual beverage, he said, "This is very pleasant, it is like the grace of Jesus." His child, who was then watching with the nurse, asked for his blessing. He answered, "The Lord bless thee, my child, with overflowing grace, now and for ever." This was one of the last sentences that was distinctly heard from his lips.

Through the two next days he continued almost or quite unconscious, with little change; and as his medical attendant thought it possible he might continue, after rallying so repeatedly, for several days, or perhaps weeks, his son thought it right to return for a day or two to his parish, where a person was dying, who greatly desired to see him. He had scarcely left more than an hour, when a change began to appear. From ten o'clock till five, all of us were gathered round him, uncertain how soon the moment of parting would come. The expression was one of languor and weariness; but his eye was clear and bright, calm and solemn, looking upward towards heaven. He was still unconscious of the presence of those around

him, but the dull, heavy expression in his times of torpor
had entirely passed away ; and it seemed as if the spirit,
in holy expectation, were waiting each moment for its
summons to the presence of the Saviour.  A few minutes
before five, the breathing, which had been slower and
slower, suddenly ceased.  It seemed as if life were gone,
but, after a pause of nearly a minute, with one sob the
breath returned again.  Six or seven times this affecting
pause was repeated.  A shade of deeper awe seemed then
to pass over his countenance, which presently was lighted
up with an expression of radiant joy.  The breathing
was noiseless, his eye grew brighter and brighter, and at
length the breath parted, and returned no more.  The
light still lingered in his eye, and those who watched
around his pillow scarcely knew the moment of his departure, when his spirit forsook the body, to be " at home
with the Lord."


The funeral took place the following Thursday, March 7.
It was an affecting scene.  A large number of his parishioners filled the churchyard, many of whom were
weeping for their loss, and most of the neighbouring
clergy showed by their presence their deep respect and
love to his memory.  There were also present many
beloved brethren, as deputations from various Societies,
the Church Missionary, the Jews', the Foreign Aid, the
Evangelical Alliance, and the Irish Church Missions ;
who came to testify the grief of thousands, his fellow-
labourers in these works of love, at the removal of one
so justly dear to the Church of Christ.  The language
in which one of them described his own feelings, expresses those which were shared by many hearts.

"When they bore the coffin in at the gateway, through
the rows of parishioners, to whom he had so often published the gospel of peace, the grief of his removal was
swallowed up in thankfulness for his finished labours,
and the full proof of his ministry. And when, after
an anthem had been sung, and the service read by his
aged brother, we gathered round the open grave, and
the sun-beam broke through the gray clouds of a March
morning, and the song of the mounting lark reminded us
that it was spring-time on the earth, I felt as if, instead
of weeping with those that wept around that grave, we
were called to rejoice with the ransomed spirit. When
the funeral was over, many returned to the Rectory,
where fervent prayers were offered up for the family, the
parish, and the Church, as affected by this dispensation.

" Very solemn it was to enter the vacated dwelling ; to
view those apartments, filled from the floor to the ceiling
with his noble library, to find one's self in the very chamber where he had often prevented the dawning of the day,
with prayer and meditation,—the chamber visited by so
many happy thoughts, and from which had issued so
many profitable books and fraternal letters. It was like
finding one's-self in Enoch's homestead, to tread for once
the fields and garden-paths, where in other days he had
walked with God."

Funeral sermons were preached, the following Sunday,
at Watton Church; in the morning, by the Rev. E. Auriol,
from Rom. viii. 38, 39 ; and in the afternoon by Dr.
M'Neile, from Matt. xxv. 23 ; and have since been published, accompanied by a short account of his last hours,
drawn up by his son. Many other sermons were also
preached, in other places, on occasion of the bereavement.
At Sierra Leone, especially, when the tidings of his death

arrived, it was made the occasion of a public tribute to
his memory, and of his services to the cause of Christ in
that colony, in a sermon by one of the native African
missionaries.   Only a few months later, a native convert
in Ceylon, who had been named after him at his baptism,
also fell asleep in the faith of the gospel.   The various
religious Societies, in whose cause he had laboured,
expressed their deep sorrow for their loss, by public
minutes, and addresses of affectionate condolence to his
bereaved family.   The following is an extract from the
minute of the Church Missionary Society, which was the
first to engage his services, and always held so large a
place in the deepest affections of his heart.

   " On receiving the intelligence of the decease of the
Rev. E. Bickersteth, the Committee feel a mournful pleasure in reviewing his invaluable services to this Institution, and in expressing their deep sense of the loss thus
sustained by the Society, by the Church, and by the cause
of Missions in the world.

   " It appears from one of his Jubilee Tracts, that the
Farewell Sermons of Henry Martyn were among the earliest circumstances that kindled the Missionary spirit of
Edward Bickersteth.   Being endowed with a vigorous and
ardent mind, enjoying also a constitution capable of much
labour and fatigue, and trained in the legal profession,
Mr. Bickersteth brought at once to the service of the
Society the very talents most needed at that stage of its
proceedings.   The duties connected with this institution,
which was then rapidly rising in public estimation, would
have proved overwhelming even to the robust frame of
Mr. Pratt, had not his youthful friend then come in to
succour him ; which he did with all the affection and
devotedness of a son labouring with a father in the Gospel.

And yet further, in the ordering of Providence—as it were, both to test and to mature the Missionary powers of Mr. Bickersteth—a sphere of foreign exertions immediately presented itself; requiring, although but temporarily, very great personal and domestic sacrifice.

" The results of Mr. Bickersteth's visit to West Africa are given in an admirable document, which appears in the Appendix of the Society's 16th Report. Its value consisted, not only in its immediate relation to Sierra Leone, but as opening to the Members of the Church at large various important principles, and many scarcely less important details, connected with Missionary work.

"From this date—1816 to 1831—Mr. Bickersteth was entirely identified with the Committee, as holding the office, first of Assistant Secretary, and afterward of joint Clerical Secretary to the Society. During this period, beside the routine of official duties, he was frequently engaged in extensive journeys, advocating the Society's cause both in the pulpit, in public meetings, and in smaller social parties. His published works, also, at this time, were greatly conducive to the interests of the Society, especially the two earliest—on " the Word of God," and on " Prayer ; " which productions, it is well known to his friends, were the result of his studies for the pulpit, and the solace of his devout spirit during his extensive journeys for the Society. . . . It may be truly said that this institution enjoyed his earliest affections, a great share of his best exertions, and his latest prayers.

" While the Committee deeply and affectionately sympathize with his bereaved widow and family, and with the Church at large, in the loss of Edward Bickersteth, yet they delight in contemplating the example of one who, being stedfast in faith, joyful through hope, and

rooted in charity, passed through the waves of this troublesome world with a greater measure of public affection
and respect than most men, even good men, enjoy. It
is their consolation to remember that the Master whom
he so faithfully served was pleased to honour, support,
and comfort him to the last; and that he is now safely
arrived at the land of everlasting life, and has there
exchanged our recent Jubilee for his eternal Jubilee in
the Church triumphant."

It would be easy to multiply similar testimonies to Mr.
Bickersteth's character and labours, not only from the
other societies, which had shared his zealous activity, but
from Christians of other bodies, or even of a different
school of theology. A generous and striking tribute to
the eminent love and holiness, which marked his life, has
appeared lately in the pages of a high-church Review.
A strong dissent from his views, on several points of doctrine and practice, is prefaced by these emphatic words.
" We must acknowledge that we shall find it difficult to
point to many living examples of equal excellence. We
know not the man in the present day, whom we should
look upon as a more faultless model of Christian excellence. His virtues and piety were far above the ordinary
attainments of Christian men, and approached those of
the saints of old. The list of names most honoured in
the Church for their saintliness would not be dishonoured
by the addition of the name of Edward Bickersteth to
their number....If out of the abundance of the heart the
mouth speaketh, there is in his life a noble testimony to
the state of that heart; for every word is instinct with a
spirit of love and faith, and humbleness of mind, and zeal
for God, which cannot be misunderstood. Here is no
cant and shibboleth of party; but something which rises

above them all, in the earnest tendencies of Christian love
towards God and man ; something which fails, indeed,
through infirmity of human judgment, but sanctifies even
its very failures." *

A still fuller testimony, founded on personal intercourse, has been borne to him in a funeral sermon, by
one of his Dissenting brethren, with whom the Evangelical Alliance had brought him into close intimacy.

" Mr. Bickersteth was strongly, because conscientiously
attached to his own Church.  He loved her liturgy ; he
approved her three orders of clergy ; he rejoiced in her
connexion with the State.   In all these points I differed
from him ; differed decidedly and hopelessly. But I would
renounce my nonconformity, if it disqualified me from
doing justice to the religious convictions, or paying a
tribute of affectionate homage, to the exalted piety of
such a churchman as my departed friend. . . . . . .

" Our friendship, indeed, was not of long standing.
But it became to me the source of much spiritual benefit,
partly in the communications which passed between us ;
but chiefly as it set before me a character so pure, elevated,
and heavenly, as I had scarcely ever contemplated before.

" By nothing was he more distinguished than by the
fervent love to Christ, which glowed in all his actions,
and breathed in all his words.   If in every mind there be
a master principle which subordinates and harmonizes all
other elements of character, this was that principle in
his.   He often reminded me of the primitive martyr
Ignatius, of whom it is reported that he cried continually
—My Love is crucified—such seemed to be the constant
affection he bore to Christ.   It was impossible to sit with
him in council, or to converse with him in the familiar

* English Review, Oct. 1851.

intercourse of friendship, without perceiving how it ran
through all his thoughts, gave a complexion to his sentiments, and governed his discussions. That Christ should
be glorified was not simply necessary to his happiness, it
was his happiness itself.

" His works, some of which have obtained an extensive
circulation, are written on various branches of Christian
truth and duty. With some of his sentiments it is to be
expected that independent minds, accustomed to judge
for themselves, will not be able to concur ; and perhaps
candour obliges me to say, that I cannot agree in some
of his prophetical speculations. I make this observation,
however, with much diffidence. In matters of the highest
moment, in the prominently evangelical character of his
writings, in the strenuous zeal with which they uphold
in their integrity and fulness the fundamental doctrines
of the Reformation, in the unction that pervades them,
in the practical character of most of them, in their holy
tendency, their candour towards opponents, their faithful
dealing with professors, and the universal charity they
display towards his fellow Christians, I deem them
worthy of all admiration. . . .

" The grace of spiritual-mindedness was conspicuously
seen in him. Though few men were better informed on
public events, or more observant of their course, it was
at once apparent to those who heard his conversation,
that his citizenship was not on earth. He viewed these
in their aspect on the coming and kingdom of Christ.
Of this he delighted to speak, and of every thing connected with it. His mind was supremely occupied with
the truths and glorious prospects which the word of God
reveals ; and he led the conversation of his fellow-Christians to these hallowed and ennobling themes.

" How wise he was in council, and how unassuming in manners; what power and fervency he possessed in prayer, and what deep insight into the things of the Spirit; how rich and varied his experience, and how familiar his acquaintance with the revelations of Eternal Truth; how cheerful his temper, how confiding his faith; how his very countenance beamed with an inexpressible gladness, as though it had caught, like that of Moses, a superabundant splendour from communion with God, I need not commemorate, since it was known to all."*

When such a witness has been borne to Mr. Bickersteth's character by comparative strangers, it is difficult for one, so closely linked with him by years of daily intercourse, to review it, however briefly, without the risk of unseemly praise. Yet it is a duty and a privilege to glorify the grace of Christ, where it has been brightly manifested; and a few remarks on the main features of his life and labours may perhaps be naturally expected at the close of such a biography.

The excellencies, which marked the character of Mr. Bickersteth, were eminently fruits of the gospel of grace. His natural temper, to judge by the few hints that remain, was cold, reserved, and rather unamiable. A vigorous and unbending will gave promise of the untiring energy, which marked his whole course; but all those gentler graces, which adorned his later years, were victories over natural disposition, and direct fruits of the Holy Spirit in his heart. It was a change like that which transformed the son of thunder, who had called for fire from heaven on the Samaritan villagers, into the Apostle of love. The doctrines of grace, which he enforced so zealously, were no separable accident of his life. They were

* The Parting Prayer, a Funeral Sermon by the Rev. Dr. Steane.

the mould into which his judgment and affections were cast, the soul of his daily experience, and inwrought into the whole texture of his inward being.

His early life was an instance of the Divine blessing on natural industry, when once sanctified by true religion, and joined with a simple devotedness to Christ. His powers of mind, though decidedly above the average, had none of the brilliancy of original genius ; and his worldly prospects, on leaving home, were of a very humble and moderate kind. But godliness, in his case, had the promise of the life that now is, as well as of that which is to come. Simple faith and earnest diligence opened before him a widening field of usefulness ; and even before his entrance into the ministry, he had purchased to himself a good degree, by his various labours in the cause of Christ.

After his ordination, during the fourteen years of his connexion with the Church Missionary Society, he was rising continually to greater eminence among his fellow-Christians. The close of the first volume will have shewn how great a share he had in reviving a missionary spirit throughout the Church of England.

On his removal to Watton, his labours were varied in their character, but not less abundant than before, and equally blessed by the great Lord of the harvest. There were few works of Christian benevolence, whether in the Church of England, or bearing on the general cause of religion, in which he had not some important share. The change in his views of prophecy, which soon followed, was regretted at the time, by many of his friends, who associated a Millennarian creed with fatalism, rashness, and spiritual extravagance. Many, who loved and admired him, feared some abatement of his zeal in the

cause of the Gospel, or at least some loss of valuable influence, gained by his former labours. Their fears proved
entirely groundless. His new conviction, that the triumphs
of the Church were only to be looked for at the return of
the Bridegroom, was accompanied with no diminution,
but rather an increase, of missionary zeal. Many, who at
first viewed that conviction as a serious error into which
he had fallen, were themselves convinced, before his
death, of its truth and importance. Others, without following his example, learned to dissociate prophetic studies
from any necessary connexion with sloth, wildness, and
extravagance. His catholic spirit hindered any breach
of affection, even where there was a lasting difference of
judgment. The steadiness of his Christian course, and
his unwavering zeal in every good work, banished suspicion, when it was ready to arise, and raised him higher
and higher in the confidence and esteem of his fellow-
christians.

Mr. Bickersteth was gifted with practical wisdom in
no ordinary measure. It arose mainly, perhaps, from the
union of two very different causes,—his early training as
a lawyer in habits of business, and his peculiar singleness
of eye, in seeking the glory of Christ, the result of habitual communion with the Saviour. Some, who admire
his glowing affection, may be disposed to question his
claim to this contrasted excellence. The doubt is natural,
and almost inevitable, in those who have viewed him
only from a distance, while their own judgment may
have differed widely from his on several points of main
importance. A high churchman, or one from the extreme ranks of dissent, however just and candid in recognizing the excellencies of his heart, must naturally
reckon Mr. Bickersteth's judgment, on many ecclesiastical

questions, highly defective. Such friendly censures, which his Memoir has already elicited, tend greatly to neutralize each other. It is plain that, without any indecision or vagueness in his own views, he occupied a mean between two remote extremes. But even among his own brethren, the Evangelical clergy, who shared alike his zeal for the Protestant teaching of the Reformers, and his attachment to the Church of England, there are many who would possibly decide the question against him, because they dissent strongly from his views of prophecy, or regret his warm support of the Evangelical Alliance. On these two points he was doubtless in a minority among his brethren ; and in general, those Christians who concurred with him most fully in one of them, disagreed with him on the other. It is, however, no safe test of superior wisdom, to sail always with the general stream. In questions of this kind, where good and holy men still differ, the final appeal must be to a higher tribunal than religious majorities. It is at least conceivable that the true reason of his apparent singularity may have been a deeper insight, on the one hand, into Divine truth, and on the other, a greater catholicity of thought and feeling, than is common among Christians ; and that, although these graces had been separately attained by many others, few had learned to combine them in the same measure.

When tried, however, by a less disputable standard, the main tenor of his personal conduct, and his counsels to friends, his practical wisdom was of no common order. It was prized most highly by those who knew him best. To myself, though with habits of thought naturally very diverse from his, it appears, after years of daily intercourse, one of the most prominent and distinguishing features of his character. Its influence, indeed, was

owned far and wide in the church of Christ.   There was
no one, perhaps, to whom his fellow-Christians looked
up, with a stronger sense of confidence and repose in his
judgment.   His advice was sought by thousands at home,
and by foreign Christians of almost every land, when
questions arose involving the interests of pure and un-
defiled religion.   His conduct in private affairs was
marked by the union of prudence and liberality.   There
is perhaps no Christian minister of his generation, whose
correspondence, occasioned by daily appeals to his judgment, and entreaties for his counsel, ranged over a wider
sphere, or would yield ampler tokens of the wisdom from
above, in all the features described by the Apostle,—'first
pure, then peaceable, full of mercy and of good fruits,
without partiality, and without hypocrisy.'

When the Tractarian School arose within the Church
of England, Mr. Bickersteth took an early and decided
part in resisting its progress, and exposing its dangerous
tendency.   Many of his later writings were occupied,
more or less, with this great question ; and his Diary
sufficiently shows the depth and force of his convictions.
But his spirit of love made him slow to impute evil, until
its presence was very manifest.   If his judgment were
sometimes at fault, it was usually in the case which Milton
has described so well, when "though Wisdom wakes,
suspicion sleeps at Wisdom's door," and resigns her charge
to Simplicity.   This temper of mind, however, when
joined, as in him, with a stedfast adherence to the gospel,
though it may involve occasional error, is far more attractive and beautiful in itself, and more adapted to
commend sound doctrine to others, than that excessive
suspiciousness, which often grows up in times of intense
religious strife, and veils its own deficiency in the grace

of candour under the plea of a zeal for the truth. From
this unamiable fault Mr. Bickersteth was peculiarly
free. His candour might sometimes be excessive, but
his charity never failed. Whenever he thought a principle at stake, he was bold and unflinching in his adherence to Scriptural truth and the doctrines of grace.
But he delighted to recognize spiritual religion, even in
sections of the Church, or schools of thought, with which
he had in general little sympathy ; and to honour religious sincerity and moral uprightness, wherever they
were found. And hence many, who were disposed to
regard evangelical truth as the mere shibboleth of a
party, from the real or fancied bigotry of its professors,
were almost compelled, in his case, to discern its higher
character, as a secret well-spring of Christian zeal and
wide-hearted love.

The various works, in which his later years were occupied, would together form an epitome of the recent history of the Church of Christ. His first love to the
Church Missionary Society never slackened, but many
other institutions came to share in his active labours.
One of these, with which his name has been most
intimately connected, is the Evangelical Alliance. No
one, but the most prejudiced, even of those who differed from him the most in their judgment of its expediency, could doubt that the motive which prompted
him was an unfeigned desire to promote the union of
all true Christians, and to advance the Church one
step nearer to the standard of our Lord's own prayer :
" that they all may be perfect in one, that the world may
believe that Thou hast sent me." He was warmly attached to the Church of England, because he believed it
the fullest witness to the truth of God on the face of the

earth, and our main bulwark against the national triumph of superstition and ungodliness. But his heart
yearned for affectionate intercourse with all those servants
of Christ, however they might differ from his judgment
in minor things, in whom he discerned the image of his
Saviour; and few have entered more into that prayer of
the Apostle, or exemplified its spirit more fully in their
practice—" Grace be with all those that love our Lord
Jesus Christ in sincerity." The most feeble and imperfect attempt at greater union, seemed, therefore, in his
eyes, more agreeable to the mind of Christ, than that
practical contentedness with strife and division, as a fatal
necessity, which had prevailed so long among professing
Christians. With these feelings, he willingly devoted his
strength to a difficult and unpopular work. He bore
cheerfully, as an appointed cross, that frequent reproach
of want of judgment, on account of the limited success
of these efforts, which might fall perhaps more justly on
the general body of the servants of Christ, for their lower
attainments in that grace of brotherly love to their fellow-
Christians, which always shone in him with peculiar
brightness. There was none, perhaps, of his many labours, which he looked back upon with deeper thankfulness to God in his dying hours.

The work, however, which had the foremost place in
his efforts during the two last years of his life, was the
Irish Church Missions. He may even be viewed as a
martyr in their cause. The daily and hourly pressure
upon his thoughts, in connexion with this infant society,
was the immediate occasion of that disease, which removed him to his rest. In the Alliance he had been
earnest to cultivate Christian love and union, for their
own sake; and had been deemed unpractical by those,

Y 2

who were less keenly alive to its importance, apart from
any outward work, as an object worthy of direct cul-
ture, and the secret fountain of all healthy activity
in the Church of Christ.    But in these missions he
shewed himself prompt, above most of his brethren,
to discern the outward work, which it was peculiarly
seasonable and important for the Church to pursue,
and full of practical energy in carrying it on.    He felt
deeply that the gospel was the only true cure for the
miseries of Ireland.    He had an intense hatred for that
hollow expediency, which led our Statesmen to endow
Romish idolatry, and aim at securing national peace by a
sin against the God of holiness.    In the dreadful famine
that quickly followed, he heard the voice of God, calling
His people to pity the souls, as well as the bodies, of the
dying peasantry of Ireland, and to undo the national sin
by their private efforts in spreading the simple and pure
gospel.    And hence he threw his whole heart and soul
into the work, for which the providence of God, by fearful
judgments, had made so wide an opening.    He rejoiced,
with deep and holy joy, when a streak of light was seen
amidst the dark cloud of ignorance and superstition, that
had brooded so long over the sister island.    His prayers
have been largely answered since his death.    The work
on which he set his heart, and for which he laboured
amidst reproach and obloquy, has borne fruit beyond the
fears of its adversaries, or the most sanguine hopes of its
friends.    It is now even of national importance ; and is
likely to prove the most signal instance, in these days, of
God's blessing on the prayer of faith and the labour of
love.

The principles, which had guided Mr. Bickersteth
through life, shone out clearly in his last illness, and

sustained him in his dying hours. Even the occasional
wandering, which resulted from the nature of his disease,
left the graces of the Spirit as transparent as ever, and
rendered them still more touchingly beautiful. The
intervals of consciousness were marked by quiet, humble
thoughtfulness, tender affection, and unclouded peace.
The subjects of which he spoke, as this chapter will have
shewn, were his confidence in Christ alone, the comfort
and preciousness of the gospel, the finishing of his work
and his desire to enter into rest, his longing for the good
of his parish, his sympathy with distant labourers in
the vineyard, his sense of deep unworthiness, the presence
and grace of the good Shepherd, and anticipations of coming glory. His death was an illustration of the promise
—" Mark the perfect man, and behold the upright—for
the end of that man is peace."

It was his constant desire, and his dying admonition,
that Christ alone should be glorified, both in his life and
his death. To Him alone the praise is due of every excellence that shone forth in His servant. It was the love
of Christ, and the deep sense of pardon through His
cross, which changed a temper cold, reserved, and unamiable, into a pattern of tender sympathy, and moulded
the rugged energy of his early boyhood into the ripened,
earnest diligence of unwearied love. To the Saviour
we would render praise for the combination of Christian
graces, which marked his life, and shed their fragrance
around his parting hours. In the words of a noble
friend, "no man in his own generation, and few in any
other, have served God in a more consistent course of
signal usefulness." May all of us, who retrace his course
in these pages, have grace to follow him, as he followed
Christ, and join in the thanksgiving and prayer, which

his lips had so often uttered, before he was removed to his Saviour's presence ;—" And we also bless Thy holy name for all thy servants, departed this life in Thy faith and fear ; beseeching Thee to give us grace, so to follow their good examples, that with them we may be partakers of Thy heavenly kingdom."


THE END


*L. Seeley, Printer.*